SOCIAL PERCEPTIONS OF
PEOPLE WITH DISABILITIES
IN HISTORY

SOCIAL PERCEPTIONS OF PEOPLE WITH DISABILITIES IN HISTORY

By

HERBERT C. COVEY, PH.D.

*Colorado Department of Human Services and
College of Continuing Education, University of Colorado at Boulder
Boulder, Colorado*

CHARLES C THOMAS • PUBLISHER, LTD.
Springfield • Illinois • U.S.A.

HV1552
.C69
1998

Published and Distributed Throughout the World by
CHARLES C THOMAS • PUBLISHER, LTD.
2600 South First Street
Springfield, Illinois 62794-9265

This book is protected by copyright. No part of
it may be reproduced in any manner without
written permission from the publisher.

©*1998 by* Charles C Thomas • Publisher, LTD.
ISBN 0-398-06837-2 (cloth)
ISBN 0-398-06838-0 (paper)

Library of Congress Catalog Card Number: 97-38919

With THOMAS BOOKS careful attention is given to all details of manufacturing and design. It is the Publisher's desire to present books that are satisfactory as to their physical qualities and artistic possibilities and appropriate for their particular use. THOMAS BOOKS will be true to those laws of quality that assure a good name and good will.

Printed in the United States of America
MS-R-3

Library of Congress Cataloging in Publication Data

Covey, Herbert C.
   Social perceptions of people with disabilities in history / by Herbert C. Covey.
      p. cm.
   Includes bibliographical references and index.
   ISBN 0-398-06837-2 (cloth). -- ISBN 0-398-06838-0 (pbk.)
   1. Handicapped--History. 2. Handicapped in art. 3. Handicappped in literature.   I. Title.
HV1552.C69   1998
305.9'0816--dc21

97-38919
CIP

To Marty, Chris, and Kelly

PREFACE

This book was written to provide an overview of major historical contexts and to describe how historical occurrences shaped the nature of disabilities. It introduces the reader to the topic of the social history of people with disabilities and provides basic background information on disability in prior centuries. It presents major notions for understanding general social trends regarding people with disabilities. The book provides an overview of some of the major trends that directly influenced people with disabilities. It was written to increase our knowledge and consciousness of presentations of people with disabilities and to fuel further inquiries on the topic. Many of our contemporary images and ideas about people with disabilities cannot be applied to people with disabilities who lived in earlier times. Other images and ideas can be traced back to earlier ideas about the nature of disabilities and the people who have them. It has been my hope to present the rich texture of presentation regarding disability from earlier times in such a way that images of people with disabilities are more meaningful to people with disabilities, scholars, and other readers of this book.

It provides a general survey of how people with disabilities were perceived in western history. It draws on art, literature, and historical information from earlier times. The span of time selected for study focuses on the Middle Ages through the nineteenth century. The period of the Middle Ages was selected because it represents a watershed of ideas regarding people with disabilities and significant changes in artistic representations of all people, including people with disabilities. In prior centuries individuals were relatively insignificant and artistic images were relatively sterile. The church exercised so much control over art and literature, that individuality found little representation. The Middle Ages represents a period of change in both artistic techniques and attitudes toward people with disabilities. It was at the close of the Middle Ages that artists and authors began to portray the individual characteristics of people with disabilities. During the Middle Ages artists began to present detailed and individualistic characteristics of their human subjects. The late Middle Ages gave rise to the use of perspective, as human subjects began to be presented in natural contexts. The thirteenth through the fifteenth centuries saw increased effort to depict subjects as individuals and as they actually appeared (Hofstatter, 1968). People with disabilities were included in this shift but stereotypes and traditions continued to influence the manner in which artists and authors represented them. The Middle Ages also represent an interesting time regarding the social interpretations and relationships between people with disabilities and those without, although many people acquired disabilities during the life span.

When the Middle Ages came to a close and the Renaissance flowered, a new orientation on life developed. Life in this world took on a new importance. The focus on the individual that emerged with the Renaissance brought attention to people and their characteristics. Some of the humanist focus brought about by the Renaissance also affected notions and images of people with disabilities. As societies turned toward understanding humankind, a natural curiosity grew about people with disabilities. People with disabilities increasingly became the subject of art and literature. Art during the Renaissance and particularly that of the later northern Renaissance sheds much light on how people with disabilities were perceived and treated by their respective societies. The centuries that followed the Middle Ages and Renaissance were characterized by accelerated social change and social upheaval, which in turn caused dramatic changes in many perceptions about people with disabilities.

The study ends with the nineteenth century for several reasons. First, the nineteenth century represents century of great importance to people with disabilities. This was the century of Darwinism and major scientific breakthroughs that changed some of the paradigms used to interpret the nature of disabilities. This was the century that led to many reforms in the care and treatment of people with disabilities. It was the century that fostered some of the stereotypes about people with disabilities that have only recently been challenged in contemporary society. The study's scope does not continue through the twentieth century because there already exists a considerable body of information about people with disabilities during the twentieth century.

The twentieth century is one in which considerable legislative, medical, and legal materials are available. While the twentieth century is undoubtedly an important one, it needs to be addressed as a separate topic.

Some historians and scholars may take issue with the broad scope of this work, suggesting that significant details and subtleties will be lost in a book covering the Middles Ages and ending in the nineteenth century. They may also argue that each region, with its unique traditions and culture, or each of the periods or centuries encompassed in this book deserves intensive, thorough coverage in a separate volume. All of these points have merit but this work is not intended to be a detailed or period specific piece but an introduction to some of the basic presentations of people with disabilities over the centuries. Only by studying presentations and images of people with disabilities over such a lengthy period is it possible to determine whether these views and presentations were short-term or lasting. No other work presents such a broad social overview on which more detailed studies can be based. While there are many excellent texts on specific disabilities, works that cover a broad range are absent. This study is meant to be a survey of the social landscape and a catalyst for further research.

Although this book might, in the eyes of some, represent a sizable effort at covering the topic of disability, it in no way fully covers the topic. Nor does the book represent all of the experiences that people with disabilities have had over the centuries. Rather it, to borrow a clichÈ, only scratches the surface. Anyone who decides to study the topic should be prepared for great voids in information. Hopefully this study helps fill some of the previous voids.

HERBERT C. COVEY

ACKNOWLEDGMENTS

As an independent scholar, I do not have the professional contacts that academe affords. This makes the help I do receive even more important. In this regard, I am deeply indebted to the following people and their respective institutions for providing valuable assistance: Ulf Hedberg, Director of Archives, Gallaudet University Library; Kris McKusker of Special Collections and Marty Covey of the Western History Archives at the University of Colorado Norlin Library; Ms. Chantal Corr of the Colorado Department of Human Services; Ms. Alperine of the Institut National de Jeunes Sourds de Paris; Mr. Henk Betten of the Netherlands. I want to thank Dr. Steven Hey for his early suggestions and involvement in the conceptualization of this book. It almost goes without saying, the book would not have been possible without the assistance of many.

I also want to thank the following museums, publishers, libraries for their permission to reproduce the works included in this text including the Louvre, Philadelphia Museum of Art, Yale University, Prado, Museum Boijmans Van Beuningen, Bibliothèque Nationale (Paris), Vatican Museum, New York Public Library, Boston Museum of Fine Arts, British Library (London), Oeffentliche Kunstsammlung Basel Kunstmuseum (Basel), The Harvard University Art Museums, Library of Congress, University of Colorado Library - Special Collections (Boulder), Wellcome Institute Library, (London), Springfield Museum (Springfield, MA), Museum of Naples, Kupferstichkabinett (Dresden), Birmingham City Museums and Art Gallery (Birmingham, England), Gallaudet University Archives (Washington, DC), Bayerische Staatsbibliothek (Munich), National Gallery of Urbino, Manchester City Art Galleries (Manchester, England), Yale Center for British Art, and the Cleveland Museum of Art.

I am also deeply appreciated of my spouse, Marty; my daughter, Kelly; and son, Chris. They are the real reason and source of inspiration for why I do what I do. They have been tolerant and supportive throughout this study. Without them, I wouldn't have the support and encouragement so important to independent scholars.

CONTENTS

Page

Preface vii

Chapter 1. The Changing Social Contexts of Disabilities 3

2. People with Physical Disabilities 45

3. People with Leprosy 89

4. People Who Were Mentally Ill 123

5. People Who Were Blind 163

6. People Who Were Deaf 195

7. People Who Had Developmental Disabilities 235

Epilogue 273

References 279

Name Index 293

Subject Index 303

LIST OF FIGURES

Figure 1. Bruegel the Elder, *Charitas,* 1559, Museum Boijmans Van Beuningen, Rotterdam.

Figure 2. Francisco Goya, *Something Rare,* captioned "Mother showing her deformed child to two women," 1814-1817, Louvre, Paris.

Figure 3. Pieter Bruegel the Elder, *The Cripples,* 1568, Louvre, Paris.

Figure 4. Jacques Callot from his series of etchings entitled *Vagabonds, Crippled Beggar,* early seventeenth century, Bibliothëque Nationale, Paris.

Figure 5. Hieronymous Cock, *Beggars,* mid sixteenth century, Philadelphia Museum of Art: SmithKline Beecham Corp. Fund for the Ars Medica Collection, Philadelphia.

Figure 6. Thomas Rowlandson, (*Mathew Bramble's Trip to Bath: The Circus Hill, Mathew Bramble's Overturn,* 1766, Yale Center for British Art, Paul Mellon Collection.

Figure 7. Francisco Goya, Captioned "He carries his patrimony in his sack of flesh," c. 1803-1824, Prado, Madrid.

Figure 8. Théodore Géricault, *A Paraleytic Woman,* 1821, The Philadelphia Museum of Fine Arts, SmithKline eecham Corp. Fund for the Ars Medica Collection, Philadelphia.

Figure 9. Jose Ribera, *The Clubfoot* or *Boy with a Club-Foot,* 1642, Louvre, Paris.

Figure 10. Johannes Wachtin, 1517 woodcut from Hans Gersdorff's *Feldtbuch de Wundartznev,* The Philadelphia Museum of Fine Arts: SmithKline Beecham Corp. Fund for the Ars Medica Collection, Philadelphia.

Figure 11. Raphael Sanzio, *The Cripple,* early sixteenth century, Vatican Museum, Rome.

Figure 12. Jacques Callot, Lieure Varie Figure Gobbi, New York Public Library, New York.

Figure 13. Annibale Carracci, *Hunchback,* 16th-17th centuries, The Trustees of the Chatsworth Settlement, Devonshire: photograph Courtald Institute of Art.

Figure 14. Rambert, *Debauche et Luxure,* 1851, Bibliothëque Nationale, Paris.

Figure 15. Diego Rodriquez de Silva y Velasquez, *Don Baltazar with a Dwarf,* seventeenth century, Henry Lillie Pierce Fund Museum of Fine Arts, Boston.

Figure 16. Margin drawing from *Exeter Pontifical,* fourteenth century, British Library, London.

Figure 17. Nicholas Manuel Deutsch, *Saint Anne Between Saint James the Elder and Saint Roch,* 1484-1530, Oeffentliche Kunstsammlung Basel Kunstmuseum, Basel, Switzerland.

Figure 18. Hans Holbein the Younger, *Portrait of a Leper,* 1523, The Harvard University Art Museums, Cambridge, Massachusetts, Meta and Paul J. Sachs Collection.

Figure 19. Claes Jansz Visscher the Younger, *Procession of Lepers on Copper Monday,* 1608, Philadelphia Museum of Art, SmithKline Beecham Corp. Fund for the Ars Medica Collection, Philadelphia.

Figure 20. Albrecht Dürer, *Melancolia* I, 1514, The Philadelphia Museum of Art: Purchased by Lisa Norris Elkins Fund, Philadelphia.

Figure 21. Attributed to First Antwerp Woodcutter, *Christ Casting Out Demons,* 1487, Philadelphia Museum of Art: SmithKline Beecham Corp. Fund for the Ars Medica Collection, Philadelphia.

Figure 22. Hieronymus Bosch, *Ship of Fools,* late fifteenth century, Louvre, Paris.

Figure 23. William Hogarth, Plate VII from *The Rake's Progress,* 1735, Library of Congress, Washington, DC.

Figure 24. Wilhelm von Kaulbach, *Madhouse,* 1835, The Philadelphia Museum of Art: The Muriel and Philip Berman Gift, Philadelphia.

Figure 25. Daniel Chodowiecki, untitled group of heads from Johann Gaspar Lavater's *Fragmente,* 1774-1778, Special Collections, University of Colorado Library, Boulder.

Figure 26. Sir Charles Bell, *Maniac in Chains,* 1806, Wellcome Institute Library, London.

Figure 27. Théodore Géricault, *The Insane Kleptomaniac* (also known as *The Insane Kidnapper*), c. 1822, Springfield Museum, Springfield, Massachusetts.

Figure 28. Pieter Bruegel the Elder, *The Parable of the Blind Leading the Blind,* sixteenth century, Museum of Naples.

Figure 29. Louis-Léopold Boilly, *The Blind,* 1825, Philadelphia Museum of Art, SmithKline Beecham Corp. Fund for the Ars Medica Collection, Philadelphia.

Figure 30. Sir John Everett Millias, *The Blind Girl* 1856, Published by permission of Birmingham City Museums and Art Gallery, Birmingham, England.

List of Figures xvii

Figure 31. Pieter Bruegel the Elder, *The Blind Beggar,* about 1564, Kupferstichkabinett, Dresden.

Figure 32. Unknown artist, *Austria - A Cafe for Deaf Mutes in Vienna,* Nineteenth Century, Gallaudet University Archives, Washington, DC.

Figure 33. Unknown artist, Illustration from the *Prayer Book of Hildegard of Bingen,* late twelfth century, Bayerische Staatsbibliothek, Munich.

Figure 34 Raphaël, *The Dumb Woman,* 1506, National Gallery of Urbino.

Figure 35. Jacob de Gheyn, *Master and Pupil,* 1599, Manchester City Art Galleries, Manchester, England.

Figure 36. Unknown artist, Abbe Epée, Date unknown, Institut National de Jeunes Sourds de Paris, Paris France.

Figure 37. Unknown artist, *J.R. Pereire and His Pupil Marie Marois,* Unknown, Institut National de Jeunes Sourds de Paris, Paris France.

Figure 38. Unknown artist, *Treatment by Electricity,* 18th Century France, Institut National de Jeunes Sourds. Paris, Paris France.

Figure 39. Unknown artist, *Illustrating the Lord's Prayer with Signs,* nineteenth century, Gallaudet University Archives, Washington, DC.

Figure 40. Daniel Chodowiecki, untitled group of people from Johann Gaspar Lavater's *Fragmente,* 1774-1778, Special Collections, University of Colorado Library, Boulder.

Figure 41. Daniel Chodowiecki, untitled plate of girl from Johann Gaspar Lavater's *Fragmente,* 1774-1778, Special Collections, University of Colorado Library, Boulder.

Figure 42. Diego Rodriquez de Silva y Velasquez , *The Jester Calabazas,* c. 1633, The Cleveland Museum of Art, Leonard C. Hanna, Jr. Fund, 1965.15, Cleveland, Ohio.

Figure 43. Unknown artist, *Wild Boy of Averon,* unknown, Institut National de Jeunes Sourds de Paris, Paris France.

SOCIAL PERCEPTIONS OF PEOPLE WITH DISABILITIES IN HISTORY

Chapter 1

THE CHANGING SOCIAL CONTEXTS OF DISABILITY

What does it mean to be a person with a disability? People with disabilities are individuals who have physical or mental impairments that make it more difficult for them to achieve certain goals. Disability refers to the consequences of an impairment, that is, any restriction or lack of ability to perform an activity in the manner or within the range considered appropriate for nondisabled persons. A disability is a functional limitation that interferes with a person's ability to walk, think, hear, learn, or see. It is a characteristic of an individual in the same sense as hair color or height but it also indicates that the individual has more difficulty in achieving certain goals or objectives. This difficulty may stem from the disability itself or sociocultural factors in which the disability is reacted to and interpreted.

Culture plays an important role in defining, interpreting, and evaluating disabilities. It is commonly understood that the meanings attached to disability differ among cultures and within cultures, and over time. A disability has a social character because culture and society define, and in some cases, impair or impede people with disabilities from accomplishing their goals and objectives. Some individuals perceived as having a disability might be able to achieve their goals if society or culture did not hamper their efforts. Disabilities are closely linked to situations and barriers imposed by society, culture, the environment, and oneself. A handicap is the social disadvantage that results from an impairment or disability. A handicap is not determined by an individual's physical limitations, but instead reflects the social consequences of that disability.

This book is about disabilities and cultural-historical discourse about them. From the very beginning it is important to realize that differences in discourse on disability, even within the same culture and social context, are likely to occur. Disabilities such as blindness and developmental disabilities were perceived and discussed differently and in similar ways during the same periods. Jessica Scheer and Nora Groce (1988: 23) once commented, "Throughout human history, societies have defined what did and did not constitute a disability or handicap, and these definitions have changed over time." For example, some people who are deaf believe very strongly that they are not disabled but simply different. Their disability is more an indication of society's intolerance and suppression of their method of communicating (sign language) than a functional limitation. Being culturally defined, a disability is not simply a fact, such as being blind or deaf, but a complex set of meanings, reactions, and interpretations reflected in what has been written and artistically depicted.

People with disabilities have been members of every society (Scheer & Groce, 1988). However, the constant presence of people with disabilities, especially those with physicaly disabilities, is often overlooked (Scheer & Groce, 1988). Experts estimate that between 2 to 10 percent of all of humanity is disabled to some degree. In the United States alone the National Institute of Medicine estimated that in 1991 one in seven people or many as 35 million people had disabilities (Sharpiro, 1993). Global estimates are about 245 million, or one per every 6 to 7 people have at least one disability. Only about 15 percent of people with disabilities had them at birth, thus most people acquired disabilities over the span of their lifetimes. What separates human beings from other species is the ability to attach meaning to those people with disabilities. Societies do not ignore people with disabilities but rather develop sets of responses based on abstract notions about what it means to have a disability or be disabled. With this attachment of meaning come a variety of responses ranging from full acceptance and integration to total rejection, separation, and persecution.

Societies have run the entire gamut of human responses toward people with disabilities ranging from outright genocide to adoration. Societies have treated people with disabilities as evil beings. For example, during World War I, the allies believed the withered arm of the Kaiser was responsible for his quest for power. Centuries earlier, the British attributed the alleged evil character of Richard III to his disability of having a crooked back. In contrast are situations when disabilities have been associated with positive characteristics. For example, Americans attributed Franklin Roosevelt's greatness to his overcoming his disabling disease. At times societies have neglected them and other times they have been used as scapegoats. They have experienced indifference and invisibility but also have been paraded in front of others as sideshow curiosities. Even with recent loosing of social attitudes toward disability, societies have not afforded people total access to jobs, opportunities, and other benefits and experiences that society has to offer. This has resulted in a perceived need for laws protecting their rights and the demands for access and control over their lives.

To understand how they lived in the past, it is important to know how familiar they were to their respective societies. Societal familiarity with people with disabilities has shifted over time. Sometimes they have been isolated and other times they moved about in relative freedom. They were essentially familiar to the general publics to which they belonged. Familiarity by definition infers to know, recognize, and understand. It can foster acceptance and tolerance. When people become unfamiliar to society, the result can be misunderstanding, rejection, and intolerance. Societies have had differing degrees of familiarity with people with disabilities. Today people have lost their familiarity with people with disabilities (Scheer & Groce, 1988). Nondisabled peoples' familiarity with people with disabilities may be improving but on the whole they still represent a relative unknown. People do not always know how they should treat and react to people with disabilities. They also do not know how they should expect to be treated by people with disabilities.

Initially, people with disabilities lived in relative social autonomy unless they were viewed as threatening. Over the course of time, some disabilities were judged to require social responses, such as restriction or isolation. The restriction and isolation of people with disabilities , especially during the intolerant Victorian period, resulted in them becoming less familiar to the general public. As societies isolated and institutionalized people, people with disabilities became less familiar. With this shift, misunderstanding, fear, and other negative reactions to people with disabilities arose. As we locked up, isolated, and segregated people, the perception of their lives became one of speculation and mystery rather than based on fact and experience. As the curve of social isolation increased, so did misunderstanding.

Relative to history, we know very little about how people with disabilities lived and were perceived in their respective societies. When historians have written history, they have not focused on people with disabilities. Consequently, the story of their roles and positions in their respective societies has yet to be told. Yet, we know they have been active participants in the building of western civilization. Societies have not relegated them to isolation in asylums, hospitals, institutions, and back streets. Contemporary scholars have only started to explore how these relationships and others have played out in social history. The ground for historical inquiry is rich and relatively unexplored. For example, McBride (1985: 41-42) commented, "Sprinkled across the pages of medieval writings are such maladies as mental disorders, physical deformities, blindness and eye diseases, deafness and ear diseases, impediments of speech, baldness, foul odors." The same can be said for works of art over the centuries.

ENDURING SOCIAL PERCEPTIONS OF PEOPLE WITH DISABILITIES

When reviewing historical information on social interactions involving people with disabilities, certain enduring perceptions, attitudes, preconceptions, and stereotypes emerge. Some of these social perceptions are specific to certain disabilities during specific times. For example, blindness and mental illness have gone through periods when they were romanticized. In contrast, physical disabilities have never been romanticized.

As Subhuman

A major social perception of people with disabilities was that they were subhuman. Being subhuman could mean many things. For instance, a social perception people have held about people with disabilities was that they were, or became wild animals. Throughout the centuries, people believed that people with disabilities were less than human. People have believed that people with disabilities were closer to wild animals than humans. They have assumed that as disabilities became more severe, the people having them became more animal-like in constitution and behavior. This perception has surfaced in many of the characterizations of people with mental illness. They were presented as being wildmen, savages, wildwomen, or animals from antiquity through much of the nineteenth century.

This perception is clearly illustrated in the biblical tale of King Nebuchadnezzar who, according to legend, became like a wild animal with claws, hair, and animal behavior. Nebuchadnezzar was the archetype of the animal-like nature of people who were mentally ill (Pouchelle, 1990). For people with mental illness, this perception continued well into the nineteenth and twentieth centuries. In a similar vein, folktales describing people becoming transformed into werewolves, common during the Middle Ages and later centuries, reflect this perception. There were traditions and legends that claim that wild animals have supposedly raised and nurtured abandoned or lost children. For example, people have credited wild animals for raising "feral" children. The mythological ancestry of feral children traces back to at least antiquity (Fiedler, 1978). Greco-Roman legend tells of Thyro, who was raised among cattle, the god Zeus who was suckled by a goat, and Romulus and Remus who were nurtured by a wolf.

For people who were deaf, there was a very old perception that there is a link between speech and human nature, including reason. Saint-Loup (1993:386) observed, that many medieval citizens thought that speech was what separated, "humans from animals." Saint-Loup linked this view to the

Christian belief that it was through the gift of speech that God separated humans from animals. People concluded that because animals lack speech, people who were deaf often were without speech and thus were less human and more animal in nature. This social perception of people who are deaf, being savage or animal-like has, in Lane's (1992) opinion, had staying power in western societies. During the Middle Ages people saw those with leprosy (Hansens Disease) as being more animal than human. Medieval and even earlier accounts and descriptions of the disease refer to the victims as having animal transformations. The history of the disease leprosy makes several references to people with the disease becoming similar to elephants, foxes, lions (as in "leotine"), and serpents. The noted medieval English medical scholar Bartholomew Angulus reflected this perception when he described a form of leprosy as being serpentine. He observed that leprosy transformed the individual's skin into that of a snake.

Within the same subhuman perception, western societies have thought of and labeled people with physical disabilities or deformities as monsters or monstrosities. This was certainly the case in Medieval and early modern Europe where people labeled infants with deformities as changelings and perceived them as subhuman monsters. This perception flavored the treatment of infants and survived from the Middle Ages through the eighteenth century. The origins of the word monster are moneo which means to warn and monstro which means to show forth, as in divine providence. People viewed those judged as being physically different as foretelling the future. Ancient societies occasionally interpreted children with deformities as being good or bad omens. The word was also used in standard medical practice for people with medical abnormalities (Bogdan et al., 1982). The term monster became so widely accepted that it was used in many medical treatises on people with disabilities or deformities.

Another tradition related to the subhuman perception of people with disabilities was that of the wildman and wildwomen. Wildmen and wildwomen of the Middle Ages were literary and artistic figures. Wild people were hairy, half-animals, violent, noncommunicative, brutish, naked, who lived in the woods and avoided human contact. Bernheimer (1952:12) wrote of wild people, "It was a habit in the Middle Ages to let many lunatics go free unless they were believed to be obsessed and subject to the exorcism appropriate to their case." Instinct and their immediate needs drove their actions rather than social constraint or norms. Their hairy bodies symbolized strength, godlessness, and lack of intelligence. Examples in art of this perception include *Hercules as a Wild Man* from the manuscript of Robert de Blois from the thirteenth century, the German artist Martin Schongauer's (1446-1488/86) fifteenth century engraving *Wildman with Coat of Arms* along with several of his escutcheons (Minott, 1971). St. John Chrysostom was depicted as a wildman in a woodcut from Fyner's edition of the *Lives of the Saints* (1481). Pieter Bruegel the Elder's (1520-1569) painting titled *Play of the Death of a Wildman* is based on a story of a wildman. Albrecht Dürer's etchings *The Abduction of Proserpina* and *The Coat of Arms of Death* (1503) contain wildmen. The High Middle Ages produced literary characters, such as Silvester (Merlinus Caldonicus) from the *Vita Merlini* by Geoffrey of Monmouth, who were wild and insane. Edmund Spenser's third book of *The Faerie Queene* (1590) also referred to a wildman.

Societies have viewed people with developmental disabilities as inhuman, subhuman, or biological throwbacks. People saw them as being something less than complete humans, which meant they were denied their rights. They were treated and perceived as being more similar to animals than humans. Their being viewed as animals had major implications for their care and treatment. Historically, animals were assumed to be devoid of feelings and were able to endure the elements, such as temperature extremes and hunger, more so than humans (Scheerenberger, 1982). Evans (1983:115) wrote, "Throughout history, it was widely held that retarded and insane persons could, because of their 'animal nature,' withstand physical hardships such as extremes of temperature that would kill a normal person." If they could withstand such hardships, it was rationalized, they required little care or attention. Consequently, they were neglected and deprived of humane treatment and care.

As Having Special Gifts or Compensations

Another social perception was that people with disabilities are often compensated for by nature, supernatural forces, biology, or God with special abilities that offset the disability. They were thought to have added sensory powers, such as a sixth sense, spiritual awareness, musical talent, prophetic gifts, more focus, more sensitive hearing, improved memory, great judgment, foresight, and other desirable traits. For example, people who are blind have been frequently viewed as having extra powerful senses of hearing, insight, touch, and smell. People who are mentally ill have been seen as having divine insight or having supernatural powers. Some societies viewed people with small statures as being oversexed or good luck omens. Some European communities saw people with developmental disabilities as good omens who brought good luck to the community. Legends and mythology contains tales of gods and humans with godlike attributes who were sometimes disabled.

Examples of gifts are numerous, such as the perception that people who were blind had special gifts. Homer's gift of poetry was viewed as a divine compensation for his blindness. In addition, people saw those who were blind capable of providing good advice and having patience (Koestler, 1976; Monbeck, 1973). In southern Slavic folk tradition, they were believed to be chosen by God and given power to create (Vukanovic, 1985). One of the special gifts that received much attention was the gift of prophecy. Societies have thought that people who were blind were able to foresee the future and make predictions. For instance in the Bible Ahijah, a blind prophet, foresaw the death of Jeroboam's son and the end of his reign (I Kings 14: 1-18). People with developmental disabilities have been seen as being holy innocent. That is, they were innocent children of God who were not capable of doing any harm. They were also viewed as possessing supernatural powers. People who were mentally ill have been viewed as having direct connections with God (Robins, 1986).

Another example of compensation was the perceived link between insanity to creativity. For instance, in the fourth century BC, Aristotle wondered why so many of the brightest artists, poets, and philosophers, were melancholic (Angier, 1993). The famous scientist and astronomer Tycho Brahe (1546-1601) kept a dwarf who also had developmental disabilities for entertainment and advice on astrological events. Brahe thought the individual could shed insight into the nature of the universe (Krishef, 1983). Numerous contemporary studies have concluded that highly creative people often have more mood disorders, manic depression, and major depression (Angier, 1993). Jamison (1993) contends that several manic depressive, depressive, and bipolar individuals were highly creative. She maintains that some of their most creative work was completed during extreme shifts from depression to manic states of mind. Jamison (1993: 50) commented, "A possible link between madness and genius is one of the oldest and most persistent of cultural notions, it is also one of the most controversial." This was particularly true during the Renaissance when there was a great interest in the relationship between madness, depression, and genius. This interest dwindled and by the eighteenth century people thought balance and rationale mattered more than inspirational and emotional extremes. This pendulum swung back and peaked in the nineteenth century when the Romantics emphasized the emotional and spontaneous nature of genius.

As Evil

Historically, people with physical disabilities have been perceived as being evil. Summarizing literature, Kriegel (1987) proposed that literary images of physically disabled people fall into general themes. The images are the demonic cripple, such as Shakespeare's *Richard the III* (1597) and

Melville's Captain Ahab. Meyerson (1948) concluded almost 50 years ago the easiest way to characterize an adult as a villain was to cripple them. Closely linked to the perception of people being evil is their being viewed as dangerous. They have been associated with murder, horror, violence, and danger (Bogdan, et al. 1982). An often cited example of the linkage made between disability and evil is Shakespeare's portrayal of *Richard III.* Shakespeare's Richard III illustrates that the disability and evil were one and the same. He characterized Richard III as having a deformed body and evil personality. The truth is King Richard III did not have the disabilities attributed to him by Shakespeare (Sharpiro, 1993). Shakespeare simply created Richard's disabilities as a literary tool because this association was already familiar in western societies and he wanted to please Queen Elizabeth. Shakespeare's Richard III buttressed existing public perceptions of people with disabilities as being evil.

Others besides Shakespeare associated physical disabilities or deformities with evil. For example, the scholar Francis Bacon (1561-1626) believed that persons with deformities were commonly vengeful and ill-tempered. He believed they returned to the evil nature that was visited upon them (Barker, 1971:210). He also believed that persons with deformities were commonly ill-tempered and vengeful. In sharp contrast was the opinion of Robert Burton (1577-1621) who thought physical deformities and disabilities could improve the person's personality (Barker, 1948). Burton declared that although deformities and imperfections of body hurt many people, they could be comforted by the fact that such imperfections of the body did not harm but rather improved the personality.

Authors and scholars from other centuries furthered this association. Herman Melville's character Captain Ahab from *Moby Dick* (1851) lost his leg to the white whale and became an evil and obsessed individual. Robert Louis Stevenson's Long John Silver from *Treasure Island* (1882) was an evil personality with a physical disability. His wooden leg, during the course of the story, became the symbol for evil (Nelson 1994a). Numerous other examples of the connection between physical disability and evil are interwoven in western literature and social perceptions. For example, in the children's tale *Hansel and Gretel* (1893) the wicked witch limped.

A related theme is the long tradition of viewing light as good and darkness as bad. For example, the *Old Testament's* book of Genesis instructed, "And God saw the light, that it was good." Traditionally, people have associated light with good and darkness with the unknown and evil. Darkness connotes death, sin, punishment, and fear. Within this cultural context and social tradition, societies have assumed that people who were blind live in a world of darkness. Authors Milton, Charles Dickens, Victor Hugo, and others have depicted blindness as a state of darkness. Associated with the assumption of darkness was the related concept of inherent evil. Just as light was associated with all that is good, darkness was associated with all of that which was evil. Panofsky (1967:109) commented:

> Blindness is therefore always associated with evil, excepting the blindness of Homer, which served supposedly to keep his mind uninvited by sensual appetites, and the blindness of justice which was meant to assure her impartiality. Both these interpretations however are foreign to classical as well as medieval thought.

As Being Worthy of Pity and Charity

Another social perception of people who have physical disabilities was that they should be pitied and offered charity. This notion was born out of the Christian tradition which emphasized charity towards the disadvantaged (Schadewaldt, 1967c). Societies have often gone to great lengths to pity and feel sorry for people with disabilities. For instance, people have pitied individuals with developmental disabilities based on the belief that they were unhappy and suffering. People have pitied them because it was assumed that they were unable to live normal and meaningful lives. They were seen as being unhappy because they understood their limitations and the fact that they could never have what others had. In contrast, others have perceived people with developmental disabilities as not having any realization of their disabilities. They do not know any better or they are not cognizant of the larger world. Thus, people saw them as not having any feelings about their disabilities and did not comprehend what happened to them. Some perceived them as existing in a world of ignorant bliss, unaware of what they are missing in life, a perception that applied to other disabilities. The most common social attitude toward people who were blind were pity and sympathy. Experts have observed that showing pity toward people who were blind is a very old idea that can be tied to early Christian practices (Monbeck, 1973). To pity a blind person was socially acceptable for centuries. This pity was often out of proportion to the abilities and needs of the individual.

Many plots in western literature depict people with disabilities as being self-pitying and never being able to accept their disabilities. This self-pity, some authors would lead us to believe, results in some cases to resentment and hatred toward life and the world. The theme of self-pity is even taken to the extent that we are led to the conclusion that many people with disabilities would rather be dead than continue their lives. This conclusion is untrue and being pitied is far from the minds and wishes of most people with disabilities. Rather, many view pity as a barrier to the integration and social acceptance as full participating members of society. The perception of feeling pity can interfere with communications, isolates, and is oppressive.

Pity has frequently resulted in acts of charity. Presentations of charitable acts directed towards people with disabilities are numerous in art and literature. For example, Pieter Bruegel the Elder (1525-1569), in a pen and ink drawing, entitled *Charitas* (1559), shows numerous acts of charity. The drawing shows various beggars and people with physical disabilities receiving bread, clothing, medical care, and wine. Many of the recipients of charity were shown with crutches, amputations, or significant physical deformities, such as the individual reaching for bread in the right foreground. The wide-brimmed circular hats and clothing worn by some of the individuals suggest they had leprosy. Individuals who were infirm were shown receiving care in houses lining the background of the drawing. Individuals being punished in stocks also received attention in the background. In the far background the dead were shown being buried. The figure of Saint Elizabeth of Thuringa, known for her charitable acts, stands in the center of the work.

Literature also has linked physical disabilities with acts of charity. This social perception is best illustrated by Charles Dickens' Tiny Tim. The depiction of Charles Dickens' Tiny Tim in *A Christmas Carole* (1843) was written to evoke the reader's pity and empathy. Dickens guided the reader into feeling sorry for Tiny Tim and his plight. The reader is moved into not only feeling sorry for him but also wanting to do something to help because he deserves a better fate than disability or death. According to Kriegel (1987), Tiny Tim incorporates one of the basic themes in literature regarding people with physical disabilities, the charity cripple.

As Scapegoats

Societies have made people with disabilities into scapegoats. People with disabilities have represented a convenient group to blame for a number of problems. Societies have blamed them for droughts, crop failures, wars, diseases, unexplained deaths, blights, economic downturns, and a wide number of social ills. Historically, societies have found them to be an ideal target, as they have not always been able to defend themselves from accusations. Western civilization contains many examples of people with disabilities serving as scapegoats. For example, Frazer (1935:255) describes how Greeks during the sixth century BC treated them as scapegoats:

> When a city suffered from plague, famine or other public calamity, an ugly or deformed person was chosen to take upon himself all the evils which afflicted the community. He was brought to a suitable place, where dried figs, a barley loaf, and cheese were put into his hand. These he ate. Then he was beaten seven times upon his genital organs with quills and branches

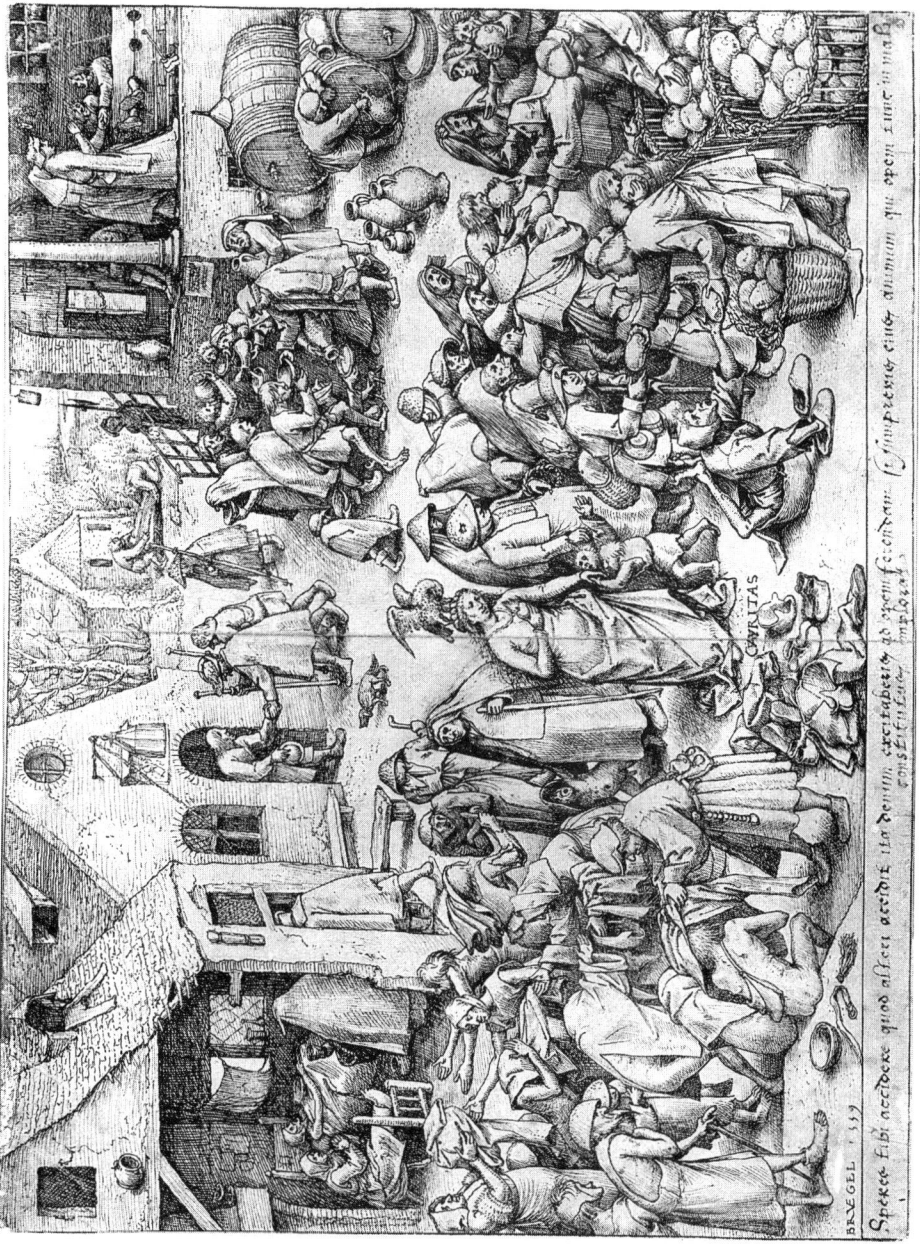

Figure 1. Bruegel the Elder, *Charitas*, 1559, Museum Boijmans Van Beuningen, Rotterdam.

of the wild fig and other wild trees, while the flutes played a particular tune. Afterwards he was burned on a pyre of wood of forest trees and his ashes were cast into the sea.

Although contemporary western societies do not blame them for plagues, droughts and other calamities, the theme has endured to the present. Today, the general public sometimes scapegoats and blames people with disabilities for contributing to governmental debt, wanting special privileges, promoting laziness, and ripping off the system.

As Being Entertaining

Since antiquity, societies have placed people with disabilities on exhibition for entertainment. Societies did not hesitate to put people, particularly those with physical deformities or mental illness, on public display for amusement and financial gain. Societies have acted if they have a social appetite for people with disabilities and deformities. The practice of displaying people spans from antiquity through the Middle Ages and was raised to an art form in the nineteenth century. For example, the ancient scholar and commentator Seneca described how the Greeks viewed people who had disabilities:

> Look on the blind wandering about the streets leaning on their sticks, and those with crushed feet, and still again look on those with broken limbs. This one is without arms, that one has had his shoulders pulled down out of shape in order that his grotesqueries may excite laughter. [Cited by Payne, 1916: 242-243]

The entertainment value of people with disabilities persisted long after antiquity. For example, in the seventeenth century the Elizabethans exhibited people for amusement (Despert, 1965). During the reign of Elizabeth I, the English had a great interest in what they labeled "raree shows." For example, Shakespeare's Trinculo stated:

> Were I in England now (as once I was) and had but this fish painted, not a holiday fool there but would give a piece of silver: there would this monster make a man; any strange beast there makes a man; when they will not give a do it to relieve a lame beggar, they will lay out ten to see a dead Indian. (*The Tempest*)

Public exhibitions of people who were mentally ill or who had developmental disabilities rivaled the "raree" shows at Smithfield for public curiosity and amusement. The period of the English Restoration made people who were mentally ill, as Fiedler (1978:280) concluded, "stellar attractions." Societies often have perceived people with mental illness or who were insane as being entertaining and amusing. It is well-known that caretakers of people in asylums displayed their wards for a fee. For example, in sixteenth and seventeenth century England, MacDonald (1981) noted the Bedlam asylum put people on display to address the public's fascination with insanity. The hospital was immensely popular as a source of entertainment until 1770. According to McGrew (1985) the fee for Bedlam was a penny a head and receipts for a year indicate that 96,000 people toured the facility for entertainment. In the eighteenth and nineteenth centuries, people with developmental and mental disabilities were increasingly isolated from public view. Because of their isolation in residential schools and institutions, their isolation seemed to fuel public fascination and the willingness to pay to see them. Physical and behavioral differences became more fascinating for the paying public at the same time people with severe developmental disabilities, major physical differences, or mental illness were being institutionalized. In the eighteenth century, the caretakers of Paris' asylums frequently subjected people to public showings and tours on Sundays. Public showings at Salpîtrière held a particular fascination as ragging and naked women drew big crowds (Jones, 1980a). However, not everyone who visited the asylums went for entertainment (Scull, 1993).

Over the centuries, people with physical disabilities and deformities were typical sideshow and circus attractions (Bogdan et al., 1982). For instance, people with spastic disorders were popularly perceived as clownish. Exhibitions of people increased in popularity from the sixteenth century onward, possibly reaching a peak between 1850 and 1900 (Stroman, 1982). The Victorians raised the practice of exhibiting people to a science. Nineteenth century showmen, such as P.T. Barnum, used the sideshow to display people with deformities and disabilities. People who were microcephalic proved to be ideal subjects for manipulating the public imagination and curiosity. Accompanying many of these people were fabricated stories of them being the missing link or genetic throwbacks, or coming from exotic places. In the age of the great African explorers such as Burton, Livingston, and Speake, there was a special fascination with exploration and people from "exotic" cultures. Consequently, there are many recorded instances of people of color, such as Africans, Asians, and South Americans with disabilities or deformities being displayed as curiosities and "freaks" (Lindfors, 1983). In the minds of racist entrepreneurs, Africans who were microcephalic were ideal for casting into the role of being the "missing links" between ape and humans.

Some of the people displayed became internationally famous, such as Hiram and Barney ("The Wildmen from Borneo"), Maximo and Bartola, William Henry Johnson ("Zip"), the "Aztec Children," the "Wild Girl of Yucatan," the "Missing Link," and the "Wild Australian Children." Their exhibitors fabricated elaborate stories and tales about their lives. These stories typically involved references to the people on exhibit as coming from exotic lands and being biological links between apes and humans. Bogdan (1986) noted that most of the people exhibited had microcephaly, possibly because it was easy for exhibitors to accent their differences by shaving their heads. Bogdan (1986) pointed out, the medical and scientific communities supported the explanations advanced by exhibitors. Social Darwinism and other scientific theories of the time validated the claims of the exhibitors. Often doctors or scientists would examine these people with much fanfare and substantiate the fabricated claims of exhibitors. The public response to these "freak shows" was enormous. Lindfors (1984) estimated over 100 million people saw William Henry Johnson ("Zip"), who was microcephalic, during his seven decades of being on exhibit.

All of this would change with the rise of modern medicine and social reform movements of the late nineteenth century. Both advanced the notion that people with disabilities or deformities should not be displayed because it was inhumane. By the twentieth century, doctors, reformers, and scientists started to define people with disabilities and deformities as "sick" and "needing pity." The general public eventually lost much of its appetite for viewing people who were different. Public displays of people with disabilities became rare and eventually lost their appeal and faded from acceptable practice.

An artistic example of an individual being used for entertainment would be Francisco Goya's drawing that shows peoples' fascination with a baby that was physically different. The drawing shows a mother displaying her child to two gossips. The baby is nude and rests on a blanket suggesting that this is not the first instance of her displaying the child. Displaying children with deformities at fairs and markets was common practice in Goya's time. Sanchez and Sayre (1989) noted that Goya drew the child with great compassion.

As Being Poor and Beggars

An enduring social perception of people with disabilities has been their association with poverty and begging. This social perception is witnessed by the many representations of people who had disabilities show them as impoverished and or begging. People have generally assumed that those with severe disabilities were poor because of prolonged illness. The historian LeGoff (1990: 321) concluded, "Being poor, sick, and a tramp were almost synonymous in the Middle Ages, and hospitals were often situated at bridges or mountain passes over which wanderers had to go." Medieval communities typically released all the people they could not tie up or shut away to the

Figure 2. Francisco Goya, *Something Rare*, captioned "Mother showing her deformed child to two women," 1814-1817, Lourve, Paris.

streets. Sick people and vagabonds integrated with pilgrims and merchants and wandered about the countryside (LeGoff, 1990). Communities were not always tolerant and often drove people out of town during the Middle Ages. The church took in some of them, but only for short periods. Others had to rely on begging and travel (vagabonding) to survive.

Prior to Europe's industrialization, most persons with disabilities were integrated into community roles, protected by ties of kinship and participation in wider social networks (Stone, 1984). Societies accepted begging if it was done by the deserving poor, which included those with disabilities. With increased industrialization and urbanization, begging became less socially acceptable. Social acceptance became linked to one's ability to work and contribute. Societies did not view begging as work and people dependent on begging were increasing judged negatively. What social meanings were attached to poverty and begging? Historically, societies have classified people who were poor into two broad categories. There are those poor who for reasons beyond their control, such as fate, sickness, misfortune, accident, birth, or old age. These were the poor people for which the general public found compassion and tolerance. Historically, people with severe disabilities have been classified into this group of the deserving poor. Their poverty has been viewed as justified given their assumed limitations. In a sense their disabilities provide a rationalization for their poverty. Then there were the poor that were the second type who were the undeserving poor. The undeserving poor were so because of life choices. For example, these were the people who were seen as lazy and unworthy.

A concern for poor people and the perceived risk they allegedly posed for society is an enduring theme in western history. In addition to humanitarian responses to illness or disability such as attempting to cure, offering care, compassion, etc., societies also attempted to control, isolate, and otherwise sanction people who were disabled. Communities tolerated the poor seeking alms and begging but only to a certain point. Some passed restrictions on vagrancy and begging. For example, in 1553, 60 pounds was given to lazar-houses in London on the condition the residents did not beg within three miles of the city's limits (Clay, 1909). Describing the plight of people who were insane and their reliance on begging, Scull (1993: 11) commented, "...the deranged beggar was a familiar part of medieval landscape, wandering from place to place, community to community, in search of alms." He then added, "Other lunatics relied on their families as a primary means of support."

During the Middle Ages, communities tolerated begging as a means for people to survive and make a living. It was a period that witnessed the rise of organized beggary (French, 1932). For example, as competition for alms increased and conflicts among groups of blind beggars occurred, people established guilds and brotherhoods at the close of the Middle Ages. Begging became an organized enterprise and in some communities corporations of beggars were established (Paulson, 1987). These early structured organizations appointed powerful leaders, developed rules, and created languages that only members could understand (French, 1932). The extent to which people who were blind depended on begging was so established that in 1377 a guild for blind beggars was established in Padua Italy. This guild was established to regulate begging and was so well-organized that pensions were provided to elderly-blind beggars. Other guilds were established in Europe, such as in Palermo, Italy in 1661. In Medieval Europe, people who were blind were also granted sole rights to selling amulets and selected prayers to support themselves (Gowman, 1957:106).

The church took an active role in either promoting acts of charity directed toward the needy by its followers or directly providing charity or care to the poor. Regarding the latter, the church would develop an expansive system of charitable organizations to serve people who were needy. This would dramatically change with the Reformation when Protestants and particularly the English confiscated church property and dismantled the power of religious brotherhoods and monasteries to administer to the poor. In England, following the wars of Henry VII and throughout the reign of Henry the VIII, the numbers of beggars reached such great proportions that public attitudes changed toward begging. Beggars who were blind increasingly were viewed with suspicion and hate. The success of some beggars who were blind was such that many people did not trust them. All of this eventually helped lead to the establishment of the poor laws and care for the poor by Queen Elizabeth in 1601. The Poor Laws of Elizabeth the I reflect the magnitude of the existing social problem of begging in England (Gowman, 1957). The laws allowed justices of the peace to name respected people from each parish to oversee the poor. These overseers could make levies on the parishioners to supply relief for older, sick, and people with disabilities. The English Poor Laws were enacted in part to limit the number of vagrant unemployed persons in any given locale by restricting their rights to beg. Similar restrictions occurred in the colonies when communities adopted English Poor Laws of 1536 and 1601 (Rothman, 1971; Stone, 1984).

Circumstances for beggars did not change much during the modern period, as begging continued to be widely practiced due to the persistence of poverty. Begging was to flourish in the modern period, in spite of modest efforts to curb its growth. The begging grew so much that the eighteenth century was known as the begging century. Garrison (1960: 351) provided a sense as to what it was like in some sectors of society to be blind and have to beg for survival:

In the eighteenth century, blind beggars were so numerous that they often fought and jostled for standing room in places where they were likely to receive alms. At its annual fairs it was customary to utilize the blind, decked out with asses' ears, peacocks' tails, and pasteboard spectacles, as objects of amusement.

No one really knows how many people who had disabilities turned to begging to survive. Many strong images created over the centuries show them as begging. Begging was not the only means of survival that people with disabilities have turned to and led productive lives without begging. It is less evident that alternatives to begging were available to those with less severe disabilities and with support systems that permitted people to work in crafts and trades. Apart from entertainment, such as music, few if any presentations of people with physical disabilities depict them as working even though many certainly did. Begging, for better or worse, was to become strongly associated with people with disabilities. Although not generally condoned today, begging by people with disabilities was socially accepted and supported for many centuries.

Consequently, the strong association between disability and begging resulted in artists creating numerous images of people with disabilities as beggars. These presentations contributed to the social perception that people with disabilities either were or were likely to become beggars. People who were blind, deaf, had leprosy, and most typically physical disabilities were popular subjects for artists depicting begging. Examples include the Italian artist Francesco Traini's (1321-1365) *A Group of Beggars* which shows a number of subjects with canes and deformities begging. Cornelius Buys' *Feeding the Hungry* (1504) shows a line of hungry people and a person with physical disabilities begging in the forefront for bread. Pieter Bruegel the Elder (1525-1569) painted a courtyard scene of a group of five people in his *The Cripples* or as it is sometimes called *The Beggars*. Bruegel showed the group heading in different directions, which has no known explanation. It has been proposed that they had just completed and were leaving a conversation. Bruegel presented them wearing foxtails, wooden stumps, crutches, and shapeless headgear. Wearing foxtails was common for people who had leprosy in Bruegel's time (Hughes & Bianconi, 1967). Gauthier (1964) observed that the five subjects are wearing different hats, including a bishop's mitre, crown, helmet, which symbolizes the church, nobility, and military that were major sources of influence. In the background a woman is shown walking in the background carrying a begging bowl. Her costume suggests that she has leprosy. Bruegel seems to be drawing attention to, in the opinion of some the misery and difficulty of having to live by begging (Seidel & Marijnissen, 1971).

Figure 3. Pieter Bruegel the Elder, *The Cripples,* 1568, Louvre, Paris.

The artist Jacques Callot (1592-1635) *Vagabonds* contains several etchings of beggars with disabilities. Callot, opening the door for the later artist Francisco Goya, devoted much of his attention to the consequences of war. Callot was horrified with what happened to people in wars and used his art as a social commentary of his times. Many of his works present street people who were victims of the war, such as soldiers who were amputees. The following etching shows a veteran who has lost his right leg to war. Battlefield surgical techniques of his period were successful enough that some soldiers survived battlefield amputations and returned to society. Other illustrations of beggars with physical disabilities abound in western art. For instance, Rembrandt, perhaps influenced by the works of Callot, also drew a number of beggars he observed in the streets of Dutch towns. Rembrandt lived during Holland's golden years which was a time of great socioeconomic contrasts between the very rich and the extremely poor. In 1589, Amsterdam attempted to teach beggars trades, as did Leiden in 1596, but eventually banned beggars from its streets.

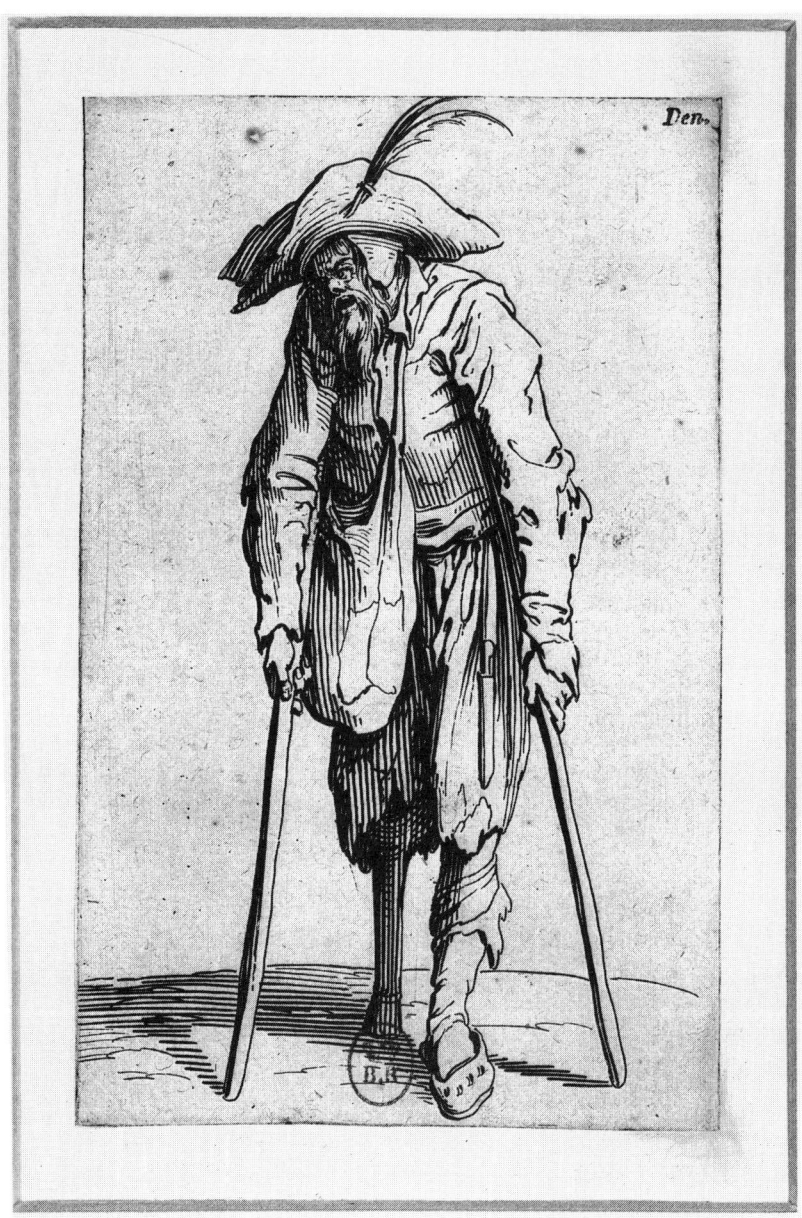

Figure 4. Jacques Callot from his series of etchings entitled *Vagabonds, Crippled Beggar,* early seventeenth century, Bibliotheque Nationale, Paris.

The association of blindness with begging represents another major enduring social perception of people who were blind. One of the most frequently assigned role for people who were blind has been that of beggar

(Best, 1934; Monbeck, 1973; Ross, 1951). The relationship between blindness and begging was so strong that being blind and a beggar were viewed as virtually one and the same for centuries (Levy, 1872). In ancient times, most people who were blind were beggars (Monbeck, 1973). Evidence shows that begging was a common occupation for people who were blind in Hebrew Times (Farrell, 1956). The *New Testament* makes numerous references to Jesus meeting people who were blind beggars. Among some beggars, blindness was viewed as an asset, they frequently collected more alms than people with other disabilities. Their success was due in part to the perception of their lifelong dependence on other people for survival. Historical records reveal that people who were blind were comparatively successful in collecting alms. For example, Paulson (1987:8) found the statutes of the Quinze-Vingts (France) from the mid-fourteenth century include provisions governing the begging expeditions blind residents were to make for the profit of the entire community. The provisions included sections requiring them to share collections with people less successful at begging.

People who were blind also enjoyed special begging privileges during the Middle Ages (Gowman, 1957). In the Slavic countries folk traditions encouraged the favorable treatment of and respect for people who were blind (Vukanovic, 1985). Besides folk tradition, the church supported and condoned their begging. In several instances, the church gave them ideal locations near the entrances for begging. For example, St. Ambrose permitted them to beg on church grounds and gave them ideal locations at the entrances of churches to ensure their collections were high.

Other Social Perceptions of People with Disabilities

Over the centuries other social perceptions of people with disabilities have persisted. One enduring perspective was to see them as children. The social perception of them being children was particularly true for those with developmental disabilities or mental retardation (Bogdan & Biklen, 1977). Perceiving them as children robbed them of their rights, responsibilities, and status. Viewing them as children, resulted in people treating them in condescending or patronizing manners (Davis, 1961). Other social perceptions of people with disabilities include the view that they were damaged, defective, and less socially acceptable than nondisabled people (Phillips, 1990). Another perception is they prefer to be with their own "kind." This latter view is sometimes stated by people who have disabilities, such as some people who are deaf. Nelson (1994a) identified the social perceptions of super crip, sinister, evil, criminal, economic burdens, better off dead, maladjusted, and unable to live successful lives as being other perceptions of people with disabilities. They have been perceived in some periods such as the Middle Ages, along with sinners, Jews, heretics, criminals, as being doomed and damned. For example, in medieval art such as the early Bamberg Dome's tympanum of the Portal of the Princes, the stone carver grouped a person who is deaf with other outsiders and evil characters as being damned (Fischer & Lane, 1993). In addition, some folk traditions taught people to distrust those who had lost their physical abilities, as the loss represented an outward sign of their moral weakness (Saint-Loup, 1993).

People with developmental disabilities have been viewed as being prolific and sexually hyperactive. Because of their assumed lower moral intelligence, poor judgment, and subhuman characteristics, they were seen as sexual predators frequently wanting sex. Hence, the public concern during the late nineteenth century and continuing to the present was that their sexual activities needed to be restricted. In a similar vein, they were viewed as the product of degenerate families, which formed a major part of the lower economic strata. During the nineteenth century, people thought "degenerate" families spawned disease, disability, dependency, and social misfits, including criminals, paupers, and biological, inferior people. People with developmental disabilities were included in these groups of perceived racially inferior and hypersexual people.

Other social perceptions about people with developmental disabilities were advanced. For example, they have been viewed as burdens to society because in severe cases, they required help from others to survive. They have been labeled, in modern slang, "vegetables" who are incapable of accomplishing anything of social value. Because of their disabilities, they have been perceived as never becoming "complete" individuals. Along similar lines, some people have viewed them as occupationally incompetent and have been perceived as being incapable of handling even the simplest of tasks. They have been perceived as being blissfully ignorant and happy (Evans, 1983). This social perception held that people with developmental disabilities are generally happy because they did not know what is going on around them. They were perceived as being carefree and having no responsibilities. They were also seen as being devoid of normal sentiments and having diminished powers of sensory acuity.

Societies have perceived people with physical disabilities as being unattractive or ugly. This social perception can be traced back to at least the ancient Greeks who placed value on the ideal human form. From the Greeks onward, any significant departure from this bodily ideal was open to criticism. Authors have used this perception as a literary tool. For example, authors frequently have juxtaposed people with physical disabilities or deformities against beauty. The nineteenth century novels, such as Mary Wollstonecraft Shelly's *Frankenstein* (1818) and Victor Hugo's *The Hunchback of Notre Dame* (1834) pair people with major physical disabilities with beautiful women. The authors contrasted the ugliness of physical disability with the attractiveness of women to refine their story lines.

Many scholars on the subject of disabilities concur that people with obvious disabilities have been cast into deviant social roles by the larger society (Bogdan & Taylor, 1989; Davis, 1961; Goffman, 1963; Longmore, 1985b). For instance, people have viewed those who are deaf as being social deviants and clannish (Lane, 1992). The crux of why this is so rests primarily on the inability of either group to effectively communicate with the other. The identification of people, for whatever reason, as being deviant always implies negative connotations and rejection. However, it would be wrong to conclude that rejection and labeling people with disabilities as deviants are universals among all nondisabled people. To the contrary, there have been and continue to be people who do not reject nor label people with disabilities as deviant. Recent research by Bogdan and Taylor (1989) found examples of accepting relationships, the ability to attribute thinking to the other, seeing individuality, and interacting between people with and people without disabilities. They found that family members, friends, and caretakers often were very accepting of children and adults with disabilities. Their research subjects saw the whole person and not just the disability. This same pattern probably existed in the past.

Societies react to people with disabilities as being liabilities. For example, societies have viewed people who were blind as uselessness and helpless (Koestler, 1976; Monbeck, 1973). Historical evidence does not support this perception and people with disabilities have been economic contributors to their respective societies. In a related vein, Scheer and Groce (1988) raised an important point about the social perception of people with disabilities. Some social scientists assume that the disability results in a certain degree of marginality for the individual. That is, people with disabilities are automatically marginal to their societies. This Scheer and Groce argue is inaccurate because it ignores the positive and valuable roles people with disabilities have performed in their societies.

This brief inventory does not exhaust all of the social perceptions societies have held of or reactions to people with disabilities. It does underscore a fundamental point that regardless if the perception is negative or positive, the perception nevertheless serves to separate and distinguish people with disabilities from those who lack them. It is important to note that while some of these perceptions are shared and cut across the different types of disabilities, others seem to apply to specific disabilities.

COMMON EXPLANATIONS FOR DISABILITIES

For any historical review of disabilities, it is important to review some of the popular beliefs about what caused disabilities. People's beliefs about what caused disease or disability have run the gamut over the centuries. One explanation was that supernatural forces caused disabilities, such as curses, spells, supernatural beings, gods, witches, and a broad range of forces. For instance, some people have thought that mental and emotional disorders could be caused by the evil eye (Hand, 1980). Periodically, people also have assumed witches could bring about blindness, deafness, physical disabilities, mental disorders, and a number of other disabilities. One of the most lasting explanations for disease and disability is that both were reflective of the powers or will of the gods or God's. People were born with disabilities because of divine forces. Consequently, priests, shamans, spiritual healers, and others were frequently involved in healing and early medical practice.

A prevailing view for much of history has been that illness was divinely ordained as punishment for sin (Rubin, 1974). In the Judeo-Christian tradition, God inflicted disease or disability on individuals or groups. Hand (1980:60) observed, "Crippling of children at birth and other forms of disfigurement are thought of as having been brought on by divine displeasure." God inflicts disabilities on people under a number of pretexts, such as punishment for sin, as an instructional tool, as an act of power, as a warning, to defend people, and enforce morality. People viewed sickness and disease as God's punishment (Hand, 1980). The belief that God's inflicted disability as a retribution for the sins of people lasted for centuries. For example, the Puritan Increase Mather (1684) provided several examples of children born with disabilities that were the result of God's divine retribution (displeasure). Later, his son Cotton Mather echoed this belief in his sermons and writings. Christians have generally believed that disability was a means by which moral doctrine was expressed.

People have also associated magic, sorcery, enchantments, spells, charms, evil spirits, and witchcraft with disease and disability. Western societies have thought that supernatural beings, such as spirits and demons, caused disease (Garrison, 1960; Meaney, 1992). For example, Germanic and Anglo-Saxon folklore contain many references to elves causing disease and illness. Some believed disease was the result of elf shot. Elf shot was when elves threw darts that produced illness in the victim (Meaney, 1992). Other references to demons, magic, spirits, and witches abound in western societies. For example, medieval theologians concluded that incubi and succubi existed and had carnal relations with sleeping persons. This belief became undisputed dogma and served as a ready explanation for infants being born with disabilities or deformities, as they were the products of such sexual encounters.

Public attention was also directed toward witches and heretics. The witch-hunting manual entitled the *Malleus Maleficarum* published in 1485 served as a complete guide for the discovery, examination, torture, trial, and treatment of people believed to be witches. People believed witches caused disorders, disease, and disabilities in people. For example, some thought that witches caused victims to have "fits." These fits were thought to be hysterical possessions by the devil. The idea of possession by a demon was an old notion that people used to explain mental illness and in some cases epilepsy (Burstein, 1956). Burstein (1956:21), summarizing the general historical context of medicine from 1500 to 1700, noted that any disease might be attributed to the workings of spirits or witchcraft, but there were certain outstanding groups, such as diseases of the nervous system, apoplexy, paralysis (partial and general), epilepsy, and hysteria, were specially attributed to witchcraft. For instance, William Drage's *Daimonomageia* (1665) elaborates extensively about the role of witchcraft in promoting disease. However, not everyone subscribed to demonic and witch-based causes of disability and disease. Henry Cornelius Agrippa (1486-1535), Paracelsus (1490-1541), Johann Weyer (1515-1588), and Reginald Scot (1538-1599) among others boldly challenged demonic and witchcraft explanations for disease and disability. The Swiss physician Paracelsus proclaimed mental diseases had nothing to do with evil spirits or demons, and that one should not study exorcism to cure the insane (Burstein, 1956).

The physician Galen (b. 129 AD) would create the prevailing medical paradigm for understanding the body and disease that lasted for centuries. Galen was a master at compiling ideas from a variety of sources and putting them into a comprehensive system of medicine. He transformed the earlier works of Hippocrates (460-377 BC) into his framework. Scholars thought all substances were made up of the four elements of fire, air, water, and earth. According to Galen, the human body converted the four elements into bodily fluids that were referred to as humours. The humors were blood, phlegm, yellow bile, and black bile. Galen thought the body was healthy when the four body qualities of hot, cold, dry, and moist were in harmony or perfect equilibrium. Scholars assumed that each of these qualities had its own temperament. The lack of or preponderance of any humours led to disability or disease. Scholars and physicians saw illness and disease, including some forms of disability, as resulting from humoural imbalances (Talbot, 1967a). Treatment of illness was, in essence, an effort to restore the imbalance of the humors. Galen's theory of the four body humours would be rediscovered, dominate, and be relatively unchallenged in western medicine from the twelfth to sixteenth century (Stannard, 1985). Later influential medical authorities such as Joannes Plaearius (eleventh century), Arnold of Villanova (1235-1312), Henry of Mondeville and Guy de Chauliac (1300-1368) all ascribed to the humoural theory. Beyond the sixteenth and through much of the nineteenth century, medical practice remained grounded in humoural theory, which basically ignored external sources of infection (Wells, 1964). Paralleling the humoural theory was the idea that internal organs, such as the spleen, intestines, stomach, and liver, also contributed to illness, including mental disorders. For example, people thought hysteria was due to the movement of the uterus inside the female body.

Historically, violence and accidents have always been major sources of disabilities. Wars have been major disablers of people. Western history can be viewed as a series of deadly and disabling wars that, although not fought on the scale known today, nevertheless played havoc on the health of the populace. Notable wars that led to disabilities include the numerous crusades that resulted in disease and disabilities for surviving crusaders. Many crusaders returned to Europe blind. Saint Louis was so moved by their numbers that he founded a hospital in 1254 in Paris for crusaders blinded by their campaigns in the Holy Land. The term hospital comes from the Hospitallers, which was a religious and military order that sent numerous crusaders to fight in the crusades, only to have them return wounded and often disabled. In addition, many surgeons learned their craft on the battlefields of Europe. Surgeons performed amputations, with varying degrees of success, for centuries. Famous battlefield surgeons, such as Ambroise Pare (1510-1590) and Richard Wise (1622-1676) were known to have performed several amputations a day. Advances made by Pare, such as his method of ligature resulted in more successful amputations of limbs and consequently more people survived and lived with disabilities. The war surgeon Dr. Larrey of Napoleon's Grand Armee allegedly performed 200 amputations in 24 hours at Borodino during the Napoleonic Wars (Haggard, 1932). Improvements in surgical techniques undoubtedly allowed more people to survive the ravages of war and live with disabilities.

Folk theories on the causes of deformities and disabilities included the belief that congenital disorders were due to maternal impressions the mother had on the unborn child (Eberly, 1988). For example, if the mother was frightened by something, the unborn child would take on characteristics of the source of fright. People linked marital fright or marking to congenital deformities, such as deafness. A mother's fear of giving birth to a child who was deaf resulted in her having a deaf child. People believed that a mother would come into contact with a deaf child that made her fearful and consequently give birth to a deaf child. People held this view well into the nineteenth century.

In folklore, children born with congenital deformities, such as cleft palate, might be viewed as a product of pairing between the human and animals or demons (Eberly, 1988). People believed that hybrids between humans and other animals existed. The belief in the link between evil spirits or parental misconduct and the birth of children with disabilities is widespread in western history. The belief was present in preindustrial and industrial Europe and America (Winthrop, 1959). Other variations on this belief have been advanced, such as people have believed that violent events occurring during pregnancy could cause disabilities and deformities. Societies have viewed disabilities as the result of moral transgressions. Societies have advanced other folk theories. For instance, in the Netherlands, "monsters" were viewed in folk wisdom to be the products of God's reaction to copulation during menstruation (Hand, 1980).

Astrological and celestial theories have fueled beliefs about what caused disabilities and deformities. Since the time of the Babylonians, astrology has played a role in explaining phenomena including disease and disability. During the Middle Ages, scholars linked the body and health with the cosmos. Medieval scholars proposed that particular planets and signs of the zodiac governed parts of the body and placed emphasis on the zodiac as an explanatory tool and predictor of events. People believed the different parts of the body corresponded with the zodiac and the movement of planets and stars affected behavior and health. Building on Galen's' theory of body humors, medieval scholars believed that astral influences were linked to bodily humors. Those people born under certain astrological conditions had propensities toward certain humors that were affected by changing astral influences.

Historically, people have linked the normal process of aging to the development of disabilities. People have perceived that as people aged and particularly by the time they reached old age, their senses became diminished, their mental functioning declined, and they lost physical mobility. Over the centuries, many cultural representations on the subject showed old age as a time in life of decline and disability. Writers, artists, and scholars typically depicted older people as having disabilities. They represented disabilities by illustrating older people as needing canes, crutches, and assistance. They often characterized old age as a time of misery and decline, as the individuals became increasingly disabled. Physical decay became a major motif during the Middle Ages (Covey, 1991; Huizinga, 1952; Tristram, 1976). It was an era in which people strongly associated the passage of time with decay (de Beauvior, 1972) and death (Aries, 1985; Stannard, 1977.) During the fifteenth and sixteenth centuries (and perhaps earlier), people interpreted this decay as a sign of human failure. Later, Elizabethan playwrights wrote of the physical infirmities that were considered an inevitable accompaniment of the aging process. By the end of the seventeenth century, Restoration comedy writers were obsessed with the idea (Mignon, 1947). In later centuries people continued to view decay as a product of aging, with each progressive age of life bringing its share of disability to the individual.

The process of decay appears in several works that influenced western thought over the centuries. For example, the book of Ecclesiastes characterizes old age in terms of physical decay (Kastenbaum & Ross, 1975). In the thirteenth century Roger Bacon thought, as did others of his time, that every day is a step toward old age and that disease accelerated the process (Freeman, 1965). Shakespeare's play *As You Like It* has the character Jacques state, "And so from hour to hour we ripe, and ripe, And then from hour to hour, we rot, and rot, And thereby hangs a tale" (Act 2, Scene 7). Other authors associated aging with physical decline, such as Congreve, Wycherley, Dryden, Etherege and others. Early New England writers also acknowledged the process of decay and viewed aging as a time of misery and pain (Fischer, 1978). Demos (1986) provides examples of the "natural infirmities" of old age identified by the influential Cotton Mather. Mather went into great detail and described weak teeth, weak backs, buckling legs, and other aspects of physical decline (Demos, 1986).

Diseases and resulting disability have been attributed to a number of other explanations. For instance, medieval medical thought is laced with references to worms causing disease and illness (Pouchelle, 1990). Bald's *Leechbook*, written during the tenth century Anglo-Saxon period identified worms (wyrms) as a cause of illness. As difficult as this is to understand today, it is possible to see why Anglo Saxons and others would have reached this conclusion. Meaney (1992:14) commented, "Any people living in unhygienic conditions would see intestinal worms of many kinds, passes in the faeces." He added, "Blowfly maggots can infest infected wounds, and squeezed out blackheads and boils have the form if not the substance of worms." According to Philippe Aries (1974), the medieval French had a view euphemistically termed *les oeuvres naturelles*, the operations of nature. This view held that all human bodies contain worms that eventually consume the individual.

MAJOR HISTORICAL TRENDS THAT HAVE AFFECTED PEOPLE WITH DISABILITIES

Several social changing contexts have framed the history of disability. Major changes in western history, such as the rise of Christianity, the move toward secularism, rise of the importance of the individual, and the development of modern science, strongly influenced people with disabilities. To understand disabilities, consideration must be given to understanding some of the major forces emerging and operating during the development of western civilization.

The Rise of Christianity

In a broad sense the growth of Christianity gave rise to a more humane interest in the plight of common people, including those with disabilities. Christianity basically taught that compassion towards others was important and human life was sacred. But at times, Christianity could respond with cruelty and intolerance toward anyone who was different, including people with disabilities. For instance, some Christians interpreted disabilities as evidence of sin, as signs of pacts with the Devil, or as evidence of heresy. One Christian tradition views people with disabilities are not innocent victims but guilty of violating God's will. They were seen as paying for the original sin or the sins they had committed, and the sins of the world. Specifically, they were seen as sinners or the offspring of parents who sinned. Aware of this, the church enforced God's will and passed judgment on people with disabilities by viewing and treating them as sinners. Church officials were frequently involved in the diagnosis of mental illness (sometimes mental illness), epilepsy, leprosy, and other disabilities or diseases that resulted in disabilities. In policy and action, the church made moves to punish, separate, and exclude them from the rest of society and the workings of the church. For example, the church restricted the rights of people with disabilities to be buried on church grounds, become married, and become priests or monks. This tradition also characterized people with disabilities as unclean.

The second Christian tradition was based on compassion and understanding. According to the second tradition, people with disabilities were innocent victims of misfortune. The church's role was to be the protector and benefactor for the downtrodden and disadvantaged. This tradition viewed people with compassion and charity. Christianity influenced society in many humane ways, such as helping to decrease the practice of infanticide. Furthermore, a number of church sponsored facilities, hospitals and other organizations arose during the Middle Ages and following centuries. Talbot (1967a) concluded the fundamental change in social conditions brought about by Christianity was most noticeable in its attitude toward the poor and suffering. This found expression in the institution of houses of hospitality where orphans, widows, the homeless, the old, and those who had no means of subsistence could find shelter. In Medieval England, the poor (including many people with disabilities) became highly dependent on the haphazard and sporadic traditions of Christian charity and almsgiving (Scull, 1993).

By the sixteenth century the church's role would change dramatically. A series of clashes and wars between the church and the state over power and control dramatically changed the way the poor were dealt. The church lost much of its control and authority to the state. The sixteenth century struggle for control between the state and church, according to Andrew Scull (1993), resulted in a reduction of funds available to care for the poor. Church sponsorship of facilities and care declined. Furthermore, the public developed a greater sense of unworthiness of those people seeking charity. Society increasingly condemned the poor and condemnation became acceptable during the last third of the sixteenth century. The refusal to give alms became acceptable custom. Towards the end of the eighteenth century the church's influence over society further declined. Modern science and medicine began to undercut the church's role as healer of the body and mind. Trained doctors and nurses replaced priests and nuns as care providers. The explanatory power of science and medicine supplanted the sacred explanation for disability.

The growth of Christianity gave rise to new methods and centers of religious healing and treatment. Shrines, relics, saints, monasteries, and the underlying belief that God was the ultimate force behind healing fueled the church's involvement in treating illness, disease, and disability. Christians believed sickness was the result of the fall of man (original sin). Interpretations on whether actions of individuals resulted in disease because of the fall or the fall itself indiscriminately varied (Siraisi, 1990). Christians viewed miracle cures and healings as testimony for the power of God and the effectiveness of sacred over secular modes of healing. The power of God to heal through the church would be an enduring theme in the rise of Christian Europe. In response, countless believers undertook pilgrimages and sought the healing powers of religious relics. Paxton (1992) noted that people prayed directly to God for the recovery of the ailing and performed rituals of healing through anointing or laying on of hands. According to Gordon (1991:145), "People invoked the aid of saints as intercessors for acute and chronic illnesses, disabilities, emotional disorders, and accidental injuries."

Numerous artists throughout the Middle Ages and periods that followed portrayed miracle cures in many of their works. Examples include the Italian artist Duccio di Buoninsegna's (d. 1319) *Jesus Opens the Eyes of a Man Born Blind*, Masolino Da Panicale's *Healing of the Cripple* (1425), and Massaccio's *St Peter Healing the Sick by the Fall of his Shadow* (1427). Artists following the Middle Ages also illustrated miracles, such as Anthony Van Dyck's (1599-1641) painting *Christ Healing the Paralytic* (1619) and Rembrandt's (1606-1669) etching *Christ with the Sick Around Him, Receiving the Children* (1649). Giovanni Battista Tiepolo's (1696-1770) painting entitled *Christ Curing the Blind* shows Christ under a tree curing a blind man in front of witnesses.

Christians took pilgrimages for a number of reasons including for pardon of sin, assurance of deliverance from damnation, penance, boredom, freedom from servitude and imprisonment, emotional release, and healing. To the medieval mind, the pilgrimage was one of the most powerful sources of help with the cure of disease (Rowling, 1968) and a great number of pilgrims were disabled or assisted friends or family members who were (Herzlich & Pierret, 1985). Jacques de Vitry's thirteenth century book entitled *Exempla* provides insights into the social life of the late thirteenth century France. Commenting on pilgrimages, de Vitry told the following story:

> I heard that many lame and deformed persons assembled at the tomb of a certain saint to be cured. But when they had been there two days and still not been healed, they refused to leave, because of the priest. But they disturbed the church and interrupted the divine office. The priest addressed them: "Do you want to be healed, so that you can go and run of your own accord?" They replied: "We do want that, Sir." Then said the priest: "Throw away all your canes," and when they were thrown away: 'Wait a little until fire is brought. For he who is the most disabled amongst you must be burnt. Then I will cast the ashes of his body over the others and they will be healed." Each and every one of them now became very afraid that he would be judged to be the most disabled, and thus be burned. Each began to force himself to such an extent that they all at once began to run away. Not one of them remained who did not leave the place without a cane; fear added wings to their feet! How wretched are they who fear the fire of this life and fly from it, but have no fear of the fire of hell. [Cited by Wortley, 1992:62]

The church often has used people with disabilities to serve its purposes relying on moralistic and humane traditions. People with disabilities have, in a sense, been moral pawns of the church. When societies needed to find blame for plagues and other calamities, people with disabilities provided a ready pool of scapegoats. For instance, when it was convenient, the church saw infants born with deformities or disabilities as products of sin. The church also used people with disabilities as subjects of miracle cures. It taught that often the benefactors of miracles were people who were blind, deaf, insane, or physically disabled. Christians with disabilities and their families have historically provided alms and donations to the church in the hope that their circumstances would improve. The church used these same people and their disabilities as reminders of the wages of sin. The church instructed that God afflicted disabilities on people for sin and identified people with disabilities were living examples of God's punishment. Likewise, people with disabilities have benefited from the church. Much of the humane treatment and care of people is directly linked to the teaching and practices of the church. The Christian tradition identified them as particularly deserving of compassion and charity (Park, 1991).

Humanism

Western curiosity and inquiry about human existence in this world erupted in a new way at the close of the Middle Ages. The Renaissance gave rise to the philosophy and body of thought called humanism. The fourteenth and early fifteenth centuries were the age of the first humanists, Boccaccio and Petrarch. They moved intellectual thought from the rigid doctrines of the Middle Ages to a renewed respect for the teachings of the ancient Greeks and Romans. The human body became interpreted differently, which had consequences for people with disabilities. It was also during this time that people, such as Calvin, Knox, Luther, Wycliffe and other religious reformers, increasingly challenged the authority of the church. Here the focus shifted from the afterlife to the human being and life on earth. Life in the here and now became the focus of scholarship and the arts. The importance of the individual, including those with disabilities, came to the forefront.

The Renaissance and rise of humanism provided the foundation for modern thought. During this great awakening, a new leisure class developed, scholars were active, artists prolific, musicians creative, and poets productive. It was a period of discovery and people increasingly relied on native languages instead of Latin to communicate. The result was a spreading of knowledge that was previously unavailable to the masses. Mass printing also allowed for the spread of information to more people. The structure of the human body became important to understand. Many of the great artists of the time, such as Leonardo da Vinci (1452-1518), Michaelangelo (1475-1564), Albrecht Dürer (1471-1528) became interested in the body and how it functioned. Later, the Enlightenment would rely on the ideas of the Renaissance humanists. The Enlightenment ideas of Rousseau and the Encylopedists gave rise to empathy and compassion for the neglected and downtrodden such as prisoners, slaves, oppressed, and people with disabilities (Kanner, 1960-1961).

The values of humanism led to increased public interest and involvement in the affairs of people with disabilities. Humanism represented a shift from public indifference to social action. This public action helped fuel the establishment of formal institutions designed to provide long-term care or custody of people with disabilities. Overall humanism allowed for humane and charitable treatment and interpretations of people with disabilities. Humanism also drew attention to human form and function, which represented a return to the physical ideal expressed by the ancient Greeks.

The Rise of Modern Medicine

In the beginning of western history, disease, or disability were viewed in moral and religious contexts. When people sought explanations for disabilities or corresponding cures, they turned to religion, astrology, folk, and other nonscientific based bodies of belief and knowledge. With the development of modern medicine, the abilities to consistently and accurately identify and diagnose ailments improved over time. This was critical because early medical treatments were based more on authority and conjecture than observation. Among early physicians misdiagnosis was the rule rather than the exception. This was partially due to the training physicians received. Medical students and surgeons were trained by instructors and manuals that were often grounded in misconception rather than fact. Illustrations in early medical texts were often inaccurate and misleading. Theories on the causes of ailments were also incorrect and undoubtedly, many people died as a result of medical interventions based on false notions.

Over time modern medicine and science would supplant preexisting explanations for medical phenomena and disabilities. This shift in orientation can be witnessed on several fronts. For example, the development of the medical and scientific notion of contagion would come to shape peoples' views on disabilities. The idea that disease and disability might be contagious was applied in the case of leprosy, where societies treated people with the disease as if there was a strong possibility of catching the disease. Societies also applied the notion of contagion to mental illness and believed that people would spread mental illness. Consequently, people tried to distance themselves from the victims of disease. As history progressed, increasingly connections were made between exposure and contraction of disease.

The historical development of medicine and its impact on people with disabilities would warrant a separate volume. However, there were key developments that were more important than others. One was the Hippocratic theory which served as the basis for western medical practice for the next 1500 years. The Hippocratic tradition was captured in the 60 Hippocratic writings, known as the *Corpus Hippocraticum*. The *Corpus* includes about 60 treatises attributed to Hippocrates and represents much of the foundation for medieval medicine. The Roman physician Galen (129-200 AD) *Ars Magna*, was essentially based on the Hippocratic system of bodily humours. His system was influential and the whole of medieval medicine may be described as Galenic.

Many theories of the causes of illness were available to the medieval practitioner and so were treatments. To the medieval mind, almost everything in the natural and spiritual worlds had curative powers. Everything was virtually a cause or cure for some ailment. A case in point is the notable Saint

Hildegard of Bingen's (1098-1179) suggestion that deafness could be cured by cutting-off a lion's ear and holding it over the patient's ear (Thorndike, 1923: Vol. 2, 145). She also thought that the heart of the weasel when dried and placed in the ear could cure deafness. Physicians and other care providers relied on a number of approaches such as astrology. Astrologers linked the constellations to prognosis and diagnosis. For practitioners studying the stars and planets was a great tool because it could easily be integrated with any number of explanatory schemes for behavior and health, such as the stages of life, magic, and medicine (Burrow, 1986; Covey, 1991; Dove, 1986).

The advances of the sixteenth century provided the foundation for modern medicine in the seventeenth and eighteenth centuries (Ehrlich, 1986). Medical science made a quantum leap in 1628 with William Harvey's (1567-1657) book on the circulation of the blood. Nevertheless, people continued to view demons, spirits, and witches as causing disease, illness, and disability. Physicians during the seventeenth and eighteenth centuries clung to medieval notions about the causes and treatments of diseases and disabilities. Physicians continued to rely on mystical and superstitious explanations for treatments and cures. Dunning (1992:92) provides one example, " ... the drama of death by hanging nurtured superstitions, that the blood of one executed, for example, could heal epilepsy and leprosy, or that touching the corpse could cure glandular tuberculosis, ulcers, and tumors." Some of these practices continued in the nineteenth century (MacKinney, 1965). Doctors continued to rely on cautery, bloodletting, herbs, and crude surgery, although refinements were made.

The Rise of Institutions and Hospital Care

Paralleling the evolution of modern medicine was the rise of institutions, such as hospitals and asylums, devoted to caring and treating people, including those with disabilities. The rise of these institutions had a profound effect on the lives of people with disabilities. It is known that the Egyptians constructed temples over 4,000 years ago to treat people for a variety of ailments. The Greeks had temples that were used to treat but not care for people. In 325 AD, the Roman Emperor Constantine ordered the construction of a hospital in every cathedral town. One of the first hospitals built under this directive was St. Basil at Caesarea, which was completed in 368 to 372. Byzantine and Moslem hospitals would be established between the eight and twelfth centuries.

Medieval monks established monastic infirmaria and the medieval hospitallers their hospices to care for people (MacKinney, 1965). Early hospitals' primary purpose was to look after people who could not take care of themselves and not necessarily treatment. The main task was to keep people alive and as comfortable as possible (Park, 1991). These early hospitals were repositories of a wide variety of the sick, disabled, old and poor. For example, Clay (1909:65) reported that St. John's at Canterbury in 1084 served, "...a hundred poor, who by reason of age and disease cannot earn their bread; and again, as a hundred hunched brothers and sisters blind, lame, deaf and sick." Medieval hospitals in England served many functions including hospitality for travelers of all classes, as educational establishments, and looking after the poor, old, and sick (Rawcliffe, 1984). For instance, St. Hans Hospital in Denmark held the mentally ill, oldest, and weakest of Copenhagen's poor people.

The rise of hospitals reflected a growing tendency to isolate the ill, poor, and those having disabilities from society. Institutionalization would, over the centuries, become an acceptable response to people with disabilities until the mid-twentieth century. The rise of hospitals, asylums, and other forms of institutions helped undercut the important role the family played in caring for people with disabilities, such as mental illness. Some people with severe disabilities found themselves at least one step further removed from the mainstream of society. Sometimes this was a step in the right direction and sometimes in the wrong.

Social Darwinism

The development of the theory of evolution in the nineteenth century had a profound effect on the perceptions of minority groups and people with disabilities. During the nineteenth century many people believed that society was declining and one of the main reasons for this decline was the growth of genetically "inferior" people. This viewpoint was best articulated by the Social Darwinists. The Social Darwinists and Spencerians viewed that social and cultural progress evolved along lines similar to biological evolution. Social Darwinists held that the survival of the fittest witnessed in the animal and plant worlds also applied to individuals, groups, and societies. An offshoot was degenerational theory which held that social decline was due partially to crossbreeding of superior with inferior peoples and the migration of inferior races of people to the western world. The perspective held that genetically inferior people were more prone to illness, disease, and disability. Consequently, they saw people who had disabilities and particularly those with developmental disabilities as genetically inferior and thus lower on the evolutionary scale.

Before the nineteenth century, societies typically viewed disabilities as an individual phenomenon. The stigma associated with the disability rested solely with the individual. With the rise of Social Darwinism in the nineteenth century, the perceptions of "good family lines" and "good breeding" became important. Disability became more of a family, rather than an individual-based phenomena. The nineteenth-century family perceived itself as a close biological unit. It was the sum of each family member's thoughts and actions. The deficiency, disability, or deformity of any one member announced to the world the weaknesses shared by the whole family. Consequently, this was an era when parents hid mentally ill, developmental disabled, deformed, and physically disabled children in attics and cellars (Calvert, 1992). Besides being hidden, they were shipped off to other locations, or placed in isolated institutions and forgotten. Some parents feared that imperfect children could destroy wedding prospects for siblings. The belief was that prospective marriage partners might view siblings with developmental disabilities as evidence of weak genetic stock within the family. As Calvert (1992:138) concluded, "A single child's deficiency became the entire family's guilt and shame."

In a separate but related initiative, several late nineteenth century Americans were captivated by the concept of degeneration. The concept of degeneration has been linked to the work of Richard Dugdale. In 1877, Dugdale published his influential study, *The Jukes: A Study of Crime, Pauperism, Disease, and Heredity*. This study tied various forms of negative and antisocial behavior to the Juke family. Dugdale concluded that these problems illustrated that some families were genetically prone to problems. Other writers of the same period, such as Oscar Culloch and Henry Goddard, echoed Dugdale's conclusions. According to this view, efforts then should be made to curb the growth of families that carried these negative tendencies, such as sterilization or physical isolation. All of this cumulated in the eugenics scare in the first third of the twentieth century, which took actions to restrict people judged to be from inferior genetic backgrounds. For example, Pennsylvania enacted a sterilization law in 1905 that was applied to a variety of people but largely directed toward those who were mentally ill or had developmental disabilities. Other states created similar provisions and almost 30,000 people would be sterilized over the next 50 years in the United States (Krishef, 1983).

Other Social Trends and Historical Events That Affected People With Disabilities

Over the centuries, numerous other key events and trends influenced the social context for people with disabilities. Macrosocial phenomena such as plagues, inventions, wars, famines, the collapse of the old feudal world, and other occurrences have shaped the social context of disability. For example, the roles of the family and community in the provision for and care of people with disabilities changed over the centuries. Responsibility for caring for people with disabilities has historically rested with the family or extended family (Funk, 1987). Families have been the first line of response to disabilities of their kin. When the family was not involved, local communities assumed, often reluctantly, responsibility for people with disabilities. Initially, communities simply tolerated people with disabilities as long as they were not dangerous. If support or care was provided, communities did so informally.

Hanks and Hanks (1948) suggested five decades ago that individuals who were disabled had more social participation and physical protection in small-scale, relatively egalitarian communities (societies) where cooperation takes precedent over competition and productivity is fairly equal. These folk societies did not develop elaborate systems of measuring individuals and individual success. Thus, people with disabilities were not perceived as being dramatically different from others but rather as members of the community. As societies moved from folk to urban structures, there was a shift from informal to more formal and organized responses to providing care. This shift paralleled efforts by centralized governments to require local communities take responsibility for needy people, including those with significant disabilities. For example, the English Poor Laws of the early seventeenth century mandated local communities to take financial responsibility. Reluctantly, some communities provided care but often through the lowest bidder who did not always have the interests of their clients in mind. Providers frequently mistreated and neglected people under their care. Abuses by unscrupulous private providers led to increased government involvement in the provision of care and treatment.

The development of Utilitarianism as a philosophy and way of life influenced thinking regarding people with disabilities. To Utilitarians, the usefulness of something determines its value. Consequently, societies employing this philosophical viewpoint judged people with disabilities as having diminished usefulness and hence social worth. Societies relying on this perspective have seen people who are diseased or disabled as burdens because they could not contribute to the welfare of the group. Societies killed or abandoned individuals judged as nonproductive (Abt, 1965; Newman, 1991). This perspective became most obvious during the industrial revolution when one's value was determined primarily by the ability to work.

The industrialization of the eighteenth and nineteenth centuries played a role in shaping the lives of people with disabilities. As the industrial system developed, so did the role of government. The industrial revolution fueled a shift from the family-based economy to one based on industrial production.

With the social shift to industrialization, Utilitarianism resurfaced and people increasingly tied one's social value to whether one could work. Phillips (1990: 853) commenting on work and disability noted, "Since the cornerstone of the American cultural ethos is the work ethic and adulthood and social value are conferred on those who contribute their labor (ability) to the society, those who are not perceived to be capable of such contribution may be devalued." Consequently, people with severe disabilities or limitations became devalued.

Industrialization and technological change in concert with urbanization fostered increasing intolerance of bizarre and disruptive behavior. Consequently, people who were different and particularly those who were seriously mentally ill experienced less social tolerance and increased restrictions in their lives. Institutes for the care, education, and treatment of people with disabilities were founded and expanded. Marketing became an important facet in these institutes, as traditional ways to assist people were abandoned in favor of more professional alternatives. The overall result was a commercialization of care and education of people with disabilities.

THE CHANGING SOCIAL CONTEXTS OF DISABILITIES

This brief overview of the general social contexts and perceptions of people with disabilities suggests that numerous social and cultural factors shaped the contexts in which people with disabilities lived. Within these changing social contexts, certain social perceptions endured and continue today. Among these are the social perceptions that people with disabilities are more similar to animals or less than human than those people without disabilities. Although most would disagree with this perception today, it has had a long tradition in western thought. Other enduring negative social perceptions include their being seen as children, deviants, sinners, sick, worthy of pity, scapegoats, entertaining, and beggars. These social perceptions served to separate, isolate, and alienate them from the rest of society. But not all social perceptions have been negative and some have worked to their advantage. For example, one perception has been that they have special powers and abilities that compensate for their disabilities. Whether these enduring social perceptions were positive or negative is less important than the idea that the peoples' individual differences were lost in the shuffle.

Given the wide variety and wide prevalence of disabilities in society, it should come as no surprise than the explanations for disabilities would also be varied. Historically, multiple explanations for disabilities have coexisted without much controversy. One of the oldest explanations linked the presence of disability to sin or for non-Christians maligning the gods. With the rise of modern society, sin became less popular in favor of secular-based explanations. For example, the theory of bodily humors provided a secular explanation for some disabilities that would last for almost 16 centuries. People also speculated that witches, demons, and other evil powers could cause disabilities, particularly during the sixteenth and seventeenth centuries when there was much public concern about witches and witchcraft. Eventually, biology and race would be adopted as major explanations for disability in the nineteenth century. While the variety of explanations is interesting in its own right, it is equally interesting that many of these explanations coexisted without much controversy. In the fourteenth century, one could adopt a combination of moral, Christian, humoral, folk, and astrological explanations that could be totally compatible. Regardless of what explanations people adopted, their explanations were always interwoven with the general concerns of society. When sin was a concern, explanations were based on sin and morality. When evil and witchcraft were concerns in the sixteenth and seventeenth centuries, people viewed spiritual forces as causing illness and disabilities. When biology and race were a general social concern in the nineteenth century, they both became important explanations for disabilities. The concerns of societies flavored the explanations people used for explaining disabilities in their respective times. In this regard, reviewing the history of people with disabilities in western societies reveals that certain developments had major and lasting impacts. A person's illness (Herzlich & Pierret, 1985) or for that matter disability cannot be separated from macrosocial phenomena. For example, since antiquity there has been a pathological viewpoint that has had a pervasive influence on social perceptions. It arises from the belief system of western culture that reveres bodily perfection as a significant value (Gliedman & Roth, 1980; Van Cleve & Crouch, 1989). The notion that disability as a disease or defect is prevalent and pertains to individuals with a wide variety of disabilities. People, and particularly those with physical disabilities or deformities did not fit the mold of the perfect body image. This body ideal had an enduring impact on people with disabilities than spanned several eras.

The development and growth of Christianity also had profound and lasting impact on social perceptions of people with disabilities. As noted previously, the Christian church shaped the context in which disability was interpreted for centuries. The church could be supportive and compassionate at times and damning and punitive in other times. It promoted charity and was instrumental by developing systems of care but it was also exclusionary and labeled them as evil. Importantly, the church was the first entity apart from the family to provide organized care to those in need including those having disabilities or chronic illness. This care would eventually be replaced by private charity as the church's influence declined. These private benefactors supported hospitals and asylums until they in turn gave way to public support. In due time governmental entities, such as local communities and the state, would become a main mechanism for supporting care for many but not all people with severe disabilities. The public confidence in medicine and science grew, the belief that humans could intervene and change the course of lives became dominant. The history of disabilities has been at times very much an obsession on the part of many societies to treat disabilities. Historically, families were the primary source of care for the disabled family members. The family served as the primary economic unit and members with disabilities were simply trained to contribute to the well-being of the family (Farber, 1986). With the rise of science and medicine, the family increasingly lost control over its members who had disabilities. Increasing government and professionals intervened to provide services (sometimes at the request of families or communities), whether custodial or treatment.

The rise of institutional and professional care physically removed some people with severe disabilities, such as developmental disabilities and mental illness, from the mainstream. When once they were part of society, they were removed to locations that separated them from the mainstream. In isolating them, societies restricted the information the general public had about them. They became distant groups rather than unique individuals. Commenting on people with disabilities in American society, Sheer and Groce (1988:33) noted, "Americans have lost familiarity with disabled people, so common in small-scale societies." When people are removed from the mainstream they become less familiar. They more easily assume stereotypical labels in the absence of direct experience and social contact. It is simply much easier to attach stereotypes to people whom you know very little. In contrast, it is more difficult to attach stereotypes to people for whom you are familiar and coexist. Familiarity breaks down stereotypes. In a related vein, the links between genetic inheritance, race, and disability represent a major change in the social perceptions of disabilities. Knowing the role genetics plays in causing disabilities is one thing but attributing one's social status on the basis of perceived genetic makeup is another.

Characteristics of people with disabilities are often more a function of social perceptions than actual conditions of individuals (Gartner & Joe, 1987). People react to disabilities based on stereotypes rather than actual experience, although many eventually become disabled to some degree through the normal aging process. When people act and react to people with disabilities based on stereotypes, they gloss over those characteristics that make each individual unique. They lose sight of many of the details that make each person human. A disability is only one aspect of an individual. In history, people have often forgotten that the individual always is more than the sum of their disabilities. Historically, people with disabilities have made clear their desire to be full and fair participants in society. Their desire for participation and fair treatment may be one of the main constants in the history of western civilization.

Chapter 2

PEOPLE WITH PHYSICAL DISABILITIES

Physical disabilities take many forms and have a wide variety of causes. Physical disabilities include impaired mobility and speech problems. Impaired physical functioning may be due to injury, birth, disease and may require adaptive devices such as braces, wheelchairs, or crutches. Speech problems (not included in this book) may interfere with communication with others and result in social isolation. People learn to adapt to some physical disabilities without difficulty but other physical disabilities are severe and difficult. We all become physically disabled to a degree as we age. Most people lose some of their mobility, agility, hearing, visual acuity, sense of touch, coordination, and sense of balance. Many things happen during the course of a lifetime that can result in physical disabilities. Disease, poor diets, accidents, injuries, and illness may result in physical disabilities. Often physical disabilities are dependent on social perceptions and restrictions placed on individuals more so than actual physical abilities or disabilities.

This chapter covers the general subject of people with physical disabilities. It focuses on major causes of physical disabilities in the past and is devoted to major disease-based causes of physical disabilities. Today we do not generally link, as did people of the past, diseases such as tuberculosis, rickets, and syphilis with physical disabilities. This was different in the past and people often connected these diseases with disabilities. They more easily made connections because these disabling diseases were more widespread. Modern western medicine has eliminated or brought under control some of these major disabling diseases, such as rickets and tuberculosis to the extent that people with these diseases are uncommon in western societies.

PHYSICAL MOBILITY

A dimension that unites all of the types of physical disabilities is that individuals have difficulty in moving from one location to another or physically performing ordinary tasks (motor skills). The importance of mobility should not be underestimated when reviewing physical disabilities in history. Physical disabilities are very much a function of the interplay between the individual and the physical environment. To a person in a wheelchair, a rampless building entrance takes on a different meaning than when access is readily available. Many of the perceptions and views of people with physical disabilities and the views they hold of themselves are dictated by environmental influences that have affected individual locomotion and physical mobility. For example, Goya's drawings of wheelchairs would not have been possible or practical without streets capable of accommodating wheeled devices, such as carts and chairs. The freedom of individual movement shapes the context in which people frame the meaning of physical disabilities.

Before the advent of adaptive devices to help with mobility, many people with severe physical disabilities had to crawl to move about. Societies generally looked upon crawling as a means of human mobility with disfavor. Historically, societies have associated crawling with animals. For example, the *Old Testament* character Nebuchadnezzar crawled like a mad animal. This negative social perception of crawling continued for centuries. Karin Calvert (1992: 32) wrote, "American colonists regarded crawling as a demeaning, animalistic form of locomotion beneath the dignity of any human being." She added, "Moving about on all fours was fit only for beasts, savages, wild men, the insane, and the subjugated as a token of their subjugation."

With mobility being an issue for some people with physical disabilities, adaptive devices were developed over the centuries to help people move. For most of history, the most common of adaptive devices were staffs and crutches. In art and literature, the most frequently used symbol of people with physical disabilities was the cane or crutch. In addition, artificial limbs have been used for centuries to help people address the issue of mobility. Numerous representations of these devices used to aid people in moving about are found in art. For example, a crude form of a crutch can be found in the medieval manuscript of Gerald of Wales. The drawing shows a man on his knees using two handblocks as adaptive devices (Brooke, 1985:27). Crutches and adaptive devices to aid mobility were common in many medieval Italian paintings depicting the great works of the saints. Other examples were provided by the late medieval artist Hieronymus Bosch (1450-1516) who paid ample attention to crutches. In one engraving, at the

Bibliothüque Nationale in Paris, he portrayed several people with physical disabilities using an assortment of crutches and canes. Later Pieter Bruegel the Elder (1525-1569) copied Bosch, an artist he greatly admired. People with physical disabilities were not generally taken care of in Bruegel's time and were frequently regarded as the embodiment of God's punishment for sin. They had to wander around the streets hoping to receive alms from those who were charitable. The Flemish artist Hieronymus Cock (1520-1570), after the style of Bosch, engraved a collection of 31 sixteenth century beggars and their respective means of mobility. Cock actually copied Bruegel's rendition of the earlier Bosch drawing and added more detail (Moskowitz, 1962). The engraving is titled *Beggars* because begging was the only occupation available to many people with physical disabilities in Cock's time. The work serves as a catalogue of some of the devices available to sixteenth century northern Europeans. The devices demonstrate a variety of creative solutions to the problem of mobility. Some of the beggars shown in the engraving are dressed in fool's costumes and carry begging bowls, instruments, or tools needed for the streets of Europe. The musical instruments are lutes, a hurdy gurdy, and a harp (Karp, 1985). Cock presented a wide variety of physical disabilities and deformities in the engraving including spinal deformities, leprosy, clubfoot, missing limbs, rickets, and others common in his time. Another example, centuries later, of drawings of adaptive devices would be Francisco Goya's many sketches of people using crutches. Goya frequently wrote notes to accompany these sketches, such as "So are useful men likely to end." This drawing shows an older man in a bent posture, possibly from osteoarthritis, who is supported by crutches.

Besides crutches and crudely designed devices, another common form of device used to move people with physical disabilities was the litter. A litter is basically a plank with handles at both ends that were used to carry people. Until streets permitted the use of wheeled devices, the litter was a common mode of transportation for people with physical disabilities (Kamenetz, 1969). The ancient Greeks and Romans relied heavily on litters for carrying people, including injured soldiers. Some ancient litters, called palanquins, were covered so as to protect the person being transported from the sun and weather. Some early litters incorporated chairs into their designs. Although wheels were sometimes used, there is little evidence that they were commonly attached to litters in Greece or Rome. Numerous artistic presentations of litters exist in western history. Bosch included them in several of his paintings as did the British cartoonist Rowlandson in his late eighteenth century satirical work on *The Comforts of Bath*. Eventually, litters lost favor but continued to be used on a temporary basis in modern times as stretchers.

The wheelbarrow, invented in China, was introduced by returning crusaders. Wheelbarrows were used to transport people with physical disabili-

Figure 5. Hieronymous Cock, *Beggars,* mid sixteenth century, Philadelphia Museum of Art: SmithKline Beecham Corp. Fund for the Ars Medica Collection, Philadelphia.

ties by the twelfth century and continued through the remainder of the Middle Ages. Lucas Cranach the Elder's (1472-1553) painting the *Fountain of Youth* (1546) shows a variety of adaptive devices available in the sixteenth century. The work shows people being transported to the legendary Fountain of Youth for miracle cures and rejuvenation. In the bottom left foreground, an example of a wheelbarrow is being used for transportation. People are using a litter in the area just above the wheelbarrow. A large cart with six people in need of a cure is also presented in the painting.

The Renaissance witnessed the addition of wheels and rollers to household furniture. Furniture-makers sometimes modified furniture to help people with disabilities to move around. They continued to develop more sophisticated adaptive devices and means of transportation during the sixteenth and seventeenth centuries. For example, the Frenchman Jean Jacques de Renouard, concerned with moving people from floor to floor, invented the flying chair that lifted people from level to level. In addition, designers incorporated cogwheels into the designs of some of these seventeenth century devices to make it easier for the individual to propel themselves (Kamenetz, 1969). Self-propulsion freed people from dependency on others to get from place to place and helped expand such devices to a broader range of people who could not afford hiring assistants.

During the seventeenth and eighteenth centuries, furniture-makers created bath chairs that incorporated wheels into their basic designs. The bath chair was commonly used in the town of Bath, England because many sick or disabled people came there to be cured in the mineral baths. These chairs typically required at least one assistant because of their design and heavy weight. Eventually, they designed the chairs in a way that allowed the occupant to turn the wheels. This change allowed people to move more independently of others and self-propulsion became a reality. It would be centuries before modern lightweight materials would be used in the manufacture of wheelchairs. The cartoonist Thomas Rowlandson (1756-1827) drew one in a 1798 print. Made of wood and a variety of materials, the bath chair is thought by some to be the predecessor to the contemporary wheelchair (Kamenetz, 1969). Rowlandson enjoyed poking fun at people with gout because the disease was associated with wealth and overconsumption. The wealthy were more likely to have gout in his time because of their diets, which contained many sweets and fortified wines that promoted the buildup of uric acid and consequently resulted in gout (Baskett & Shelgrove, 1978). In the following pen, ink, and watercolor drawing Rowlandson depicts overweight wealthy people with gout falling down Circus Hill at Bath England.

In the early nineteenth century, Francisco Goya's made many sketches of people living in the streets of Spain and France including presentations of some of the adaptations that people made to be mobile. Goya did not title

Figure 6. Thomas Rowlandson, (Thomas Rowlandson, *Mathew Bramble's Trip to Bath: The Circus Hill, Mathew Bramble's Overturn*, 1766, Yale Center for British Art, Paul Mellon Collection.

many of these works but did provide short commentaries. The following drawing shows a man with a case of what would have been known as elephantiasis on a flat wheeled cart. The low profile of the cart would have been more suitable to the rough streets of Goya's time. The design of the cart is a relatively simple board with four wheels. He drew the man with an oversized nose and smile, the latter possibly symbolizing his desire to reap profits from his disability. Goya included the comment, "He carries his patrimony in his sack of flesh." Later in his career Goya would draw other sketches of wheelchairs and adaptive devices. In one chalk drawing entitled *Yo lo he visto en* (c. 1824-1828) he drew a man in a cart that was pulled by a dog. While in Bordeaux, France between 1824 and 1828, he sketched a man with a much more elaborate device that must have struck him as extravagant compared to the previous drawing. The sketch is captioned, "Beggars who get about on their own in Bordeau." The chair has two large wheels in the front and one on the back that was used for steering. The man sits upright and displays more independence, as indicated by the caption.

The French artist Théodore Géricault (1791-1824) provides a later image of a woman in a wheelchair entitled, *A Paralytic Woman* (1821) that shows a

Figure 7. Francisco Goya, Captioned "He carries his patrimony in his sack of flesh," c. 1803-1824, Prado, Madrid.

relatively well-to-do woman in her wheelchair. The drawing is most likely a depiction of a woman he observed during his stay in London. The chair required a porter to move. The porter walks while she sits facing backward. A young woman looks back and recoils at her as the she passes. The chair is simple in design and has large wooden wheels. It looks heavy and the woman is dependent on the porter to pull her through the streets. Karp (1985) noted that the woman in the chair seems to be trapped by her cloak and conveys a sense of isolation.

EXPLANATIONS FOR AND TYPES OF PHYSICAL DISABILITIES

The variety of causes of physical disabilities are too numerous to mention here and would require volumes. Disease, genetics, and accidents all have and continue to contribute to the population of people with physical disabilities. Some causes of disabilities have varied over history in significance,

Figure 8. Theodore Gericault, *A Paralytic Woman,* 1821, The Philadelphia Museum of Fine Arts, SmithKline Beecham Corp. Fund for the Ars Medica Collection, Philadelphia.

prevalence, and degree. For instance, in the sixteenth century, syphilis was a major disabler of people in Europe. Today, syphilis is not the scourge and disabling disease that it was in the sixteenth and seventeenth centuries. Medications have effectively reduced the disabling aspects of the disease for those people obtaining treatment. Tuberculosis was a major disabling disease in the nineteenth century. Today it is comparatively insignificant for most people in the western world, although there are recent indications powerful drug resistant strains are beginning to emerge. Although there were numerous causes for physical disabilities, it is possible to briefly touch on major ones, such as those resulting from injuries.

Some physical disabilities result from injuries or physical traumas, such as physical blows or oxygen deprivation. For example, cerebral palsy, also known as cerebral diplegia, is a permanent neuromuscular disability. Cerebral palsy is almost always present from birth and is generally associated with difficult or first births. The London physician W.J. Little (1810-1894) described it in the nineteenth century. Some people experience spinal cord injuries that lead to physical disabilities. Spinal cord injuries and poliomyelitis are the most common causes of paraplegia and quadriplegia. Spinal tumors and infections, and injuries can result in spasms, loss of muscle tone, limpness, impaired mobility, and other physical disabilities. Throughout much of history the day-to-day accidents that resulted in fractures, dislocations, and broken bones became disabilities for many people before modern medicine. Injuries as a result of wars have been major disablers of people. A case in point is the U.S. Civil War that forced the nation, especially the South, to deal with significant numbers of people with war-related physical disabilities (Sharpiro, 1993). In addition, people have purposively injured others to disable them. For example, it is known that some medieval parents injured or disabled their children so that they could earn more begging (Payne, 1916). In seventeenth-century France, this practice was so common that Saint Vincent de Paul started a shelter for disabled children.

Genetic factors can cause people to have physical disabilities. For example, muscular dystrophies and atrophies are groups of genetically-caused and primarily pediatric diseases. Genetically-caused disabilities include ataxia, cystic fibrosis, and spina bifida. Spina Bifida is a malformation of the neural tube that forms part of the spinal cord and results in scoliosis. One example of a genetic or congenital deformity and limited disability is what is commonly known as clubfoot. The Greek physician Hippocrates was familiar with clubfoot (Garrison, 1960). Centuries later Galen described clubfoot as being either congenital or acquired (McGrew, 1985). One of the most recognized painting of a person with this disability is Jose Ribera's (1591-1652) *The Clubfoot* also known as *Boy with a Clubfoot*, located at the Louvre. This work shows a boy with a deformed hand and clubfoot (infantile hemiplegia). Ribera chose to portray the boy as a happy youth unconcerned or caring about his physical disability. The viewer sees a normal happy child, who just happens to have a physical disability. The boy smiles at the viewer and Gauthier (1964) commented, he seems to take pleasure in showing his physical deformity. The subject was not looking for sympathy nor was he cast in a religious context seeking a miracle cure. Rather, he was an ordinary boy with his walking stick on his shoulder. He holds a card that requests alms. This work reflects the artist's ease with the subject and represents a natural and somewhat charming look at a boy with a disability. Its realism matches the Spanish taste for realistic portrayals of people who were beggars, physically disabled, or mentally ill.

There are numerous accounts of people having other congenital deformities and corresponding disabilities in history. For example, in the seventeenth century, Matthew Buchinger was born without hands, feet, legs, and thighs. He would become a famous and successful calligrapher in England. Following accepted practice of his century, he exhibited himself to add to his

Figure 9. Jose Ribera, *The Clubfoot* or *Boy with a Clubfoot*, 1642, Louvre, Paris.

income. John Valerius was born without arms in England in 1667 and was exhibited in 1705. He was well-known for his physical dexterity and was depicted in numerous prints during the seventeenth century (Clair, 1968). Martha Bagshaw, an American, was born without arms, was also exhibited throughout England during the early years of the nineteenth century. Other people lacking arms and legs with corresponding disabilities lived and thrived. In 1788, the Reverend Wesley described his visit with an individual named William Kingston:

> He highly entertained us at breakfast by putting his half naked foot upon the table as he sat, and carrying his tea and toast between his great and second toe to his mouth, with as much facility as if his foot had been a hand and his toes fingers. He writes out all his own bills and other accounts. He then showed me how he shaves himself with a razor in his toes, and he can comb his own hair. He can dress and undress himself except for buttoning his clothes. He feeds himself by holding the fork or spoon in his toes. He cleans his own shoes, can clean the knives, light a fire, and do almost every other domestic business as well as another man. [Cited by Clair, 1968:136]

A major disease that affects the central nervous system is poliomyelitis. Poliomyelitis is a disease that does not usually result in paralysis or disabilities for most people. Polio is most likely to affect the leg muscles than the arms. The late medieval artist Hieronymus Bosch provides an example of polio in western art. Bosch showed the gaits of paralytic and poliomyelitic in his *Procession of Cripples*. In this work Bosch uses humor and satire in his presentation. Centuries later Sir Walter Scott (1771-1832) recorded his personal experiences with polio. In 1789, Michael Underwood issued a second edition of his *Treatise on Diseases of Children* that added a new section on a difficult to describe disease. He observed that the disease primarily attacked children following a fever and led to debility. Later, (1808) Christopher Carlander reported that several children had developed the disease.

Multiple sclerosis is another well-known disease that results in physical disabilities. Diabetes mellitus is a disturbance of metabolism caused by an insufficient supply of insulin that is manufactured by the pancreas. Unless controlled, the disease in the fifth and final stage can result in blindness (cataracts), heart disease, loss of limbs through amputation, and other disabling results. Physicians may have known about the disease for over 4,000 years (McGrew, 1985). From almost the beginning of medicine, sweet and large amounts of urine have been observed by physicians, such as the Greek Aretaeus of Cappadocia (2nd century AD) and the Arabic physician Avicenna in the eleventh century. Modern treatment for the disease began with Dr. Thomas Willis, who was the physician for King Charles II (1630-

1685) of England. Parkinson's disease or shaking palsy is a disease of late middle life. Hippocrates mentioned it as did later ancient physicians Celsus and Galen. Galen indicated that he only saw the condition twice (Skinner, 1961). The disease causes the person's limbs to shake. In more advanced stages the person's gait becomes awkward as the disease progresses along its downhill course.

From this brief overview of some of the causes of physical disabilities, it should be evident that there were many causes for disability in western history. Other causes, not described include cancer, scurvy, meningitis, myasthenia gravis, Huntington's chorea, and myotonia atrophica. Coronary disease also resulted in disabilities, as people have been physically disabled by strokes (cerebral vascular disease), cerebral arteriosclerosis (hardening of the arteries of the brain), and heart attacks. Gangrene infections were prevalent in Anglo-Saxon England and led to many amputations (Rubin, 1974).

PEOPLE WITH PHYSICAL DISABILITIES IN ANTIQUITY

Little is known about how people with physical disabilities lived in antiquity. One can speculate that they did not fare particularly well. For example, historians have concluded that infanticide and exposure were common reactions to people with physical disabilities or deformities in antiquity. It is known that the Greeks exposed and destroyed children born with deformities or disabilities (Bender, 1970). However, this was not always the case. The ancient Hebrews did not expose children with deformities but considered them gifts from God (French, 1932). At times, ancient societies seem to focus more on creating disabilities rather than caring for people with them. For example, ancient laws sometimes resulted in the creation of disabilities. The ancient *Code of Hammurabi* (2000 to 1501 BC) made provisions for numerous corporal punishments that maimed and disabled people disobeying the *Code*. The *Code* did not pay equal attention to helping or the rights of people whom had become disabled. Bender (1970) noted the *Code* indicated that tongues that lied were cut out, eyes could be destroyed, and hands removed for certain offenses.

Some ancient ideas about people with physical disabilities would shape western thought for centuries. For example, Greek culture placed high value on the perfection, beauty, and symmetry of the human form. The Greeks promoted the ideal image of the human body and its movement. This ideal image did not include deformities or disabilities. Instead, the image was of strong, muscular, smooth, athletic, young bodies that were correctly proportioned. The body image of the Greeks was a yardstick and those people not measuring up were stigmatized. The ideal image of the body went beyond physical appearance; it also extended to the mind. Consequently for centuries people with physical disabilities or deformities were compared to an ideal in body and mind. The Greeks thought a sound body was linked to a sound mind (Meyerson, 1948). If an individual had a crooked body, then it followed they had a crooked mind and personality. One's physical state reflected one's inner state. This ancient notion would resurface during the modern period with the rise of physiognomy.

Exceptions to the ideal existed in Greek folklore, such as the Greek god Hephaestus who was a contradiction to the emphasis on the ideal body. Hephaestus was a legendary Greek god who limped on deformed legs. Hephaestus was exposed by his mother who was ashamed by his lameness. The other gods often laughed at his limping in several literary works, such as Homer's *Iliad* (900 to 800 BC). Artistic renditions of him from the period show him with stunted legs, deformed feet, and a strong upper body. However, he was also characterized as being intelligent and was heroic on many occasions. He gained strength through the attention others paid to his disabilities and deformities (Newton, 1989). Hephaestus was not the only figure with a disability in Homer's *Iliad*. The *Iliad*, II (216-219) also describes an individual named Thersites who was the ugliest person in camp, physically disabled, hunchbacked, and had a deformed skull.

Another Greek idea that lasted for centuries was the belief that events occurring during pregnancy could result in disabilities or deformities. Aristotle (384-322 BC) thought that deformed children were *lusus naturae* (jokes of nature). He believed that sudden blows to the pregnant mother (intrauterine traumas) could lead to malformations because such events made lasting impressions on pregnant women. This notion of maternal impression was expanded from physical trauma to include fears and experiences. Other Greek ideas, such as the body humours (covered elsewhere) would also influence western thought and perception about people with physical disabilities for centuries.

The Romans adopted Greek culture and inherited the notion of the veneration of the human body as an ideal. They valued physical perfection and did not respond particularly well to people having physical deformities and disabilities. For example, evidence exists that ancient Romans sold people with physical disabilities or deformities in the markets as novelties and servants. The Romans thought such physical characteristics entertaining. Historians have noted the Romans also exposed and killed children born with deformities or disabilities. The practice may have been so widespread that legislation was deemed necessary. According to French (1932), Romulus, the legendary Roman Emperor created a law that any misshapen or monstrous child should be exposed only after being shown to five neighbors and their consent secured. He was not opposed to the idea of exposure but wanted it controlled to protect those falsely accused of having disabilities or deformities. Other laws set parameters for this practice, such as the Roman Law of 12 Tables, which empowered fathers to act as sole arbiters of the fate of their "defective" children.

What care people who had physical disabilities received resided with families and communities. A few exceptions existed, such as a wealthy woman named Fabiola (d. 399) who established a hospital in Rome that admitted people with deformed faces, blindness, and were poor. However, people with physical mobility problems were not a particular concern for the Romans who did not assume any responsibility for ensuring that they were able to move about Roman streets (Gardner, 1993). Transportation and mobility of people were viewed as the responsibility of the individual or family and not the Roman government. The Romans developed a few adaptive devices to help people stay mobile but on the whole paid little attention to their needs.

PHYSICAL DISABILITIES DURING MIDDLE AGES

Medieval perceptions of people with physical disabilities were strongly influenced by the church and ancient philosophical notions about the nature of the body and illness. Medieval peoples' views of physical disability were always cast within a context of Christian morality. People continued to associate sin with disability. Those having disabilities were typically viewed as being immoral. The medieval concept of the body, with its physical imperfections, was that it was merely a vessel used to transport the soul to heaven, hell, or limbo. During the Middle Ages the notions of Christian charity toward people with physical disabilities reached full fruition. When socioeconomic circumstances were favorable, usually under the auspices of church officials, people performed charitable acts for people with disabilities. The Middle Ages witnessed the establishment of many church organizations and facilities devoted to the care and treatment of people who were ill, some of whom had physical disabilities. However most of the charity directed toward people was as alms. Many people believed that they could gain God's favor through charitable acts toward those in need, including those with disabilities. Thus, the giving of alms and charity were common to the medieval landscape.

Several medieval works of art that address physical disabilities demonstrate a strong Christian influence. Healing and curing people with physical disabilities were popular subjects of artists over the centuries. For example, in the cloister of Santa Maria Novella in Florence there is a fourteenth century presentation of the wonder of St. Dominicus. The work, from the school of Giotto (1266-1337), has several frivolous figures but also numerous people with physical disabilities. The work depicts the miracles performed by the founder of the Dominican order, Saint Dominicus (d. 1221). The painting shows several persons with deformities, muscular atrophies, leprosy, and blindness. A child with partial paralysis is also displayed. A woman in the background has a hand displayed in a claw-like position. Another example is a sixteenth century wood panel at the National Gallery of Art in Washington which depicts the Book of Mark's story of the *Healing of the Paralytic*.

During the Middle Ages, numerous attempts were made to cure and care for people with physical disabilities. Medieval medical and folk treatments for people with physical disabilities covered a full range of theories and practices. Some efforts involved Christian faith and were spiritual in orientation. For instance, many medieval citizens went on pilgrimages to holy places hoping they would benefit from miracle cures. Many medical and folk cures were also available. Galen's humoural theory continued to be popular and people continued to be subjected to bleedings, purges, herbs, drugs, and strange diets. One folk treatment tied directly to physical disabilities and worthy of note was the practice of swaddling. For centuries, people attempted to prevent physical disabilities by the practice of swaddling infants. Swaddling involved wrapping an infant tightly in cloth to the point that the child could not move its arms, legs, and body. On occasion, adults wrapped and bound children so tightly that they prevented normal bodily functioning. Swaddling cloths were sometimes not changed for days. People thought swaddling was beneficial because families could easily manage wrapped infants because they were immobile. Many infants were injured and were sometimes killed from being tossed about while they were in their swaddling cloths (de Mause, 1974a).

Besides the advantages to child care, people practiced swaddling for other reasons including their belief that it prevented skeletal deformities. Specifically, many people thought that rickets could be prevented by swaddling. To prevent bones from bending and bowing, adults tightly bound infants, to rigid boards, to keep their limbs straight. The medieval physician Bartlolmaeus Anglicus (c. 1230) thought this practice was beneficial in this regard. People swaddled infants for centuries under the false assumption that unless infants were kept straight they would walk on all fours and develop bent limbs (Marvick, 1974). People believed that infants ran the risk of degenerating to an animalistic state unless their posture could be controlled. Today it is known that swaddling infants, at a minimum, delayed psychological and physical development and may have actually increased the risk of rickets.

Medieval citizens once viewed Saint Anthony's Fire as a source of disability, deformity, and death. Saint Anthony's Fire, ergotism, or erysipelas (Greek for red skin) is caused by eating bread made from moldy rye flour infected with the ergot fungus (claviceps). Ergotism was one of several possible bread-induced hallucinogens and illnesses found among the poor during the Middle Ages and Renaissance (Camporesi 1989). Ergotism could and often did result in the loss of limbs for those people with the disease. People called the gangrenous form Saint Anthony's Fire, Hidden Fire, or Devils Fire (Haller, 1993: 718). The association of the disease with fire was made because it gave the individual an intense burning sensation. Artistic presentations of people with the disease include Johannes Wachtin's (1517) woodcut found in Hans Gersdorff's widely distributed medical text *Feldtbuch de Wundartznev*. It shows a young ergot victim with a flaming arm appealing to Saint Anthony for a cure. A pig, symbolic of Saint Anthony, rests behind the Saint's cape. St. Anthony holds a cane capped by a large letter "T" that stands for the Friars of the Blue Tau and is the Greek symbol for Saint Anthony. Another example is Grunewald's *Altarpiece for the Covent of St. Anthony in Isenheim*. Matthias Grunewald (1455-1522) was commissioned between 1508 and 1516 to create an altarpiece on Saint Anthony's Fire. The commission for such a large of work is testament to the importance people attached to the disease in Grunewald's time.

PHYSICAL DISABILITIES DURING THE MODERN ERA

Following the Middle Ages, modern medicine and science arose and diminished the power and control of the church. Church power, especially in the eighteenth and nineteenth centuries, yielded to more secular-based explanations for disease, deformity, and disability. Most of the historical record of disabilities comes from the centuries following the Middle Ages. Some diseases and genetic causes leading to disabilities warrant special consideration. Each of these diseases or causes of disabilities seems to have been dominant during certain periods in history or have received special attention. Syphilis mattered little during the Middle Ages but increasingly became important during the fifteenth and sixteenth centuries. Rickets was relatively unimportant until the industrial revolution helped usher it in on the working classes. Syphilis, rickets, and tuberculosis have all had their special place in the history of physical disabilities. Yet, other disabling diseases, such as arthritis, seem to remain in the background never really moving to the forefront.

Figure 10. Johannes Wachtin, 1517 woodcut from Hans Gersdorff's *Feldtbuch de Wundartznev*, The Philadelphia Museum of Fine Arts: SmithKline Beecham Corp. Fund for the Ars Medica Collection, Philadelphia.

People with Abnormal Curvature of the Spine

A number of factors may cause abnormal curvature of the spine, such as spinal bifida which is a genetic disorder. Regardless of the cause, people with severely curved spines called scoliosis when curved to one side, have historically been referred to as "hunchbacks." Other causes such as, poor diet, and disease can also result in abnormal curvature of the spine. One common cause was a form of tuberculosis that attacks the spine was known as Pott's disease. In 1779, a London surgeon named Percival Pott published a pamphlet on spinal caries. Spinal caries (tuberculosis) would be named Pott's disease to recognize his early efforts at describing this disease.

People with severe curvature of the spine have been consistently characterized in western societies as villains and deviants. One notable example of this were the legends surrounding England's King Richard III. Richard III, the last Plaganet King of England was accused of murdering several people during his ascension to the throne of England in the fifteenth century. Richard has always been cast as an evil person with a hunchback. Not just a hunchback but a treacherous one whose most heinous act was his alleged murder of his two child nephews in the tower of London. Richard III is also credited with the murders of his wife Anne Neville, brother George, King Henry VI, and his son Edward. Evidence exists that Richard III did not have severe curvature of the spine and a limp arm but rather was a person of frail stature with possibly one shoulder slightly higher than the other (Richards, 1983). In addition, he may have had no role in the murder and treachery attributed to him and his brief ascension to the throne. Chroniclers and playwrights, most notably Shakespeare in his tragedy *Richard III*, characterized Richard as an evil and sinister individual (Jones, 1980; Kriegel, 1987).

In addition to the association between evil, another important social perception was that of the person with a hunchback which was a pitiful individual who needed charity from others to survive. The Italian artist, Raphael Sanzio's (1483-1520) painting entitled *The Cripple* presents an individual with severe curvature of the spine with other physical deformities. The painting is highly realistic and was probably based on a person Sanzio had seen. The individual reaches up to the others asking for alms. Here the message was one of pity and charity.

Another set of images of people with severely curved spines was provided by the engraver Jacques Callot. Callot was a famous French engraver who made many drawings of people and characterizations of people. The following two sets of drawings are cartoons of people with hunched backs. Callot seems to be making fun of people with the characteristic. One figure is making a toast and the second strumming a mandolin in Florence, Italy.

Figure 11. Raphael Sanzio, *The Cripple*, early sixteenth century, Vatican Museum, Rome.

Callot depicted the figures in a grotesque fashion to add to the humor but also to insult and demean.

279, 407-426 — LES GOBBI

411.- Le buveur vu de face 1er état

412.- Le buveur vu de dos 1er état

413.- Le duelliste aux deux sabres 1er état

414.- Le duelliste a' l'épée et au poignard, 1er état

415.- L'homme au gros ventre, orné d'une rangée de boutons. 1er état

416. L'homme au gros dos orné d'une rangée de boutons. 1er état

Figure 12. Jacques Callot, Lieure Varie Figure Gobbi, New York Public Library, New York.

66 *Social Perceptions of People with Disabilities*

In sharp contrast to Callot's figures of people with hunched backs is Annibale Carracci's (1560-1609) *Hunchback*. Annibale Carracci united high renaissance monumentalism with Venetian warmth. His drawings of people were realistic and delicate. His sensitive chalk drawing shows a young man with severe curvature of the spine. Carracci is not humorous or mocking the

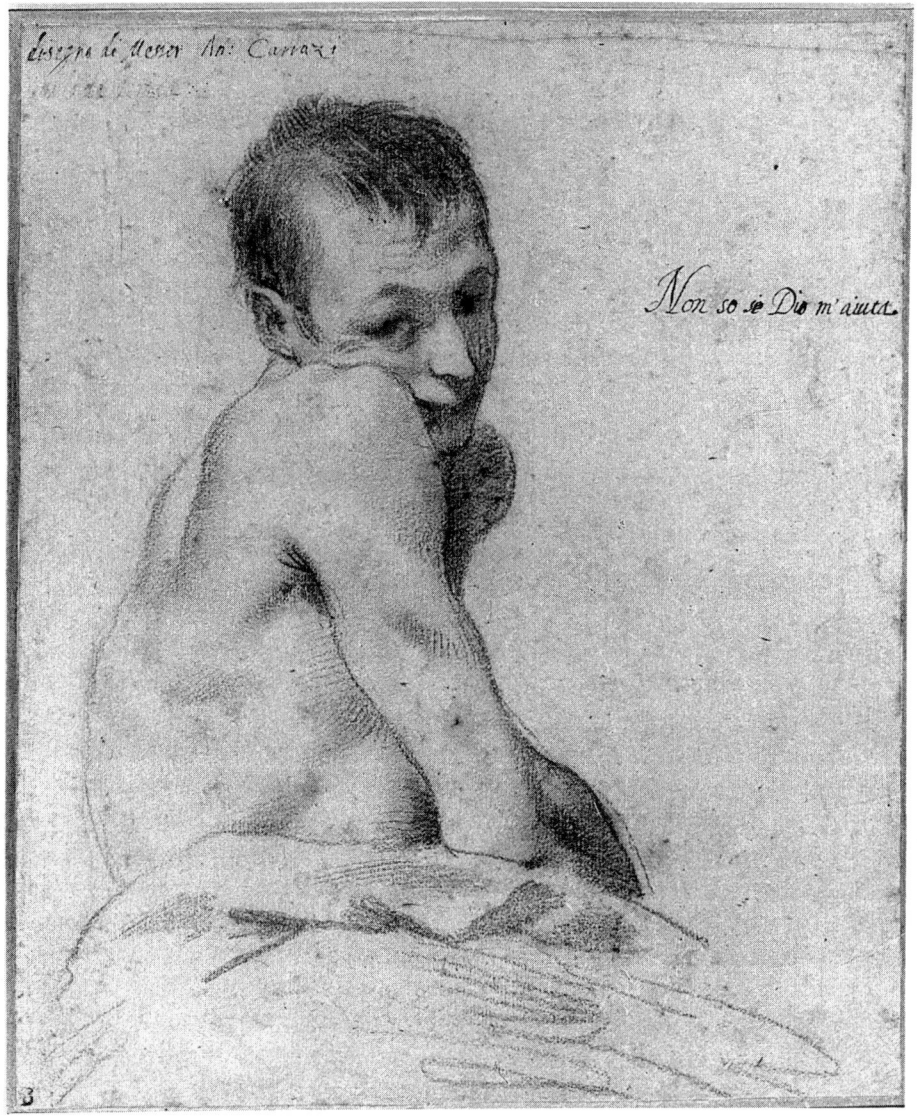

Figure 13. Annibale Carracci, *Hunchback,* 16th-17th centuries, The Trustees of the Chatsworth Settlement, Devonshire: photograph Courtald Institute of Art.

subject but showing a person with feelings. The subject looks back at the reviewer and provides a sense that there is much more to this individual than outward appearance. The same sensitivity shown toward this subject was present in his numerous chalk drawings of people who were blind.

The nineteenth century author and social commentator, Victor Hugo (1802-1885), developed one of the most lasting and engaging literary characters with severe curvature of the spine in his *Hunchback of Notre Dame*. Hugo was fascinated with people that he viewed as being peculiar. He wrote with compassion about people who were mentally ill and who had developmental disabilities. He also stressed the "bizarre" aspects of deformity and disability in his characters. Hugo attended college in Madrid where an individual who was deaf, had a small stature, was speechless, and had a number of disabilities including a severely curved spine named Corcorito worked as a porter. Hugo used this individual to create several literary characters including Quasimodo. In western literature, Quasimodo is probably the most recognized figure with this characteristic of an abnormally curved spine. Solomon (1968) persuasively concluded that Hugo based his Quasimodo on a hereditary disorder known as neurofibromatosis scoliosis.

Syphilis

Today, we do not typically think of syphilis as deforming and disabling people. Modern medicine has, at least for the present, effectively controlled the disease. This was not always the case. Syphilis, also known over the centuries as the pox, was a deforming and disabling disease caused by a virus. It is included in this review of people with physical disabilities because of its debilitating effects on the individual's mind and body. In its advanced stages, syphilis could result in loss of senses, insanity, blindness, paralysis, physical impairments, disfigurement, and dead or diseased offspring. Syphilis, like many of the disabling diseases described in this book, has been an enduring disease throughout the Middle East and Europe. However, there is little evidence of it in ancient Egypt but there is some proof of it existing in the ruins of ancient Roman Pompeii (Stage, 1987). Further evidence of it is found in the Old Testament book Isaiah 3:16-17, which makes reference to an ailment thought by some to be secondary syphilis (Stage, 1987). Some authorities have argued that the book of Leviticus has a description of Job's sickness, which includes ulcers and aching bones, that is evidence of the disease among the ancient Hebrews (Quetel, 1990). Other ancient references were made by ancient scholars such as Hippocrates, Celsus, Galen, and Paul of Aegina. However, these scholars may have been describing any number of diseases other than syphilis that were common.

The disease was named by the Italian poet and physician Girolamo Fracastoro (Fracastorius) who wrote a well-known and immensely successful Latin poem entitled *Syphilis Sive Morbus Gallicus* in 1530. The poem is about a mythical shepherd named Syphilis who was punished with the French Disease for not respecting the gods (Stage, 1987). Fracastoro created the name Syphilis to represent the disease that was pandemic in Europe at that time that was known as morbus gallicus. By the seventeenth century the term *ives venerea* (venereal disease) was used as much as morbus gallicus to refer to the disease (Arrizabalaga, 1993). People eventually popularized the term syphilis during the late eighteenth century.

Over the centuries, people have offered various explanations for what caused the disease. They have proposed that soldiers eating human flesh, people having sexual intercourse with horses, immoral behavior, and sexual relations with people who were leprous caused syphilis. Astrologers interpreted the conjunction of Saturn and Jupiter in the sign of Scorpion and the House of Mars on November 25, 1484, as the astrological starting date and cause of the epidemic that followed. During its pandemic stage at the beginning of the sixteenth century, doctors continued to identify causes for the disease including corrupt air, breast-feeding, kissing, and coitus (Quetel, 1990). People also thought that God also punished debauchery by inflicting the disease. Common to many of the causes has been the association, justifiably so, between the disease and sex (sin). By the late fifteenth and early sixteenth centuries, doctors recognized that sex with infected partners was related to the onslaught of the disease. By the eighteenth and nineteenth centuries, multiple theories about the cause of the disease persisted. It was not until the 1880s when researchers found the bacterial source (treponema pallidum) that people began to understand the real cause of the disease.

Syphilis was clearly present in Europe over the centuries but failed to make serious inroads into the general population. This would all change at the close of the fifteenth century and the disease would spread like wildfire across Europe. Quetel (1990:4) summarized the spread of the disease, "The terror began in Europe with the appearance, at the very end of the fifteenth century, of a new disease which was far more horrifying than leprosy and the plague—because of its novelty, its profusion of symptoms, its extreme contagiousness, the suffering it caused, and the fact that (in the early years, at least) it was often fatal." The disease became particularly pronounced and spread rapidly upon the return of Columbus from the New World. Over the centuries, this coincidence has led many scholars to speculate that the disease in a more virulent form was transmitted by Columbus' sailors from the new to the old world (Stage, 1987; Arrizabalaga; 1993). Other explanations for the rapid spread of the disease have been proposed that suggest that the more virulent form was simply a mutation of the disease that coincidentally occurred about the same time as Columbus' return.

Social reaction to the spread of the disease paralleled some of the responses to leprosy. By the 1490s many Europeans loathed the disease. For example, the town of Lyon, France passed laws that people with leprosy and those effected with the great pox were to be expelled. Countries and towns took similar measures throughout Europe, such as Geneva (1496) and Scotland (1497). In Paris, during the late fifteenth century, people with the disease built a shanty-town, similar to those built by people with leper colonies on the outskirts of the city. Quetel (1990) described a decree operating in Paris that specified that pox-sufferers had to report within 24 hours to authorities so they could be listed and paid a small sum of four sous. Under threat of hanging, they were expected to leave the city and not return until they had been cured. Parisians with the pox had to report to authorities within 24 hours and stay at home or live at the premises at Saint Germain des Pres. In 1497, the Scots gave people with the disease in Edinburgh two choices: banishment to the island of Inch Keith or getting branded with a hot iron on the cheek. In Germany and Switzerland they were prohibited from entering public inns, bathhouses, and even leper colonies (Nikiforuk, 1993). Children found with syphilitic ulcers were beaten in some communities, as townspeople thought they contracted the disease from swearing too much (Nikiforuk, 1993).

By the beginning of the sixteenth century, syphilis was pandemic in Europe. It was within this context that Europeans began to blame each other for causing the disease. The Italians, English, Turkish, and other Europeans called it the French Disease (French Scabies), and the balding that occurred in its advanced stages the French Crown. When the conquering troops of French King Charles VIII undertook his Naples Campaign in 1494, they called it the Italian or Neapolitan Disease. Local residents undoubtedly believed the French brought the disease to them. The conquered Romans called it the French Disease and believed the French had brought the disease to Italy. The Flemish and Dutch, who went to war with Spain, called it the Spanish Sickness. The Portuguese called it the Castellan Sickness. The Russians named it the Polish Disease. People from Turkey called it the Christian or Castellan Disease. The Indians and Japanese called it the Portuguese Disease (Andreski, 1989). As was often the case, disease and corresponding disabilities were attributed to outsiders or foreigners and in particular different peoples and classes. Usually, the immigrant, the foreigner, or the downtrodden were viewed as the source and purveyor of diseases and disabilities.

During the course of the disease's rampage throughout western societies, people made attempts to cure what was considered to be a baffling disease. Many doctors did not know what to do with the disease and frequently avoided treating people. Others made attempts at treatment, such as using mercury or quicksilver. Mercury may have first been used in 1496 by the Veronese physician Georgio Sommariva (McGrew, 1985). It was also known as salivations or the salivary cure because practitioners promoted the patient's salivation to rid the body of poisonous phlegm and saliva. It was given to patients in large quantities as ointments, orally, and in vapor baths from 1500 onward. Beyond the disabling effects of the disease, the individual faced the destructive effects of the mercury treatments. The prolonged use of mercury, fatal in large doses, resulted in permanent damage to patients, such as the loss of teeth, muscular shaking, and paralysis. Mercury probably did as much harm to the patients as the disease. In addition to mercury, people used all of the traditional purges, cautery, ointments, bloodletting, gaiac, sarsaparilla, and other treatments for diseases and disabilities. The strong negative stigma attached to the disease and those with it resulted in different medical and social treatments. European hospitals were known to exclude people with syphilis and many found it difficult to find hospital care. For example, in the seventeenth century, hospitals such as SalpÍtriÈre and BicÍtre excluded pox victims. For many, beggars' prison was a more likely option than the hospital. Yet, some communities seemed to show compassion and special hospitals were established to serve people with the disease (Park, 1991).

Artists and authors from the period addressed the disease. References to the disease were numerous from 1500 onward through the nineteenth century. For example, Sebastian Brant's (1494) poem *The Ship of Fools (Das Narren Shiff)* contains a woodcut that addresses the subject of the great pox. Desiderius Erasmus (1465-1536) referred to it in his *Colloquia* (1523). The scholar Erasmus thought a person was not well-heeled unless he or she had the disease. The author Francois Rabelias (1494-1553) referred to it in his work *Gargantua* (1532). Albrecht Dürer (1471-1528) drew *The Syphilitic* in the early sixteenth century to illustrate an early medical article on the subject. Dürer devoted much attention to the subject of syphilis because the disease was spreading all over Europe. He was reportedly afraid of the disease and may have had it, as evidenced in a few of his nude self-portraits. In his *The Doctor's Dream* (1497-1499) he alludes again to syphilis. Dürer's woodcut *The Men's Bath* also presents the disease.

Some have concluded that by the mid-sixteenth century, the disease began to decline in virulence and frequency of occurrence (Quetel, 1990). What occurred was a major shift from fear of contagion to a moralistic-based interpretation. The rise of Puritanism in the seventeenth century coincided with the continued spread of syphilis. This was a period of great religious reform and people with the disease were reacted to in silence or contempt. Quetel (1990) concluded that the disease became defined in a stricter moral and religious context. The spreading of the disease provided Calvin and other Protestant reformers with a convenient illustration of what happened to those straying from the Christian moral life. The presence of the disease helped promote the reformers' efforts to narrow sexual freedom and eliminate what they defined as sinful behavior.

Syphilis drew the attention of artists and authors in the seventeenth century. Miguel de Cervantes (1547-1616) described the pox in his *The Deceitful Marriage (Novelas ejemplares)*. The work described a young man who catches the pox from his young bride. Seventeenth century Elizabethan theaters were often located in the same districts as the brothels, thus playwrights, actors, and their audiences would have been very familiar with syphilis and other venereal diseases. Shakespeare referred to the pox in several of his plays. In *Henry IV* (Part 2) Falstaff states: "A man can no more separate age and covetousness than he can part young limbs and lechery. But the gout galls the one and the pox pinches the other... A pox of this gout! or a gout of this pox!"

Shakespeare made another reference to syphilis when his Lucio, in *Measure for Measure* (1623) proclaimed, "Thy bones are hollow impiety has made a feast of thee." Giovanni Casanova, the great eighteenth century Venetian lover, had the disease along with several others including gonorrhea, chancroid, and herpes (Stage, 1987). Casanova's memoirs are descriptive of the disease and its prevalence throughout Europe. Voltaire's (1694-1778) eighteenth century masterpiece *Candide* (1759) described the disease. Voltaire thought the disease was not so much a badge of sexual prowess but a common enemy of humanity. Authors continued to write about the disease in the nineteenth century. Personal accounts of the disease were relatively abundant, such as those by Alphonse Daudet (1840-1897), Charles Baudelaire (1821-1867), John Keats (1795-1821), and playwright Oscar Wilde (1856-1900).

During the eighteenth century, moral interpretations started to be replaced by medical and scientific explanations but licentiousness and the disease continued to be viewed as one and the same. The evolution of the disease from a moral to a medical problem resulted in increased emphasis on treatment of the symptoms and the search for a cause. The disease was somewhat romanticized during the late eighteenth century, as it was viewed as the price paid by those taking many lovers (Gussow & Tracy, 1970). During the nineteenth century the disease continued to be linked to morality and the wages of sin. An example of the link to morality was by the nineteenth century artist Rambert who created a number of engravings focused on moral themes. The following engraving presents an individual disabled by advanced syphilis. The subject is shown with his vial of mercury hanging around his neck. He looks back at his lustful and debauched life as he is

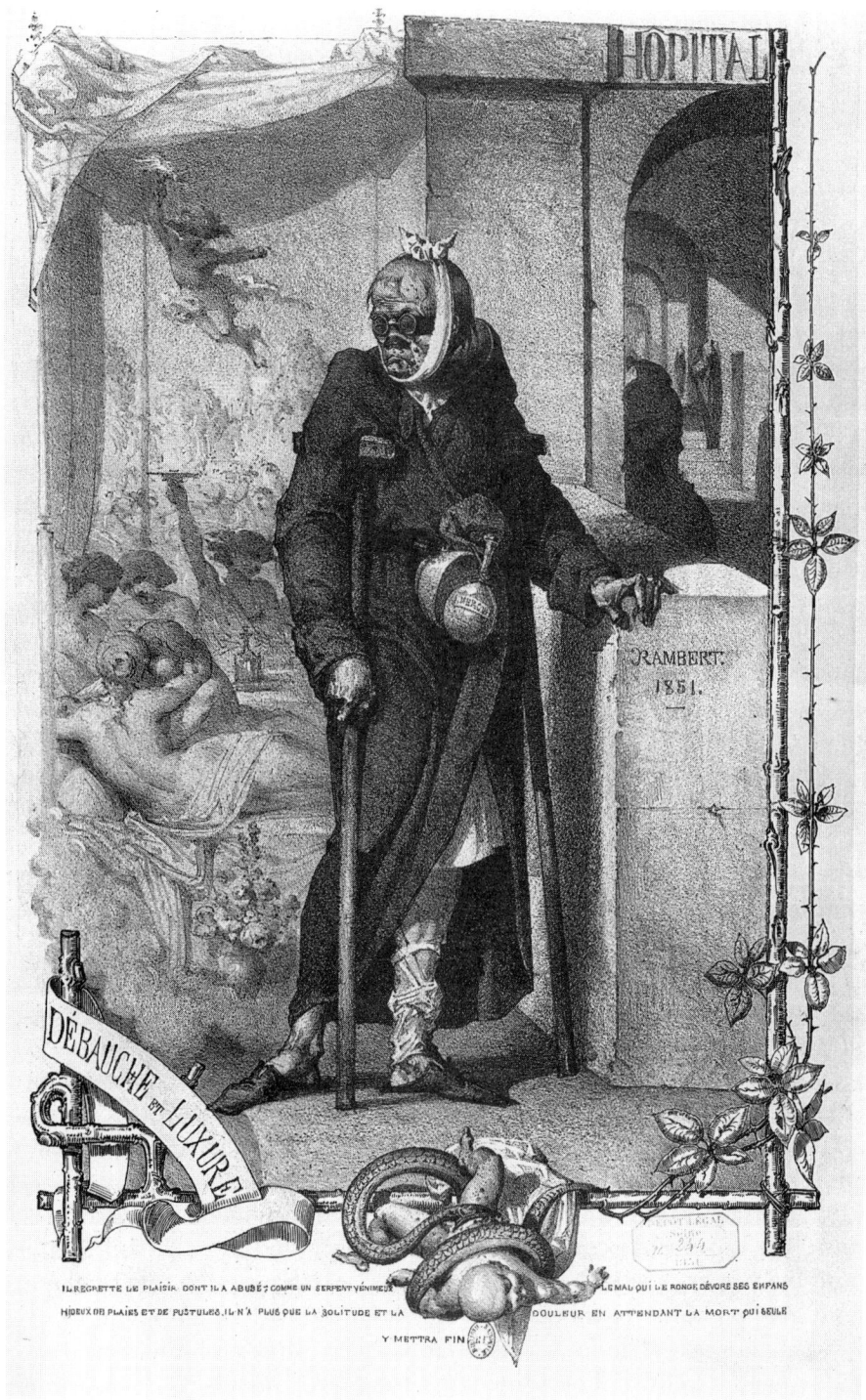

Figure 14. Rambert, *Debauche et Luxure*, 1851, Bibliotheque Nationale, Paris.

opening the door to a hospital. The physical disabling and deforming effects of the disease are evident. Besides the crutch, his sight is impaired and his physical stance is altered. He wears a bandage on his head. He displays a loss of cartilage in the nose. A baby is in the foreground being devoured by a serpent, perhaps symbolic of his descendants being consumed by the disease. Underpinning the message of the work is the Christian interpretation of venereal disease as the result of immoral and unchristian behavior.

Rickets—The English Disease

Rickets is a disabling disease that is caused by a vitamin D deficiency. It is due to the abnormal metabolism of vitamin D and secondarily to calcium and phosphate deficiencies. Rickets is a bone disease that deforms and disables children during the first two years of life. In the past, the disease was known as the twilight disease because of its association with darkness and the lack of the sunlight. This association was not coincidental, as the lack of exposure to sunlight plays a critical role in the evolution of the disease. Rickets is more abundantly found in areas lacking adequate sunlight and among people with poor diets. Lacking vitamin D, people with the disease developed disabilities and deformities, such as alterations in the pelvis and leg bones. Their bones could not support body weight and became curved and bent. Rickets appears to be a relative newcomer to the list of diseases that can result in disabilities. No evidence exists that rickets was present among ancient populations (Steinbock, 1993). However, in the second century AD Galen did describe a disease as deforming the skeletons of infants and young children. Although present throughout western history, the disease increased dramatically during the Middle Ages. A medieval artistic example of the disease is Hans Bergmaier's *Virgin and Child* (1500) shows a number of physical deformities such as a square head, bowlegs, Harrison's Groove, protuberant abdomen, and other characteristics of infantile rickets (Garrison, 1960). It peaked during the industrialization of northern Europe and in the nineteenth century. The absence of sunlight caused by industrial smoke, coal dust, and narrow streets prohibited sunlight from reaching the streets of cities and people. These factors helped account for the magnitude of the disease in industrialized English communities and London was particularly hit hard (Wells, 1964).

Folk cures for rickets have been plentiful over the centuries. For example, children showing signs of rickets received radical forms of treatment (Calvert, 1992). People believed that sleeping in the bent fetal position was commonly viewed as a cause of rickets during the seventeenth century. Parents placed emphasis on stretching and keeping children straight to keep them from growing up bent and misshapen (Calvert, 1992). People believed swaddling infants prevented the disease by keeping the infant's body straight. Ironically this practice would have contributed to the prevalence of the disease because wrapping infants up limited their exposure to sunlight that would have increased their likelihood of developing the disease. As late as the eighteenth century, some people clung to the belief that children with rickets were changelings and should be mistreated, killed, or abandoned (Haffter, 1968). Folk medicine also suggested that passing the individual through the father's legs, or pulling people through splits in trees, or through mounds of earth were cures (Hand, 1980). The fact that none of these practices were effective did not deter people from using them.

Tuberculosis–Scrofula–Consumption

Tuberculosis is an infectious disease that is caused by the bacteria called mycobacterium tuberculosis. Tuberculosis can be a chronic infection that affects the individual for years but in acute forms can lead to death within a few days. While tuberculosis can occur in almost any part of the body, it most frequently occurs in the lungs because people contract the disease by inhaling the tubercle bacilli from others. It most frequently attacks people who are run down, malnourished, and are unable to fight off the disease. The disease started to flourish in the nineteenth century when people crowded into the cities to work under poor and dirty conditions. The rise of textile industry hit women working in the mills particularly hard and promoted pulmonary tuberculosis (Johnston, 1993). Tuberculosis, also once referred to as consumption, was a leading cause of death in sixteenth and seventeenth centuries (Forbes, 1979). In the history of civilization, no other disease has killed more people. Researchers have found evidence of the presence of tuberculosis in ancient cultures (Johnston, 1993). The Egyptians and Greeks wrote about it or presented the disease in art. The poet Homer provided a possible early description in about 800 BC. Hippocratic writings from 400 BC described a disease called phthisis, which was the Greek term for consumption. It was attributed to exposure to evil air (Johnston, 1993).

During the Middle Ages, scrofula was a historical term that was used to describe a form of tuberculosis that resulted in inflamed and disfiguring bumps (tumors) on the neck. When the term scrofula was in vogue, the distribution of the disease was influenced by a number of religious and social factors as much as the actual occurrence of the disease. According to Johnston (1993), medieval Europeans suffered considerably from the disease and frequently mentioned scrofula and its treatments in their medical and surgical text. The disease was also known as the King's Evil because people believed it could be cured by the royal touch. Accounts abound of people being cured by royal touch. Following the Middle Ages little changed regarding the understanding and treatment of the disease. During the sixteenth and seventeenth centuries, the link between the disease and royalty was rigorously pursued, royalists viewed the royal touch as a sign of divine right (providence). It was evidence of the link between God and the line of monarchs. Antiroyalists seeking to overthrow the monarchy in England (Stuarts), such as the pilgrims, sought to discredit the royal touch as a cure. Opponents to the crown disproved of the effectiveness of the royal touch and hence the link between the monarchy and God (French, 1993a). When Robert Koch in 1882 isolated the bacteria that caused tuberculosis and hence scrofula, the term became obsolete.

Late in the eighteenth century, as was also the case for syphilis, people started to romanticize tuberculosis. They adhered to this view through the Victorian period through the early 1900s (Gussow & Tracy, 1970). It was romanticized and some even suggested that consumption, as it was called then, benefited the romantic and creative side of its victims. For example, the literary figure of Camille quietly and romantically died from consumption in the arms of her lover. Real death from tuberculosis was not anything similar to this romanticized image. It was painful and can be likened to drowning in one's own blood. This fact did not stop many creative and artistic people in the nineteenth century from romanticizing the disease. Nineteenth century authors thought the disease would add passion to their writing. Victor Hugo (1802-1885) was encouraged by others to contract the disease to improve his writing (Nikiforuk, 1993). Lord Byron (1788-1824) also wished to die from consumption to improve his poetry and prose. In the 1830s and 1840s, to have consumption was to have good form. This attitude was fostered by the fact that many famous people of the time, such as Frederic Chopin (1769-1854), John Keats (1795-1821), Nicolo Paganini (1782-1840), Robert Louis Stevenson (1850-1894), Henry David Thoreau (1817-1862), and Elizabeth Barrett Browning (1806-1861), were known to have had the disease.

This romantic view of the disease as attacking the sophisticated and refined of society present throughout the eighteenth and first half of the nineteenth centuries eventually gave way to the view of the disease as the plague of people who were poor and inferior. It was no longer fashionable to have the disease as it was associated with the down and out. It became viewed as the disease of the dirty and unclean masses. People came to see it as a disease of genetic and moral failing. This represented a major shift from the highly romanticized view of the disease. The poor could not resist the disease, as they were overworked, malnourished, lived in close quarters, and did not have access to health care. The last decades of the nineteenth century the disease became identified as the people's plague, as it struck the poor and working classes. Crowded industrial centers served as breeding grounds for the spread of the disease.

During the nineteenth century, people tried to make moral sense out of the disease. Victorian ideas about virtue and morality played a role in shaping social perceptions of people with the disease. Noting that the disease was more common among the working poor, nineteenth century experts concluded that immoral living and degenerate life-styles led to consumption. In the 1840s many held the belief that the disease was caused by one's misbehavior. Scholars also observed that the disease tended to run in families and concluded that it could be inherited from parents of "racially inferior" backgrounds. Racism and ethnocentrism, as is so often the case with disease and disability, played an important role in how people with the disease were perceived. Nineteenth century scholars observed that African Americans were susceptible to the disease and had resulting high mortality rates. African Americans were characterized as being unclean and carefree and thus good targets for disease. In addition, people thought that Eastern Europeans and in particular those of the Jewish faith, were inclined to have the disease. This conclusion was based on higher incident rates and the social perception that their smaller stature and girth made them more susceptible to the disease. Experts attributed these observations to the genetic "inferiority" rather than the poor living conditions experienced by both groups. Eventually, eastern European and African American populations were viewed as a health menace and steps were taken to isolate them from the mainstream. Immigrants who were diagnosed with the disease were denied entry into the United States. These attitudes, rampant among the medical establishment, undoubtedly influenced both African Americans and Eastern Europeans' willingness to seek medical assistance, as those seeking help could be adversely treated.

By the close of the nineteenth century major breakthroughs regarding the biological cause of the disease would be uncovered. The German scientist Robert Koch discovered the tubercle bacillus in 1882 and changed the paradigms used to explain the disease. His discovery of the bacilli made the disease no longer a mystical disease. The discovery raised the hope of people that something might be done to cure the disease. In 1890, Koch announced he had found a cure by injecting bacilli into patients with the disease. This proved to be a disaster and may have accelerated the deaths of many hopeful patients. The search for a cure would continue in the twentieth century.

The nineteenth century witnessed the rise of sanitariums to treat and cure the disease. Edward Livingston Trudeau, a successful physician, was dying from tuberculosis. He moved to upstate New York to spend his remaining years. Much to his surprise he felt better in the fresh mountain air and decided to establish a sanitarium for people with the disease. He built the first cabin in 1884 and from that time forward people who could afford it flocked to his sanitarium. He believed in the healing power of nature including plenty of bed rest, fresh air and good food. Following the lead of Dr. Trudeau, sanitariums would become major industry over the next 50 years. Many efforts at providing facilities to care for people with the disease were well-intentioned. However, in 1893, officials established a sanitarium on Blackwell's Island in New York. Known as consumptive's prison, the real purpose of this facility was not to treat people but to remove them from society to prevent the spread of the disease.

Arthritis

Arthritis, a disease that in severe cases can disable people, takes two basic forms, rheumatoid (early middle age) and osteoarthritis (old age). Authorities have established its current prevalence to be between one to two percent of the adult population but its prevalence in earlier times debatable (Duncan & Leisen, 1993). Arthritis disables but does not kill. Arthritis is a generic term for any disease that produces swelling in the joints and pain in the limbs. Over the course of a life span, many people develop some degree of osteoarthritis or degenerative arthritis. The most severe form of arthritis is rheumatoid which affects the joints in the hands, feet, and arms. It results in severe pain, stiffness, and deformity.

The history of arthritis has been lengthy and can be traced back as far as Neanderthal populations and more recently to the Egyptians in about 2900 BC (McGrew, 1985). The Hippocratic writings refer to the disease (Ehrlich, 1986). The Roman Emperor Constantine IX (980-1055) suffered from arthritic symptoms in his feet, shoulders, and hands. Researchers have found that arthritis and rheumatism were common impairments in Anglo-Saxon England (Kealey, 1981). Other medical descriptions of the disease may include those written by Bartolemeus Anglicus (thirteenth century), Thomas Sydenham (1676), and W. Heberden (1770). In the seventeenth and eighteenth centuries, scholars suggested arthritis was a consequence of gonorrhea. In 1640, Dona Francisca Henriquez de Ribera, the countess of Cinchona brought Peruvian bark back to Europe that would eventually become named after her (Cinchona Bark). The bark's active ingredient was quinine which helped relieve the symptoms of arthritis (Ehrlich, 1986).

Shakespeare made no reference to the disease but acknowledged changes resulting from osteoarthritis. In his 1611 work *The Tempest* (1: ii) he wrote these lines for Prospero, "The foul witch Sycorax, who with age and envy was grown into a hoop." In contrast, it is difficult to identify arthritis in early art, as details such as swelling of hands and joints would not be discernible.

The realistic paintings and drawings of the seventeenth century paintings however suggest the presence of the disease. Flemish painters (1400-1700) presented deformities in the hands of people who were otherwise ordinary in appearance, which suggests that they were representing arthritis (Klepinger, 1979.). Peter Paul Rubens (1577-1640) included examples of the effects of rheumatoid arthritis in some of his paintings (Appelboom et al.,1981; Ehrlich, 1986) including his *Sir. Theodore Mayerne* (1629), *Saint Matthew* (1609), *Drunken Sleeping Satyr* (1610), *Susan and the Elders* (1614), *Marie de Medic* (1622), *The Infante Isabelle* (1625), *The Crowning of the Hero* (1627), *The Holy Family with Saint Anne* (1633 to 1635), and *The Three Graces* (1638-1640). He illustrated the disease by painting his subjects with swelling of the finger joints in their hands and wrists, which was indicative of rheumatoid arthritis.

It is widely accepted that Rubens suffered from rheumatoid arthritis and included presentations of the disease in his self-portraits. His self-portraits, spanning the decades, portrayed his own progression to advanced stages of the disease. By the 1620s his own arthritis had progressed so far that it was a major element of many of his works. He may have included it in some of his works to present his signature, as was common among painters of his time. By 1638 he was often bedridden and needed a walking stick. In 1640, he would write that his, "... hands are paralyzed for more than one month without hope I might still use my brushes; with the warm season an improvement can occur"(Appelboom et al., 1981: 486). The great nineteenth century impressionist Auguste Renoir also had severe arthritis. His disease increasingly affected his paintings after 1888 and his paintings became more shapeless as his arthritis progressed (Appelboom et al., 1981). Perhaps some of his impressionistic style might be attributed to his arthritis. He continued to paint well into old age and eventually could only paint by having someone tie his paint brushes to his forearms.

People with Little or Large Statures

People of little or large stature have traditionally been considered to be disabled. However, some people may disagree. Other than being proportionately different from the general population, they are not as individuals always disabled. In some cases disabilities may accompany little or large statures, but normal ability is more the rule. They are included because, regardless of their abilities, because they have much in common with people who have disabilities. Societies have restricted, stereotyped, honored, displayed, treated them as novelties, discriminated, and frequently acted and reacted to them in ways very similar to people with disabilities. Today, dwarfism or people with exceptionally little or large statures can be considered disabilities.

The dwarfism can be caused by at least 150 conditions, such as genetic factors and diseases affecting the kidneys, heart, lungs, and intestines. Hormone imbalances, severe stress or emotional deprivation all can lead to dwarfism. Thyroid hormone deficiency may be congenital or acquired. Hormone deficiencies may cause growth failure in addition to other problems. People sometimes experience an underproduction of human growth hormone by the pituitary gland or have thyroid gland deficiencies. Today, both deficiencies can be successfully treated. Dominant or recessive genes, skeletal disorders, metabolic disorders, chromosomal mutations, disease and other factors can also cause dwarfism. Nutritional deficiencies eventually will cause poor growth and intestinal disorders may lead to poor absorption of food. Failure to absorb nutrients leads to growth failure. Abnormal formation or growth of bone or cartilage can cause short or large statutes.

Being proportionately little stature does not always result in disabilities for the individual, rather disabilities are often in public perceptions and reactions. People of little stature have always been relatively statistically rare, so when they are in the public they draw public attention and reaction. For some people, having little stature can also be disabling. Specifically, movement can be impaired, facial deformities can be present, severe arthritis, rigidity, hearing loss, respiratory problems, fertility problems, and other characteristics may accompany dwarfism. In addition, people are confronted with a world on a different scale based higher heights and longer distances for reach and stride.

Several social perceptions have been advanced regarding dwarfs. For instance, western cultures attach great importance to height and size. Traditionally, people who are taller and bigger are associated with power and success. Consequently, those who are little or shorter are assumed to be less powerful. People with dwarfism are looked on as marvels, freaks, and human curiosities but not powerful or worthy of respect. Furthermore, people have reacted to them with insensitivity. For example, it is not uncommon for people to treat them according to their size rather than age. They have been treated like children and not adults. They also have been seen as magical and bringers of good fortune (Eberly, 1988). People have seen them as sterile, concupiscent (sexually very active), and giving birth to children of little stature. They have also been perceived as being marvels. For instance, in Gaspar Schott's book entitled *Physica Curiosa* (1662), they were considered human marvels.

Fairy tale images of people of little stature abound in western culture and folklore. Fairy tale images of fairies, goblins, trolls, leprechauns, sprites, gremlins, brownies, pixies, gnomes, Lilliputians, munchkins, hobbits, and sylph are widespread in folklore and culture. All of these images have been applied to people who were little. In addition to stereotypes normally attached to dwarfs, an entire set of mythical and fictional characteristics are also associated with them. Some of these stereotypic images and assumptions have been positive, such as those ascribing special powers, and others have been negative.

People have also perceived dwarfs as being entertaining. The royal courts of Europe collected many individuals for entertainment, to be servants, jesters, or fools. For example, in 1572, the Emperor of Germany presented three of them to King Charles IX of France (Stroman, 1982). Queen Elizabeth I had Mrs. Tomysen. Blocked opportunities, prejudice, and discrimination undoubtedly directed some of them to the entertainment industry where they were exploited. With an absence of suitable work, some unquestionably saw being placed on display was a good opportunity to earn a decent living. It should be noted that the numbers of people with dwarfism would have exceeded the demand. Most dwarfs were not put on display but lived, worked, and carried out their lives in the mainstream.

How did dwarfs live in antiquity? Evidence shows that the Egyptians used pack trains at the time of Pepi I to transport them and people and with disabilities from central Africa to Egypt where they were valued as entertainers and curiosities (Ross, 1951). Some were celebrated personalities and judged as important people. Even the deities incorporated them. For instance, Egyptian artists portrayed the gods Ptah and Bes as people (beings) of little stature (Fiedler, 1978). The Pharaohs surrounded themselves with dwarfs. They liked to have them around as court jesters and advisors. Dwarfs were frequently deified, as was the case of the Egyptian Ptah, an achondroplastic dwarf (Eberly, 1988). Egyptian figurines of people who were dwarfs have been found dating to the V Dynasty 2470-2320 BC. For instance, a painted limestone group from about 2500 BC is of a man named Seneb and his family. Seneb's small stature (achondroplasia) is shown in contrast to the proportions of his normally sized spouse and children. His spouse embraces him, as both sit on a bench. Overall, Schadewaldt (1967a) concluded Egyptian society treated them well.

During the Hellenistic period they were highly prized and were included in feasts. The Greeks sometimes credited them as being oversexed, which was occasionally discussed in literature and depicted in art (Shapiro, 1984). The Romans actually tried to stunt the growth of children by using lime salts. Dwarfs were valued in the homes of the powerful and wealthy Romans. For example, the emperor Augustus had a dwarf named Lucius. Lucius was about 24 inches tall and weighed about 17 pounds. Lucius and other dwarfs in the emperor's court were kept for entertainment and as servants. Their roles in wealthy households are witnessed by the artistic record from the period that typically depicted them as servants (Roth & Cromie, 1980).

Centuries later the courts of the Middle Ages and Renaissance typically had dwarfs as members and servants. For example, the Bayeux Tapestry (1070) celebrating the battle of Hastings shows Turold's groom as a dwarf managing two horses. The French dwarf Triboulet was a famous court jester of Louis XII. Centuries later the figure Triboulet was used as a main character by Victor Hugo (1832) in his *Le Roi s' amuse*. Hugo depicted Triboulet as deformed, hunchedbacked, jealous, a court fool, and hateful of the King. Hugo's characterization bears little resemblance to the real person named Triboulet. In 1580, Lucrezia Borgia gave a banquet at which servants served two dwarfs with the fruit for amusement of the guests (Robins, 1986).

The practice of including dwarfs in the courts of Europe trend continued in early modern times. From 1400 to 1700, the most noteworthy occupational role for dwarfs was in the service of kings and queens. One of the most famous dwarfs of the sixteenth century was Will Sommers who served as the court jester for King Henry the VIII. Sommers was well-known for the many jokes and tricks he played on Cardinal Wosley. In Spain, Catherine de' Medici was fascinated with dwarfs and had at least three of them in her court named Merville, Bezon, and Augustin Romanesque. In 1578 and 1579, she had five dwarfs in her court (Clair, 1968). Charles V of Spain had a dwarf named Cornelius of Lithuania. The tradition of royalty keeping little people around their courts continued in the seventeenth century. The dwarf Richard Gibson (1615-1670) became a page for Charles I and Queen Henrietta Maria. One of the most famous was Jeffery Hudson of Oakham (1619-1682) who entertained the court of Charles I. Another notable dwarf was Archibald Armstrong, who was the court jester to James I of England. Armstrong was probably the most famous of all court dwarfs. He was also known for the many court quarrels that he typically instigated. Although he made many enemies at home and abroad, he was able to maintain his position when Charles I became King. Eventually he would be discharged from the King's service and retired with considerable wealth.

Others lived in the courts of Europe. According to Fiedler (1978:20), Spanish court records from the seventeenth century refer to people of little statute as *gente de placer*, which meant amusements for the aristocracy. Well into the eighteenth century the Spanish courts continued to keep dwarfs. Catherine de Medicis had six. With Philip V the custom died in the Spanish court and eventually grew out of vogue. The last dwarf in the royal court of France died in 1662. In 1741, a dwarf named Nicholas Ferri was born who later would become a member of the Polish court under King Stanislas. The practice of keeping dwarfs for amusement, as servants, or as advisors was virtually absent in the nineteenth century. Only the Russian Czars continued the practice in the nineteenth century (Clair, 1968).

There are several examples of dwarfs in art, particularly from the seventeenth century when they were especially popular among the courts of Europe. Artists such as Raphael, Mantegna, Bronzino, Carreno, Mora, Goya, Carpaccio, Van Dyck, and Veronese all created representations of dwarfs. Venetian artists Paolo Veronese and Caraccio painted many dwarfs. Other examples, include Juan van der Hamen y Leon's (1596-1631) *Portrait of a Dwarf* which shows a bearded subject of the 1620s Spanish court of King Philip IV. In northern Europe, Jan Weenix (1640-1719) painted a person of short stature with a hunchback. The artist depicted the person wearing a tall hat and a monkey on his shoulder. The artist also showed the individual with a tray of trinkets to sell. Other images include Giacomo Ceruti (1720-1750) painting of a dwarf. Velasquez(1599-1660), royal court painter to the King of Spain, paid considerable attention to people who were dwarfs. His works including dwarfs were his *Portrait of Sebastino de Morro* (1643), which shows the subject seated on the ground. Another of his paintings of a dwarf is entitled *Don Diego de Acedo* (1644), or "El Primo," which means cousin. El Primo held a high position as assistant to the king's chancellery. Velasquez surrounded him by books and turning a large folio. His portrait of *Franciscano Lezcano* (1643-1645) is another portrait of an entertainer dwarf. One of his paintings and perhaps his most famous is entitled *Las Meninas* (1656), which means the maids of honor. This painting is located in the place of highest honor in the Prado Museum. The work depicts the royal infant Margarita Teresa in the center of the painting. Velasquez includes a achondroplastic male and ateliotic female in the scene. Velasquez displayed a mastiff to provide the viewer with some sense of scale. Artists frequently scaled people of little stature with dogs, "normal" sized people, pets or space to give a sense of dimension. He also included himself as a painter in the left of the work and the King and Queen in the rear as a mirrored reflection. Velasquez's painting of *Don Baltazar Carlos with a Dwarf* represents another example of a typical Velasquez depiction of a dwarf from a royal court. The dwarf is located in the lower foreground and is holding a silver rattle and an apple.

Literature has also included references to dwarfs. For example, Charles Dickens' Miss Mowcher in *David Copperfield* is a nineteenth century depiction of a person of little stature in literature. Miss Mowcher proclaims:

> "You are a young man," she said nodding. "Take a word of advice, even from a three-foot nothing. Try not to associate bodily defects with mental, my good friend, except for solid reason." I gave Miss Mowcher my hand, with a very different opinion of her from that which I had hither to entertained." [Cited by Ransou, 1986:13]

People with Physical Disabilities 83

Figure 15. Diego Rodriquez de Silva y Velasquez, *Don Baltazar with a Dwarf*, seventeenth century, Henry Lillie Pierce Fund Museum of Fine Arts, Boston.

The nineteenth century witnessed a shift in the perception of dwarfs. Until the nineteenth century, dwarfs were frequently associated with mythical and mystical powers. They were marvels of humanity. In the nineteenth century the Victorians essentially demythed them. The Victorians put them in exhibits and marveled but also pitied them. Lost was the perception that they had special magical powers and charms. For example, General Tom Thumb was a major worldwide curiosity but was not viewed as having mythical powers. People saw him as a quirk of nature.

In contrast to dwarfism is gigantism which is often the dysfunction of the pituitary gland that leads to excessive growth. The upper limit appears to be about 8 1/2 feet in height. Another growth dysfunction is acromegaly which is a progressive disease in which the hands and feet grow as well as the lower jaw. The facial features also thicken. A tumor in the pituitary gland may cause too much growth hormone to be secreted. This results in unusually rapid growth and tall stature. Growth hormone excess, also called acromegaly, may be treated with medication or surgery. Other causes include Marfan's and Klinefelter's syndromes. Many people with this characteristic die at a relatively young age, typically in their twenties.

Similar to the folklore and mythology surrounding dwarfs, people of exceptionally large stature have been perceived as being mysterious and mythical. For example, for centuries people believed that people in the past were larger in stature. Mythology and legend frequently referred to communities of giants. Greek and other ancient Middle Eastern mythology is abundant with tales of giants. Holy scripture also made many references to giants. The Bible mentions races of giants including the Rephaim, Anakim, Emin, and Zonzonim. Genesis refers to the giants in the days of Noah. There is also the well-known Old Testament story of David and Goliath. Academics have speculated on the heights of biblical giants, such as the noted French scholar Henrion who calculated Adam's height at 123 feet 9 inches, Eve at 118 feet, and Noah at just over 100 feet (Clair, 1968).

The royal courts of Europe were fascinated with people of large stature. The Tudors and Stuarts were fond of people of large stature and men of exceptional size were embraced by these two royal lines. Walter Parsons, William Evans, and Anthony Paine were three of the better known individuals who joined the English court. During the seventeenth century it became fashionable to have people of large stature as emblems of power. For example, King James had Walter Parsons, King Charles I had William Evans and even the nonroyalists such as Cromwell had Daniel (Parkinson, 1977). In the eighteenth century, Irish show giants became popular. Frederick II of Prussia recruited persons of large stature to join his elite military corps.

In art, stone masons carved a figure of a woman who is acromegalic on a flying buttress of Rheims cathedral in the thirteenth century (Garrison, 1960: 183). The legendary giant Druon Antigon was carved as a forty-foot figure in 1534 by Peter van Aelst, a court painter for King Charles V. The Tyrolian artist Ambras Schloss painted a acromegalic giant in 1553. Two effigies made of wickerwork and plasterboard named Gog and Magog were displayed in London in the sixteenth and seventeenth centuries until they were destroyed in the great London fire of 1666. In the eighteenth century, Goya painted "monstrous" creations as giants. He used scale to project our inner fears.

To a degree, people of large stature have been treated in dehumanizing ways. Societies have depersonalized them and treated them as objects of curiosity. For example, the famous English physicians John and William Hunter were involved in body snatching of people who were different. John Hunter bribed an undertaker to obtain the corpse of an Irish individual of large stature who had made his name as a circus attraction in London. Many anatomists were after the body to add to their collections. The man's body ended up in Hunter's hands, in spite of the man's wish to be buried at sea. The unfortunate Irishman's skeleton is still on display in the entrance to the Royal College of Surgeons in London and serves as a preview of the Hunter medical collection housed there (Dunning, 1992).

PEOPLE WITH PHYSICAL DISABILITIES OVER THE CENTURIES

Western societies typically have had numerous social perceptions of and reactions to people with physical disabilities. Most of these social reactions have been negative and at times destructive. In antiquity, evidence suggests that people with physical disabilities did not fare particularly well. People were sold into slavery or killed at birth. They were also used for entertainment and at a minimum were restricted by law. Having a physical disability or deformity did not conform well with the ancient values of the ideal image of the human body. This ideal image was to have lasting influence on perceptions of people throughout western history.

The Middle Ages continued to be difficult for all but a few people with physical disabilities. Early medieval communities saw people as God's children but as the Middle Ages unfolded people became more punitive. People with physical disabilities became the targets of scapegoating, misinformation, and ill will. When begging became a problem or fear of contagion was high, communities frequently restricted their participation. A few communities allowed people to earn their livings through crafts and trades but how common this practice was is unknown. For better or worse the Middle Ages was a time of begging and many people with disabilities had to turn toward the streets to survive. The church, family, and feudal power shared responsibility for people but did so in differing and inconsistent degrees. This would change with the modern era.

The medieval feudal system would eventually erode for a variety of reasons, such as explosive population growth, costly wars, urbanization, development of private enterprise, and the rise of the nation state. The development of the nation state and government helped shift responsibility for people with physical disabilities (all disabilities for that matter) away from the feudal powers and medieval church to secular government. In addition, the central role of the medieval church in defining, interpreting, and caring for people with physical disabilities would erode. It is with the rise of the modern nation state, development of cities, expansion of private enterprise, and other social changes, that the context of physical disability also changed. The ability of centralized government to intervene in the lives of people and communities resulted in an increased sense of social responsibility for people considered to have disadvantages, such as the poor, old, infirm, and people with significant physical disabilities. This new sense of social responsibility was not extended to all types or forms of disabilities or the diseases that caused them. For example, while communities established almshouses for people who were born with congenital deformities, the same communities avoided people who were disabled by syphilis.

As modernization and industrialization came into full swing, societies placed increased emphasis on one's ability to work and contribute. Thus, more energy and effort went into teaching people trades. When some of these efforts failed, the social reaction was to look for reasons for failure, such as the perceived biological inferiority of people with physical disabilities. The modern era gave rise to the importance of work in the lives of people with physical disabilities that continues today. Families and communities continued to provide care to people. Even with the efforts of family and the community, western history is best characterized as being inhospitable toward people with physical disabilities, even those not needing assistance. For those diseases that resulted in disabilities, such as syphilis, the public response was typically one of outright rejection and restriction. Although inhospitality was the rule, exceptions existed. For example, throughout most of American history, people were inhospitable to people with disabilities. However, in 1636, the Pilgrim Courts provided provisions to maimed soldiers (Farrell, 1956). After the Revolutionary War, peoples' attitudes softened and soldiers were provided pensions if they were disabled during the war. The government established marine hospitals in 1798 for sailors with disabilities. The Continental Congress passed the National Disability Law on August 26, 1776 which had provisions for half pay to the physically disabled.

Throughout these changing social contexts some perceptions of people with physical disabilities remained constant. They have been historically classified into the stereotypes of being evil, subhuman, dependent, always seeking a miracle cure, and others. What is lost in many of these enduring perceptions is that each person, while sharing some characteristics with others, is both human and has individual characteristics that go well beyond their outward appearance or physical disabilities.

Chapter 3

PEOPLE WITH LEPROSY (HANSEN'S DISEASE)

In extreme cases, Hansen's disease, or as it is more commonly known as Leprosy, is one of the most disabling and deforming diseases. Leprosy, until recently, also has been one of the most misunderstood of human diseases. Many misconceptions regarding its nature and misdiagnosis frame its long history. The disease is only rivaled by mental illness in the degree of misunderstanding and misconceptions about its cause, methods of spreading from one person to another, and treatment. Even in contemporary societies, it is common to find misunderstandings about the disease and its disabling effects. Many contemporary beliefs regarding leprosy would be remarkably familiar to people living centuries ago.

Leprosy or Hansen's disease is a chronic infectious disease involving the skin and nerves that may also affect other tissues. It is a bacterial infection that affects the nervous system and can disable and deform people. The cause is Mycobacterium Leprae, which is a bacterium that is a second cousin to the tuberculosis bacterium. The Mycobacterium Leprae is slow-growing and may take up to 20 years to incubate before making a visible or physiological impact on the individual. Contrary to popular opinion, it is not terribly contagious and only about 10 percent of people exposed to it actually get the disease (Nikiforuk, 1993). Clinical manifestations of the disease vary from individual to individual with early symptoms appearing three to five years after infection with some cases showing effects within six months (Carmichael, 1993). Leprosy takes two basic forms, lepromatous and neural. Lepromatous is recognized by the numerous nodules and lesions containing bacilli that form on the skin, frequently on the nose. Neural leprosy may result in facial paralysis. The body's reaction to the Mycobacterium has a bearing on the nature and the form the disease takes, as differences in immunity systems result in various forms of the disease.

The disease, if unchecked, is progressively disabling and may lead to permanent disabilities, such as blindness. The disease results in a loss of neural sensation and can lead to local paralysis of the muscles. People with it may unknowingly suffer injuries that in turn lead to necrosis from secondary infections. Leonine forms of the disease cause skin damage. Their skin becomes thickened and furrowed due to the formation of thick scar tissue. Correspondingly, there is a gradual withering of certain parts of the body that may result in deformed feet and what some have characterized as a "claw hand." Secondary infections from syphilis, frostbite, diabetes, or injury often account for some of the characteristics associated with the disease.

Leprosy remains a baffling disease because how and why the disease spreads still are not fully understood. The mode of transmission of the disease remains unclear. Some experts believe the disease spreads through the respiratory passages or by the skin. They contend that poor living conditions, close contact, poor diet, and other factors promote the disease (Richards, 1977; Rubin, 1974). Genetic factors may also be an important influence on the degree of susceptibility. It has also been baffling because, until modern times, it has been difficult to diagnose. Before the sixteenth century, reliable diagnosis and accurate descriptions of the disease were both rare (Gussow & Tracy, 1970). Over the centuries, medicine has done little to dispel the myths about leprosy. Physicians misdiagnosed the disease frequently (Anonymous, 1977; Brody, 1974; Kealey, 1981; MacArthur, 1953; Rogers & Muir, 1946; Rubin, 1974). Early physicians often confused the disease with other skin ailments, such as fungi, eczema, pellagra, ringworm, syphilis, and psoriasis (Cohn, 1989; MacArthur, 1953; Tullis, 1977; Wells, 1964).

Although it is present in the western world, the numbers of people with the disease are small. In contrast, the World Health Organization estimates of its presence in developing countries range from 10 to 15 million people (Cohn, 1989; Gussow, 1989; Gussow & Tracy, 1971a; 1971b; Anonymous, 1977; Anonymous, 1978; Zivanovic, 1987). India has the highest number of people with the disease followed by Brazil. The actual number of cases is probably higher, as some people with the disease do not seek medical help because of cost, availability of care, ignorance, or the fear of being socially stigmatized. In addition, because of its long incubation stage, some people with the disease may not know they have it because it can take many years for symptoms to develop.

Throughout most of history to be diagnosed with the disease had major implications for the individual. Diagnosis was serious business, as it had life altering social implications for those judged to have the disease. Some communities, having determined that importance of the diagnostic decision, established panels to review suspected cases. Representatives from the church, physicians, and people with the disease were typically members of these panels. Regarding the medieval diagnosis of leprosy, Brody (1974:59) wrote, "It was a prediction of disfigurement and death, and what is perhaps more terrifying, it separated a man from society because of the infection he carried outwardly and the moral corruption that lay within him."

General social perceptions and stereotypes have surrounded leprosy and the people with the disease. These social perceptions have been relatively consistent over the centuries and some persist to the present. Perhaps no other human disease, since the periodic outbreaks of plague and the recent rise of the HIV epidemic, has provoked stronger social responses and stigma. Some experts have argued that the stigma attached to the disease is far more damaging to the individual than the disease. Commenting on the disease, Saragin (1971) concluded that it is difficult to imagine a socially created status more damaging to self-esteem and added that even the word "leper" is frightening. The stigma and stereotypes regarding leprosy often have shaped public policy. This was the case in the United States when the government created a large and isolated asylum for about 400 people who had the disease in the early part of the twentieth century (Gussow, 1989). While the majority of responses to people with the disease have been negative, the presumption that stigma always has negative consequences for people is not always true for leprosy. Historical evidence indicates that some communities treated people with the disease with compassion and understanding (Stringer, 1973; Gussow & Tracy, 1971a).

People have viewed those with the disease as being unclean. As will be noted in the following sections, the Judeo-Christian tradition characterized them as dirty and unclean. Many references in the Old and New Testaments refer to people with leprosy as being unclean and impure (Lewis, 1987). The medieval church considered them sinners and filthy, even though throughout history most people were not particularly clean by today's standards. Beyond the religious bases for viewing people with the disease as unclean, people had other reasons for this perception. Undoubtedly, fear of contact drove part of this perception. The most common social response people have to leprosy has been fear. Dols (1983: 891) wrote of leprosy, "To the western mind, no disease is so fearsome and horrible as leprosy." People have feared leprosy over the centuries because they thought it was a highly virulent disease with horribly unpleasant effects. People assumed that the disease was easily transmitted through the breath, physical contact, or sex. Fear of leprosy, in the absence of real scientific understanding, was an expected response. Given how the disease in its advanced stages can disfigure and lead to death, people naturally feared it.

People have perceived people with leprosy, similar to others with disabilities, as having heightened sexual desires and behaviors. The disease continues, even today, to convey a sense of moral perversion (Dols, 1983). People have frequently associated people with disabilities with paranormal sexual desires. The association between leprosy and sex surfaces on many fronts. For example, medieval authorities proposed that uncontrolled and wanton sex was a cause of the disease. In the Christian view, God afflicted leprosy on people as a punishment for excessive and wanton sexual activity. Given the strong public association with the disease and lust, people saw those with the disease as having strong sexual urges and appetites (Brody, 1974; Burt, 1982; Jacquart & Thomasset, 1988). Some have suggested that increased sexual activity may have occurred for some in an effort to have one last fling, before banishment from society. During the Middle Ages it was also true people did not always distinguish between venereal disease and leprosy, thus the association between sex and leprosy was exaggerated (Jacquart & Thomasset, 1988).

PEOPLE WITH LEPROSY IN ANTIQUITY

Apart from rare references to people with the disease, we know very little about how people were cared for, social perceptions of them, and efforts to educate them in the ancient world. Depictions of them do not exist or are rare, so we are limited to the few written descriptions. Although we have very limited knowledge about people with leprosy in ancient times, it is known that they lived in ancient Africa and Asia, including Egypt (Skinsnes, 1964b), India (Browne, 1990; Skinsnes, 1964a), Rome (Manchester, 1984), and China (Rogers & Muir, 1946). Currently, scientists believe the disease began in Africa and was present in the Mediterranean Basin (Carmichael, 1993).

Some scholars have questioned whether leprosy was as prevalent as suggested by the Old Testament and other ancient writing. Others have concluded that leprosy was not common and did not exist in ancient Egypt or Persia before Alexander the Great but existed in the Far East, India, and Central Africa (Dols, 1979). Part of the difficulty in knowing the existence and extent of the disease is because during ancient history diagnosis was primitive and imprecise. People frequently confused it with other illnesses. Yet, some ancient descriptions of the disease are consistent with nodular leprosy (Anonymous, 1977). Whether the leprosy described by all ancient writers is the same as the leprosy today is uncertain (Gussow, 1989). Similar to later periods, evidence exists of stigmatization of people with the disease was common among ancient cultures. Regardless of the accuracy of the diagnosis, the larger noninfected society treated people perceived as having the disease differently. For example, authorities know that the Egyptians referred to leprosy as "death before death" and sent people with the disease to the

City of Mud to live out their lives (Nikiforuk, 1993). The ancient Hebrews also treated people with the disease differently.

The original spread of leprosy to Europe may have occurred through Asia or Africa. Some have placed its introduction into Greece in 480 AD following the conquest of Darius by Xerxes (Skinsnes, 1964a). The Greek scholar Hippocrates, who was fairly comprehensive in his descriptions of disease, did not describe the disease around 400 BC (Carmichael, 1993). Later Aristotle did in 345 BC. Contemporary authorities have suggested that Greek and Roman military excursions into Asia and Africa contributed to the spread of the disease northward. Some authorities claim Alexander the Great's India Campaign in 327-328 BC may have spread the disease to ancient Greece (Browne, 1990). Records show the ancient Greeks commonly described leprosy about 200 BC (Rogers & Muir, 1946). When true leprosy reached Greece, people knew it as Elephantias because they thought people with it had skin texture similar to an elephant's skin. Others have linked the introduction of the disease to much later in history. Some suggest that it was generally unknown to much of Europe until Pompey's soldiers carried it from the East in 62 (Anonymous, 1977; Browne, 1990; Dols, 1979; Skinsnes, 1964a). Later the Roman physician Galen inaccurately described the disease in 180 AD (Dols, 1979; Skinsnes, 1964a). During antiquity and after the fall of the Roman Empire, little progress was made over the following centuries in understanding and treating leprosy (Kalisch, 1975).

The Judeo-Christian tradition makes many references to leprosy and was critical in influencing later perceptions and interpretations of the disease. The Bible alone makes about 50 references to the disease (MacArthur, 1953). Some scholars have judged leprosy to be the most important disease mentioned in the Old Testament (Garrison, 1960). The Old and New Testaments provided an important mechanism for interpreting the disease in a moral context for centuries. However, it is incorrect to assume that all of western attitudes and practices find their basis in this tradition. Multiple references to leprosy exist in the Old Testament including Exodus; Deuteronomy; Genesis; Kings, Leviticus; Numbers; and Chronicles. Some have suggested that Old Testament references to Tsara'ath and lepra are unlikely references to true leprosy (Anonymous, 1977; Browne, 1990), undoubtedly this was the case. It would be erroneous to assume that the Old Testament's reference to leprosy conforms with contemporary understandings of the disease. For example, there is no mention of leonine faces, ulceration of the extremities, or loss of digits characteristic of advanced leprosy (Anonymous, 1977). Authorities generally agree that biblical leprosy may not have always represented the disease as we know it (Garrison, 1960; Skinsnes, 1964c; Stringer, 1973). Early writings do not always refer to deformities, loss of feeling, destructive physical changes, blindness, nor paresis (Lewis, 1987).

In pre-Christian antiquity, the Old Testament had little influence on thoughts on Middle-Eastern and Greco-Roman ideas about leprosy (Skinsnes, 1964b). Rather, custom and culture influenced practices and attitudes, the legacy of the ancients and in particular the Greeks and the Hebrews were their writings on the subject of leprosy. These works, abundant with misconceptions about the disease and its effects, served as the foundation for the treatment and care of people with the disease through the Middle Ages and early modern period. The New Testament refers to leprosy in the books of Luke; Mark, and Matthew. The New Testament characterizes leprosy as a condition that turned its hosts white as snow. In contrast to the Old Testament which treats leprosy as an abomination, the New Testament views it as a metaphor of divine salvation (Gussow, 1989). The New Testament characterized, following the wisdom of the Old Testament, considered leprosy highly contagious but easily cured by divine intervention. The role of Jesus as physician-healer in the New Testament resulted in an emphasis on the treatment and cure of the disease rather than the simple diagnosis and control characteristic of the Old Testament (Tullis, 1977). Many references in the New Testament are made to Christ healing lepers. According to Tullis (1977:474), Jesus touching the leper carried several symbolic meanings, "1) His love and concern extended to immoral (leprous) persons as well as to moral ones; 2) He showed contempt for the fear and helplessness commonly manifest toward physical disfigurement; 3) the act of healing accompanied a laying-on of hands..." Luke 17:12 reads, "...as he entered into a certain village there met him ten lepers, which stood far off... And when he saw them... Jesus healed the lepers." Jesus' miraculous cures of people with the disease was a lasting image in western history.

Ancient and early Christian peoples essentially considered leprosy to be a moral disease (Brody, 1974; Richards, 1977). Leprosy, for much of the Christian tradition, was regarded more as a sin than a disease (Anonymous, 1977). Early Christians believed that by giving them leprosy God punished people for sinful behavior (Brody, 1974; Burt, 1982). The disease comes to the surface as a reflection of the individual's inner sinful character. Thus, the person with the disease was showing inner sinfulness. Unlike the Christian tradition, Middle Eastern medical texts and teachings over roughly the same and later periods did not morally censor the affected (Dols, 1979). The Middle Eastern peoples were seemingly more tolerant of people with the disease.

PEOPLE WITH LEPROSY DURING THE MIDDLE AGES

Experts on the disease once thought that leprosy was a late immigrant to Europe. In the past historians suggested the returning crusaders brought it from the Middle East. Today authorities agree that leprosy was well-established long before the crusades. Historical evidence shows that leprosy was already present in Anglo-Saxon England (Clay, 1909; Rubin, 1974) and even Roman-British archaeological excavations dating back to the fourth and fifth centuries indicate the disease was present (Richards, 1977). It was also present in the Middle East during the early Islamic period in the sixth century (Dols, 1979) and in northern Europe (Garrison, 1960). Gregory of Tours described French leper houses and people with leprosy in 560 (Garrison, 1960; Jacquart & Thomasset, 1988). Early Irish, French, Anglo-Saxon, Welsh, and other European literature prior to the crusades refer to people with leprosy. English officials found hospitals for people with the disease in Nottingham between 625 and 638. In 757, Frankish King Pepin issued a decree making marriage of people with leprosy illegal and grounds for divorce. Irish records from the tenth century and Anglo-Saxon evidence indicate the disease was present throughout the British Isles (Richards, 1977).

While experts agree that leprosy was a familiar disease in medieval Europe (Richards, 1977), expert opinions vary as to its prevalence during the period (Gussow, 1989; Mac Arthur, 1953; Richards, 1977; Robins, 1986; Clay, 1909). Authorities have suggested that the disease may have reached its apex during the twelfth and thirteenth centuries (Le Goff, 1990; Clay, 1909; Rubin, 1974). They base this conclusion on the finding that the number of facilities established to care for people with the disease were numerous during the twelfth century. For example, in the mid-twelfth century, France had about 2,000 leprosariums and England and Scotland about 220 to serve approximately 1.5 million people with leprosy. In all, there may have been as many as 19,000 leprosariums in medieval Europe. Some would point to the large number of these hospitals as evidence that the disease must have been widespread and common to have warranted so many hospitals. Given the frequency of misdiagnosis, it is difficult to know with certainty if the people actually served by these hospitals actually had the disease.

During the Middle Ages, the perceptions of people with the disease were deeply rooted in ecclesiastical tradition (Gussow, 1989). The perceptions found within this tradition, described earlier and flavored how people with the disease were responded to during the Middle Ages. Leprosy must, at least through the Middle Ages, be viewed within the context of Christian morality. In regard to this tradition, leprosy stands as somewhat of a contradition because it was a sickness of sinners but also given special grace by God (Brody, 1974). During the Middle Ages, people with leprosy came to symbolize the spiritual corruption in the world. People viewed leprosy and mental illness as either tests of martyrdom, purgation, or punishments for sin (Neaman, 1978). The strong moral connotation of leprosy would result in a dilemma during the Middle Ages and the period of the crusades. Crusaders, from 1095 to 1270, contracted the disease during their campaigns in the Middle East. When they returned to Europe, society should have treated them as heroes because they had fought in the service of God. However, because of their leprosy, society considered them sinners and damned. Their fighting in the Holy Wars guaranteed salvation and forgiveness for sins, but this contradicted the moral definition of people with the disease as being sinners. Society did not know whether to avoid or embrace them. One contemporary scholar has suggested that this circumstance did not pose any difficulties for returning crusaders and they were not ostracized (Dols, 1983).

Early Christians created few, if any, artistic renditions of people with leprosy. However, the Old and New Testaments provided a legacy that fueled the creation of many symbolic images of the disease and its interpretation over the centuries. Old and New Testament characters, such as Job and Lazarus, served as models for telling the Christian story. One of the most common stories serving a subject for artists was the many accounts of Christ healing people with the disease. These accounts were a popular theme by the Middle Ages and later centuries. Cosimo Roselli's (1439-1507) Sistinian Chapel in Rome which has a scene depicting the sermon on the mount that shows Christ healing a person with leprosy. Artists depicted stories of healing of people by figures other than Christ over the centuries. For instance, Han's Holbein the Elder's (1460-1524) picture of *Saint Elizabeth* shows the saint ministering to three people with leprosy. Presentations of *St. George and the Dragon* represented the perfect allegory of the fight between the faithful and leprosy. Richards (1977) observed that many of the hospitals in Scandinavia were dedicated to St. George due to the staying power of the disease in northern Europe.

The Christian tradition includes enduring stories and major figures that were linked to leprosy. The Biblical leprous beggar named Lazarus goes to heaven while the rich man who pays him alms goes to hell. Lazarus of Bethany, brother of Mary and Martha who Jesus raised from the dead, became one of the patron saints for the disease (Mac Arthur, 1953). This happened even though he was not diagnosed as ever having the disease (Gron, 1973; Rubin, 1974). An example work was painted by Paolo Veronese (1528-1588) who shows the leprous Lazarus as a person with crutches and bandages wrapped around his head and ankle. The biblical patriarch Job was pronounced a leper because of the swellings that affected him (Mac

Arthur, 1953). Job was one of the primary figures representing leprosy in the Bible, although some have suggested he may have suffered from scabies or possibly a venereal disease (Gron, 1973). The medieval French artist Jean Fouquet's (1420-1481) miniature entitled *Three Friends Offer Their Consolation to Job* from the fifteenth century *Heures of Anne de Bretagne* is a fine depiction of Job's leprosy (Gron, 1973). The German artist Albrecht Dürer's painting entitled *Job* is another example. According to Gron (1973), Dürer emphasized the submission of Job to his fate in the work. Other representations of Job also carry the theme of Job's submission to his fate and show Job's spouse trying to comfort him. Artists also linked the charity of *Saint Martin* to leprosy. Examples include, Jan van Bruegel the Elder's (1568-1652) painting of Saint Martin shows the saint on a horse with one of the individuals in the scene having leprosy. Following the Middle Ages, Anthony Van Dyck's (1599-1641) *St. Martin Dividing his Cloak*, Peter Paul Reuben's (1577-1640) *Charite de Saint Martin* at Windsor Castle also depict the Saint in the presence of people having the disease.

Besides healing, medieval Christianity took an active role in diagnosing and reporting cases of leprosy. Consequently, the church imposed many of the prevalent attitudes toward people with leprosy. Within the context of Christianity, priests were often involved in diagnosing leprosy, as it was considered to be as much a disease of the soul as it was of body. William Cowper (1731-1800) wrote, "When nations are to perish in their sins, 'Tis in the church the leprosy begins" (Richards, 1977:5). In addition, church care for them did not cease upon diagnosis. Early church leaders, such as St. Francis, preached that it was one's duty to serve people with the disease. What was it like to be a person with leprosy in early Christian society? St. Gregory of Nysse (332-400) provides one description:

> They have no friends but each other, united as they are in misery; that which makes them despised of others unites them in a close bond among themselves; repulsed on all sides, they become by their union a people in themselves...Are they not excluded from public assemblies and feast days, like murderers, parricides, fated to be perpetual exiles, and even more unhappy than these. For murderers are at least permitted to live with other men; these are driven away like enemies. They are denied the same roof, the same table, the same utensils with others. Moreover they are barred from the cleansing waters for public usage, and there is a fear that even the rivers may be inflected with their malady. [Cited by Brody, 1974: 80]

The moral connotations of the disease were expressed throughout medieval history. For instance, Pope Gregory the Great (540-604) viewed people with leprosy as heretics, as did the scholar Isidore of Seville (560-

636). The medieval scholar and monk Bede also associated leprosy with heresy (Brody, 1974). The moral connotation of leprosy would continue well into the Middle Ages. For example, the famous and comparatively enlighten fourteenth century physician Henri de Mondeville viewed the disease as shameful and morally a sign of corruption (Pouchelle, 1990).

During the Middle Ages, more than actual observation, belief and misunderstanding influenced how people perceived leprosy. Typically, society saw people with the disease as untrustworthy, wrathful, malevolent, unclean, hopeless, and suspicious. To the medieval citizen, leprosy meant a long, disfiguring, and inevitable death. Given the perceived horrors of the disease, it should come as no surprise that people usually tried to avoid contact with those having the disease. Medieval citizens worried they could contract leprosy from associating with people with the disease. People have assumed leprosy to be highly contagious, which was certainly the case during the Middle Ages (Jacquart & Thomasett, 1988). Although, many physicians during the Middle Ages did not believe leprosy was highly contagious (Brody, 1974), people feared the disease because it meant a slow death that could last for decades. Their fear resulted from it not only being a physical death but also internal spiritual and social death. Consequently, people have generally distanced themselves from people with the disease.

Officials frequently made special provisions for people with leprosy in medieval law. A case on point, laws sometimes prohibited them from drawing up wills and inheriting wealth. The lack of property rights put many at the mercy of society. Clay (1909:56) noted, "When pronounced a leper in early days, a individual lost not only his liberty, but the right to inherit or bequeath property." After the Norman Conquest and clearly by the close of the thirteenth century, leprous individuals did have some property rights in England (Rubin, 1974). Yet, the situation differed in medieval France where communities denied the privileges of ownership to them (Brody, 1974).

The people with leprosy were at the mercy of society. Society developed other prescriptions and restrictions to control their activities and behavior. Throughout Europe, communities implemented a large number of prohibitions for people with leprosy. For instance, some people believed leprosy could be spread through the breath, thus people with the disease were only permitted to communicate when they were downwind (Brody, 1974; Jacquart & Thomasset, 1988). Some communities required people with leprosy to avoid well-traveled roads and forbade them to enter markets, taverns, churches, and other public structures without special permission. Communities also prohibited them from washing in local streams, touching babies, and using public drinking cups. In medieval England, church officials excommunicated people who had the disease because they were outside the community of humanity.

Restrictions over people with leprosy varied among communities. In Scotland, some communities hung or transported people with the disease, while others permitted them to travel about as they pleased (Nikiforuk, 1993). However, in 1427, the Scottish Parliament decreed that people with the disease could enter the burghs three times a week but never during fairs or market days (Stearns, 1944). According to Kealey (1981), in twelfth century England, people with leprosy were not ostracized and separated from society. Kealey noted that during this period in England clappers and bells were not found. It was also true that not everyone viewed the disease as highly contagious during this period. Although authorities established separate hospitals for them, these hospitals were open to a wide variety of nonleprous patients. The fear of leprosy evolved in the centuries that followed the twelfth for reasons are open to speculation. In 1346, King Edward issued an edict expelling people with leprosy from the city limits of London. He did this because of his fear the disease would spread but also because of his concern that they were becoming a public nuisance for wanton begging. In 1375, King Edward of England tried to restrict the mobility of people with leprosy. Through his actions he helped perpetuate one of the great myths of leprosy that it is highly contagious. Later Henry I, great grandson of Edward the I, had people with leprosy burned alive.

In some communities, authorities passed laws to restrict the personal freedoms of people with leprosy, including mobility. A case on point is the 1,276 assizes of London that proclaimed that people with leprosy could not reside in the city (Clay, 1909). Writs for the right to expel people with leprosy were also common in medieval England. However, there is some evidence that the enforcement of such laws differed by locality (Rubin, 1974). Commenting on medieval France, Le Goff (1990) noted that legally people with the disease had the rights of healthy people except in Normandy and Beauvaisis. Furthermore, some authorities claim laws governing them had no more force than other patients of hospitals and no one could be forced into hospitals against their will (Mac Arthur, 1953). It is also important to note that many medieval people with leprosy resisted efforts to place them in hospitals because of the decayed and deplorable conditions they found in these facilities (Rawcliffe, 1984). For example, patients at the medieval Kingston leper house revolted and demolished their building and fled to the roads (Mac Arthur, 1953). In sum, Clay (1909:136) characterized people with leprosy contacts with the outside world as, a various "...mixture of strictness and laxity."

One of the most dramatic social restrictions on people with leprosy was their segregation from mainstream society. They were separated from society for at least eight centuries (Richards, 1977). This separation, primarily fueled by ignorance and fear, may have been functional. Kealey (1981:104) concluded, separation would have provided medieval society with a means to limit begging. It may have also contributed to their sense of membership, as individuals with common interests were pooled together. One author takes this notion a step further. Kealey (1981:103-104) commented, "Inevitably lepers tended to gravitate toward one another, probably impelled as much by some sort of biblically directed sense that this is what they should do as a desire for uncritical, sympathetic companionship."

To denote the segregation and separation from society, societies implemented elaborate rites of passage during the Middle Ages to mark the passage from the living to the world of the living dead (people with leprosy). Medieval society developed a set of rituals that were used to diagnose, segregate, and label people with leprosy. The church promoted and was often actively involved in these rites of passage. Under Pope Alexander III, the Third Lateran Council (1179) issued a decree that urged the segregation of people with leprosy from society and appropriate ceremonies of separation. The decree stated the church should segregate people with the disease and that they were to be buried in separate cemeteries. The Council also authorized the construction of special chapels and cemeteries inside hospitals that in effect closed people with leprosy off from the rest of the world (Le Goff, 1990). During the Middle Ages, the responsibility for segregating people rested with the local church and village elders (Manchester, 1984).

The rite-of-passage of people with the disease being expelled from the community were common. In Anglo-Saxon and medieval England, officials sometimes issued writs (orders) of separation to people with the disease. In France, separation ceremonies differed little from burial services. Officials sprinkled earth on peoples' heads signifying they were buried from the world (Rogers & Muir, 1946; Talbot, 1967a). One medieval account of the rules that people with leprosy must live by was:

> After formal separation from the church, priests typically read the new rules that would govern people with leprosy for their remaining lives. Officials forbid the person to share the company of others in the church, market, mill, bake house, and tavern. If people with leprosy wanted to buy items, they must touch the articles with their sticks. They could only receive items in their begging bowls and nothing should touch their hands or feet. Their dress and warning rattles or bells must declare them to have the disease and their feet must always covered (shod). If he stopped to talk to someone on the road he must stand to the leeward, and he must avoid narrow lanes that might bring him close contact with others. Apart from the companionship of his spouse, the only company he now may keep in life, or in death, was that of other people with leprosy. [Cited by Richards, 1977: 50-51]

These ritualistic separations from the mainstream were not limited to the Middle Ages. Some communities continued to ritualistically separate people from society in the sixteenth and seventeenth centuries (Le Goff, 1990).

Restrictions were not limited to travel, place of residence, religious practices, and property rights, authorities also placed restrictions on marriage and the family. Typical of the experiences of people with other disabilities, officials tried to restrict their rights to marriage and having children. In addition, the diagnosis of leprosy could be grounds for divorce. Dols (1983) has likened their legal status as being similar to people who were mentally ill, especially in areas of marriage and divorce. However, officials sometimes treated them comparatively well. Again, local customs resulted in a wide variety of responses.

In addition to fear, another contributing factor to their segregation was linked to their begging. Those people with the disease often needed to beg to support themselves. Since their income often came from begging, many citizens considered them a public nuisance. Because of their numbers, town officials found it convenient to deal with them as a concentrated group rather than an endless series of individuals. Authorities made efforts to restrict begging by people with the disease. In England, restrictions on begging by people with the disease would occur in 1348, 1367, 1372, and 1375 (Bayless, 1977). Even when authorities allowed begging and almsgiving, people were not always generous with their donations. This is illustrated by the medieval Scottish practice of customarily sending people with the disease donations of spoiled pork or salmon (Stearns, 1944).

While not a restriction, it is nevertheless important to know that persecution and scapegoating of people with the disease occurred. Society blamed them, similar to heretics, the insane, Jews, and other minority groups, for social and economic calamities, such as disease and famine. For instance, in 1315-1318, officials blamed and persecuted Jewish people and those with leprosy for a great famine in France (Le Goff, 1990). King Philip V (1316-1322), facing limited resources, widespread poverty, horrible living conditions, and famine accused people with leprosy of poisoning wells across France. Haggard (1932: 15) stated Philip's order, "Let us collect in one place all of the people with leprosy and burn them, and so often as more appear, let us burn them also, until the disease is eradicated." The result was hundreds of people were burned at the stake and their property confiscated. Charles the V of France took similar actions and complained that they were overtaking Paris.

In contrast to efforts to limit and restrict their lives, medieval societies sometimes showed compassion to people with the disease. In the twelfth century, at least in England, there was a strong sense of charity and sympathy for people with leprosy (Mac Arthur, 1953). Queen Matilda, spouse of

Henry I, was known widely for her charitable acts toward them. She allegedly kissed and washed the feet of people with the disease (Rubin, 1974). The English King John (1204) allowed people with leprosy to have a portion of all of the flour sold at the market. The church sometimes took an active role by encouraging grace toward people with leprosy. For example in 1163, the Bishop of Exeter allowed them into the markets to seek alms and collect food. Officials judged them to be among the deserving poor and gave them special begging privileges.

In the absence of scientific method and modern medicine, medieval peoples' thoughts on the causes of leprosy ran the gamut of hypotheses. Medical authorities suggested a number of causes for the disease including that it was sexually transmitted or was spread by simple association with other people with the disease. Authorities also proposed that bites of venomous worms, eating rotten fish, drinking unclean wine, and eating rotten or melancholic meat led to the disease. Other explanations were readily available, such as conception during menstruation, imbalances of bodily fluids (humors), and leprous wet nurses (Brody, 1974; Parr, 1945; Rubin, 1974). The Franciscan monk, Batholomaeus Angelicus postulated in 1246 that the disease was hereditary in origin. The medieval physician, Bernard of Gordon, proposed there were many causes including sex with a leprous woman. At the close of the Middle Ages and beginning of the modern era, some experts proposed that consumption of rotten fish caused leprosy (Carmichael, 1993; Richards, 1977; Skinsnes, 1964a). This idea would survive well into nineteenth century in Scandinavia.

During the Middle Ages, authorities characterized people with the disease as having strong sexual desires. They also saw a link between leprosy and venereal disease (Brody, 1974). Western and Arabic scholars had a long tradition of scholarship that linked leprosy to venereal disease (Jacquart & Thomasset, 1988). Some medieval doctors believed it spread through sexual contact. They concluded that having sex with women with the disease caused it to spread (Jacquart & Thomasset, 1988). In addition, people with leprosy were viewed, as was so often the case with people with disabilities, as having tremendous sexual appetites. People saw them as being sexually promiscuous. It may have been more a situation, as suggested by Nikiforuk (1993), that once a person learned they had the disease, they may have become more sexually active out of a fear of being sexually isolated from the general population. Wanton sex may have represented a last hurrah for some, pending their being housed in a leper community.

Some authorities on the disease have noted that treatment of adulterers in the Old Testament parallels that of people with leprosy (Skinsnes, 1964c). Scholars have traced this theme as far back as the writings of Aretaeus of Cappadocia who was a contemporary of the physician Galen. Girolamo

Fracastoro (1478-1553) and Paracelius (1493-1541) were two later scholars who also made the connection. Fracastoro went so far as to believe that leprosy and syphilis were identical. Paracelsus even proposed that syphilis developed from a combination of leprosy and another disease (Brody, 1974). The excessive sexuality attributed to people with leprosy was unfounded and in reality, leprosy causes weakness and a drop in activity.

Medieval Care of People with Leprosy

Misdiagnoses of the disease undoubtedly affected the perceptions of the effectiveness of medical care and treatments people received. Because misdiagnosis of leprosy was common, some medieval physicians would have incorrectly interpreted their medical interventions as effective when they were actually treating acute illnesses other than leprosy. For example, the effectiveness of the Sacrens Ointment in treating leprosy is evidence of misdiagnosis. Physicians and care-providers made the ointment with mercury and a fatty base that would have been somewhat effective for controlling syphilis. Because some patients responded to the ointment, it is likely they may have had syphilis instead of leprosy. In the Middle Ages, diagnosticians' misdiagnosis of leprosy resulted in individuals being stigmatized as having the disease when they did not. For example, the physician John of Gaddesden in his *Rosa Anglica* (1314) wrote:

> No-one is to be adjudged a leper and isolated from all his fellows until the appearance and shape of his face be destroyed. And therefore "cancer" in the feet and a foetod skin disease should not be taken as proof of the disease even when accompanied by a nodular eruption, unless this be on the face. And because many are leprous before the appearance of these signs, be it known that they are three signs common to every form of leprosy. [Cited by Rubin, 1974:155]

The thirteenth century Franciscan Bartholomaeus Anglicus (Kalisch, 1975) testified that persons with the disease had, "...redde whelks and pymples in the face, out of whom offene runne blood and matter; en such the noses swellen, and ben (become) grete, the vertue of smellynge faylyth, and the brethe stynkyth ryght fowle." The late thirteenth century physician Bernard of Gordon's *Lilium Medicinae* (1303) observed that accurate diagnosis was critical to the patient. The medieval physician Guy de Chauliac (c. 1363) expressed concern over misdiagnosis of leprosy. He noted that the damage to the individual could be great because communities often confined people (Clay, 1909). Guy de Chauliac's text *Chirurgicalis Medicinae* (1363) was an influential medical text on leprosy during the late Middle Ages. In this work, de Chauliac made two important points about leprosy. First, anyone misdiagnosed should receive a certificate of freedom from the disease. The benefit being they would then be free from all of the negative sanctions and restrictions from society. Second, communities should isolate people diagnosed with leprosy when the diagnosis was beyond question (Richards, 1977). He was not optimistic that much could be done to cure the disease. Consequently, he instructed medical personnel to tell patients that they would be redeemed in heaven, as there was salvation after death.

All of this is not to suggest that accurate diagnosis was impossible. The description of the tenth century Persian physician Avicenna represents one of the first accurate depictions and diagnosis of the disease (Carmichael, 1993). His tenth century *Canon of Medicine*, provided a description that was commonly used by medieval doctors. However, accurate descriptions of the disease were uncommon. For example, medieval medical texts labeled the sores on the legs of people with leprosy as "mesles," a term that was sometimes confused with the acute disease measles. According to Kim-Farley (1993), eventually the term lost its connection with leprosy and became a term for the disease we know today as the measles.

Medieval physicians used a wide variety of treatments to care for but not necessarily cure the disease. Some medieval physicians admitted their inability to effectively treat the disease. For example, the English physicians Bartolomeus Anglicus (d. 1250) and Bernard of Gordon both acknowledged the difficulty in curing the disease except through the intervention of God (Rubin, 1974; Talbot, 1967). Other doctors suggested that carrying religious relics and using herbs could ward off the disease. For example, Mediterranean peoples thought that leprosy could be cured by blood sacrifice (Hand, 1980). Medieval efforts also included magical and medical treatments. Medieval doctors tried herbal and chemical cures such as Chaulmoogra (hydnocarpus) oil that they applied to the patient's body. The benefits of these and similar efforts were minimal and varied from patient to patient (Cohn, 1989). Because authorities made the connection between leprosy and humoral theory, they often directed treatments toward dealing with the overabundance of black bile. To accomplish this, they let blood. The medieval French physician Mondeville describes the practice of letting blood for leprosy and added that red wine should accompany the treatment (Pouchelle, 1990). Medical authorities also instructed people to eat fresh food, purge, and drink medicinal waters. Islamic physicians during this same period were also trained in the Galenic tradition and believed the disease was caused by an imbalance of bodily humours. Medieval bathing was viewed by some as a cure for leprosy. One account was provided by an early Christian pilgrim to Palestine in 570 AD:

We went to a city called Gadava, which is Gibeon, and there, three miles from the city, there are hot springs called the Baths of Elijah. Lepers are cleansed there, and have their meals from the inn there at public expense. The baths fill in the evening. In front of the basin is a large tank. When it is full, all the gates are closed, and they are sent in through a small door with lights and incense, and sit in the tank all night. They fall asleep, and the person who is going to be cured sees a vision. When he has told it the springs do not flow for a week. In one week he is cleansed. [Cited by Dols, 1983: 904]

This account underscores the medieval belief that cure was a combination of physical treatment and spiritual intervention. This approach was based on the belief that the treatment of the disease involved spiritual and physiological aspects. To address the spiritual aspects of the disease, the church established and maintained leprosariums. The mission of these medieval church hospitals were primary ecclesiastical rather than medical and the emphasis was more on care than cure. These hospitals frequently charged fees for care (Clay, 1909). Communities also provided more and better facilities for clergy and the affluent than lower income groups. This fact may have served to limit the number of people with leprosy entering hospitals. According to Richards (1977), financing the care of people with leprosy was a combination of fees, alms giving, begging, the church, and the finances of the patients. Many administrators expected people with leprosy to surrender all of their possessions to help pay for their care.

Because the disease was linked to the soul and sin, the church pursued religious cures of the spirit. Some Christians viewed religious relics as effective treatments for leprosy. The bones of Saint Milburga (d. 715) were exhumed in 1101 and were believed to cure people with the disease (Kealey, 1981). Some Christians thought that by associating with symbols of the Virgin Mary they would be cured from the disease, as Christians saw her as a pure alternative to carnal lust. People, who developed strong spiritual relationships with her could be cured (Burt, 1982). Numerous locations could be found throughout Europe for pilgrimages, such as Compostella and Saint Gilles in France served as major shrines for people with leprosy and other disabilities (Kealey, 1981). Christians viewed Saint Elizabeth (1207-1231) of Hungary as the patron saint of leprosy. People knew her from her charitable work and service to people with the disease.

Some people thought that the royal touch was a miraculous cure for leprosy and other diseases. The custom was to bring subjects to the King and he would cure them by his touch. Other responses were the same treatments used for other diseases and disabilities. For instance, Hildegard of Bingen (1098-1179), the famous twelfth century Benedictine abbess, recommended using the white lily for curing leprosy (Stannard, 1985). She chose the white lily according to the doctrine of signatures which held that disease and corresponding cures shared common physical features. Because healthy skin was white, she concluded the white lily was a good treatment for the skin and cure for leprosy. She also thought that the soil of anthills had curative powers for leprosy and devised uses for the soil as a treatment (Thorndike, 1923, Vol. 2:147).

If custodial care was the best that could be done for people with the disease, then communities needed to build hospitals. With the apparent lack of successful treatment, public efforts focused on simply isolating and caring for people with the disease. Hospital and care facilities predate the Middle Ages. During the fourth century, a wealthy man with leprosy named Zodicus built the first hospital, Constantinople, that cared for people (Nikiforuk, 1993). Saint Basil of Caesarea established a place to care for people between 369 to 372. The Bishop of Nona built a leper house in Edessa in the mid-fifth century. Evidence shows that lazar or leper houses and hospitals were very common during the Middle Ages. The number of leprosariums may have numbered in the thousands throughout Europe during their peak. A case on point was the city of Toulouse in Spain which had a population of about 25,000, seven leprosaria, and 12 hospitals during the late Middle Ages. Around 625-638, authorities established the Blyth Leper Hospital in Nottingham, England (Skinsnes, 1964a). Later, authorities established leprosariums at Saint Gallen in 759 and at Moutien in 871. The Cid established the first Spanish leprosarium at Palenca in 1067 (Skinsnes, 1964a). Officials founded Leonard's Hospital in Northampton before 1087 (Richards, 1977). In London St. Giles established a leper house in 1101. Officials founded hospitals at Rochester and Harbledown England around 1100 (Clay, 1909). In 1181, the Earl of Chester founded a private hospital for people with leprosy in Coventry (Rubin, 1974). In 1227, Louis VIII willed 100 sous to each of France's estimated 2,000 leper hospitals (Le Goff, 1990). In England, the chief building period for hospitals occurred about the middle of the thirteenth century. However, the British built fewer hospitals than communities on the continent, suggesting that the disease was less prevalent in the isles or perhaps less readily diagnosed (Rubin, 1974). Considering the large number of hospitals founded during the Middle Ages, some authorities concluded that leprosy was fairly common in Europe. However, Rogers and Muir (1946) note that some of these institutions never served people with the disease and fear of the disease may have led to serious overexaggeration of its prevalence (Mac Arthur, 1953).

Typically, the hospitals had walls, private gardens, chapels, cemeteries, and were located outside town limits. For example, the Scottish located them outside the walls of the towns. In Scotland, these hospitals were poorly endowed, which forced some inhabitants to beg to survive (Stearns, 1944). Historians viewed this practice of building outside towns as an illustration of how people with leprosy were outcasts and segregated from society. It should be noted most hospitals, even for people without leprosy, were located outside the towns' walls (Kealey, 1981). In addition, hospitals for people with the disease also served other needy and sick (Clay, 1909; Rubin, 1974). Despite the isolation inferred by the location and structure of these hospitals, there is evidence that they may have been more open than one would assume. Evidence exists that these hospitals were fairly open to other members of the person's family. Officials allowed family members to visit and stay in these facilities (Mac Arthur, 1953). During the Middle Ages, some communities allowed the privileged classes to live outside the leprosarium (MacKinney, 1965).

Medieval Depictions of People with Leprosy

Despite the relative familiarity of leprosy in medieval society, medieval authorities' descriptions of the disease are simplistic and often inaccurate. The same could be said about artists and writers' characterizations of the disease, which was based on secondary information rather than direct observation. Even when direct observation occurred, one could never be sure that the person truly had the disease or some other ailment. Artistic and literary portrayals focused on the symbolic and moral views rather than on observation. As Saul Brody (1974) noted, medieval descriptions of the disease bear little resemblance to modern notions about the disease.

One medieval way to identify people with leprosy was by their clothing. Some communities expected people with leprosy to wear special clothing to warn of their disease. The clothing allowed others to identify and keep great distance from approaching those with leprosy and also to identify people for discriminatory purposes. The clothing served other purposes besides being a warning, such as symbolizing the fact that the person was a moral and social outcast (Richards, 1977). Long robes, gloves, horns thrown over the shoulder, were typical features of the general costume (Rubin, 1974). Rules required that footwear be worn because it was thought bare feet would spread the disease. People with the disease wore ankle length tunics of russet (a coarse reddish brown cloth) with long sleeves that were closed at the wrist, with cowls, and capes of black cloth. People sometimes sewed yellow crosses to their capes or vestments (Carmichael, 1993). They wore gloves with gray or white wool robes and masks were sometimes worn over mouths. The French sewed the letter "L" into the garments. Gron (1973) found that red signs in the shape of a goose or duck foot were sometimes worn over the person's chest. Communities even had social expectations on how the clothing was worn. Clay (1909:175) cited the statutes of St. Julian's that people with leprosy ought, "...as well in their conduct as in their garb, to bear themselves as more despised and as more humble than the rest of their fellow men...." In some communities people with the disease carried long poles that they used to point to things that they wanted to purchase in the markets and also to retrieve alms cups that had to be distanced from them (Carmichael, 1993).

Some communities supplied garments and clappers to people with leprosy (Rogers & Muir, 1946). As part of this costume, depending on local custom, a clapper, handbells, rattles, castanets, or bell was also often used to warn of the their approach. When shaken, these clappers created loud warning clicks. Paintings by Rembrandt (1631) and Cornelius Matsy (1540) show that the use of clappers and rattles continued in the sixteenth and seventeenth centuries. The costume sometimes had bells and still survives in the carnival dress in certain regions of Germany (Schadewaldt, 1967b). Clothing requirements eventually disappeared with the decline of the disease. In sharp contrast to the previous medieval images are those of later centuries that depict people with leprosy in ordinary clothing. For example, Rembrandt's *Uzziah Stricken with Leprosy* (1635) shows the leprous Uzziah in an eastern turban and royal clothing common to the seventeenth century. Later, J.A. Welhaven and Bevalet's nineteenth century drawings of people with leprosy also show them in ordinary clothing. Absent are the clappers and bells common in the Middle Ages. As far as clothing contributes to stereotypes and stigma, it appears people with leprosy were able to shed the burden of the medieval and repressive clothing as the disease declined.

An English illumination found in the margin of the *Exeter Pontifical* from the fourteenth century shows a costume of a person with leprosy. The work shows a woman in a full robe with the wide brim hat. She holds a bell that she used to warn others of her presence and to gather alms. She sits on a mat. Above her head is a banner that reads, "Sum good, my gentyll mayster, for God sake." The artist marked her face with the spots to depict the condition of leprosy. Nikifrouk (1993:38) commented:

> Most medieval painters and lithographers relied on inaccurate biblical descriptions of leprosy as pepper-like red spots in order to avoid examining the real thing. The first painter to capture the physical and moral despair of the leper was the Italian artist Francesco Traini in 1355. His dark fresco *The Triumph of Death* shows eight angry lepers and beggars with bandaged limbs and melted noses. One holds a scroll that reads, "Since prosperity has abandoned us, Death, medicine for every pain, Course and give us now the Last supper."

Figure 16. Margin drawing from *Exeter Pontifical*, fourteenth century, British Library, London.

Other medieval art and literature contain numerous examples of leprous people. Brody noted that medieval writings are abundant with references to leprosy. He (1974: 191) wrote, "Writers of the fifteenth century continue to connect leprosy with sinfulness, and lust, being perhaps the most sensational of sins—is encountered with great frequency." "Medieval lepers," as noted by Brody (1974: 49), "...are very much like people with leprosy in medical treatises: The faces of both types are covered with modules, their breath stinks, and they speak with altered (and usually hoarse) voices."

An example of a medieval literary work that refers to leprosy is the poem *Amis and Amiloun*. *Amis and Amiloun* told the tale of a knight who contracts leprosy, is rejected by his lady, and is forced to beg for survival. John Gower's text *Confessio Amantis* (1390-1393) inferred that leprosy is punitive in the case of Constantine. According to the tale, Constantine learns that his leprosy can be cured by bathing in the blood of children. The emperor ordered that children be sent to him so that they could be sacrificed for their blood. Later, dreaming, Constantine sees Peter and Paul who inform him that Silvester can heal him. Constantine finds compassion for the children and frees them. Silvester cures him by converting him to Christianity. The Scottish schoolmaster Robert Henryson's (c. 1425-1500) fifteenth century poem *Testament of Cresseid*, which is a sequel to Chaucer's *Troilus and Criseyde*, described the leprosy of the character Cresseid in great detail. The following passage uses worms and toads as classical references to death and decay. The impending death of Cresseid led her to write in her will:

> When this was said, with paper she sat down,
> And in this manner made her testament:
> Here I bequeath my body
> with worms and toads to be rent;
> My cup and clapper and my ornament,
> And all my gold the leper folk shall have,
> For burying me in the grave when I am dead. [Cited By Richards, 1977: 7]

Just as they were popular subjects for medieval authors, they were equally popular for medieval artists. As noted before, artists knew very little about them and relied on stereotypes and secondary sources to portray them. During the Middle Ages, artists began to portray them on a human scale. Medieval medical illustrations of the disease were often diagrammatic (Richards, 1977). In these images, artists frequently presented people with leprosy in their costumes. To artists, this was a quick way to inform the viewer that the subject had leprosy. Medieval artists' representations of people with leprosy generally conformed to copies from other artists rather than reality. Medieval artists' representations of leprosy were inaccurate. Brody

(1974: 47-48) concluded, "Similarly, in manuscript illuminations and early woodcuts, people with leprosy are conventionally represented with numerous spots, small circles, or other marks intended to depict lesions on their bodies." Artists paid little attention to anatomical accuracy because they had the overriding purpose to give the viewer a symbol that could be immediately understood.

Other examples of art and architecture that carry images of people with the disease include the medieval *Tower of the Leper* found in Acosta, Italy. While people with the disease were common subjects of drawings, sculptures of people with possible leprosy were relatively uncommon. One late fifteenth century exception, however, can be found at the Musee de L'oeuvre Notre-Dame in Strassburg, France. According to Rousselot (1967), the head of man resembles facial paralysis resulting from neural leprosy. Giralomo Muziano's (1528/30-1592) painting of Jesus and his disciples healing the sick at the gate of the temple found at the Uffizi Gallery in Florence shows a person with leprosy. Nardo di Cione Orcagna's (1343-1365) fourteenth century fresco at Pisa, titled *The Triumph of Death*, shows various deformities resulting from leprosy. In the fourteenth century, Pietro del Donzello's work, *Charity of Saint Martins,* also includes a person with leprosy with a deformed hand. The Renaissance (1400-1500) witnessed the onset of several artistic works on the subject of leprosy (Kalisch, 1975). Renaissance artists were the first to begin to display the neurological symptoms of leprosy in the extremities in the fifteenth and sixteenth centuries (Gron, 1973). However, during this period, syphilis was rampant in Europe and it is difficult to tell if artists were presenting leprosy or syphilis. Sandro Botticelli's (1445-1510) painting at the Vatican titled *The Sacrifice of the Leper* and Cosimo Rosselli's (1439-1507) *The Leper's Supplication to Jesus* also at the Vatican are representative works.

The Decline of Leprosy at the Close of the Middle Ages

Although the prevalence of the disease is difficult to determine (MacArthur, 1953; Wells, 1964), experts believe leprosy raged during the twelfth to the middle of the thirteenth centuries. By the middle of the thirteenth century it started to decline (Rubin, 1974). One scholar estimated the percentage of people with leprosy in the general population might have been around one percent (Tullis, 1977). Others have concluded that about one in 200 may have had the disease in England (Kealey, 1981; Wells, 1964). Regardless, whatever the level of leprosy was, experts believe it dramatically declined near the end of the Middle Ages. It continued to decline during the fourteenth and fifteenth centuries and almost disappeared at the close of the Middle Ages (Carmichael, 1993; Le Goff, 1990). Currently, most authorities are in agreement that it basically disappeared in Europe during the sixteenth century (Gussow & Tracy, 1971b).

The decline of leprosy was not evenly spread across Europe. According to Rogers and Muir (1946), in England it disappeared in the sixteenth century (Gussow & Tracy, 1970). However, it persisted in small pockets across Europe, such as in Ireland up to 1775. In France, it was still common at the end of the sixteenth century and continued until about 1789. It had sufficiently decreased by the close of the seventeenth century to the extent that Louis XIV abolished leper houses and was able to direct endowments to other charitable causes (Garrison, 1960). Even with these major declines, leprosy persisted in Scandinavian countries well into the nineteenth century.

Authorities do not agree on what caused the decline of the disease. Some have suggested a number of factors may have been responsible, such as improved sanitation, acquired immunities, segregation of people with leprosy from society, rise of tuberculosis, improved diet, and improved living conditions (Rubin, 1974). Some experts argue that the Black Death assisted in the decline, as many people with leprosy fell victim to the plague (Richards, 1977). The Black Plague of 1349 would have been particularly harsh to people with leprosy, as they were generally in poor health (Clay, 1909). Others have suggested the cold weather and increasing supplies of woolen textiles in Europe may have diminished leprosy (McNeil, 1976). Better diagnosis by physicians probably contributed to the decline of the disease. This is because the slow development of the disease meant that people with leprosy could unknowingly spread it before they were separated from the general population (Rogers & Muir, 1946). Some experts note that the decline of the disease coincided with urbanization and corresponding rise of pulmonary tuberculosis (Manchester, 1984; McNeil, 1976). As urbanization progressed, population densities increased and the threat of tuberculosis emerged. Tuberculosis, a competitive cousin of leprosy, thrives in densely populated areas. The slow developing mycobacterium lepra was not able to win the biological race to infect human hosts compared with the more aggressive tuberculosis bacterium. People contracting tuberculosis gained some immunity to leprosy. The same is not true for those contracting leprosy, as tuberculosis was the leading cause of death for people with leprosy.

The disappearance of leprosy from medieval Europe may have affected other groups. Some have noted that the alms formally bestowed upon people with leprosy became available for other needy groups, including people with disabilities and older and invalid people. Michael Foucault (1965) has made the connection between attitudes toward madness and the disappearance of leprosy between 1200 to 1400. As leprosy disappeared from Europe, he concluded mental illness became the new outcast segment of society. According to Foucault, a social vacuum was created by the decline in the number of people with leprosy at the close of the Middle Ages. People with mental illness would fill this void and the facilities designed to serve those with leprosy.

PEOPLE WITH LEPROSY DURING THE MODERN PERIOD

By the modern period, leprosy was not the significant disease that it was during the Middle Ages. It continued, however, to receive public attention. The beginning of the modern era essentially marked the end of the leprosy era, as the disease was mostly a medieval phenomenon. Those people with the disease during the modern era continued to face restrictions and other negative social reactions that were medieval in origin and tone but not to the same degree as their medieval counterparts. The most significant conclusion reached about the sixteenth century is that, for all practical purposes, people witnessed the virtual disappearance of leprosy in Europe and it never became important in North America. The disappearance of leprosy, as noted by Gussow (1989), also corresponded within the context of decline of the power and prestige of the medieval church. However, leprosy remained a moral disease and was linked to sin.

Public fear of infection continued to isolate people from the rest of society during the sixteenth and seventeenth centuries. This continued even though the odds of encountering people with the disease were increasingly rare. Even though uncommon, the disease continued to capture the attention of physicians, writers, and artists. In spite of the attention it received, there were no great advances in the care and treatment of the disease. The same could be said about the eighteenth century. The only advance made was that some medical writers were more accurate in their descriptions of the symptoms of the disease (Kalisch, 1975).

Although few people were known to have the disease, artists created numerous works representing people with the disease during the sixteenth and seventeenth centuries. A dramatic shift in these images occurred. They were shown in much broader contexts than in the past and would be shown as human beings and not as walking dead. Bernard Von Orley (1496-1542) triptych contains a patient holding a leper's bell with a deformed hand, and having deep lesions on his face (Antwerp Museum of Fine Arts). Another work by Orley titled *Judgment Day* depicts a person with the disease seated in the right panel. Han's Holbein the Elder's (1460-1524) painting of Saint Elizabeth shows the saint ministering to three people with leprosy. Nicholas Manuel Deutsch (1484-1530) painting of *Saint Anne Between Saint James the*

114   *Social Perceptions of People with Disabilities*

Elder and Saint Roch. God is depicted in the traditional location of above all in the upper center of the painting. In the bottom right foreground are the faithful and nobility. To the left foreground are four individuals who have different diseases and disabilities. The well-dressed woman has a tumor on her forearm. The figure closest to the center has an advanced case of leprosy. The individual's arms are crossed and he has lost his fingers on his

Figure 17. Nicholas Manuel Deutsch, *Saint Anne Between Saint James the Elder and Saint Roch*, 1484-1530, Oeffentliche Kunstsammlung Basel Kunstmuseum, Basel, Switzerland.

right hand. His leg is deformed by the disease and his face shows signs of partial paralysis. His hands have been reduced to stumps, arms are supported by linen slings wound around the neck, and his legs have major deformities. This is a brutally realistic depiction of the disease and accents the horror of massive deformity to the viewer. This depiction parallels other works by Deutsch in its style and portrayal of the negative aspects of sin, disease, disability, and death.

In sharp contrast is Hans Holbein the Younger's (1497/98-1543) *Portrait of a Leper* drawn in 1523. Holbein's work is a realistic chalk and watercolor depiction of the face of a man with the disease. The work shows a young man whose leprosy has not progressed to an advanced stage. The back of the drawing indicates that the subject died that year but not the cause of his death (Moskowitz, 1962). The drawing is simple and direct. Holbein made no value or moral statements about the man but simply depicts him with as he was with his eyes focused on the viewer. Absent is the judgmental tone found in earlier representations of people with the disease. Holbein has created a simple and nonjudgmental portrait of this individual who happens to have leprosy but was first and above all a person. Holbein is not attempting to horrify us as Deutsch did, but show us the human side of the individual. Absent are the moral overtones obvious in the work by Deutsch. In comparison to Holbein's image, is Rembrandt's (1606-1669) *Uzziah Stricken with Leprosy* (1635). Rembrandt depicted the biblical figure Uzziah. The biblical story of Uzziah, a King of Judah, tells of him inappropriately burning incense in the temple of the Lord. A priest of the temple tries but fails to stop him. God strikes him with leprosy for the sin of assuming priestly functions (2 Kings 15: 1-7; 2 Chronicles 26: 1-23). Rembrandt, a master of the effective use of light, draws the viewer to the stricken hands and face of Uzziah in a style typical of Rembrandt's other works. Being the King of Judah, Rembrandt shows him in royal clothing.

One of the most interesting modern illustrations of people with leprosy and local custom from this period comes from northern Europe. Many communities allowed people with leprosy to parade into town and seek their alms for the year. Processions of people with leprosy into towns on holidays were a theme for northern European artists of the seventeenth century. The seventeenth century Dutch artist Claes Jansz Visscher the Younger's (1568-1652), *Procession of Lepers on Copper Monday* (1608) remains one of the best depictions of the custom. This etching shows a group of people with leprosy parading through town. Visscher showed children in the work that is uncommon in most representations of leprosy. The children may or may not have had the disease. As dictated by custom, people knew the first Monday after the first Sunday following Epiphany as Copper Monday. On this day, the citizens of Amsterdam allowed people with leprosy to march through town to collect

Figure 18. Hans Holbein the Younger, *Portrait of a Leper,* 1523, The Harvard University Art Museums, Cambridge, Massachusetts, Meta and Paul J. Sachs Collection.

yearly alms. The day was also a celebration for the carpenter's and printer's guilds. They delivered coppers to the leper house to help support them. Although authorities outlawed the custom in Amsterdam in 1604, Visscher chose it as the subject for this etching four years later (Karp, 1985).

The people in the etching wear the costumes of people with the disease as well as carrying alms cups, clappers, and bells. Visscher drew them as having short statures and general appearances of being cherub-like. Except for differences in dimension, the viewer might conclude that a group of children

Figure 19. Claes Jansz Visscher the Younger, *Procession of Lepers on Copper Monday*, 1608, Philadelphia Museum of Art, SmithKline Beecham Corp. Fund for the Ars Medica Collection, Philadelphia.

had gathered together. The people with the disease lose their individuality in the huddling group. This is a group that is festive and not in any way threatening.

Other northern European artists, such as Adrien van Nieulandt's (1587-1658) *Yearly Procession of Lepers in Amsterdam in 1604* also represented this custom. Other presentations were made, such as David Teniers the Younger's (1610-1690) *Deeds of Misercorde* illustrates one of the beggars as having leprosy. Dutch seventeenth century portraiture occasionally portrayed the directors of charities, including those involved with leper hospitals. Werner Van den Valckert's (1580/85-1627) portrait of the governors of a leper asylum titled, *Four Governors and the Master of the Leper Asylum*, Amsterdam (1624) shows the governors with their charitable roles symbolized by objects on a table. The secretary has his pen and paper, treasurer a money bag, the warden the keys, and a picture of Lazarus hangs in the background.

Nothing about the disease or people with it stands out in the eighteenth century. Social perceptions and reactions continued as they had in prior centuries. The same cannot be said about the nineteenth century, which would bare witness to new ideas about the disease. Although leprosy in Europe and North America was uncommon during the nineteenth century, leprosy remained a social concern. People continued to view leprosy as a very contagious venereal disease. The moral aspects of the disease became reemphasized in late nineteenth century thought (Brody, 1974). Possibly as a by-product of the Victorian concern for morality that came into vogue during the middle of the century.

Although scientists probed into the possible causes of the disease, no progress was made during the eighteenth and early part of the nineteenth centuries. It was only toward the end of the nineteenth century that any advances occurred when spectacular discoveries were made in bacteriology. Diagnoses common in the Middle Ages progressed little over the centuries that followed until 1850 (Richards, 1977). The same was true for explaining what caused the disease. One school of thought believed that hereditary caused the disease. Scholars based this perspective on the observation that the disease sometimes ran in families or specific geographic areas. Proponents of this view noted that contact with people with the disease did not always result in contracting the disease. They concluded the disease must be hereditary and was passed from one generation to the next. Other nineteenth century explanations focused on environmental factors or infection. One theory, proposed by the Norwegian leprosy authorities Danielssen and Boeck in their *Traite de la Spedalsked ou Elephantiasis des Grecs* (1847) proposed that eating bad fish led to leprosy. They based their conclusion on the observation that the disease seemed to be more prevalent in coastal communities and fishing villages in Scandinavia. They proposed that the disease was mostly inherited in that related people tended to contract or not contract the disease. Danielssen repeatedly inoculated himself with the disease but never succeeded in developing the disease. Based on his observations, he wrongly concluded that some aspect of the disease was genetically inherited. Only with the discovery by the Norwegian Gerhard Armauer Hansen (1841-1912) of the true medical cause of leprosy in 1873 did the disease become understood (Gussow, 1989; Stringer, 1973). This discovery was to be the major milestone in understanding the nature of the disease and his discovery forever changed views of the disease (Larsen, 1973).

Social Darwinism and the Disease

To understand how societies perceived leprosy and people with the disease in the nineteenth century, it is important to acknowledge the important influence Dawinism had on viewing people, disease, and disability. The nineteenth century was to witness the rise and popularity of Social

Darwinism, which provided a theoretical basis and rationale for the order of things, including the prevalence of disease and disability among foreign populations. Leprosy attracted attention in the nineteenth century as a foreign and highly contagious disease often found among "inferior populations" (Gussow, 1989).

While the disease in the western world had declined at the close of the Middle Ages, such was not the case for the remainder of the world. The nineteenth century was a period of colonial imperialism by western nations. Nineteenth century imperialism fueled the uncovering of the disease in native populations. Missionaries, imperialists, colonialists, and others found leprosy in the colonial world. When coupled with western ethnocentrism and the popular Social Darwinism, leprosy became a symbolic reaffirmation of the racial superiority in the nineteenth century mind. Westerners saw leprosy as a disease of impoverished and inferior peoples. This theory provided a rationale for suppressing the cultures and people of the underdeveloped (colonial) world. Ignoring the many references to the high prevalence of disease in western literature, many nineteenth century people thought of leprosy as a foreign disease that was associated with poverty (Volinn, 1989). When expeditions found leprosy in the populations of underdeveloped countries, they viewed its presence as evidence of the existence of inferior peoples (Gussow, 1989). They believed the developed west had evolved into a higher stage of evolution that included some immunity to the disease. To illustrate how the rationale worked, one can turn to the Hawaiian Islands. The Hawaiian Islands experienced an outbreak of leprosy during the mid-nineteenth century that led to accusations that imported "racially inferior" Chinese laborers were spreading the disease to the native islanders (Gussow & Tracy, 1970). All of this led to an alarmist concern for the disease. Summarizing the alarmist perceptions and fears of the time, Gussow and Tracy (1970: 437) concluded, "Certain races and peoples, notably the Chinese, Asiatic Indians, and Blacks–the Yellow and Negro races–were coming to be identified as leprosy-prevalent populations, and the fear was rapidly growing that Europeans have ceased to show the immunity from its attacks which was once thought to be their privilege."

This fear of foreigners and the spread of leprosy was irrational but nonetheless real in the nineteenth century. Some nineteenth century medical authorities estimated that the numbers of people with the disease would explode, if unchecked, in the United States to as many as 500,000 people (Gussow & Tracy, 1970). Leprosy was not alone in this regard, people also feared those with mental illness and other disabilities judged to be linked to genetic inheritance. Notable exceptions in the care, perception, and treatment of people with the disease existed in the nineteenth century. Father Damien de Veuster drew worldwide attention to people with the disease when he joined a colony of people with the disease on the Hawaiian islands. He became devoted to teaching the rest of the world to view them in more humanistic terms. Father Damien contracted the disease shortly after having joined the colony and eventually died. His well-publicized infection and later death helped spread the public perception and fear that the disease was highly contagious and not hereditary, as some nineteenth century scholars had thought (Gussow & Tracy, 1970). While his work with people with the disease was admired for its humanity, his death fueled negative perceptions.

In the United States, American officials did not really define leprosy as a problem until 1880 (Gussow, 1989). It is somewhat surprising that it was ever defined as a problem at all, given its rarity. Even humanitarian and progressive groups viewed leprosy as unique and different from other diseases or disabilities. Kalisch (1972: 489) noted, the "Progressive Era produced in the United States resulted in the enlightened amelioration of stigma surrounding such illness as insanity, tuberculosis, and syphilis, but failed to break through the barrier of stigma surrounding leprosy." This is witnessed by several decades of debate and policy formation during the Progressive Era and cumulated in the building of a leprosarium in Carville Louisiana in 1921. Officials established the facility even though there were only 278 known cases of leprosy in the country.

By the nineteenth century, artists represented the disease without the heavy moral themes common in the past. They attempted to create objective and realist representations of people with the disease. As the disease became defined in scientific and medical rather than moral terms, images of people with it also changed with increased scientific and medical understanding. Illustrations of people with the disease became increasingly scientific in tone and purpose. Only medical and scientific texts contained images of people with the disease. These texts were not generally available or of interest to the general public. Coupled with the rarity of the disease in the general population, the eighteenth and nineteenth century citizen was free to imagine what people with the disease appeared and what their corresponding disabilities were like. The public had only those images of the disease linked to stereotypic works created in previous centuries rather than more realistic works based on direct observation. Artists, such as J.A. Welhaven and Bevalet, created images of people with the disease for medical and scientific texts in the nineteenth century. A collection of nineteenth century illustrations of people with the disease was done by Bevalet in 1836. Danienssen and Boeck's text on the subject entitled *Traite de la Spedalsked*, published in 1847, has several scientific drawings of people with the disease. All of the moral overtones present in medieval works are absent in these drawings and the emphasis is placed on accurately depicting the disease and individual.

PEOPLE WHO HAD LEPROSY OVER THE CENTURIES

Leprosy represents one of the most interesting of all diseases that can result in disability. Many myths and misperceptions about the disease have shaped social perceptions and reactions to people with the disease. The very nature of the disease, with its prolonged incubation period and wide array of symptoms, only fueled public misunderstanding. For those with the disease, the misunderstandings have been historically overwhelmingly catastrophic. We also know that some people were able to handle difficult situations and negative social stereotypes.

The role of people with the disease was functional for Christian society. By virtue of being considered a sinful outcast, they served as a symbolic representation of evil. Leprosy was a warning to all living that their sinful lives might result in God's punishment. They reaffirmed one's commitment to and fear of God. The person with the disease served as a signpost of the moral and Christian view for those tempted by sin. Similar to other disabilities, leprosy carried a moral connotation that it was only able to shed in the late nineteenth century. Leprosy was a disease heavily burdened by metaphorical trappings (Brody, 1974; Gussow, 1989).

Departing from Brody's view is Gussow (1989) who contended that powerful social forces, such as racism and imperialism, as well as social institutions contributed to the prolongation of the stigma attached to the disease rather than medieval teachings. According to Gussow (1989), leprosy does not have its equivalent in the other disabling diseases. We do not fear other disabilities, such as being deaf or blind, as leprosy was once feared. One does not fear acquiring deafness from the deaf or blindness from the blind in contrast to the fear of contracting leprosy from other persons. One fears the person with leprosy out of uncertainty, misinformation, tradition, self-preservation, and ignorance. Finally, Isle Volinn (1989:1157) wrote, "Society's perception of an occurrence as dangerous as well as epidemic brings about a broad gamut of exclusionary measures." This was certainly the case for leprosy which was seen as contagious and something to be feared. Proclamations for the expulsion of people with the disease were common during the later Middle Ages (Rawcliffe, 1984). People with the disease were judged as being disruptive, along with other groups such as epileptics and people with severe mental illness.

Disabilities and disease have, at times been treated and reacted to with a sense of urgency. This was certainly true for leprosy. One side of the swing of the pendulum, people have generally overreacted to people with the disease. People built numerous leprosariums, wrote about the disease, and feared it over the centuries. All of this represents an overreaction compared to the relatively few people who may have actually had the disease. This overreaction continued well into the nineteenth century even in America, which constructed an unnecessary leprosarium in Carville, Louisiana. The current social reaction of the general public to HIV positive individuals (not withstanding the relatively slow response of Government and Medicine to formulate a strategy and funding for AIDS treatment and research) is certainly an overreaction based on fear and ignorance on the disease and how it is spread.

Chapter 4

PEOPLE WHO WERE MENTALLY ILL

Mental illness refers to disorders of perception, cognition, emotion, and behavior. Disorders can be mild or severe, acute or chronic, and can be caused by defects in mind, body, or both. Typically, the diagnosis of mental illness is the determination that an individual is impaired in his or her capacity to think, feel, or relate to others. Although mental illness and insanity (madness) have been persistent concerns in western history, little consensus exists over their nature (Porter, 1987). Even in contemporary times mental illness continues to be an elusive entity, because people do not always know where to draw the line between sanity and insanity. This was not always the case and there have been eras, such as the Middle Ages when, differences between the sane and mentally ill were more evident.

Throughout history the identification of people as being mentally ill has always involved considerable judgment. This judgment has been based on criteria that were found in the historical context in which it occurred. People always identified mental illness relative to social context in which it occurred. These social contexts have changed over the centuries. The labeling or identifying of insanity has been primarily a social act (Szasz, 1961). The study of the history of people who were mentally ill is one of the social construction of labels. However, labeling a person as mentally ill or insane does not account for all that we may observe or know about mental illness.

Gender has always played a role in the social perceptions of madness and insanity. Gender also influenced artistic representations of insanity, asylums, and people who were mentally ill. For example, in western thought, hysteria has long been associated with females. Egyptian papyrus, Hippocrates and other ancient writings linked hysteria to females. The ancients believed the uterus moved throughout the female body and associated this movement with hysteria. By the Middle Ages and Renaissance, people thought hysteria was caused by sprits or the devil. Centuries later, in the eighteenth and nineteenth centuries, it was associated with a condition known as the vapors, which was common to excessively refined women. Nineteenth century men did not have the vapors. Regardless of perceived cause, it was perceived as uniquely female in origin.

With some exceptions, during the centuries leading to the eighteenth, mental illness, and madness was predominantly male phenomena. Male images dominated representations and the characterizations of madness. Although females images existed, such as the hysterical woman, male images were at the forefront. In scholarly works, male representations dominated writings. This would change during the close of the eighteenth century, the madwoman supplanted the madman as the image of insanity. The brute half-animal and half-man image of insanity was replaced by the frail and vulnerable madwoman. Reform movements in the eighteenth and nineteenth centuries helped drive the shift from male to female images. Showalter (1985) concluded that reform movements of the late eighteenth and early nineteenth centuries were born out of a concern for the poor treatment and care of frail mentally ill females rather than for males found in asylums. Before the eighteenth century, the public viewed people who were insane as animals and brutes, who required chains for control. By the close of the eighteenth century, people increasingly viewed them as objects of pity and needing care. It was during this time the general public perceived women as being more vulnerable to insanity than men. Showalter (1985: 7) commented, "Women were believed to be more vulnerable to insanity than men, to experience it in specially feminine ways, and to be differently affected by it in the conduct of their lives." This trend continued in the nineteenth century and women dominated representations of insanity.

Gender mattered in other ways regarding mental illness. For example, the Victorians were obsessed with sex and females were not to express their sexuality physically or behaviorally. In the male-dominated Victorian ideal, females should be void of sexual feelings and emotions. Victorian medical responses to perceived inappropriate sexual behavior could be drastic. Well into the nineteenth century, men, often with the support of females, took drastic measures to repress female sexuality. Physicians, usually male, applied harmful medical interventions to women for normal menstruation and menopause. Physicians made efforts to delay menstruation, such as prescribing cold showers and nonmeat diets. Physicians injected lye water into rectums or vaginas of menopausal women. Some physicians gave clitoridectomies to control women (Showalter, 1985).

In the nineteenth century, female insanity was romanticized in that it was beautiful, angelic, melancholic, irrational, emotional, and frail. Three characters dominated female images of insanity: Ophelia, Crazy Jane, and Lucia. Ophelia was a major character in western literature and art. William Shakespeare's Ophelia fed the erotomania of the Elizabethans. Ophelia was suicidal and full of love melancholy. Ophelia also was a compelling figure for Victorian artists. Harriet Smithson's *Ophelia* (1830) wears a black veil that symbolizes mystery and sexual intrigue. The straw in her hair represents Bedlam, the English symbol for madness. The English pre-Raphaelites presented Ophelia as the drowning Ophelia. Examples include John Everett Millais' (1852) and Arthur Hughes' (1852) versions of *Ophelia*. Millais' rendition shows Ophelia surrounded by flowers. Artists, since the Renaissance, used flowers to symbolize female sensuality. The drowning Ophelia incorporates water that symbolized the female because fluids were traditional symbols for the female. Crazy Jane, Crazy Ann, and Crazy Kate were other popular images of insanity during the romantic period.

Melancholy or depression deserves special attention as a mental illness because of its history as a gender-based mental illness. The syllables "melan" comes from melos that meant black and the "choly" from chole that meant bile. Thus, people used melancholy to refer to a black bile that was believed to be secreted from the liver. People sometimes refer to melancholy as the love madness. Melancholy has been a topic of interest for scholars for centuries. The ancient Greeks and Romans were very concerned with melancholy. The Roman physician Galen associated melancholics with Atlas because he bore the burden of the world on their shoulders (Rosen, 1968). In antiquity Jewish and early Christian people thought melancholics, since the Old Testament (I Samuel 14-23), could be cured by music. In the tenth century scholar-nun Hildegard of Bingen viewed melancholy as the original human disease (Neaman, 1978). It was in Hildegard's time that people characterized melancholics as being dark, shaggy, immobile, silent, solitary, depressed, and suspicious. They saw the condition as being temporary, as opposed to mania, which they viewed as enduring.

By the Renaissance, melancholy would become the sole domain of women. Since then melancholy has been essentially a female image in the western tradition and mania, epilepsy, and frenzy were typified as being male. Even when late medieval writers and artists depicted male melancholics, they took on "feminine" attributes (Gilman, 1988). Around 1500, writers started to popularize the association between love and melancholy. This resulted in increasing numbers of broken hearted women proclaiming themselves as being melancholic (McDonald, 1981). Melancholy was thought to be influenced by astrological events and cycles. It was at the close of the Middle Ages when Albrecht Dürer drew *Melancolia I* in 1514. This work became archetypal female image of melancholy. Melancholy takes on a highly symbolic form with Dürer's drawing. In his time scholars thought that melancholy was philosophically-based in contrast to believing it was an internal psychological state. In the centuries following the Middle Ages, scholars would increasingly view it as a psychological state of mind. The print illustrates much of the symbolism known to artists of the period. For example, the sleeping dog represents the inability to act and the hourglass symbolized time. This and many other presentations of melancholy include dogs, which

Figure 20. Albrecht Dürer, *Melancolia I,* 1514, The Philadelphia Museum of Art: Purchased by Lisa Norris Elkins Fund, Philadelphia.

according to Gilman (1988) also symbolized the most sensitive of all beasts. Melancholia's head rests on her hand as she sits. She is insular to the rest of the world and her face is dark, which fits with the association of melancholy with black bile.

Other images of female melancholic exist. Henry Fuseli's (1741-1825) *Crazy Kate* (1806) depicts the love melancholic Kate, who according to Gilman (1982) became the standard icon for love melancholy. The images of Crazy Kate or Crazy Jane marked the association between irrationality and the female over the last half of the eighteenth century. Before this period, the image was essentially male (Showalter, 1985). Jean Baptiste Camille Corot's (1796-1875) *La Mélancholie* (1850-1860) shows melancholy as a seated woman in a formal dress. Edgar Degas' (1834-1917) *La Mélancholie* (c. 1874) depicts a melancholic woman. Vincent Van Gogh's (1853-1890) *Sorrow* (1882) was a portrait of a female melancholic.

Gender also surfaces with the hysteria which is one of the oldest identified mental illnesses and has long been associated with females. The term hysteria is derived from the Greek word for uterus, ustera. Hippocrates coined the term hysteria in 406 BC (Evans, 1983). The ancient Greeks believed that the uterus moved around in the woman's body and caused the condition known as hysteria. By the Middle Ages and through the Renaissance, physicians thought hysteria was caused by evil spirits, even the devil. In the eighteenth century it became associated with the vapors which was common to over-refined women. During the nineteenth century mental health professionals, who were almost exclusively male, became obsessed with what they perceived as a predominantly female condition, hysteria. The world famous therapist Charcot conducted highly orchestrated presentations of female hysterics at Salpêtrière in Paris. Professional treatment of female hysteria went to extremes in the nineteenth century. For example, physicians put female hysterics in solitary confinement or subjected them to electrical shocks. Evans (1983: 38) described the treatment of one patient at Salpêtrière, which was considered to be the state of the art hospital for mental illness in the nineteenth century:

> She had hysterical attacks, which pressure on the ovaries often arrested. When the attacks persisted, however, and in, an effort to calm her blatant sexuality, her doctor cauterized her cervix. This operation, which was all the more painful because she also suffered from vaginismus (spasm of the vaginal muscles) was repeated four times for reasons that are not specified. They then treated her with ether, to which she became addicted.

EXPLANATIONS FOR MENTAL ILLNESS

The factors believed to cause mental illness and insanity over the centuries are too numerous to identify here but fall into general categories of natural and supernatural. Supernatural explanations for mental illness and insanity include divine retribution, magic, destiny, witchcraft, demonic possession, astrological, sin, lack of faith, and God's will. Natural explanations include diet, genetics, biology, trauma, nurturing, health, physiology, and other natural causes. Explanations linked to nurture include all of the experiences people have and how they were raised. Some explanations for mental illness found more favor than others during specific periods. For a large segment of history, multiple explanations coexisted, sometimes harmoniously and other times in direct conflict with each other.

The relationship between mental illness and witchcraft warrants some elaboration. Many scholars have studied the characteristics of people defined and persecuted for witchcraft (Larner, 1981). For example, historians Keith Thomas (1971) and Alan MacFarlane (1970) suggested the social vulnerability of lower-class women in late medieval society encouraged accusations of witchcraft against them. It was the fourteenth century when we witness the mentally ill becoming increasingly viewed as witches and consequently persecuted (Alexander & Selesnick, 1966). During the period, Pope John XXII issued a Papal Bull in 1326 titled *Superillius Specula* that labeled magicians and heretics as witches. One hundred and fifty years later Pope Innocent VIII issued a Bull in 1484, titled *Summit Desiderantes*, which was one of the most rigorous attacks on witchcraft. The Bull condemned ritualistic magic as heresy. In 1487, Heinrich Kramer and Jacob Sprenger wrote the *Malleus Maleficarum*, which was to become an influential witch-hunting and prosecution guide. Under the auspices of this manual, communities put to death many people for witchcraft who were actually mentally ill (Robins, 1986). These mentally ill were consumed and swept-up by the obsession over witchcraft for the next three centuries.

Not everyone jumped on the bandwagon to persecute people defined as witches. In sharp contrast to the witch-hunters were the physicians Johannes Hartlieb (1455) and Johann Weyer who argued against the existence of witches and changelings. Almost 80 years after the *Malleus* was published, Johann Weyer (Johannes Wier), with his 1563 courageous publication *De Praestigiis Daemonum (The Deception of Demon)*, rebutted the *Malleus*. He argued that witches were only melancholic old women, feeble of intellect, and simply mislead by the devil (Rosen, 1968). He argued that those called demonics were not possessed, but were mentally ill. Alexander and Selesnick (1966: 88) observed, "Weyer fought to prove that mental diseases are neither supernatural nor sacred and that it was his right as a physician to treat people so affected." Others besides Weyer, such as Reginald Scot, shared similar opinions of witchcraft, but these views went against the grain of public opinion (Szasz, 1970). Nevertheless Scot's *The Discoverie of Witchcraft* (1584) helped popularize Weyer's views on witchcraft. Scot also concluded that many older women accused of witchcraft were actually mentally ill, incompetent, or insane and infected with "melancholie." He proposed that they presented themselves as witches because of the power it afforded them in their communities.

Concern over witchcraft and demonic possession peaked during the sixteenth and seventeenth centuries (Rosen, 1968). For example, Richard Napier's seventeenth century clinical notes on his mental patients reveal that slightly over half of his 500 clients thought they were bewitched (MacDonald, 1981). During this period, people continued to see witches as possessed by the Devil. Later, witches would become increasingly viewed as being products of hysteria, ignorance, and foolish minds. The Protestant Reformation fueled witch-hunting activities among the Protestants who approached the issue with a vigor equal to that of the Catholics. Some communities put suspected witches who were actually mentally ill to death. Key Protestant leaders such as Calvin and Luther voiced the opinion that people who were insane were possessed by Satan.

PEOPLE WHO WERE MENTALLY ILL IN ANTIQUITY

The ancient Greeks described a wide range of human behavior as representing mental illness or insanity. The Greeks initially thought that madness was a consequence of some external force, such as the gods. They thought that the divine powers intervened frequently in human lives. In Greek culture, heroes go insane and frequently this madness had therapeutic value. The Greeks considered madness an important link to the supernatural or spiritual world and thus people who were insane were set apart from the rest of society. Common lore held that priests and poets communicated with the gods by inspired madness and sacred enthusiasm. Examples are numerous such as Plato's *Timaeus* that describes the relationship between the divine gift of prophecy and madness. The Greeks interpreted artistic madness as possession by the muses. However, as Rosen (1968:86) observes, "But it is clear from various sources that the madman, even when regarded as in some way touched by the divine, was a person to be shunned." Other public responses included spitting at mentally ill, as it was thought to repel contagion. Stoning of people who were mentally ill also occurred and was referred to in Aristophanes' play *Birds*.

The second Greek explanation regarding mental illness was that it had natural and physiological causes. Some Greeks believed physiology and not divine power caused madness. From Plato on, madness was viewed as running contrary to rationality. Following the lead of Plato, people saw madness as being opposed to reason and something that was undesirable. Greek literature refers to mental illness in several works. Homer's (9th century BC) poems told of Ulysses plowing sand and Ajax killing sheep instead of his enemies. Homer portrayed Odysseus as feigning madness by yoking a bull and a horse to plow sand that he later sowed with salt. Aristophanes' (448-335 BC) *Frogs* describes homicidal mania when the slave Xanthias goes insane when asked to pay his bill by a host. The Greeks often associated their gods with madness. For example, Dionysus was a god known for his power to inflict madness on others.

Hippocrates (c. 400 BC) classified mental illness into epilepsy, mania, melancholia, and paranoia. He viewed the brain as a spongy material capable of absorbing vapors from other parts of the body into the hollows of the skull (Sullivan, 1986). His *Corpus Hippocraticum* forwarded the idea that mental illness and epilepsy were not holy diseases but similar to other diseases (Schadewaldt, 1967b). From then on, many people viewed mental illness as a physical sickness of the body and organs. They believed that natural causes accounted for mental illness and not divine intervention. Beyond the works of Hippocrates, one of the major legacies of the Greeks was the humoral theory of disease. The humoral theory viewed the human body as composed of four humours, blood, phlegm, yellow bile, and black bile. Imbalances of these four bodily humours produced mental illness, illness, and disease.

Ancient legal systems made special provisions for people who were mentally ill. Under Greek and Roman law, people with mental illness had no legal capacity (Gardner, 1993). They were viewed as lacking understanding, similar to children. This may not have been important for some. Gardner (1993:170) commented on Roman law:

> Of course, it is possible, and indeed extremely likely, that many people who were born mad or became mad, were never specifically declared to be so, simply because the occasion never arose when the question of their insanity became important. That is because, as I have remarked elsewhere, for many people—mainly those with little or no material wealth—the necessity to prove their status and competence may never have risen.

Besides limiting their rights, the Romans divided people with mental illness into two groups, those judged dangerous and those who were not. Regarding the care of people, Gardner (1993) noted that those seen as not dangerous were left to the care of relatives and friends. Those judged to be dangerous were restrained or placed in prison. To the Romans, insanity was a family problem but those seen as dangerous were a community issue. McGrew (1985: 192) wrote:

> The serious disturbed were kept under restraint at home. The less serious roamed abroad, though if not guarded, they were likely to be mistreated. The evil spirits (keres) who were thought responsible for all disasters not only could enter people to make them insane but also could fly out to enter others. As a result, the disturbed, whether merely eccentric or wildly psychotic, were feared and shunned. Spitting was thought to ward off the spirit, and clods of stones would be thrown at the insane to drive them away. So long as the insane kept to themselves, they were left alone, but when their presence became threatening, and they could not be driven away, they were tied up or imprisoned.

PEOPLE WHO WERE MENTALLY ILL DURING THE MIDDLE AGES

The Middle Ages signals the first time in history when considerable amounts of information become available on people who were mentally ill. For example, various twelfth and thirteenth century scholars commented on what they saw were causes of mental illness. For instance, the twelfth century physician Bartholomew of England proposed that there were a variety of causes of mental illness, such as passions of the soul, sorrow, great thoughts, and the bite of the mad dog. In the thirteenth century, the physician Arnold of Villanova thought anger, too much fasting, different types of blood, and other phenomena could explain mental illness. The humoural theory of Galen and Hippocrates also continued to be a popular explanation.

These and other rather broad based sets of explanations continued to be framed in the context of the medieval church and morality. People continued to interpret madness as God's punishment for sin. From the thirteenth century onward, madness was placed in the hierarchy of vices. The Middle Ages were a period of great instability and social disintegration. Following the thirteenth century, social mobility was increasing with the rise of trade and private enterprise. The cities were growing, literacy was expanding, and interest in ordinary lives was developing. In addition, the world was changing and the future largely unknown. The last vestiges of the feudal order were disappearing and some people thought the end of the world was near. Consequently, people saw madness was increasing, which was a forbearing of things to come. The social climate was ripe for seeing madness everywhere.

Medieval Christianity sometimes interpreted mental illness in a positive vein, as reflective of one's extreme belief in or connection with God. For example, there was a belief that melancholics and some people who were mentally ill held powers similar to saints, such as talking in tongues or predicting the future. Spiritual possessions helped account and explain behaviors and psychological states of mind not understood by ancient and medieval societies. With Christianity, as Screech (1985: 25) noted, "Madness and Christianity go hand in hand." Scholars have associated religious fervor with madness (Porter, 1987; Robins, 1986). The medieval scholar Erasmus described Christianity as a form of madness (Pressman, 1993).

Others who were mentally ill were seen as possessed by evil spirits. People in the Middle Ages viewed madness increasing in the world, therefore the end was near. Christians sometimes viewed those having visions as possessed by evil spirits. Late medieval artists, such as Mathis Grunewald (1470/80-1528/30) and Hieronymus Bosch (1450-1516), portrayed the linkage between religious revelation and madness. Bosch showed mental illness as demonic possession. Their works titled *The Temptation of Saint Antony* connected madness with religious revelation. Demons abounded and madness loomed everywhere and took many forms. For example, the Last Judgment has been a popular subject for centuries during the Middle Ages and Renaissance. In many of the depictions of the Last Judgment, stone carvers and artists showed the damned as mentally tormented, anguished, or ill.

The medieval church exercised power to define and interpret the nature of mental illness. Besides providing the moral and spiritual guidelines for defining mental illness, the church, with the exception of the family, was a primary care provider to people with mental illness. The church provided diagnosis, faith cures, and other care services. It took an active role in constructing hospitals and confining people. Not only did the church have the social organizational capability to define and care for the mentally ill, it also provided a rationale for the existence of insanity. The church viewed people with mental illness as sinners, being possessed and caught up in a battle between the forces of good and evil for their soul through the eighteenth century (MacDonald, 1981).

Within this framework, the boundaries among heresy and mental illness, as well as, witchcraft, were often blurred. The church used the three interchangeably to meet its needs as it saw fit. Heretics were obviously insane, likewise, the insane could be heretics. The same was true with witches. The medieval church used whatever rationale was convenient to persecute those people not adhering to church doctrine. The Catholic and later the Protestant churches did not hesitate in labeling the mentally ill, heretics, and witches interchangeably to serve their purposes. It was in the interest of the church to use broad based and inclusive boundaries when defining the three groups.

This allowed the guardians of the faith to go after virtually anyone who strayed from the accepted path. The equating of mental illness, witchcraft, and heresy also helped reaffirm the conviction that evil was everywhere.

Over the centuries the power of the church declined and correspondingly its control over people who were mentally ill. Treatment and care of the insane moved from the spiritual to medical. The physician replaced the role of the priest in these matters. As the power of the church declined, there was a corresponding rise in centralized government, science, and medicine. All three of these factors helped create the social organizational where-with-all to define mental illness and insanity. Over the centuries, science, medicine, and government became more involved with defining, interpreting, and caring for people who were insane.

Special provisions for people who were mentally ill were virtually nonexistent throughout the Middle Ages. Much of the literature of the period indicates that people who were mentally ill were known to wander about communities and the countryside without gathering much public attention. The medieval British author William Langland (1330?-1400) mentioned roaming, harmless lunatics in his *Piers Plowman*. In rural areas people who were insane roamed about the English countryside (Neaman, 1978). In a sense, they enjoyed a freedom that would diminish with the social movement to confine and treat them that emerged in later centuries. They were free to roam, as long as they were not threats to the community (Rosen, 1968). When they were judged as being harmful or dangerous, they were simply run out of town or confined. For example, towns in Germany periodically whipped and then expelled people judged to be mentally ill. Some medieval communities implemented laws that restrained those who were violent (Kealey, 1981).

Not all responses were punitive and some communities provided homes for people and a few monasteries provided limited care. For example, in twelfth century England, authorities created laws that required compassionate care of people who were insane. By the fifteenth century, asylums were open in Spain and England. These were the exceptions and most people had to receive care from friends and family or the community at large. Many people found it necessary to roam among the general populace of the community, as the church or communities provided little support. The primary responsibility for caring for people generally rested with family and friends (Clay, 1909; Rosen, 1968) and to some degree with the community (Alexander & Selesnick, 1966). Organizations, such as monasteries, only cared for a fraction of people with mental illness. During the late Middle Ages and Renaissance, public authorities took little responsibility for the insane (Rosen, 1968). Some medieval towns constructed madmen's towers or cells that would hold people who were insane, such as the Teutonic Knights hospital at Elbing. Those judged as being incurables were often doomed to iron chains and stocks at the close of the Middle Ages. But on the whole, the Middle Ages were not a period of confinement for the mentally ill, as would later be the case in the seventeenth through nineteenth centuries.

During the Middle Ages, people saw those who were mentally ill as being possessed by demons and evil spirits. The Renaissance witnessed a return to demonology as an explanation for the mind (Alexander & Selesnick, 1966). Art and literature of the period were emphasizing the individual, but insanity was still within the realm of the devil. Church and secular officials believed that demonic possession was treatable. The principle task of the church or secular practitioner was to find a way to drive the demons and evil spirits from the person's body. Artists often represented the possessed with demons being driven from their bodies and specifically their mouths. Biblical passages, such as Luke 8:26-29 and Mark 5: 1-20, supported this social perception. Medieval images of the curing of mental illness often portrayed the victim openmouthed with his or her head tilted back with demons and other spirits fleeing. Some presentations showed the spirits fleeing while others failed to include them (Gilman, 1982). The following Flemish hand-colored woodcut illustrates the belief that demons could be driven from a person who was mentally ill or insane. The print shows demons emerging from the mouth of the subject as he is being held by two men. Christ is exorcising the demons from the subject.

During the Middle Ages and Renaissance, no single treatment or approach to mental illness dominated. Renaissance scholars embraced ancient notions of mania, melancholy, and dementia, which were all linked to the theory of body humors. Physicians used several somewhat eclectic methods to cure insanity. In the period preceding the Middle Ages in pre-Christian Ireland, the Druids prepared madmen's wisps (Robins, 1986). Belief in this practice lasted until the fifth century and the beginning of early Christian Ireland. Clovewort wrapped in red thread and worn around the neck in April or October was thought to cure lunacy in Anglo-Saxon England (Rubin, 1974). Other popular techniques included cooling or heating the body, herbal therapy, dieting, hydrotherapy, trepanning, and other methods (Neaman, 1968). Authorities used or recommended exorcism or pilgrimage to treat mental illness during the Middle Ages (Rosen, 1968). In the fourteenth century, Henri de Mondeville advised the use of leeches for skin diseases, tumors, mental illness, and other conditions suitable for cupping (McBride, 1985). People also used mistletoe, peony, and hellebore to treat insanity (MacKinney, 1965; Stannard, 1985). Restraint was also available to the medieval custodians of people. For example, an early thirteenth century window at Canterbury depicts a maniac who is tied with ropes and is receiving a beating with birch rods. The second scene shows the individual cured of madness (Clay, 1909:31). During the fourteenth century, some communities whipped people

Figure 21. Attributed to First Antwerp Woodcutter, *Christ Casting Out Demons*, 1487, Philadelphia Museum of Art: SmithKline Beecham Corp. Fund for the Ars Medica Collection, Philadelphia.

who were insane (Rosen, 1968). The theologian, Sir Thomas More (1478-1535) had a lunatic flogged for looking up women's dresses while they were praying.

The Middle Ages was a period of transition for people who were mentally ill. The period set the stage for a time of persecution and confinement. Alexander and Selesnick (1966) characterize the Middle Ages as a transition from charity to bloodshed. Initially, medieval society was relatively tolerant of people who were mentally ill. Society viewed them as God's citizens. As the Middle Ages unfolded, they increasing became objects of suspicion and persecution. Part of this rejection was driven by increasing the association between sin and mental illness that occurred during the Middle Ages. Medieval society needed scapegoats for all of the uncertainty and events that were occurring. People who were mentally ill provided a convenient and easy target for peoples' anxiety about the future.

According to Foucault (1965), the end of the Middle Ages emphasized the comic as well as the tragic aspects of madness. He proposed that attitudes regarding mental illness changed between 1200-1400 with the disappearance of leprosy. As this occurred, the mentally ill increasingly became the targets of stigma and moral values, and judgment. Whereas leprosy was the obsession, mental illness became a new focus of society. Those who were mentally ill essentially filled the void left by those who had leprosy. Evidence indicates that it was really much more than the decline of leprosy that led to the increased confinement and persecution of people who were mentally ill at the close of the Middle Ages.

Medieval art and literature addressed the topics of mental illness and insanity. One of the standard medieval representations of confinement and mental illness was the ship of fools. The ship of fools was quite common in northern Europe during the sixteenth century (Gilman, 1982). It is claimed that some towns in northern Europe gathered people who were insane and hired ships to transport them away. Foucault (1965) proposed that people with mental illness were actually sent out in boats. Other contemporary historians have concluded that there is no evidence that this practice ever occurred (Maher & Maher, 1983, Midelfort, 1980). Sebastian Brandt's book (1498) *Narrenschiff (Ship of Fools)* was one of the earliest literary presentations on the ship of fools. Hieronymus Bosch's late fifteenth century *Ship of Fools* contains many of the symbols of immorality and mental illness. The work shows a Hazel branch tied to the mast, fools as melancholics, a fool's stick, and a loaf of bread that symbolizes the presence of the church (Loaf of Bread Psalm 14:4). By placing a group of fools on a boat, Bosch symbolically removed the group of fools from the remainder of society as the boat drifts.

Flemish and Dutch artists in the fifteenth through seventeenth centuries painted or drew many renditions of the cutting of stones from the mentally ill. This was a period when proverbs were abundant in northern European literature and art. People living during this period were obsessed with the virtues and vices. People also believed that those with mental illness carried

Figure 22. Hieronymus Bosch, *Ship of Fools,* late fifteenth century, Louvre, Paris.

the stones of folly in their heads. Medical charlatans and quacks worked hard to convince the public that the stones of folly could be surgically removed from the heads of people. The typical surgical scenario was that the physician made a superficial incision on the patient's head (Menden, 1969). Then the surgeon would palm a stone and at the appropriate moment toss the stone into a basket. Artistic examples include works by Jan Sanders van Hemessen (1500-1555), Frans Hals, Jr. (1581/86-1666), Nicolas Weydmans (Claes Jansz), and Jan Steen (1626-1679). Bosch's *Stones of Folly* (1480) and Theodore de Bry's (1528-1598) *Cutting the Stones of Folly* are other examples.

PEOPLE WHO WERE MENTALLY ILL DURING THE MODERN ERA

The society following the Middle Ages became increasingly intolerant of mental illness and mental disorders. For instance, in early modern England, people started to view mental illness as frightening and mysterious (Scull, 1993). It was both disturbing and seen as a threat to the existing social order. Grob (1994: 8) wrote, "Madness in early modern England was a term that conjured up supernatural, religious, astrological, scientific, and medical elements." In the past many people who were mentally ill were integrated into their communities and families. This would change and by the latter seventeenth century, as the family became less important in handling people with mental illness. Increasingly, mental illness was forced into the public domain. Institutions would be established and expanded that isolated mentally ill people into separate enclaves from mainstream society.

The shift to less tolerance of mental illness occurred during a time of social uneasiness. The social order of the Middle Ages had eroded with the rise of the modern state. The poverty of the late Middle Ages became progressively worse in the early sixteenth century. The seventeenth century was a period of social unrest and economic depression. Vagrancy, unemployment, and high prices, typify the sixteenth and seventeenth centuries. Many people, including those with disabilities, turned to the streets to survive. Similar to other disabilities, begging was a means of survival for many people who were mentally ill. In Tudor England, people referred to them as "Toms O' Bedlam." This expression inferred they were people who were discharged from Bethlem Hospital. Begging was so common, that authorities in some communities issued licenses to beg. Beggars wore mental plates that served as official identification badges on their left arms, a practice dating back to 1504. The wearing of these badges continued through the seventeenth century (Rosen, 1968).

In the centuries immediately following the Middle Ages, the notion that mental illness was linked to evil continued and grew in popularity and practice. This notion found expression in the sixteenth and seventeenth centuries through a variety of channels. For example, people continued to believe that possession by the devil was one of the main causes of insanity during the sixteenth century (Feder, 1980). As noted previously, the sixteenth and the seventeenth centuries were also periods when witch-hunting reached its peak. It was also a time that many religious leaders commented on possession and mental illness. For example, the American religious leader Cotton Mather in the late seventeenth century argued that Satan tempted peoples' moral weaknesses into madness.

Belief in demonic possession was one of several explanations for mental illness available to citizens of the sixteenth and seventeenth centuries. Religion, magic, and medicine were seen in this eclectic age as overlapping and sometimes complementary approaches to understanding and treating mental illness. Mental illness, regardless of form, became the proper business of the clergy, medical practitioners, witches, and astrologers. Physicians and others drew upon whatever theories they chose to understand and treat people with mental illness. It did not necessarily matter if explanations were incongruent but rather what tools and approaches the practitioner felt the most comfortable in using. For example, the early seventeenth century physician and astronomer Richard Napier's memoirs and notes provide many insights into the perceptions and treatments of mentally ill. Napier believed madness came in many forms. He thought mental disorders came from natural and supernatural sources. Napier made extensive notes on the patients under his care. His notes reflect the unseen world of demons and spirits and their impact on the lives and minds of his patients. Napier was very eclectic in his approach to mental illness and used a broad mix of often contradictory treatments, such as purges, vomiting, prayer, amulets, and others to deal with mental illness. This was an age that produced many religious maniacs and expert religious exorcists to heal them.

In the seventeenth century, people thought Robert Burton's *The Anatomy of Melancholy* (1621) was the definitive work on the subject of melancholy. Robert Burton, the Oxford University Dean of Divinity and himself a melancholic, wanted to write the definitive work on melancholy. Burton was one of the most widely read authors of his time (MacDonald, 1981). Drawing from over 1,000 years of literature, he described many of the theories on madness (Porter, 1987). Burton, drawing upon the Christian tradition, attributed the origin of madness to the fall of man. He proposed that little could be done for severe melancholy and mania because they were a natural part of the human condition. He proposed that only prayer might serve any benefit. Burton was so committed to his beliefs that when he applied his system to predict his death, he committed suicide rather than admit his error (Haggard, 1932).

Some believed madness could be purged through one means or another. Typical of the period was Thomas Willis' (1622-1675) influential book *The Practice of Physick: Two Discourses Concerning the Soul of Brutes* (1684). Willis was a pioneer in placing the brain at the center of human action. His studies of hysteria convinced him that the brain was the cause of hysteria and not the uterus, as was proposed in classical thought. He proposed that bloodletting, vomiting, and strong purges forcefully given had curative powers for mental illness.

Present during this age was a sense that the public had a responsibility for the care and treatment of people who were mentally ill. Communities carried out much of this responsibility. For example, in colonial seventeenth century America, the common view was that society had a responsibility to care for the poor and dependent. Church officials and women, rather than physicians, often treated sick individuals (Grob, 1994). As the age unfolded, society increasingly turned to confinement to address the needs of society and the individual. Societies defined those who were mentally ill, along with criminals and vagrants, as social marginals who needed to be removed from society. The contemporary French historian Foucault referred to this as the "Great Confinement." He proposed that the age of the Great Confinement started in 1657 with the establishment of the Hôspital Général in Paris. The hospital took in the poor, deviant, morally decrepit, and those otherwise incapable of working including the mentally ill. Andrew Scull (1989) and others have observed additional forces beyond a social concern for idleness that operated in the seventeenth and later centuries to confine people. For example, the ancient regime's attempts to tighten social organization and centralization also helped fuel confinement efforts (Midelfort, 1980: 256). It should be noted that people who were mentally ill were only a small portion of those originally admitted to these asylums (Scull, 1989). Most people continued to live in their communities. Bynam et al. (1988) also warn, "There is a danger that the attention given to madhouses, mental hospitals or (as they have more recently been called) psychiatric units has been excessive, resulting in certain distortions." A large portion of those who were mentally ill during the period were simply ignored and not confined.

Examples in art and literature of people who were mentally ill or insane are numerous in the sixteenth and seventeenth centuries. One example is Pieter Bruegel the Elder's mid-sixteenth century work that shows people who were mentally ill on a pilgrimage to Molenbeck. The drawing shows men, some appearing to be insane, escorting and in instances arm twisting a group of women who were insane toward their destination. The bagpipe, which was sometimes associated with madness, was the instrument Bruegel chose to lead the procession. Another example is Mathias Greuter's (1564-1638) *The Doctor Curing a Phantasy* which shows a possessed person being placed in an oven to dry out the spirits from his body. Peter Paul Ruben's (1577-1640) *The Miracle of St. Ignatius Loyola* from the seventeenth century also addressed mental illness.

Shakespeare addressed mental illness in a number of his plays and comedies. Shakespeare's characters Hamlet, Oedipus, and King Lear were all mentally ill. In *A Midsummer Night's Dream*, Theseus proclaims "The lunatick, the lover and the poet are of imagination all compact." In *As You Like It* (Act 3, Scene 2, lines 420-426) it is proclaimed, "Love is merely a madness; and, I tell you, deserves as well a dark house and a whip as madmen do; and the reason why they are no so punished and cured is, that the lunacy is so ordinary that the whippers are in love too." In *King Lear*, Shakespeare tells of an insane monarch who confronts his own unconscious impulses. King Lear gave away his kingdom and lost his mind. Lear's emotional and mental conditions were symbolic of the monarch's decline in power. According to Rosen (1968), Shakespeare was aware of how varying social contexts effected the definitions of what was defined as insanity. The character of Hamlet was a classic melancholic. Shakespeare scattered many references to madness throughout Hamlet.

From the mid-seventeenth century onward, there was an attempt to eliminate anything thought to be unreasonable, including people. This was the period of the Enlightenment. When society judged behaviors and attitudes judged to be irrational, people were dismissed as being insane or idiotic. During this period, abnormality provoked anxiety and anxiety action. People viewed those who were insane with benevolence, but also as alien (Porter, 1987). Society perceived them as being something different from rational beings.

In 1671, the French artist Charles LeBrun (1619-1690), the first painter to King Louis XIV in 1671 drew a series of comparisons of animal and human heads according to what he perceived as their shared features. Le Brun was a firm adherent to the enduring theory of physiognomy. He believed that animalistic inclinations were present in the shapes and characteristics of people's faces and heads. His collection of 250 drawings was compiled into two albums in 1806 (Gareau, 1992). However, not everyone bought into the theory of physiognomy. The eighteenth century English artist and cartoonist Thomas Rowlandson poked fun at physiognomy and phrenologists. Many of his popular drawings showed and characterized believers in the theory as fools and quacks.

After the seventeenth century, the trend was to continue to isolate insane people from the rest of the "sane" society. Care and treatment through the seventeenth and well into the eighteenth centuries consisted of blood-letting, starvation, flogging, terrorization, and various forms of incarceration and punishment (Robins, 1986). Terrorization was particularly popular and people were threatened with drowning, buried up to their necks, subjected to special baths, and otherwise abused. Those finding their way into jails (gaols) were often dependent upon the graces and whims of the jailers. They were the group most mistreated and abused by caretakers. This fact has led some to conclude that care was better during the early Middle Ages when they were free to roam (Alexander & Selesnick, 1966).

By the close of the seventeenth century the foundation for a more natural-based view of people with mental illness had been laid. Spiritual and supernatural explanations for mental illness increasingly lost ground to natural and scientific-based approaches. Rather than seeing people as sinners, people viewed those who were mentally ill as animals. The centuries, along with the eighteenth, brought about the image of the mentally ill as subhuman beasts (Alderidge, 1985; Scull, 1979). Medicine would supplant supernatural explanations and cures by the mid-eighteenth century. An emphasis on rationality would be the rule. In the eighteenth century, the English became increasingly concerned about the prevalence of mental illness and specifically hysteria. Numerous scholars tried to explain the perceived increase in the numbers of English citizens that were judged as being insane. A physician named George Cheyne set out to explain this rise of mental illness in English society. In 1733, he authored the book *The English Malady*, which proposed that insanity including hysteria was the result of English sensitivity, ambition, and intelligence. The English, he argued, should be proud of their plight as madness was a clear sign in Cheyne's way of thinking of British cultural superiority. If the English were prone to being hysterical, it was because they better understood the ramifications of an ever-changing world.

During the eighteenth and nineteenth centuries, the rise of asylums warrant special attention. Contemporary scholars have written volumes about the emergence of asylums and the impact on people who were mentally ill. The rise of asylums has been a controversial topic for social historians. Some scholars have viewed the rise of asylums as a move to isolate, control, and otherwise punish people. Others have seen their creation as an act of compassion, because it was an attempt to help and treat people. They believe that, in spite of problems, asylums represented a noble effort at removing people from the jails, streets, and deplorable living conditions.

The question of when insane asylums were first founded is subject to debate. Alexander and Selesnick (1966: 23) reported that as early as 490 there was a hospital in Jerusalem for the mentally ill. Lyons, France had hospitals that cared for people who were mentally ill as early as 542. The Hotel Dieu in Paris, established in 652, took care of people. The city of Sienna, Italy took care of people who were insane in 898. Other scholars have suggested later dates for hospitals. For example, Neaman (1978) noted that Arabic hospitals for the insane were present in the eighth and ninth centuries, but not until the late fourteenth and early fifteenth centuries in Europe. In 1409, a mental hospital existed in Valencia, Spain. The Spanish had a long history, partially due to Moorish influences, in the treatment of the mental illness and actually freed people from their chains long before Pinel did so in the eighteenth century. Others have noted that madhouses and mad cells were present in fourteenth and fifteenth century Germany and England (Rosen, 1968). The famous English hospital for mental illness, St. Mary of Bethlehem (Bedlam), was founded in 1450.

The sixteenth century displayed a strong societal tendency to place people who were insane in institutions. These asylums or madhouses treated people with great harshness. People continued to view those who were insane as victims of their own vices and sins. Being isolated in one of these facilities did not insulate people from public view and ridicule. During the seventeenth and eighteenth centuries, custodians charged the public fees to view patients at hospitals, such as Bethlem (Alderidge, 1985). Andrew Scull (1989: 51) stated, "Indeed, it could scarcely have been otherwise when, throughout the century, the inmates of Bethlem were exhibited before the impertinently curious sightseers at a mere penny a time, and when many a treatise on the management of the insane advocated such treatment." Seventeenth century literature contains other references to asylums serving as sources of entertainment for the children of London and officials permitted visitors to tease the patients (Despert, 1965).

Foucault (1965) concluded that up to the mid-seventeenth century, people who were insane were free to wander about society. He observed they were either cared for by their families or received no care. Insanity became perceived as a problem that required a social response, which was confinement. He proposed that asylums of the seventeenth century were not established for the mentally ill but rather for the holding of impoverished and idle poor (Ingleby, 1983). He concluded that asylums were one way to deal with the nuisance of poverty. Poverty was one of the absolute criteria for admission to Bethlem hospital (Alderidge, 1985).

Alternative explanations have been advanced such as by David Rothman who, in his *The Discovery of the Asylum*, (1971), proposed the rise of the asylum movement was due to a general sense of social upheaval. He proposed the rise of asylums may have grown out of the emphasis on order characteristic of the period following the Middle Ages and the increasing intolerance of disorder and variation. During the eighteenth and nineteenth centuries, officials increasingly questioned traditional family-based care and promoted the expansion of asylums and madhouses (Scull, 1993). Regardless of reason, more than ever before, people who were mentally ill found their way into institutions. For example, Porter (1987:20) found that, "In Britain, perhaps 5,000 people were confined in asylums by 1800; this tally had leaped to about 100,000 by 1900, and to half as many again by 1950." He (1987:20) also found that, "By then, approximately half a million mentally ill or defective people were confined in psychiatric institutions in the USA."

By the close of the eighteenth century, the conditions in many asylums were deplorable. For instance, the Hotel Dieu located next to Notre Dame in Paris was unsanitary and ripe with illness. The living conditions for those who were mentally ill were actually worse than other patients at the hospital. Jones (1980: 6-7) provides the following description of what the Bicître was like at the close of the eighteenth century:

> The Bicêtre had small cells, called loges. Each loge was about two metres square, was unheated and was illuminated only by daylight from a tiny window and from the door when open. Each was dank and humid and often contained nothing but rotting straw. A reign of terror and brutality had long prevailed at Saint-Prix. Each loge contained an iron ring to which inmates might be attached by chains. Other means of keeping order included beatings, whippings and kneeing inmates in the groin.

Regardless of the reasons why they were established, it is important to realize that the creation and expansion of asylums offered an alternative to incredible squalor and neglect that people lived in during this period. Given the alternative of virtually living in "shit" (Marcus, 1974), the rise of the asylum in nineteenth century England may have posed an attractive, albeit not altogether perfect alternative to reformers. The optimistic promise of the asylum at least offered a sanitary humane retreat from the world (Bynum et al., 1988). Andrew Scull (1979), in his *Museums of Madness*, noted that providing adequate care to the mentally ill would have raised the living standards above those living under normal circumstances. This notion of providing better shelter, food, and care did not sit well with the attitude of the times that placed heavy emphasis on people working to support themselves. People thought those who were mentally ill deserved no better living circumstances than the regular working classes of the period.

Consequently, the asylum movement was successful in removing some people from the squalor of living in the streets but often fell short of providing adequate shelter and care. Critics of the asylum movement were present from the beginning but initially never really attracted much support. Critics' arguments against asylums were muted because they could not offer suitable humane alternatives, such as community treatment (Scull, 1989). One early exception was founded by William Tuke. William Tuke established the York Retreat in 1792 as one of the earliest attempts at treating mentally ill people in a humane fashion. Tuke, a Quaker, was a devotedly religious individual who sought to treat and cure the mentally ill through strict adherence to Quaker moral teachings. William Tuke's "moral treatment" would become a model for treating and caring for people who were perceived as being insane. His York Retreat was a homelike asylum that rewarded good behavior and did not punish patients.

A contemporary of Tuke was Phillipe Pinel (1755-1826) who was a leading clinician in Paris. Pinel believed the reason why people behaved as animals in asylums was because they were treated like animals. He believed that once people were unchained, their behavior would improve. After a lengthy debate with French authorities, he was able to convince them that some patients could safely be unchained. In 1793, Pinel obtained official permission to unchain people at the Bicêtre and Salpêtrière. Pinel was careful to select those patients who had a reasonable chance of success. Freeing people from their chains did not immediately result in more humane treatment. Care within asylums continued to consist of cold showers, electric shocks, centrifuges, purges, beatings, and other treatments thought to be more punishment that treatment today. Others benefited from the unchaining. Temkin (1971: 225) observed, "Once the fetters were taken off the insane, their former prisons began to assume the character of asylums or of hospitals." He then added, "This change benefited epileptics too, for they had often been confined with the insane."

During Pinel's reforms, he and others emphasized medical examinations of new admissions, refined classification systems, and prohibited the public showings of people who were insane (Jones, 1980). The key to the new treatment of insanity was to insulate patients from the external social causes of mental illness. People generally saw the world as a confusing and chaotic place that led some to lose their rationality. Ideally, the asylum afforded temporary and rational respite from this chaotic world. Pinel's ideas were shared by Etienne Dominique Esquirol (1772-1840), who was Pinel's pupil and colleague. Esquirol's text entitled *Des Maladies Mentales* (1835) contained 27 engravings of hospital residents and many descriptions of mental illness.

Early in the nineteenth century, other reformers continued their efforts to improve conditions within asylums. The reformers were composed of harsh evangelicals and Bethamites. The old paradigm had been that people who were insane were brutes and consequently brutish treatment was the natural way to deal with them. The reformers believed that all nature was malleable and that those mentally ill could be rehabilitated. The reformers, according to Scull (1993), condemned the past, promised cures, and believed that treatment rather than punishment. They wanted to make the asylum more palatable to the family. As part of the nineteenth century reform effort, people replaced the traditional term "madhouse" by the terms "asylum" and "retreat." Reformers thought these terms reflected a more humane sensitivity to people with mental illness (Showalter, 1985). While they sought reforms, they failed to recognize the negative aspects of institutionalizing all mental patients.

John Conolly's (1794-1866) book entitled *The Construction and Government of Lunatic Asylums* (1847) provided detailed instructions on all factors that should be considered when building an asylum. Conolly was a strong proponent for what was known as moral management of people who were mentally ill. Moral management was to become a cornerstone for the treatment of people in the nineteenth century. Moral management called for the abolishment of mechanical constraints of people with mental illness. Conolly replaced restraints and chains with very close supervision and parental oversight of people. He designed buildings in very structured ways so that people could be controlled and exposed to what he viewed as positive environmental influences. An example of this rational approach was Colney Hatch Lunatic Asylum in Middlesex, England which was opened in 1851. It was the largest (1,250 residents) and most modern facility in England and was essentially a small town.

A result of the expansion of asylums was that officials brought together sufficient numbers of people who were mentally ill to single locations. The concentration of people allowed mental practitioners to easily observe and provide treatments. In addition, the rise of asylums would dramatically change public perceptions of people. The asylums fueled the belief that people who were mentally ill not only were different but more importantly that they should be separated from the general populace. From then after, officials separated many people when providing care. A few dissenting voices to this trend were present at the close of the nineteenth century. For example in 1887, Nellie Blye, the Pulitzer Prize winning reporter, spent 10 days in New York's Blackwell Island Lunatic Asylum. In her account entitled *Ten Days in a Mad-House*, she concluded that living there would have easily driven her to insanity.

Artists have produced many representations of asylums over the centuries. Images of people being confined predate the seventeenth century's great confinement, as suggested by Foucault. Sander Gilman (1982) noted that increasingly during the fifteenth century people who were insane were shown confined. Numerous examples came to the forefront during the eighteenth century. For instance, an engraving in Jonathan Swift's (1667-1745) *A Tale of a Tub*, Fifth Edition (1710) shows the inside of one of Bedlam's open corridors. The work is Swift's eulogy to the political madmen of his time. Many people in Swift's time thought that radicalism and revolutionary fervor were indicative of mental illness. Swift treated mental illness as a satiric weapon directed at the political radicals of his time. He characterized all people with mental illness as having the vapors, which was a common concern of the period that Swift wrote (Feder, 1980). Keeping with accepted practice, the print shows visitors gazing through windows at a group of patients.

One of the most important and symbolic eighteenth century artistic representation of insanity and the inside of a British asylum was by the artist William Hogarth (1697-1764). His final plate (VII) of *The Rake's Progress* is an informative view of how the public viewed the asylum and the people who lived there (Gilman, 1988: 65). The scene, typical of the renditions of the period, underscores many horrors of the madhouse that fueled the popular imagination (Scull, 1989). Bedlam was an immensely popular source of entertainment in Hogarth's time and public tours were conducted for a fee. The print shows a variety of stereotypical images, such as people who were alcoholics or had schizophrenia. Hogarth depicted people who were insane in chains in the background. In this scene, Hogarth depicts himself as an insane artist scribbling all over his walls (Porter, 1987). Hogarth depicted the stereotypic eighteenth century ideas of what it was like to be insane. Hogarth also

Figure 23. William Hogarth, Plate VII from *The Rake's Progress*, 1735, Library of Congress, Washington, DC.

included an image of an insane monarch which was a popular theme in his time. A lunatic scientist figures longitudes on the wall. A tailor is shown as insane with pride. The main character of the book, Rakewell, is in the foreground gone insane because his wealth was not earned but inherited. His physical excesses, such as gambling and drinking, have taken their toll and he has become insane.

Francisco Goya's *The Madhouse at Saragossa* (1794) is another example of a presentation of an asylum. Goya drew upon his observations from a trip to the asylum at Saragossa (Schickel, 1968). Goya's work shows a courtyard of people who were mentally ill with two men fighting in the center, as an overseer beats them. There is a striking similarity between the residents and the overseer whose job is to control them. The overseer holds his whip high as he looks upward within this context of madness. The patients wore rags or were nude. He also drew a melancholic on the left side of the work. Typical of many of Goya's social commentaries, the work is characterized by a dark background. Perhaps Goya's use of darkness in the painting reflects the association between mental illness, melancholy, and black bile.

Artistic presentations of people in asylums would change as reforms occurred. For example, in sharp contrast to Goya is Robert Fleury's (1819-1890) painting that shows Philippe Pinel unchaining the inmates of Salpêtrière. Some view the unchaining by Pinel as an act of enlightened medicine. However, it was more an act of rebellion against the leading medical authorities of Pinel's time (Scull, 1989). Thomas Rowlandson and Augustus Pugin's *St. Lukes* in their *Microcosm of London* (1809) shows a reformed asylum. It was basically a workhouse that conformed with the social emphasis on work and industrial production. Amand Gautier's *The Madwomen of the Salpêtrière* (1855) shows a courtyard of mentally ill women having different forms of mental illness, such as mania and lunacy. Unlike the earlier Goya, Gautier's work is full of light and openness. Other images of people in asylums shift from confined rooms to the courtyards and out-of-doors (Gilman, 1982).

In 1835 the German artist Wilhelm von Kaulbach drew the residents of the asylum at Düsseldorf in a work entitled *The Mad House*. He moved the subjects outside the confines of the asylum to the courtyard. Kaulbach relied on expressions and gestures to characterize the subjects and their respective forms of mental illness (Gilman, 1982). Kaulbach based this presentation on the principles of physiognomy, which held that people's state of mind could be determined by their outward physical characteristics. Medieval doctors thought that insanity was shown through their physical appearance (Neaman, 1978), an idea that continued through the nineteenth century. Gilman (1982) noted that the stereotypic subjects of religious melancholy, senile dementia (old woman), the insane philosopher with his books, insane king, and raving madwoman were depicted in this highly influential work. Numerous experts on mental illness used his drawing as a reference to understanding the types of mental illness.

The eighteenth century age of the Enlightenment and French Revolution dominated much of western thought on the relationship between mental ill-

Figure 24. Wilhelm von Kaulbach, *Madhouse*, 1835, The Philadelphia Museum of Art: The Muriel and Philip Berman Gift, Philephia.

ness and social change (Rosen, 1968). Human reason, people argued could be used to overcome the forces of nature and human action. Reason, natural law, and happiness were key foci of the period. During the Enlightenment people believed that God's divine plan for the cosmos and the natural order of things could be discovered through science and reason. The eighteenth century also witnessed an increase in emphasis on the legal, political, medical, and religious aspects of madness by the intellectuals of the French Revolution. The American and French Revolutions promoted individual liberty, popular sovereignty, national patriotism, and egalitarian values. All of these core values touched people, including those with mental illness. Scholars increasingly pointed to social causes as explanations for mental illness. To the Enlightenment scholar, insanity stood out as a sharp contrast to the rationality of the enlightened mind.

The works of the highly influential American physician Benjamin Rush (1746-1813) and Pinel concluded that dramatic social change and upheaval gave rise to mental illness. Rush thought that radicalism and revolutionary fervor were indications of madness (Porter, 1987). Scholars also made a connection between political views and madness. Some of the nobility of the eighteenth century were viewed as being mentally ill and in some cases were actually insane. For example, King George III was considered insane and eventually suffered from senile dementia. He had outbursts of insanity in 1765, 1788-89, 1801, 1804, and 1810. Beyond nobility, some believed that entire nations could go insane. For instance, the British often linked madness with politics and saw the French Revolution as an act of public madness. The British viewed the massive crowds of French revolutionaries as having delusions. To the revolutionaries, the Revolution was simply the freeing of all people, including people who were mentally ill, from the shackles of society.

During the colonial period in the United States, mental illness was not considered a serious concern. There were so few people who were mentally ill that they were not defined as a major social problem. Care for people who were mentally ill was available in the community or through the family (Grob, 1994). The colonists tried to teach people how to become self-sufficient and take care of themselves. This was a comfortable strategy because they defined mental illness as essentially a social and economic issue rather than a medical one. The colonists saw mental illness as culturally defined rather than a medical phenomenon. The colonials referred to people who were mentally ill as "distracted" or "lunaticks." Grob (1994:14) concluded that in colonial America, "Unless they threatened public safety, people who were mad resided in the community." He added, "Those able to work were often afforded the opportunity to do so."

In the eighteenth century, the English viewed mental illness as a major concern. Before the eighteenth century, the English did not treat people with mental illness as a separate category of deviance. Society treated them as part of a larger group of poor, criminal, indigent, and less successful citizens. Except for the dangerous, they were basically kept in the community. As concern for mental illness grew in the eighteenth century, informal responses became less common and institutional response more frequent (Scull, 1989). Workhouses, almshouses, and correctional facilities all became available options in the eighteenth century.

In spite of rising concern for the severely mentally ill, the focus in eighteenth century England was on nervous disorders and not people living in institutions. The English believed the "English Malady," including the vapors, hypochondria, hysteria, and other nervous disorders were major concerns. George Cheyene's *The English Malady: Or a Treatise of Nervous Diseases of all Kinds, as Spleen, Vapors, Lowness of Spirits, Hypochondriacal and Hysterical Distempers* (1733) reflects British concern during the eighteenth century. Cheyene (1673-1743), physician to Samuel Johnson, essentially wrote an autobiographical statement on his mental illnesses. He proposed that the perceived hysteria (insanity) rampant in English society was a result of English sensitivity, ambition, and intelligence. He argued the English should be proud of their plight, as their madness was a sign of their cultural superiority.

Eighteenth century experts on mental illness placed emphasis on the connection between people's appearance and their mental condition. Popular during the eighteenth century was the notion that people with mental illness looked different from those without mental illness. Insanity was part of the physiological makeup and appearance of people who were insane. By the end of the eighteenth century, it was commonplace that forms of insanity, such as melancholy, would be identified by the physical appearance of the person afflicted. Examples include the Swiss Pastor Johann Caspar Lavater's (1741-1801) influential four volume set on human physiognomy and psychopathology entitled *Physiognomische Fragmente* (1774-1778). Lavater proposed that peoples' sanity could be evaluated on the basis of their outward appearance. In his highly illustrated volumes he tried to show that physiological characteristics could reveal the state of mind of the individual. In preparing his volumes, Lavater relied more on various artistic reproductions based on stereotypes of insanity rather than on actual observation (Browne, 1985). He assumed that predispositions toward character, such as skin color, slope of the face and other physical characteristics were indicative of mental condition. He assumed that temporary expressions left permanent impressions on the face that could be interpreted. The following set of drawings from Lavater's *Fragmente* shows a number of women who had, in Lavater's judgment, different types of insanity. Their type of insanity was revealed by their outward appearance.

Lavater's work played a crucial role in altering the way society viewed people who were mentally ill. The body reflected mental illness and mental and

Figure 25. Daniel Chodowiecki, untitled group of heads from Johann Gaspar Lavater's *Fragmente,* 1774-1778, Special Collections, University of Colorado Library, Boulder.

physiological states were one and the same. Both were stereotypically represented in illustrations and in literature for decades. Gilman (1982:72) concluded, "By the end of the eighteenth century the association of madness with a specific physiognomy of insanity had become commonplace in European thought." This notion would continue through the nineteenth century. In 1801, Philippe Pinel published *Medico-Philosophical Treatise on Mental Alienation* or *Mania* that adhered to the notion that physiology reflected mental illness.

Alternate explanations for mental illness were available in the eighteenth century. For example, some authorities proposed in the late eighteenth century the idea that masturbation led to insanity. This idea would come to full fruition during the Victorian period of the nineteenth century. Influential to this line of reasoning was Samuel August Andre David Tissot's (1758) influential *L'Onanisme ou Dissertation Physique sur les Maladies produites par la Masturbation (Onanism or the illnesses Produced by Masturbation)* that linked masturbation to senility. Tissot proposed that sperm was connected with the life force and as it was lost the life force was drained. He also concluded that masturbation was life-draining and led to insanity. Keeping with later Victorian ideas and morality, the American physicians such as Benjamin Rush and John Harvey Kellogg, were strongly influenced by Tissot's ideas. John Harvey Kellogg, of cereal fame, spoke and wrote extensively on the dangers of masturbation and too much sex.

During the eighteenth century, the long standing cultural traditions of what it meant to be insane or mentally ill persisted. For example, the notion that madness was a wild beast that needed taming persisted. Consequently, authorities emphasized coercing the wild beast back to sanity. Scull (1989: 85) wrote, "...intimidation, threats, and outright coercion were commonly used to cow and subdue the madman." He (1989: 85) added, "To most madhouse keepers, fear was the most effectual principle by which to reduce the insane to orderly conduct." Whippings and beatings were common treatments in asylums. By the mid-eighteenth century, many professionals believed they could treat and cure insanity (Porter, 1987). This period also saw the rise of the view that insane people had normal people inside and that the task of care and treatment was to help to let this normal being surface. People emphasized dramatic ways to cure mental illness in the eighteenth century and placed an increased emphasis on the role of nervous systems. For example, the influential Dutch Physician Hermann Boerhaave proposed a variety of ways to cure insanity including near-drowning, hidden trapdoors that unexpectedly dropped the insane into "baths of surprise," and other traumatic measures (Scull, 1989). Benjamin Rush used restraint to increase blood flow to the brain. Under the leadership of Rush, professionals thought that traumatic assaults on the brain would shock the individual back into sensibility and rationality. Rush tried a number of mechanical devices to bring people who were mentally ill back to sanity. For example, he promoted the use of hydrotherapy, which involved the dripping or pouring cold water on the patient's head. Rush also developed a tranquilizing chair that spun its patient around to rid the body of insanity.

By the nineteenth century, the industrial revolution was in full swing. Unlike the eighteenth century which viewed insanity as total perversion and the absence of reason, the nineteenth century witnessed the moral treatment of people and the perception of them as having reason. An increased sensitivity toward mental illness emerged. People no longer viewed the "lunatic" as an animal stripped of humanity but rather a person lacking self-restraint and order in their lives. Nineteenth century authorities increasingly believed that society could restore the person through treatment (Scull, 1989). An example of the new approach toward mental illness was the French physician Jean-Martin Charcot, who was well-known for his innovative techniques and work with hysteria. During Charcot's time, concern over hysteria was rampant in Europe. Professionals and the public used hysteria as a catchall category for anxiety, panic, the vapors, and a variety of behaviors found in nineteenth century society. Scholars thought modern civilization sometimes depleted the nervous systems of people trying to cope with the challenges of a rapidly changing society. Charcot took thousands of photos of hysterical patients living in asylums. He relied on hypnosis to treat individuals and would stage presentations of his hypnotic techniques. Notable people, such as Emile Durkheim, Sarah Bernhardt, Guy de Maupassant, Henri Bergson, and Sigmund Freud, attended some of his sessions. Within this context, hysteria became a common reason for institutionalizing women during the nineteenth century, women, whom otherwise would have been ignored in prior times.

Nineteenth century authorities continued to adhere to physiognomy and classified or treated patients on the basis of their external appearances. Experts such as Charles Bell, Esquirol, and Alexander Morrison relied on well-known artists and their renditions of madness (Browne, 1985). These images were particularly important because they were used to train physicians and other care providers of the mentally ill. Artists' interpretations of moods rather than direct observation served as the models (archetypes) for insanity. Charles Bell was one of the most well-known nineteenth century authorities on insanity. He characterized insanity as an outrageous maniac and likened the insane to a savage animal who had lost human reason. Bell's *Essays on the Anatomy of Expression* (1806) characterized the people who were mentally ill as being closer to animals than humanity (Browne, 1985: 139). Bell (1806: 153-154) described the "maniac" as:

> If laying aside the peculiar expression of the features, I were to set down what ought to be represented as the prevailing character and physiognomy of a madman, I should say, that his body should be strong and muscular, rigid and free from fat; his skinbound; his eyes sunk; his color a dark brown-

ish yellow; tinctured with shallowness, without one spot of enlivening carnation; his hair sooty, black, stiff, and bushy; or perhaps he might be represented as of a pale sickly yellow, with wiry red hair: ...Bell added, death-like fixed gloom, heaviness of features, with blood working to his head, restless, inflamed eye, vacancy in their laugh.

Bell's work did little to discredit public misconceptions about people who were mentally ill. Bell thought that insanity was a beast' that could be controlled with constraint. Insanity was the loss of human reason, an animal state, a brutal being. Bell thought that distinguishing characteristics of the face distinguished the insane from the "normal" (Browne, 1985). Facial expressions revealed key information to Bell. The following drawing from Bell's *Essays on the Anatomy of Expression* shows the stereotypic view of the individual maniac as a brute animal. The poorly clothed and chained maniac is shown wild with madness. He scowls at the viewer in a fit of rage. Gilman (1988) observed that the maniac's chains are at rest. The image is male, which will change over time to become the melancholic or hysteric female.

Others in Bell's time developed comparable approaches regarding mental illness. For example, Dr. Alexander Morrison's (1825) *Outlines on Lectures on Mental Diseases* (Gilman, 1988) emphasized the faces and viewed expressions as the result of repetition and not in individual inherited features. Josef Gall (1810-1868) published his four volume set entitled *Anatomy and Physiology of the Nervous System in General and Brain in Particular* that outlined his ideas on phrenology. Bell's ideas would later influence Charles Darwin (1809-1882) whose book *Expressions of the Emotions in Man and Animals* (1873) argued there was an evolutionary hierarchy of emotions. Darwin drew heavily upon the writings of Bell and Browne. Darwin made several references to unrestrained emotions, he wrote (1873:155), "The insane notoriously give way to all their emotions with little or no restraint."

Following the lead of Darwin, people in the nineteenth century had the attitude that humans were rational beings who were influenced by natural laws (Alexander & Selesnick, 1966). The role of biology and genetics (eugenics) in the causing of mental illness was to surface in the latter part of the nineteenth century. People commonly thought that "inferior" people were products of biological mating of people from weak genetic stock. They held this view not only for people who were mentally ill but also for other groups of people with disabilities. There was a common fear of the degeneration of the masses and the ruination of society (Porter, 1987). The late nineteenth century was the period of the degenerationist school that interpreted the insane as genetic throwbacks and retrogressives. Ironically, the degenerationalists judged artists, such as the impressionists, cubists, and literary geniuses of the period, as being insane (Porter, 1987).

Figure 26. Sir Charles Bell, *Maniac in Chains,* 1806, Wellcome Institute Library, London.

Many nineteenth century artists and authors characterized people who were mentally ill. For example, Charles Dickens portrayed a person who had schizophrenia, John Jasper, in *The Mystery of Edwin Drood* (1870) and a character named Mr. Dick who was mentally ill in *David Copperfield* (1850). Dickens was very familiar with the writings of Dr. John Conolly and his nonrestraint approach to treatment. During a tour of the United States, Dickens visited an asylum in South Boston and what he witnessed formed the basis for his character Mr. Dick in *David Copperfield* (Ranson, 1986). Many of the works of the American author Edgar Allan Poe (1809-1849) addressed the subject of mental illness. The theme of insanity also surfaces in Charlotte Bronte's (1816-1855) novel *Jane Eyre* (1847) where Mrs. Rochester who is mentally ill is kept in the attic.

Artists also portrayed mental illness, such as Francisco Goya while in exile from Spain, drew images of insane people in a French asylum in Bordeaux. Keeping with the physiognomic theories of the period, Goya drew the mentally ill with fixed physiological characteristics. He frequently wrote intriguing comments to accompany these drawings such as, "Not everyone knows it, or "You should not have written for idiots." Eugene Delacroix's (1798-1863) *Portrait of Tasso* (1839) depicts the mental illness of the dissenting poet Tasso. Delacroix's Tasso is shown in repose with his head resting in his hand. Tasso is at ease and seems to be contemplating the world. Apart from the bars that separate him from other patients who are shown expressing their mental illness, the viewer would not know that Tasso is in an asylum. Théordore Géricault (1791-1824) painted 10 exceptional paintings of patients at Salpêtrière from 1821-1824 for his friend Dr. Georget, who was on the staff. He apparently was fascinated with the subjects and turned down his commissions for these paintings. Examples from this collection of paintings include *The Insane Kidnapper, The Madwoman* and *The Woman with Gambling Mania,* and *The Insane Woman.* Students were very familiar with these half-figures of insanity, as they were used for instructional purposes. Géricault interpreted insanity, not in terms of behavior nor a disease but as a state of mind (Browne, 1985). This was an idea surprisingly sophisticated for his time. Théordore Géricault's images are different from those of Bell and Esquirol as they were sensitive to the individuality of the subjects. In the works, the viewer enters the world of real people who also happen to be mentally ill. His paintings represent one of the earliest and most sensitive presentations of people who were mentally ill.

The introduction of photography into western Europe would radically change the way people who were mentally ill were perceived (Gilman, 1982). With the introduction of photography it became easier to objectively image mentally ill people. By the mid-nineteenth century, Dr. Hugh Welch Diamond and John Conolly (1794-1866) used photographic images to depict people in asylums. Conolly argued that photography was the best way to represent mental illness. Diamond was the first to photograph people who were mentally ill in the 1850s. He believed that photography was objective and free of caricaturing common to the drawings of people living in asylums. He

Figure 27. Théodore Géricault, *The Insane Kleptomaniac* (also known as *The Insane Kidnapper*), c. 1822, Springfield Museum, Springfield, Massachusetts.

viewed drawings as disfiguring and unrealistic and concluded that photographic portraits were useful for diagnostic purposes (Rosenblum, 1989). Diamond's photographs, contrary to his claims otherwise, were nevertheless were highly staged presentations based on stereotypic ideas about mental illness. Showalter (1985) characterized these "objective" images as highly staged and based on negative stereotypes of women common during the Victorian period. Kerchiefs, bonnets, shawls, untidy hair, and other props were organized by Diamond to create the stereotypic images he wanted to convey.

PEOPLE WHO WERE MENTALLY ILL OVER THE CENTURIES

The history of people who were mentally ill has been one of great variation. Social attitudes toward the mentally ill have not been uniform over the centuries. For example, the Greeks held assorted views of mental illness as did people living in the Middle Ages. It was a matter of where one wanted to place emphasis, on the spiritual, physiological, or natural basis for mental illness. Western societies have never reached a consensus on what it was to be mentally ill and what caused mental illness. Multiple explanations for mental illness have coexisted over the centuries. There were periods when societies came close to agreement but these are uncommon. Judith Neaman (1978:145) concluded, "Perhaps the major difference between medieval and modern concepts of insanity is that medieval men knew what insanity was and we of the modern era do not." The symptoms and characteristics of mental illness were obvious to the medieval mind. The medieval citizen had a prescribed sense of order, of right and wrong, what was moral and immoral. There was a homogeneity of perspective that stands in sharp contrast to today's heterogeneity of perspective that carries with it more tolerance of the boundaries of normalcy and expression. Often it has been less clear and societies have fluctuated from knowing how to define mental illness to not knowing. In the sixteenth and seventeenth centuries, societies thought that people with mental illness were so out of choice. They applied punishments and tortures to force people to become rational and come to their senses (McGrew, 1985). In the eighteenth and nineteenth centuries, people assumed they could identify mental illness by studying the outward appearance of people and specifically their heads. People linked the size and contours of the head with personality in the nineteenth century. Andrew Scull has suggested the boundaries of insanity were stretched to encompass a wider variety of socially inept and incompetent, and possibly most importantly marginal people. This expanded definition of insanity placed a wider variety of people at risk for placement in asylums. In modern society, our definitions of insanity continue to be imprecise and unclear.

Just as the definitions of mental illness and insanity have varied, so have the explanations for mental illness. In antiquity, supernatural causes shared the stage with physiological. Mental illness was seen as a punishment by the gods or God. It was seen as a curse but also as a gift. The ancients saw people who were insane as having special connections, some negative and others positive, with the gods. An alternative was the secular physiologically-based view that mental illness was due to an imbalance of bodily humours, such as black bile. In antiquity, people made a connection between the physical body and mental states. Later societies would adopt modifications of this connection between body and mind and the basic notion that one's physical appearance indicated their mental state. These ancient ideas and social perceptions carried over to the centuries that followed.

Some of these views changed with the rise of Christianity. The body and soul became viewed as interacting and were interpreted within a moralistic framework. Early Christians promoted the idea that mental illness was a punishment for moral corruption (Feder, 1980). Initially, Christianity viewed mental illness as God's punishment for disobedience and immoral behavior. Under the auspices of Christianity, mental illness evolved into a barometer for moral behavior. One's mental state was indicative of one's moral character. Sinners were afflicted with mental illness as wages for sin. Christianity also interpreted mental illness as reflecting a commitment to God. Madness struck the believers as well as the nonbelievers. Christianity often used people who were mentally ill to further its purposes. People who were mentally ill were visible symbols of sin and nonbelief. The church actively persecuted people who were mentally ill as heretics or witches. However, the church also saw them as representing objects of Christian charity. The church proposed that madness sometimes reflected a strong commitment to God. In addition, Christianity provided the first major foundation for the humane care of people.

Christianity was influential during the Middle Ages. The Middle Ages was a period when people who were mentally ill generally were free to roam about so long as they did not pose any threats to the community. Care primarily rested with feudal lords, local charity, and mostly the family. Although sometimes seen as scapegoats and sinners, people who were mentally ill during the Middle Ages were seen as generally harmless and were ignored. Seldom did they ever escape the lens of Christian interpretation. It was during the Middle Ages that explanations for mental illness expanded to include astrology, demons, and a wide variety or supernatural and natural causes. These explanations coexisted and people frequently combined explanations as well as treatments together in pseudoscientific ways.

As the Middle Ages drew to a close, societies became less tolerant of mental illness. The unsettled social conditions of the early modern period gave rise to the pointing of fingers toward anyone who was different, including those who were mentally ill. It was a period of little tolerance compared to the social climate of Middle Ages. Consequently, they became the objects of physical restraint, confinement, punishment, and persecution. Increasingly, during the seventeenth and eighteenth centuries, societies turned to confining people. While Christianity continued to be an important influence, over time, sacred explanations of mental illness lost ground to natural and medical. Mental illness became not so much a matter of possession, but one of disease.

Morality was replaced by rationality as the paradigm in which to understand mental illness. Thomas Szasz (1970) observed the religious ideology toward mental illness shifted to a scientific one. The outcome was the same. What was considered to be sin in the Middle Ages became defined as sickness in the modern world. Thus, the secularization of insanity shifted emphasis from a concern over morality to one of sickness (Feder, 1980).

With this shift to science and medicine, there was a development of a sense of social responsibility for people who were poor and/or disabled, including those with mental illness. This sense became operationalized by placing them in institutions. The locus of responsibility for people shifted from the family and local community to a group of trained professionals who claimed to have a unique capacity to understand and treat mental illness (Scull, 1989). The seventeenth and eighteenth centuries became known as the age of confinement. The confinement of people was a mixed blessing.

Some assumed that people who were mentally ill were deprived of reason and were insensitive and immune to discomfort. They were insensitive to heat and cold and lacked feelings. People assumed that because people lacked feelings and sensitivity, it was wasteful to provide them with adequate care and living conditions. Cells available to those who were mentally ill were often dark, moist, cold, and full of vermin. Caretakers did not always provide clothing and some residents were left naked in their cells. Caretakers used straw for bedding and those people judged to be uncontrollable were chained to walls or each other. Sanitation, comfort, and health were absent from these facilities. On the positive side, as deplorable as some facilities were, they represented an improvement over the alternative of living in even more squalor in the streets. Most people who were mentally ill lived outside of such facilities, for better or worse.

Before the nineteenth century, people emphasized controlling behavior and people with mental illness. During the nineteenth century, the emphasis shifted to a medical model of mental illness. People with mental illness became viewed as sick and diseased. The methods used to care and treat people were based on the assumption that people chose to be mentally ill and treatment was simply a matter of shocking them into rationality. Consequently, people were subjected to a number of traumatic treatments that would, by today's standards, be counterproductive and punitive. As terrible as treatments seem today, they were at least based on the assumption that treatment provided hope that people could be cured. This is an improvement over simply imprisoning and warehousing them, which had been the custom.

Chapter 5

PEOPLE WHO WERE BLIND

In spite of being relatively rare, people who were blind have always received more attention from the seeing public than their numbers would suggest. Art and literature are full of references to the term blind and people who are blind. This emphasis on blindness is partially due to the persistent belief that it is one of the worst disabilities an individual can have. People assume blindness has devastating and insurmountable negative effects on the individual. Shlomo Deshen (1992) concluded, "People who were blind occupy a particularly salient position in the western popular imagination. That is, they attract more public attention and imagination than other disabilities." While the hardships that accompany blindness should not be downplayed, it is clearly not as difficult to adjust to as western thought and belief imply.

One consequence of the great amount of attention paid to blindness is that it has been treated in western thought more symbolically than any other disability or impairment. Meanings attached to the disability go beyond the simple absence of sight. Perhaps it is the relative isolation or cutting off people who were blind from the seeing world that contributes to the many meanings for blindness. Deshen (1992:4) commented, "However, blindness has an essential distinctiveness and lack of ambiguity relative to other conditions." He adds, "There is an immediate visible link between the condition and its behavioral manifestations, such as an impaired mobility and lack of ability to read print." This results in well-defined stereotypes about people who are blind.

Blindness is a master status to the person who has the disability. The world has been arranged for the sighted. Blindness overpowers all of the individuals unique qualities in the perceptions and judgments of seeing others. The consequence is that many assume that people who were blind are more similar than they are different. They believe that being blind dominates the individual's state of mind. People who were blind are stereotyped into a group with a single master status, their being blind. Being blind overrides everything else an individual is or is capable of doing. People perceived them as blind first and an individual later. All of the individual differences, such as personality, aptitude, values, interest and what make a person unique are overlooked and dismissed by their being blind. This reduces people who were blind into a general stereotypical category rather than their being viewed as unique individuals.

Authorities agree that three factors dramatically affect the nature of blindness for the individual. The factors are the age of the person when blindness was acquired, the degree of visual loss, and the other collateral effects of blindness, such as loss of hearing or other characteristics that are considered disabilities. However, culture also plays an important role in how people use their bodies and senses (Hall, 1966; Montagu, 1971). Deshen (1992: 15) noted, "The impaired body is managed by disabled people under cultural conditions that include both the variable of ethnic culture common to all members of a given society, and the variable peculiar to the disabled, that of living in a situation dominated by the able-bodied." Thus, people who are blind must abide by cultural dictates but also by another layer of expectations placed on them because of their disability. At times these cultural norms or expectations run contrary to the ways people who are blind use their senses to know their world. For example, European and North American cultures tend to avoid tactile contacts and body odors to a greater extent than do people from Mediterranean and middle eastern societies (Deshen, 1992). People who are blind often need to touch things in their world to better understand them. The act of touching a person to help gain orientation, know their features, or by accident runs contrary to western culture which mandates that distances be maintained among people and especially among strangers. Thus, those with sight may perceive the touch of a person who is blind as violating cultural norms. What is certain is people who are blind relate to the world differently than people with sight and sometimes cultural norms restrict their actions.

EXPLANATIONS FOR BLINDNESS

Explanations for why people became or were blind have been numerous in western thought. The multitude of explanations for blindness parallel those for other disabilities. The oldest explanations can be found in religion and mythology. Primitive mythologies interpreted blindness as a sign of divine disfavor (Koestler, 1976). One of the most pervasive and enduring of explanations for blindness was that it was caused by sin. Evidence of blindness as punishment for sin is mentioned in the Old Testament in Job,

Deuteronomy, Psalm 66, Proverbs, and Zephaniah. In the Old Testament the Sodomites were struck blind as punishment for the sins they had committed. Individuals did not necessarily have to sin themselves but could be blind because of the sins of others. For instance, giving birth to such children served as a sign to the community that the parents had sinned in some way. At times, societies coupled parental sin with folk tradition and beliefs. Hand (1980:61), noted in southern Slavic countries people thought blindness resulted from intercourse with a vile being or sinning before the child was born. The attribution of blindness to sin posed a paradox at times because blindness was applied to the innocent infant, although the child had not sinned. Aware of this issue, the church had to find a way to not blame children born blind. The answer was to come in the New Testament that taught a man's blindness was not due to sin. Rather, as Jesus points out, the people are blind so that God's power might be displayed (John 9: 1-5).

Similar to other disabilities, people also associated blindness with sex. Jacquart and Thomasset (1988: 56) noted, "In the Middle Ages, the deterioration of the eyesight was constantly being mentioned as part of the damage caused by coitus." Strikingly similar conclusions were reached centuries later during the Victorian Age when well-known physicians proclaimed that blindness was one of the risks of too much sexual activity, such as masturbation or coitus. The famous physician and cereal potentate John Harvey Kellogg expressed many concerns about the dangers of too much sex to an individual's health during the nineteenth century. Besides sin and sex, throughout history disease was known to cause blindness. The ancient Greeks were well aware of the role of disease in causing blindness. For example, Hippocrates and Aristotle used the term glaucoma for cataract or opacity of the lens of the eye. Any grayish or greenish appearance in the dark of the pupil was labeled glaucoma. Evidence also shows that the Anglo-Saxons were quite familiar with eye disease. The lack of hygiene, Vitamin A deficiency, poor diet, smoke, proximity to animals, and other factors all contributed to favorable conditions for eye disease and corresponding blindness (Rubin, 1974) and similar conditions continued in medieval England as well (Kealey, 1981).

Opthalmia is an inflammation of the eye and the term applies to any disease that attacks the eye. A common form of opthalmia is trachoma. Trachoma is a disease characterized by the formation of inflammatory granulations on the inner eyelid, severe scarring of the eye, and in some cases eventually leads to blindness. The term trachoma means roughness in Greek and referred to the roughness of the eyelids associated with the disease. It has been one of the leading causes of blindness in history. The disease requires long-term contact among people in filthy and overcrowded areas. Trachoma is an ancient disease and scholars have found evidence of its existence in Egypt in the sixteenth century BC and in ancient Greece and Rome. Ancient treatment for the disease involved scraping the eyelids with sharkskin or other abrasives to remove the roughness.

Wars have generally contributed to the number of people who became blind. The damage inflicted by weapons in combination with that done by wartime disease resulted in many people becoming blind. Historically, war and disease have worked together to promote blindness in populations. Wars have created significant numbers of people to the extent that officials have established hospitals. For example in 1254, Louis IX provided an asylum in Paris for returning crusaders who were blind. Sensing a need to further assist soldiers who were blind, he also provided special privileges for them, such as freedom from taxation. One of the characteristics of trachoma was that it was typically spread by the movement of large armies (Karasch, 1993). This was certainly the case when armies involved in the Napoleonic Wars brought an epidemic back to Europe from North Africa. During the early nineteenth century, trachoma took a heavy toll on soldiers during the Napoleonic wars in Egypt. Trachoma eventually slowed many of the French troops serving in Egypt in 1798. Consequently, the French set up special compensations for blindness. By 1800, the disease also affected English troops. In 1818, the problem was so widespread that the British opened a special hospital for trachoma-stricken soldiers. Artists have recognized this fact over the centuries. Major artists who portrayed blindness in relationship to war were Goya and his *Disasters of War* and Callot's *Great Miseries of War*, the latter artist addressing the horrors of the 30 Years War. Trachoma was uncommon in the United States until the nineteenth century when the immigration of large numbers of people with the disease resulted in the enactment of laws to restrict their entry. In 1897, public authorities perceived the problem as so significant that they enacted laws to prohibit their entering the country.

Other causes of blindness, some real and others simply imagined, have existed over the centuries. Congenital factors cause about two percent of blindness and other factors occurring after birth cause the remainder. Accidents, gonorrhea, retinitis pigmentosa, muscular degeneration, diabetes, syphilis, and rubella (German measles) all can result in blindness. Up to 1798, small pox blinded many people. It was in that year that Dr. Edward Jenner introduced a vaccine for smallpox in England. Before the twentieth century, ocular gonorrhea may have been a major cause of blindness in newborns (Karasch, 1993). Cataracts cause the lens of the eye to become milky and cloudy and in some cases results in complete blindness. Measles (Rubella) is an acute, highly contagious, and common virus that principally attacks children. The disease can result in blindness and or deafness in the womb if contracted by pregnant women, although measles is uncommon during pregnancy. Early physicians wrote about it, such as the Middle Eastern physician Avicenna (@1000) and the English physician Thomas Sydenham. Sydenham studied the epidemics of 1670 and 1674 (Kim-Farley, 1993). Other explanations have been suggested, such as folklore linked too much crying to blindness (Hand, 1980).

SOCIAL PERCEPTIONS OF PEOPLE WHO WERE TOTALLY BLIND

Monbeck (1973) also identified pervasive attitudes toward people who were blind. These attitudes include their deserving of pity and sympathy, being miserable and melancholic, living in a world of darkness, being helpless, being fools, being useless, living by begging, unable to function, compensated for their lack of sight, being punished for some past sin, maladjusted, immoral and evil, better than sighted people, mysterious, and easily frustrated (Scott, 1969). In addition, some scholars have concluded that blindness has been trivialized. For example, Deshen (1992: 5) provided identified slogans that incorporate this view, such as "People who were blind are like everyone else; they just do not see," or "Blindness is an inconvenience, not a handicap."

References to blind being targets of humor are not abundant in Western thought and writings (Monbeck, 1973). The perceived seriousness of the impairment may have led to its not being a suitable target for writers. There are exceptions in ancient Greek writings and occasionally in later works, but they are uncommon. Occasionally, playwrights, authors, and artists made them the subject of humor. For example, humor is implied indirectly as in the parable of the blind leading the blind. The blind leading the blind is referenced in Matthew 15:14; Luke 6:39, "If one blind man guides another they will fall into the ditch." In this parable, Christ likens the Pharisees to persons with blindness. Spiritual blindness to Christianity and the corresponding darkness resulting from it symbolize sin and ignorance in western thought.

Pieter Bruegel the Elder's (1525-1569) *Parable of the Blind* is the most famous of all presentations of the blind leading the blind. It is a painting full of rhythmic composition. The local church sits in the background out of sight of the six blind men. To Bruegel, blindness was a state of the soul, the stigma of a corrupt world. Bruegel is objective and detached in his presentation of the men. In the painting, the leader has already started to fall back into the swamp. He partially crushes his hurdy gurdy. According to Marijnissen (1969), blindness was shown as irremediable state of the soul, the stigma of a corrupt world. There is also a comedic theme to the work, as men are laughable in their foolish journey. Other works that address this theme include Domenico Fetti's (c. 1589-1623) *The Blind Leading the Blind*, which, less tragically than Bruegel, presents essentially the same scene of men falling down. Pieter van der Heyden's (1637-1712) engraving *The Parable of the Blind* (1560-1565) is another example.

Figure 28. Pieter Bruegel the Elder, *The Parable of the Blind Leading the Blind*, sixteenth century, Museum of Naples.

In addition to the highly symbolic blind leading the blind, blindness was used to represent other cultural values. For example, blindfolding people so they cannot see has many symbolic meanings. For instance in art, when cupids are blindfolded in the presence of lovers, the meaning is blinded by love. The figures of Fortune and Nemesis are blindfolded because they were random. Justice was blindfolded because of her impartiality. In the story of the mocking of Christ, a popular theme for many medieval and Renaissance artists, the seated Christ is often blindfolded. The blind lover was one of the best known symbolic representations of blindness. The art historian Panofsky (1967:95) wrote, "The belief that the lover is blinded about what he loves so that he judges wrongly of the just, the good and the honorable is, of course, frequently expressed in classical literature."

The act of becoming blind or the blinding has played a highly symbolic and dramatic role in the western cultural tradition. Societies have blinded people as punishment for crime, adultery, and sin for centuries. Heroes were occasionally blinded, as was the biblical Samson who was blinded by Delilah and the Bible's book 2 Kings (6:18), God strikes an army blind to protect

Elisha. The Romans blinded Christians. In antiquity, people used mixtures of vinegar and lime that were sometimes poured into eyes. They also used ropes that were twisted around the victims' heads until the eyes came out of their sockets later in history. Blinding for certain crimes was a common punishment in northern Europe, Greece, Spain, and Brittany (Monbeck, 1973). Canute (1014) and William the Conqueror (1070) had provisions for it as a punishment. During the Middle Ages, people used hot irons to burn out eyes. Being stricken blind, such as viewing holy or unholy things was sometimes characterized in folk and religious lore as being a piercing or searing of the eyes (Hand, 1980). The Normans used blinding as a common penalty for crimes.

Legends and stories of blinding have been popular over the centuries. For example, in the ancient tale of Ulysses and the Cyclops, the latter was blinded by Ulysses and his men by the sharp end of a hot stake. The most well-known story is probably the biblical tale of Samson and Delilah. The Philistines blinded Samson to reduce his threat to them (Judges 16:21). Many artists over the centuries found this story a popular subject. For example, Rembrandt chose this as the subject of his *The Blinding of Samson* (1636). Other biblical stories tell of blinding, such as Paul blinding Elymas and Jesus' bedside cortege being blinded by angels. Another popular legend involving blinding came from the Byzantine Empire. In the sixth century, the Byzantine Emperor Justinian had his immensely successful general Belisarius blinded out of his concern over the popularity and power of the great Byzantine warrior. Justinian had the general blinded to curb his ambitions. Belisarius (Byzantine General) fought off the Goths and Vandals for Emperor Justinian in the sixth century. After being blinded, Belisarius reportedly wandered the streets of Constantinople begging. A theme central to this and other stories of blinding or being stricken blind is that becoming blind was often considered a fate worse than death (Monbeck, 1973). Many artists and authors romanticized this tale following the Middle Ages. Numerous depictions of this story include Rembrandt's 1660 rough sketch entitled *Blind Belisarius*. In Rembrandt's sketch, Belisarius was shown as a social outcast. This is in sharp contrast to Rembrandt's presentation of Homer where blindness is shown as a source of creative genius (Held and Posner, 1971). Other works on the story of Belisarius, such as Jacques-Louis David's (1748-1825) *Belisarius Begging for Alms* (1781) depicts this legend.

One of the most common perceptions of people who were blind beyond that of beggar was that they were apt to be musicians or bards. The image of the bard or musician who was blind exists very early in the western history. Farrell (1956) noted that in nearly all countries, Christian, Moslem, and Buddhist, blind bards, often led by dogs with bells to herald their arrival, found favor as they sang the praises of the countries' heroes and of the ruling monarchs. Blind musicians and court minstrels can even be traced back to the ancient Egyptians and Greeks. The Greek scholar, Pythagora, noted in his travels the important role music played in the lives of people who were blind. In antiquity, music may have been their most common profession (Ross, 1951). Literature of the period also included blind musicians. For example, Homer's *Iliad and Odyssey* VIII, tells of the singer Demodous who was a blind bard. The patron saint of blind bards and musicians was St. Hervae or Herve (d. 565) who was born blind. St. Herve lived in Brittany and legend has it was led by a white dog. He taught children to love God and was known for his songs of praise to God. Even today, musicians bring their instruments to a monastery he founded for blessing. Other famous musicians and minstrels who were blind include Ossian (c. 300) and Torlough O' Carolan (b. 1670).

The blind poet, storyteller, musician, bard, and entertainer served a useful social function as a repository of culture. People who were blind might have been ideally suited to carrying on cultural traditions because they could focus on memorizing lengthy texts to poems, tales, and legends. The need to have people who were blind serve as repositories of song, tales, and traditions diminished over time with the introduction of the printing press. The blind bard would become less common with the rise of printed materials. Books replaced memory as the medium and repository of cultural knowledge.

One of the reasons people who were blind became musicians was a general public perception that they were well-suited as entertainers. Early educators thought people who were blind had a proclivity for music. One of the most famous was Maria Theresa von Paradis who was born in 1759 in Vienna and became an accomplished concert pianist. She traveled throughout the world demonstrating her talent. Her success demonstrated that people with blindness were capable of major accomplishments. She was inspirational to others and helped educators, such as Haüy, build public support for their schools. In addition, her talent further ingrained music education as a major component of schools for people who were blind (French, 1932). This emphasis on music education can be looked on favorably or unfavorably. It undoubtedly provided musical opportunities for some but limited the opportunities for others.

In the seventeenth century genre tradition of Jan Vermeer, Ostade, David Teniers, Georges de La Tour, and Jan Steen, artists moved away from commissioned portraits to painting ordinary people. The French artist Georges de La Tour (1593-1652) focused on street life and painted blind hurdy-gurdy players in three separate paintings. The English artist David Wilkie's (1785-1841) oil painting entitled *The Blind Fiddler* (1806) is another example of the blind musician. Francisco Goya made several presentations of blindness with his drawings of people from the streets. One work from his collection

(1803 to 1812) entitled *Muy Acordes* (Perfect Harmony) depicted a couple who were blind singing in the street. In 1778, Goya etched a work entitled *The Blind Guitarist* that shows a minstrel who is blind entertaining a large group of people in the middle of a road. Another example, is by the French artist Louis-Léopold Boilly (1761-1845) who was known for his many scenes of Parisan life. His lithograph titled *The Blind* dated 1825 from the series titled *The Collection of Grimaces* (1823-1828), shows a group of three subjects who were blind. One plays a fiddle, another a flute, and we are left to speculate what the third does but most likely is the singer for the trio. The three subjects have contorted faces that they are using to try to communicate with an unseen audience (Karp, 1985). The assumption of compensation is implied in the work. Finally, the artist's focus on the outward appearance of the subjects would have fit comfortably with the scientific notion of physiognomy popular during this period.

At times, societies have associated blindness with compassion and sensitivity, and consequently romanticized blindness. For example, when Rembrandt painted his portrait of the poet Homer, he did so with a sense of romantic compassion toward blindness and its corresponding creativity. Viewing blindness as a romantic state of existence was certainly the case in the nineteenth century when, similar to tuberculosis, the romantics romanticized blindness. Sir John Everett Millias, *The Blind Girl* (1856), is a perfect nineteenth century romanticized portrayal of blindness. The painting shows a young and beautiful woman who is blind holding a younger girl in the countryside. She covers the young girl with her shawl and her left hand. The little girl looks over the shawl of the woman at a colorful double rainbow on the horizon that the woman cannot obviously see. An accordion rests on the woman's lap, reinforcing the traditional link between blindness and music. Both subjects, keeping with Victorian practice, are clothed in drapery-like garments. The young woman's face looks solemn and expressive.

Numerous other perceptions of people who were blind have been promoted over the centuries. For example, they have been characterized in folklore and literature as being fools. Those who could see easily tricked people who were blind. The three blind men in folktales were commonly characterized as fools. In a biblical story from Genesis (27: 1-27), Jacob fools his blind father Isaac into blessing him rather than his brother Esau. The French encylopedist, Denis Diderot, concluded that people who were blind had a moral code that differed from other people. To Sebastian Guillie (1819), they had distorted thoughts, sensibilities, were ungrateful, and victims of self-hate. People who were blind were seen as unhappy, depressed, and had a gloomy outlook on life. They were perceived as living in misery and having a hopeless outlook on life. A common perception was that they possessed personalities and psychologies that were different from seeing people.

172 *Social Perceptions of People with Disabilities*

Figure 29. Louis-Léopold Boilly, *The Blind,* 1825, Philadelphia Museum of Art, SmithKline Beecham Corp. Fund for the Ars Medica Collection, Philadelphia.

Figure 30. Sir John Everett Millias, *The Blind Girl,* 1856, Published by permission of Birmingham City Museums and Art Gallery Blind Girl, Birmingham.

PEOPLE WHO WERE BLIND IN ANTIQUITY

Early representations of people who were blind have been traced back to art from the Neolithic period (Vukanovic, 1985). Other representations of people who were blind have been found in ancient Egyptian art and are dated back to about 3000 BC (Monbeck, 1973). One bas-relief from the Egyptian tomb of Patenemhab dated about 1350 BC represents one of the earliest portrayals of blindness known. The details in the eyes of the work suggest chronic trachoma was a common source of blindness throughout northern Africa (Wells, 1964). The person is a harper which underscores the long tradition of associating blindness with music.

Overall, it is generally agreed on that people who were blind were not particularly treated well in antiquity. The Egyptians, however, departed from other European and Middle Eastern societies in their humane approach toward blindness. Several historians have found evidence of a humane response of the Egyptians toward people who were blind (French, 1932, Koestler, 1976; Ross, 1951). Perhaps because blindness was more prevalent in the tropical climate of Egypt, Egyptians focused not on eliminating people who were blind but on their care and treatment (Ross, 1951). Gowman (1957: 211) found, "The chronicles of Herodotus, some 500 years prior to Christ's birth make reference to the great numbers of people who were blind within Egypt, the land that Hesoid termed "the country of the blind."

The Egyptians, at least as early as 1550 BC, wrote about eye disease and treatments (French, 1932). These writings make many references to treatments, ointments, and medications believed to be effective in treating blindness (Koestler, 1976). Treatments that can be identified from these early medical references included ox livers, incantations to the gods, honey, goose fat and oil, wax, and other concoctions. Beyond care and treatment, the Egyptians also trained people in the trades of massage, music, and the arts. Those who were blind consequently represented a large portion of poets and musicians (Moores, 1987). In addition, officials allowed them to participate in religious ceremonies.

The humane response to people who were blind persisted over the centuries long after Egypt was an empire. When the Romans overran and conquered Egypt under the Emperor Hadrian in the second century, he noted that people who were blind were actively engaged in the economy in several occupations (Ross, 1951). The relative openness to blindness of Egyptian society was the teacher Didymus (308 to 395) who was blind by age five. He was an excellent scholar and became the head of the prestigious Cathehectical School at Alexandria. Didymus, who taught early Christian leaders, such as Saint Jerome, Isidorus Palladius, and Saint Antony. Saint

Jerome reportedly held Didymus in awe (Farrell, 1956). He was responsible for one of the earliest known efforts at blind education. He used wooden letters to teach himself and others how to read. It should be noted that about the same time, Asian cultures provided people who were blind with meaningful and productive roles in their respective societies.

While the Egyptians tried to make the most out of blindness by developing opportunities, the Greeks viewed blindness as a calamity, punishment, and dramatic state of existence. Many Greeks viewed blindness as a fate worse than death. They saw blindness as a punishment from the gods. This basic belief provided a rationalization for negative social practices and attitudes toward people with blindness in Greek society. For example, the mythical prophet and soothsayer Tiresias was said to have been blinded by Minerva because he had seen the goddess at her bath. In another tale Oedipus anticipated the wrath of the gods by tearing out his eyes out to get rid of incestuous and patricidal guilt.

Yet, Greek perceptions were sometimes positive. In Greek culture and folklore, blindness afforded some the gifts, such as prophecy. For example, Tiresias was given the gift of prophecy, Phineus the gift of song, and Homer the gift of poetry. Democritus, a Greek philosopher of the fourth century BC, put his own eyes out to gain understanding and insight. In Greek legend, many clairvoyants were blind (Von Hentig, 1948). These legends contributed to the enduring idea that people who were blind were compensated for with extraordinary abilities and senses.

The Greeks and Romans destroyed, as they did with people having other disabilities and deformities, infants who were blind. The Spartans formed review committees that examined newborns for imperfections (Paulson, 1987; Ross, 1951). Those judged unworthy of becoming productive citizens were abandoned or killed. According to Koestler (1976), the Athenians placed these children in clay vessels especially designed for abandonment. Later the Romans continued the practice by using baskets. The philosophers Aristotle and Plato supported this practice. Those children not killed were sold into slavery, abandoned, or forced into prostitution (French, 1932; Ross, 1951).

Care and treatment of blindness under the Greeks did not advance much but the study of blindness and sight did receive attention from scholars. For instance, Aristotle linked eyes and sight to sex in his *Generation of Animals*. He concluded that for all the regions in the head, the eyes were the most seminal. He observed that this was the only region that changes its appearance because of sexual intercourse, and those who overindulged in it had noticeably sunken eyes. The Greek physician Hippocrates identified 30 types of eye diseases (French, 1932; Ross, 1951). He and others suggested a variety of treatments, including combinations of magic, baths, ointments, prayers, hymns, and herbal treatments.

Blindness appears in several ancient Greek literary works. For instance, the hero Odysseus puts out the single eye of the Cyclops. Homer's *Illiad and Odyssey* also tell the tale of Phineus, who Jupiter blinds as punishment for his cruelties. Oedipus eventually blinds himself. Oedipus Rex tells us, "Thou wert better dead than living blind." Demodocus, the blind minstrel of Book VIII of the *Odyssey,* was blinded by the Muses in exchange for his poetic gifts.

With the rise of the Roman Empire, conditions did not improve for people who were blind. The Romans referred to people who were blind as "prisoners of blindness" because they were perceived as isolated and maladjusted (Gowman, 1957). Under the Romans, people who were deaf, "dumb," or blind were frequently grouped together, as distinctions were minimal (Gardner, 1993). This was certainly the case under Roman law. However, under Roman law, people who were blind could manage their own affairs, serve as judges, senators, and take responsible roles in Roman society. They could not legally represent others. Legal barriers prohibited them from having full rights as Roman citizens, but few of these laws were insurmountable. When compared to other disabilities, blindness resulted in the fewest restrictions under Roman law (Gardner, 1993). This may have been partially due to the importance attached to spoken rather than written language in Roman culture.

People who were blind had a difficult time surviving during the Roman empire. French (1932:40) found the following description in the *Martial Epigrams XIV*. For example, "Their refuge was perhaps an open vault, their dog the only companion of their misery, their nourishment bread fit only for dogs, their sole possessions a staff and a coverlet or mat, and a knapsack, their relief in some lonely corner." Seneca also described the dramatically poor conditions people lived under in Rome. In addition to poor living conditions, they were sometimes killed by relatives. French (1932) found that the Roman Praetorius described older and weak parents being killed by their sons; blind, squinting, and deformed children were disposed of by fathers either by the sword, drowning, or burning; and blind servants were hung to trees by their masters. References to occupations of Roman and other ancient peoples indicate that people who were blind were occasionally employed as prostitutes, beggars, rowers, seers, operators of hand-mills, and scholars specializing in the memorization of laws or sacred texts (Gowman, 1957; Jablonski, 1966).

Blindness, along with deafness, has had a long history of philosophical attention and interpretation within the Christian tradition. References to blind and blindness are common throughout the Old and New Testaments and no other disability received more attention than blindness. The Old Testament made several references to blindness in Exodus, Leviticus, Deuteronomy, Ecclesiastes, Psalms, Genesis, Kings, Isaiah, Jeremiah,

Lamentations, Zephaniah, and Malachi. Blindness, in the Old Testament, was clearly attributed to the power of God. In Exodus (4:12), God proclaims to Moses, "Who makes [man] clear-sighted or blind? It is not I, the Lord? Ancient Hebrew culture generally associated blindness with the power of God.

In Genesis 18:9-11, we read of Lot who protected two angels in Sodom against harm at the hands of the townspeople. Blindness, along with other disabilities was assumed to be the result of sin.

A major source of sin was disbelief in God. Blind is referenced in the Old Testament as in being blind to God or having a lack of understanding or faith. Biblical blindness is symbolic and used to represent the lack of Christian insight or understanding. The perception of blindness as God's punishment endured throughout the rise of Christianity. For example, Vukanovic (1985) reported the belief that people who were blind were being punished by God and served as social reminders in southern Slavic countries' folklore and traditions.

Besides punishing, God had the power to restore sight. For example, disabilities and blindness were cured during the Exodus so that revelation on Mount Sinai could be provided to healthy people. When the biblical Isaac was born, all people who were blind regained their sight (Monbeck, 1973). One of the most famous stories of God's restoration of sight was the ancient Hebrew story of Tobit from the Book of the Apocrypha. This story remained popular and was repeated over the centuries. Illustrations of Tobit lying blind with his spouse, Anna, preparing medicine for his illness were common in medieval and later art. The artist Rembrandt returned to the story several times, such as his *The Blindness of Tobit* etching (1651). His *Tobit and Anna with the Kid* dated 1626 is an example of the connection between blindness, despair, and faith. Anna returns home to Tobit holding a kid that she has earned.

Societal restrictions have frequently been applied to people who were blind, such as on the occupations they were allowed to pursue. Formal religion sanctioned some of these restrictions. For example, in ancient Hebrew culture, blindness disqualified men from serving as priests (Leviticus 21: 16-23). Other references to restrictions were mentioned in the Old Testament. In the Book of II Samuel 5: 8, it was written "No blind or lame man shall come into the Lord's house." In addition, Hebrews made no provisions to systematically educate or care for people who were blind. Apparently they were allowed to beg and it is known that some Hebrews faked blindness in order to more effectively beg. In response to this fraud, rabbis threatened genuine blindness as a punishment from God. The *Talmud* (French, 1932:58) stated, "Who ever feigns blindness should not depart this life without actually being so afflicted."

Much of the negativism toward blindness would change with the New Testament. The New Testament references to blindness includes Acts; Ephesians; John, Luke, Matthew, Peter; Revelation, and Romans. The New Testament treated blindness with more compassion. People continued to be blinded but were viewed as subjects to God's compassion. Where in the Old Testament people were assumed to be blind because they deserved it, in the New Testament their blindness was seen as an opportunity for God and Christ to show kindness and charity. This is revealed in the numerous accounts of the miraculous restoration of sight in the New Testament. The books of Mark and Luke portrayed Jesus as having great compassion for blind and disabled people. He does not just pity people who were blind but cures them (John, Matthew).

The development and spread of the Christian Church had a profound impact on people with blindness. St. John, St. Jerome, and St. Thomas all encouraged their followers to give alms to people who were blind. St. Jerome praised charitable acts toward the blind. St. Ambrose allowed people who were blind to beg and made special provisions to accommodate them. Beginning in the third century, church authorities opened hospices to serve people who were blind (Paulson, 1987). The fourth century witnessed the establishment of hospices and cloisters that cared for people who were blind (Monbeck, 1973). In 370, St. Basil became the Bishop of Caesarea. St. Basil founded an asylum for people who were blind, poor, and others in need. Saint Basil had his staff search the countryside for people to bring back to the refuge. They lived in separate living units except for prayer (Farrell, 1956). During the fifth century, Saint Lymnaeus established a refuge for the blind in Syria. St. Lymnaeus provided care to a small community of people who were blind. Patients were taught to sing religious songs with the hope that alms would result. St. Herve (d. 565) found a monastery in Brittany that provided care. In the seventh century, Saint Benard (Bishop of Le Mans) established an institution for the blind in France. In Smithfield, England St. Bartholomews admitted people who were deaf, blind, and otherwise disabled (Neaman, 1978).

PEOPLE WHO WERE BLIND DURING THE MIDDLE AGES

The Middle Ages was a difficult time for people who were blind. According to French (1932), they lived and slept under the most unworthy of conditions and grew demoralized. Not only were living conditions poor for many, but the numbers of people who were blind rose during the Middle

Ages. According to Ross (1951:37), "Blindness reached appalling proportions with the plagues of the Middle Ages, as well as the hazards of battle." He added, "The spears, arrows, and bludgeoning battle-axes used in close-in fighting of the period were no less deadly to the eye than the weapons of today." In addition, the development of medieval towns and cities created new challenges for people who were blind. The increasingly complex and urban life made traditional and rural-based social relations between the seeing and nonseeing outmoded. In rural society, communities looked out after people with disabilities, whereas as urbanization occurred, people with disabilities increasingly came into contact with more strangers. This development raised new issues regarding mobility and orientation for people who were blind. The family and community assumed different roles and functions.

During the Middle Ages, people knew very little about the eye, how it functioned, or how to effectively treat eye disease. Ocular remedies have a long history and were numerous in medieval and earlier societies (Kealey, 1981). For instance, Thorndike (1923) identified several references in ancient writings for treatments of loss of vision such as the use of lizards mixed in potions and ointments. The Anglo-Saxon text entitled *Lacnunga* has several eye remedies and salves including honey, roebuck marrow, and fox grease (Rubin, 1974). The Anglo-Saxons used leeches to treat eye disease. During the Middle Ages, if ointments and treatments failed, people would also go on pilgrimages to bring miracle cures.

One of the leading causes of blindness during the Middle ages was cataracts. Cataracts typically required surgery and surgeons have operated on them for centuries. For example, in the twelfth century, cataract operations were common in England (Kealey, 1981). Medieval surgeons typically adhered to Galen's theory of bodily humours to explain cataracts. Galen proposed that cataracts were caused by an excessive buildup of phlegm in the brain that solidified behind the lens of the eye. In a similar vein, medieval physicians and surgeons believed that cataracts were formed by a whitish liquid (humour) running down from the brain into the eyes. Medieval surgeons who specialized in eye surgery were called cataract couchers. Cataract couchers performed the specialized surgery of breaking up the solid matter and pushing it away from the pupil. Numerous medieval medical manuscripts illustrate crude cataract surgeries. Medieval renditions of cataract surgery include Guido of Vigevano's (1345) *Anathonia* which has a miniature of the surgery being performed. Surgical techniques advanced when Jacques Daviel (1676-1762), eye surgeon to King Louis XV, developed the first modern treatment of cataracts by extracting the lens.

In addition to crude surgery, the use of lens was available to some who were not totally blind. Roger Bacon was the first to propose a reading glass for visually impaired people in the thirteenth century. Bacon recommended the use of convex lenses to correct vision impairments of older people in 1268 (Farrell, 1956). Later, in the fourteenth century, several texts refer to the manufacture of spectacles (Garrison, 1960). Spectacles can be found in bas-reliefs from the fifteenth century, but may actually date to Venetian glass-workers at the close of the thirteenth century (Garrison, 1960). Artistic representations of spectacles in art include Jan van Eyck's (1390-1441) *The Madonna of Canon van der Paele*. The great Italian artist Raphael painted Pope Leo X holding a pair of concave lens. Others include Dürer's *Christ Child in the Temple* (1500), Hans Holbein the Elder's *Martyrdom of St. Bartholomew* (1503), Ghirlandaio's *Saint Jerome* in the Church of Ognissant in Florence. In 1784, Benjamin Franklin invented bifocals.

William the Conqueror (eleventh century) established early hospitals in England for people who were blind or had eye disease. State care of people began in France when, in 1254, the French King Louis IX (Saint Louis) expanded the L' Hospital des Quinze-Vingts (Almshouse for the Three Hundred) to provide care for handicapped crusaders who had been blinded by the Sacrens in 1250. The story, whose accuracy has been questioned, told that the Sacrens blinded 20 crusaders a day until a ransom was paid for by King Louis IX (Farrell, 1956). Residents of Quinze-Vingts had to comply with rules such as daily prayers, chores, and acts of piety to remain in the facility. Men and women wore long blue gowns with a lily on the breast. They were allowed to marry, were free from taxes, and maintained a right to asylum.

Other asylums serving people who were blind were established during the Middle Ages. William Elsing opened a shelter in London in 1329, and Henry de Gower founded an asylum in 1347. The town of Bruges established one in 1305, and so did Swansea, England in 1347. Medieval communities developed other responses besides institutions and asylums. Frankfort, Germany made provisions for the relief of the poor in 1437, similar relief measures were in place in Antwerp (1450), and Nuremberg (1522). German Emperor Charles V required communities to feed the poor including those who were blind. England's Queen Elizabeth I made one of the most dramatic moves with the implementation of the poor laws in 1601. These laws provided for the provision of care to the sick, blind, physically disabled, aged, poor, and otherwise needy. These medieval asylums and hospitals for people were little more than shelters. Church cloisters in the Middle Ages also cared for people who were blind and saved children who otherwise were doomed (French, 1932). Early asylums were designed to simply remove people from the streets and did not train people. With the coming of the Protestant Reformation in the sixteenth century, many of these institutions were devastated or closed because of their alliance with the Catholic church.

People who were blind appear in medieval art and literature. Many medieval farces depicted them as comic, grotesque, roguish, and villainous. Societies often reacted to them with scorn and revulsion. In some cases, they were viewed as taking advantage of their blindness to make fortunes. The idea of people using their blindness to make fortunes occurs in Medieval literature, such as thirteenth century *Le Garcon et Pareugle*. Andrieu de la

Figure 31. Pieter Bruegel the Elder, *The Blind Beggar,* about 1564, Kupferstichkabinett, Dresden.

Vigne's medieval miracle/farce story *The Blind Man and the Cripple* (1496) tells about a dying man and a devil who mistakes his excrement for his soul. One pen and chalk drawing attributed to Pieter Bruegel the Elder dated about 1564 depicts a beggar who is blind. The robed and hooded man sits while holding his alms cup. In all likelihood, this was modeled after a beggar Bruegel saw on the streets of northern Europe. It is unquestionably an accurate depiction of the subject, absent of symbolism. The man is neither glorified nor criticized.

Numerous artists used Christian themes to depict people who were blind. The theme of the miracle healing was probably the most common in this art. For example, Titian's (1477-1576) *Saint Antony Cures a Young Cripple*, Quentin Massys (1466-1530), and Pedro Berrugete (d. 1503-1504) all depicted the popular theme of the recovery of sight. Massys shows the curing of the biblical Tobias by his son, who had been instructed by an archangel to rub his father's eyes with file bile. Berruguete depicted a blind man being led by a boy praying to Saint Thomas or to his relics in a coffin to cure his master's blindness. Typically, blindness was presented within a Christian context and frequently as a miracle healing.

PEOPLE WHO WERE BLIND DURING THE MODERN PERIOD

The first major social changes for people who were blind occurred at the close of the Middle Ages. The perception and status of people who were blind had not changed appreciably since early Christianity. At the close of the Middle Ages, blindness continued to be mysterious and unfamiliar. Medical advances in eye care and treatment had made little progress. For example, some sixteenth century scholars continued to view witchcraft and demons as causing blindness. In 1583, George Burtisch published a book on ophthalmology that provided a comprehensive survey of eye surgery. In this work he provided a section identifying the causes of eye diseases that included demons, witches, and magic. He wrote:

> Furthermore, as can be proved by Holy Writ, we have many other examples, some even of our own day, and similar ones may well happen in the future, that such wicked people, who were discovered to be the Devil's instruments or tools, have not only, at the instigation and with the aid of the Devil, bewitched other people and destroyed them, so that they became absolutely blind, but they have also with the aid of their aforesaid accomplice, caused many poor people's eyes to swell and bulge out of their heads. [Cited by Burstein, 1956: 20]

Although remnants of medieval understandings of the eye and its treatment continued in the early modern era, there is evidence that progress had been made. For instance, although not useful for total blindness, spectacles were helpful for those with minor visual impairments. By the sixteenth century spectacles found widespread use in Europe, at least for those who could afford them. The main shift was not in technology or treatment but in social perception. Increasingly people viewed those who were blind as being capable of being educated. In addition, the cure of some types of blindness became possible in the eighteenth century due to medical advances. In the eighteenth century successful care of congenital cataracts was possible for some people. Blindness for those suffering from cataracts shifted from an incurable condition to a medical condition that could be altered with intervention. In a sense, blindness became demystified once it moved from the traditional spiritual explanations to the medical. With cures possible, blindness was no longer seen as predetermining one's destiny. People came to believe that medicine could cure blindness or at least improve whatever vision remained. Paulson (1987:72) summed the importance of being able to cure cataract caused blindness, "...curability modifies the imaginary conception of the blind by the seeing, and alters their status in society. Not all the blind can actually be cured, of course, but the possibility of cure changes the very concept of blindness." More medical progress was made in the nineteenth century. A series of developments in the later half of the nineteenth century continued to push medical treatment of eye disease and treatment forward. For example, the ophthalmoscope was invented in 1850. In 1882, physicians began to apply silver nitrate to the eyes of newborns.

With cures possible, people with blindness became objects of philosophical speculation. How did the mind work in a sightless versus a sighted world? These questions reached full fruition during the eighteenth century. In addition to medical advances, blindness became the subject of intense cultural interest in eighteenth-century France (Paulson, 1987). Perhaps the greatest changes occurred in the nature of the discourse about sight and the implications of the absence of sight. Philosophers and scholars, following the works of John Locke (1632-1704), George Berkeley (1685-1753), René Descartes (1596-1650), Voltaire (1694-1778), Denis Diderot (1713-1784), and Jean-Jacques Rousseau (1712-1778), Etienne Condillac (1715-1780), Gottfried Leibnitz (1646-1716), and others engaged in lengthy discourses about the nature of knowledge and sight. René Descartes' earlier *Discours de la Methode* (1637) reviewed the intellectual processes of people who were blind. John Locke's *Essay Concerning Human Understanding* (1690) described the problem of a person being born blind but gaining sight. Bishop Berkeley's 1709 *Essay Toward a New Theory of Vision* led to speculation about vision and the basis of knowledge. Philosophers wondered how knowledge could be acquired by people with disabilities. How did they learn and did learning change when sight or hearing was regained or acquired for the first time? What was the relationship between language and learning?

The main offshoot of all of this philosophical attention was the laying of a foundation for educating people who were blind. Increasing numbers of scholars and educators became interested in how to instruct people who were blind. Their instruction represented a kind of laboratory for learning how all people learned about their world. Unlike people who were deaf or developmentally disabled who were written off as lost causes when it came to learning, people who were blind were always assumed to be able to learn. Educational efforts had occurred before the eighteenth century. However, the modern period ushered in the first systematic efforts to educate people who were blind. It is this development that represents the most critical shift of social perceptions of and attitudes towards people who were blind. Evidence of adaptive teaching techniques and educational devices for teaching the visually impaired are sprinkled throughout much of modern western history. In 1517, Francesco Lucas taught in Spain and Italy by using large cut letters to instruct people who were blind. The sixteenth century Italian physician, astrologer, and mathematician Cardan, also known as Geronimo Cardano (1501-1576), wrote a book titled *De Subtilitate Rerum* (1550). This work described a device to teach reading and writing that used touch. It also included ideas on how to teach those with deafness. Cardan used wooden letters to construct words and sentences. He also used special readers which helped students memorize written materials.

Numerous publications on blind education followed. About one hundred and forty years later, Pierre Moreau in 1640 used moveable lead letters to form words. The Italian Prospero Fagnani (1590-1678), who lost his sight at age 44, published his *Commentary on the Decretals of Gregory IX* in 1661. Sections of this work refer to special provisions for the blind, widows, older people, and needy (Farrell, 1956). Fagnani thought that people who were blind should be treated like sighted people and helped on the basis of need rather than on their blindness. In 1670, Lana Terzi published a book that dealt with techniques for instructing the blind. He proposed a cipher code based on a circle of dots enclosed in a square and a system of knots on a string to teach the blind. During the seventeenth century, Abbe Deschamps published a method for working with deaf and blind children through proper placement of lips and tongue.

In 1749, Denis Diderot (1713-1784) published his *Lettres sur les aveugles à l'usage de ceux qui voient* that showed how the blind adapt to their environments by using other senses. He would be imprisoned in the Bastille for three months for this letter. Eventually, he was released to work on the *Encyclopedia*. Diderot thought the processes and results involved in learning through touch were different than those involved in sight. Much of his questioning focused on the relationship between sight and language. He assumed that blindness called into question the very nature of human existence. He suggested a way to teach the blind by touch. He believed the souls of the blind resided in their fingertips and thoughts started there. Diderot was one of the first scholars to systematically think about educating people who were blind, although he never attempted to apply his ideas in the classroom.

About the same time, a Frenchman named Valentin Haüy (1745-1822) attended a burlesque concert where ten blind entertainers were made to look like fools, wore dunce caps, played instruments with crude bows, and were teased by the audience. Offended and touched by the show, he committed himself to a lifetime of educating people who were blind. He collected all the information he could on how to instruct people who were blind. One story tells of Haüy giving a blind boy some coins. He was impressed by the boy's ability to tell the value of the coins by touch. Haüy adopted him as a student. Haüy became an influential educator of the blind in France and would eventually gain worldwide recognition for his teaching techniques. Haüy experimented with a number of techniques to teach blind students. He tried wooden blocks with little success. He experimented with using raised print which allowed some students to read. He developed adaptive reading techniques by pricking holes into letters and using embossed letters. Strongly influenced and impressed by the successes of Abbe Epee teaching deaf children, he founded the National Institute for the Young Blind in Paris (Institute des Enfants Aveugles) with 14 students in 1784. This was the first school for blind children in the world and represented the first systematic effort to educate children who were blind. The famous Louis Braille would be a student at the school.

Haüy's school did not receive government support so he needed to raise private funds for its operation. He used techniques that today would be criticized. To gain support of the French aristocracy, he held demonstrations involving his most successful students. He provided shows of their talents and abilities throughout Europe. For example, his pupils entertained and demonstrated their skills to Louis the XVI and his court. Marie Antoinette was present at some of the demonstrations. Haüy's school was built on the success of the concert pianist, the blind Maria Theresa von Paradis of Vienna. She became the rage of Paris and Europe. All of this ended with the French Revolution which virtually destroyed everything that Haüy had established. The school was strongly associated with the French aristocracy and was consequently closed. Although the school was dismantled, Haüy's students and ideas had a lasting influence on Europe.

Outside of France, the first English schools for people who were blind placed emphasis on institutionalizing students rather than educating them but eventually educational facilities were established. The first day school was founded in Liverpool in about 1790 and a similar school followed in Edinburgh in 1793. Edward Rushton opened a school called the School for the Indigent Blind in Liverpool in 1791. Johann Wilhelm Klein founded schools in Vienna in 1804 and Berlin in 1806. Klein published a textbook on educating people who were blind in 1819 titled *Textbook on the Education of the Blind*, which contained numerous, somewhat contemporary concepts, such as the use of guide dogs. Klein also proposed that students could be placed in local schools with sighted children.

The titles given to these early schools usually included the terms asylum or industrial. These terms incorporated the philosophies of the schools, which was to train people for work. The founders of a school in Bristol, according to French (1932:99) stated its purpose being "...not to employ the blind after being educated, but to teach them the means of getting a living by work." Here lies a critical aspect to these eighteenth century schools. People assumed during the industrial revolution that one's worth was tied to work and the same was true for those who were blind. Eighteenth century schools for the blind stressed preparing students for outside work. This was the industrial revolution and people disabled or not were measured by whether they could lead productive lives. Emphasis on work and industrial training was embedded in the values and psyche's of the labor classes from which students were often drawn.

In 1800, Napoleon moved to place all children who were blind in the Quinze-Vingts asylum. Following the Napoleonic Wars, the Royal Institute for Blind Children was established in the Latin Quarter of Paris. It was more a workhouse with terrible food and living arrangements than a school (Dunning, 1992). Conditions at the school improved when Andre Pigner adopted Charles Barbier's writing system of raised dots and dashes. Babier, an officer in Napoleon's army, developed a method of communicating military information in the darkness of night. His night writing system was based on a system of 12 raised dots in a cell that the reader's fingers could interpret without light.

Besides Barbier's system, many other adaptive techniques were developed during the nineteenth century. One of the major breakthroughs was made by Louis Braille. Braille was born in 1809 and died in 1852 at age 43. Braille, blinded in childhood by an awl, was a pupil at a school for the blind in Paris where he would later become an instructor. He is most famous for his adaptation of Charles Barbier's dot system which Braille reduced from 12 to six dots, which he thought could be spanned by a fingertip. He also reduced the size of the dots to take advantage of the sensitivity of his fingers. Initially his system was resisted by officials until students insisted it be accepted in 1854, two years after his death. Europe would wait until 1878 to adopt his system. Other efforts at communicating with the blind included Dr. William Moon's system which was a simplification of the alphabet that relied on touch. In the nineteenth century there would be other developments, such as the first blind printing press which was invented by Henry Robyn in 1865.

During the latter part of the eighteenth century, humanitarian concerns not only gave rise to the American and French Revolutions, but also to ideas that would affect people with blindness and other disabilities. In addition, the federal system was overthrown in favor of increased opportunities for all people to become integrated into society. People could demand more status and participation in government and society. Ideas of liberty, equity, and dignity were being applied to all people, including those who were blind or had other disabilities. In addition, in early nineteenth century America, there was a spirit of benevolence toward blindness. It was a period when there was a surge to help the underprivileged, including people who were blind. Consequently, the nineteenth century was a period of the opening of many schools for the blind. In the United States, Jacksonian Democracy with its emphasis on universal education for all children, helped usher in the establishment of schools during the 1830s. These early American schools were really multipurpose in that they also served "defective children," such as those with developmental disabilities and/or deafness.

One of the early American educational leaders was Dr. John Fischer, who was an advocate for people who were blind in the United States. Fischer traveled throughout France and returned to the United States impressed by French methods of instructing people who were blind. He selected Samuel Gridley Howe (1801-1876) to head the New England Asylum (Institution) for the Education of the Blind in 1831. The school had been established two years prior with very limited success. Fischer's selection of Howe for the directorship proved to be a good decision for the school and the education of the blind in the United States. Under Howe's direction, the school would expand dramatically when it received a large gift of a mansion by a Mr. Perkins in 1832. The school would become named the Perkins Institution and Massachusetts Asylum for the Blind. About the same time, schools were established in New York and Philadelphia.

Howe was in favor of public displaying of students and believed it was necessary to garner support for his school. His students who went on exhibitions wore green ribbons over their eyes to demonstrate that they were truly blind. He believed, typical of the times, that through training and education, they could contribute to society. While instrumental in the development of schools for the blind, Howe expressed reservation over relying too heavily on residential schools and institutions for the blind, as he valued personal independence. Howe wrote:

> All great establishments in the nature of boarding schools where the sexes must be separated, where there must be boarding in common and sleeping in congregate dormitories, where there must be routine, and formality, and restraint, and repression of individuality; where the charms and refining influences of the true family relation cannot be had, - all such institutions are unnatural, undesirable and very liable to abuse. We should have as few of them as is possible, and those few should be kept as small as possible. [Address at laying of the cornerstone of the New York State Institution for the Blind, 1866; Cited by Farrell, 1956: 60-61]

Dr. Howe's work with the blind and deaf Laura Bridgeman would establish him as a major educator of special needs children, but his success in developing public support for educating people who were blind was even more important. His leadership led to the widespread establishment of schools in several of the states, such as the Pennsylvania Institution for the Blind which was founded in 1833. Besides the personal happiness gained through education, Howe believed that education of people who were blind was a matter of economy for the community, as educated people who were blind could contribute to the community and live productive lives. More importantly, they would not be dependent on the community for support and care.

At the foundation for many of these schools and similar earlier eighteenth century views was the belief the blind should work and the key to their employment was education (Farrell, 1956). This basic underlying theme fit well with eighteenth and nineteenth century emphasis on work and production. Able-bodied people and people with disabilities needed to be productive and contribute to society. The theme of work vestiges itself in a number of schools for the blind established in the nineteenth century. The names of some of the schools reflect this perspective, such as the Pennsylvania Working Home for Blind Men (1874) and the Industrial Home for the Blind in Brooklyn (1897). Small scale industries, such as basketry, chair caning, brooms, and light manufacturing were common and the only job training available to many students.

Not everyone was convinced that special schools were the sole answer to the question of how to best educate people. William Hanks Levy, himself blind, described mobility techniques in his *Blindness and the Blind* (1872) such as the use of canes, other senses, and human or animal guides. He also argued against blind fathers keeping their children out of school in order to have them serve as guides (Koestler, 1976). By the mid-nineteenth century, residential schools, sheltered workshops, and financial aid were available to people in the United States. However, for those children who received any education did so away from their families during the important formative years in state-supported schools. They were separated from their sighted peers and often were mixed with children who were deaf. About 1900, some educators claimed that blind children could be better educated while living at home and attending day schools.

Artistic presentations of people who were blind are numerous from the modern era. Examples include Mattia Preti's (1613-1699) *A Blind Man, Youth, and Servant*, Rembrandt's *Homer Dictating to a Scribe* (1663), and Jacques Louis David's (1748-1825) *Blind Belisarius Recognized by a Soldier*. John Trumbull's (1756-1843) *The Blind Belisarius* (1778) and Benjamin West's (1738-1820) drawing titled *The Blind Belisarius Led By A Boy* (1784) are other examples of the story of Belisarius. Other examples were Francisco Goya's untitled sketches of street people such as a man with the notation, "Blind man in love with his hernia" and his painting entitled *Tio Paquete* (1820). Tio was a famous beggar who begged from the steps of the church of San Felipe in where Goya displayed his works. The artist Annibale Carracci (1560-1609) from Bologna, created a series of six remarkable portraits of people who were blind. The six portraits are realistic drawings of people who had lost their sight for a number of reasons. One drawing of a man's head, drawn in 1590, shows that he has lost one of his eyes and is blind in the other. The detail of the work, and his other portraits in the series, indicates that it was indisputably drawn from real people. The anatomical detail of the subject's head is remarkable. The work is objectively drawn so as to not incorporate any of the stereotypes of people who were blind, such as the blind beggar, that would have been popular in Carracci time. The sitter is both isolated from the world of sight but also dignified. In the lower right hand corner of the work is a detailed drawing of a human eye. Carracci included similar symbolic eyes in some of his other portraits in this series. Cavina (1989) speculates that Carracci added the eye to ensure that the meaning of the presentation would not be confused, as one could easily mistake the man for being deceased. Perhaps the eye was included to convey, as Cavina (1989) also suggests, the message of the moral superiority of people who were blind.

Some artists experienced the loss of sight and severe visual impairments. Honoré Daumier (1808-1879) underwent surgery for cataracts, which proved to be unsuccessful. Claude Monet (1840-1926) also had failing eyesight due to cataracts. His failing eyesight affected his impressionistic style toward the end of his career at the beginning of the twentieth century. Written records reveal that this great impressionist artist was reluctant to have cataract surgery in spite of reductions in his ability to see forms and colors. In 1918, Monet (Ravin, 1990:91) would write, "I no longer perceived colors with the same intensity." "I no longer painted light with the same accuracy." The impact of his loss of sight is obvious when comparing his early with latter works. The latter ones reveal increasingly blurred images and the color blue became dominant during different phases of his career. The more abstract images were probably a product of vision loss as much as changes in artistic style, as indicated by Monet's displeasure with some of his later works (Ravin, 1987; 1990). Over the years that followed, he tried a variety of glasses with little satisfaction until the very end of his life when tinted glasses seemed to help. The American artist Mary Cassatt (1845-1926) also had cataracts that required surgery, which proved to be unsuccessful. She prematurely stopped painting in 1914. Cassatt's surgery resulted in a painful infection, which was common due to crude surgical techniques of the period (Bixenstine, 1989).

Modern literature also presents blindness and characters who were blind. A popular theme of modern plays was the person who was blind gains sight (Paulson, 1987). From the mid-eighteenth to the first quarter of the nineteenth centuries, there was an abundance of works that included lovers who were blind who had their sight restored. For example, the Brothers Grimm's nineteenth century tale of *Rapunzel* describes how the prince's sight is restored by the tears of his faithful wife (Hand, 1980). In addition, the image of people with blindness moves from the comic fool of the Middle Ages to the object of sympathetic passion. Being blind or becoming blind becomes romanticized and the focus of empathy. The ancient notion that people who were blind were gifted seers and poets was reborn in nineteenth century literature. Consequently, depictions of blindness became romanticized. Other story lines were presented in literature such as Betha Plummer, who is blind in Dicken's *Cricket on the Hearth* (1881), being visited by friends.

PEOPLE WHO WERE BLIND OVER THE CENTURIES

Blindness evokes some of the strongest emotional responses from people with sight. Societies have viewed blindness as a personal tragedy. Among those who see, the assumption is made that it was better to be dead than blind (Koestler, 1976). Even people who work with people who were blind see blindness as a devastating tragedy (Lane, 1993). People who are blind, however, typically do not. All of the social perceptions are not negative. People who were blind, unlike people with other disabilities such as leprosy or syphilis, have been viewed in negative and positive terms. Unlike leprosy which carries a totally negative reaction, blindness can be perceived as having positive impacts on the individual. For example, people with blindness were perceived as having extraordinary powers, such as the ability to predict the future.

Over history, blindness has evoked strong emotional responses, not so much from those who were blind but from those who could see. A number perceptions and assumptions about people who were blind have endured over the centuries. On the positive side, they were assumed to have special gifts and talents, such as creativity, ability to reason, prophecy. Among their perceived gifts was the gift of music and they were often cast in the roles of bard and musician. Early schools also pushed students into music, for better or worse. Koestler (1976:1) summarized the lives of those who were blind:

> They were feared, shunned, pitied, ignored. Some were thought to be blessed with magical powers, others to be accursed for their sins. They were princes and beggars, bards and soothsayers, storytellers and buffoons. Some were killed as infants, others were tolerated in youth but abandoned to die by the roadside or even buried alive when they grew old and infirm. There were those who roamed the countryside in gypsy bands, living by their wits, communicating in a secret jargon. There were others who never in their lives ventured from home and hearthside. Some came under the special protection of the church or the crown, and some were thrown into madhouses, pesthouses, where they could be kept out of public view.

People who were blind were frequently characterized in art, literature, and folklore. An example is the parable of the blind leading the blind that was popular during the sixteenth and seventeenth centuries. Other folklore tales, games, poetry, and stories, such as the Three Blind Mice, and Blind Man's Bluff incorporate blindness. Those who were blind were often the fools in folklore. Their being the butt of the joke or cast as fools were common themes in these and other depictions of blindness. Two negative perceptions people held were that blindness represented evil and darkness. To be blind was to be in a state of existence that was full of mystery and unknown darkness. It was also evil, as most things in the western mind that were classified as dark were also considered evil. This social perception endured in spite of the notion that many people who were blind do not sense darkness in the same way as people who have sight. Darkness does not carry any meaning of evil or mystery for those who have never had sight. One of the most common and enduring social perceptions of people who were blind is that they were beggars. This traditional role and label of beggar is not welcomed by people who are blind today (Koestler, 1976). Rather, they abhor begging and react negatively to those that perpetuate any sense of economic dependency.

We know very little about how they lived in antiquity. What is known is that ancient societies were mixed or indifferent in their responses to blindness. The Egyptians, perhaps because of the large numbers of people who lost their sight, seem on the surface to have treated them with a greater sense of dignity than other ancient societies. They were permitted, and in fact, did integrate well into Egyptian societies. Evidence shows that they served in a number of important occupations and social roles. The Hebrews perceived blindness as evidence of the power of God. Nonbelievers, sinners, and the enemies of God were struck with blindness and it was the wage for sin. If people were blind, it was because they had earned being blind. The Greeks also interpreted blindness as a calamity and attributed it to the gods. People were punished by the gods by being blinded. They perceived blindness as a fate worse than death. In this vein, children born blind ran the risk of being abandoned, killed, or sold into slavery if the parents and authorities approved. Later, the Romans adopted Greek notions about blindness and formalized these ideas into law. Roman laws devoted to blindness were both protective but also restrictive.

The rise of the early Christian church had a dramatic affect on how societies treated people who were blind. Christianity encouraged Christians to treat people who were blind with compassion and concern. People who were blind represented an opportunity for Christians to express compassion. The Christian image of Christ or other Christian leaders performing miracle healings of those without sight evolved into a major motif during this period and continued well into modern history. Eventually, the church took on a formal and organized role of providing alms and care for people, including those who were blind. The Middle Ages continued to foster Christian perceptions of people who were blind. When blind or its related terms are used in the Bible, they are used fairly consistently in the contexts of healing and or failure to believe in God. These ideas were expressed in literature, art, and social perceptions.

It was during the modern era that public discourse about the nature of blindness relative to knowledge came to fruition. Scholars and philosophers debated the relationship between observation and knowledge. This debate helped demystify blindness in the eighteenth century. These debates along with the democratization of France and the United States, and other social changes created fertile ground for the establishment and development of separate schools for students who were blind. People devoted energy to including all people in the new social order, including those without sight. The eighteenth and nineteenth centuries saw the considerable expansion of schools for students who were blind. Even with the development of numerous schools and systems for educating students, the general public only reluctantly embraced the notion that people who were blind could lead productive lives. In the nineteenth century blindness even became romanticized by some, as being a state of being characterized by emotional insight and understanding that few with sight were able to obtain.

Blindness in social relations is characterized with a degree of uncertainty. Reasons for this include people who were blind have always been individuals and their responses to their disability have varied with circumstances, personalities, and other social factors. Everyone, blind or not, while sharing some commonalties with others, is nevertheless unique. In addition, those with sight are highly dependent on vision for relating to their world and others. So much of human interaction is nonverbal and is dependent on visual cues. To not have the tool of sight for communication and relationships is unimaginable for many sighted people. When relating to people who lack sight, the task seems difficult, as people who are blind cannot key off of visual and nonverbal cues. Third, blindness is unfamiliar and mysterious to those with sight. The conclusion people reach is that people who have sight do not know what people who are blind are able to do, how to communicate with them, and what, if any level of dependency exists.

Chapter 6

PEOPLE WHO WERE DEAF

The history of people who were deaf has been one ripe with debate and controversy, more so than probably any other groups of people with disabilities. For example, throughout history deafness, some would argue, is not a disability but simply a characteristic that makes some people different from others. Some see deafness as not a disability or even a disabling characteristic. Rather, it is simply an alternative way of communicating. Some people who are deaf see themselves as primarily visual people with their own visual language (Lane, 1992). Deafness is more than a hearing status or condition, it is an identity and sociocultural condition. To some, to be deaf means a person is only a member of a linguistic minority and little more. They are not disabled. Others would argue that people who are deaf have a right to be a member of this linguistic minority. From this point of view, people who are deaf are not disabled in any way in their own communities (Lane, 1993).

In contrast, others view deafness as a major disability. To them, deafness represents a disability and to deny this fact results in the individual who is deaf being isolated their whole lives unless they can learn to communicate with people who can hear. Lane (1993:74) wrote, "In the disability construction, deafness is associated with the absence of hearing, silence, individual suffering, personal incapacities, and achievement in overcoming great obstacles." He added, "In the minority construction, deafness is associated with a unique language, history, culture, social group, set of institutions." The dominant point of view of people who hear has been that people who are deaf are disabled (Lane, 1992). From the disability construction has grown, Lane continued, a major trouble-industry that focuses on bestowing benevolence on people defined as in need. This industry has a vested interest in serving itself as much as people defined in trouble. People who are deaf have suffered needlessly from this dominant perspective (Lane, 1992). In addition, this industry fails to include people who are deaf in providing services. They are perceived as not being able to meet the needs of their own troubled group. When hearing people imagine what it is like to be deaf, they imagine themselves to be disabled. The construction of the deaf child as disabled was legitimized early on by the medical profession and later on by the welfare bureaucracy and special education (Lane, 1993). The history of deafness is very much a discourse between those who see it as a disability and those that see it as simply an alternative life-style.

Two concepts central to an understanding of the history of people who are deaf are the concepts of deaf community and deaf culture. Several authorities have observed that people who are deaf are different from people with disabilities because they have developed a separate culture. The existence of a deaf community is generally accepted by most scholars who study people who are deaf (Foster, 1989). The deaf culture is a social construct that differs among societies over time and place. Lane (1993:77) wrote, "Deafness is constructed differently in that culture (deaf culture) than it is in hearing culture." Deaf culture is not simply defined by the larger hearing society but is shaped by members of the deaf community. Members of the deaf culture do not simply react to the rules and definitions of the larger hearing society but take an active role in shaping their own cultures. Crittenden (1993: 218) defines deaf culture as, "The view of life manifested by the mores, beliefs, artistic expression, understandings, and language particular to Deaf people." Behavioral norms govern the social interactions of individuals who are deaf within this deaf culture. Reagan (1990:76) wrote, "Among the more obvious examples of variations in behavior norms between deaf and hearing people would be eye contact patterns, rules governing physical contact and touching, the use of facial expressions, gesturing, and so on." The two groups misunderstand each other because of these differences.

There is an important relationship between American Sign Language (ASL) and American deaf culture. In the United States, ASL is the means through which norms, values, beliefs, and ideas are communicated and shared among populations of people who are deaf. The use of ASL is a shared experience that strengthens bonds among people who use the language. ASL has been a major contributor the sense of deaf pride (Chough, 1983). In addition to ASL, there are three major characteristics that are associated with the deaf community. These are attitudinal deafness, behavioral norms, and attendance at residential schools. Residential schools are the "bastions" of deaf culture because they enrich and transmit the deaf culture (Neisser, 1990). These three factors influence their values, the beliefs they hold for themselves and a strong commitment to their culture.

There are strong arguments for the profound power of a separate deaf culture (Sharpiro, 1993). Strong feelings and beliefs of the separate and distinct culture of people who were deaf led some people to suggest that separate deaf nations or states ought to be established. This occurred in France and the United States in the nineteenth century. Jean-Ferdinand Berthier (1803-1886), an outspoken advocate for people who were deaf, attempted to establish a French Deaf Nation. In the United States, some activists suggested a deaf nation where only deaf people could live should be established in the unsettled West. In the late 1850s, John J. Flournoy lobbied for land to be set aside to establish an independent and sovereign nation for people who were deaf (Crouch, 1986; Winzer, 1986). He proposed this nation would draw people who were deaf from all over the country and would afford them full and equal status that was not possible in the United States. Flournoy's efforts have been characterized as a reflection of the alienation experienced by people who were deaf in the nineteenth century (Winzer, 1986). Others have likened his ideas to be the ravings of a person on the fringe (Crouch, 1986). Although some people clearly supported Flournoy's efforts, many did not want a separate nation and did not take his proposal seriously. No establishment of a separate nation for deaf people ever succeeded, although some made attempts.

Another important concept is that of the deaf community which is a group of people who are deaf that have common interests, similarities, and activities. These deaf communities vary and are not monolithic in character. Carol Padden (1980: 92) defined the deaf community as, "...a group of people who live in a particular location, share the common goals of its members, and in various ways, work toward achieving these goals." They have separate beliefs about themselves and larger society. According to Higgins (1980) there is also a moral dimension to the deaf community. Members experience a common sense of unity and identity. Their communication techniques and languages serve to bond them together into a community distinctly unique from the hearing world (Meadow, 1972). Membership in the deaf community is accomplished by identifying, sharing experiences, and participation (Higgins, 1980). Many people who were deaf have considered themselves united by their common language, experiences, traditions, and concerns for deaf organizations. Crittenden (1993:230) observed, "Those in the Deaf community accept themselves." Deafness is considered a natural condition and there is nothing wrong with being deaf.

Susan Foster (1989) found several reasons why the contemporary deaf community has developed, all of which are linked to either the concepts of alienation or peer identification. Her list of factors includes experiences the person has within the family, school, work, and community. Clearly the lack of communication, sense of isolation, as well as positive experiences associated with other people who are deaf fosters the creation and maintenance of the deaf community. When people who are deaf interact and socialize with others, typically whom they interact with are also deaf. As Foster (1989: 233) put it, "No one is born into the deaf community." Rather, they learn how to be members in the community. It should be noted that deaf communities have been documented in many western countries including the United States (Groce, 1985), France (Fischer and Lane, 1993; Karacostas, 1993), Russia (Abramov, 1993), German (Mally, 1993), and Denmark (Widell, 1993).

A reflection of deaf communities has been the many social events organized to reaffirm their purpose and value to members. People who were deaf over history have found it necessary to create and participate in social events to break down some of the isolation that they may feel living in a hearing society. "Social events," according to Mottez (1993:27) "are integral to deaf communities." Social events provide an opportunity for people to relax, converse, and develop a sense of social cohesion. In the nineteenth century Paris, grand banquets became customary social events among the deaf community. This wanting and needing to associate with other people who are deaf is sometimes referred to as attitudinal deafness. Attitudinal deafness is when individuals will seek associations with others whom they perceive as having similar values and attitudes.

The following print from the nineteenth century illustrates what is widely known by historians that many people who were deaf sought each other out and socialized. The illustration shows a cafe scene from Vienna. A number of adults who were deaf are shown socializing. The importance of the deaf community and human interaction is implied by the illustration.

It would be wrong to assume that people who are deaf always live in isolation or only with others who are deaf. In history some communities have fully integrated people who are deaf. A case on point can be found on Martha's Vineyard. For decades, Martha's Vineyard in New England had a sizable portion of deaf residents, dating back as early as the seventeenth century, Jonathan Lambert (1694) was the first Vineyard resident who was deaf. Historically, the attitude of hearing residents of the island was accepting and they paid little attention to deafness. The entire island developed a form of sign language and was able to communicate. It was a given and people, both hearing and deaf, worked and lived together in harmony (Groce, 1985). There were no social or economic barriers for people who were deaf to overcome on the island.

The hidden nature of deafness has contributed to the generation of misconceptions and myths regarding people who were deaf (Nash & Nash, 1981). The history of people who were deaf in western societies is pretty much an unknown prior to the 1500s. Until then, they received very little attention. Before the sixteenth century, people saw people who were deaf as being similar to young children. This perception would change in the sixteenth century as some scholars made efforts to educate students who were

Figure 32. Unknown Artist, *Austria–A Cafe for Deaf Mutes in Vienna*, Nineteenth Century, Gallaudet University Archives, Washington, DC.

deaf. The real shift occurred, however, in the eighteenth century when many special schools for students who were deaf were established.

Couched in misconceptions about deafness has been a number of enduring social perceptions and stereotypes. Two major paradigms that have shaped western perceptions of people who are deaf are what have been labeled the clinical and cultural views on deafness. The clinical view has dominated most of western history. In summary, the clinical view sees deafness as an unacceptable condition that needs to be addressed. Van Cleve and Crouch (1989:6) commented:

> To physicians in ancient and medieval western societies, and perhaps physicians today, the idea of a deaf community was absurd. To them, deafness was a malady, a physical condition that should be eliminated to allow the patient to live a healthy life. This required a cure, and physicians often prescribed solutions that they believed would be successful. One of these involved making loud noises next to the ears of the deaf individual. Despite the obvious failure of this method, it was tried repeatedly and written about in medical texts.

This perspective holds that deafness is a pathological condition that should be prevented or cured. Deafness is like a disease that requires a response. The intent of this perspective is to make deaf people function like a "typical" nondisabled hearing person. In the extreme, proponents of this view believed that members of the deaf culture are failures for their inability to adapt and integrate into the larger mainstream hearing society. It was based on the value that the hearing world has a strong preference for dealing and communicating with people who were able to speak. The hearing world has built institutions, has values, and attitudes that attempt to make people who were deaf as close to people who hear as they could.

In contrast, the cultural perspective did not view deafness as a disease or even necessarily a disability. Proponents did not view deafness as a pathological condition that needed to be cured or fixed. From this perspective, people were simply different and live in a world that has a bias toward oral language (Neisser, 1983). Proponents of this view observed that people who were deaf cause people who were not some social discomfort. Adherents to this view sometimes believe that people who were deaf preferred and should live with people who were also deaf in separate cultures. There have been periods when this cultural view of people who were deaf dominated. For most of the nineteenth century, people lived and flourished under a cultural-oriented model. They taught and were taught sign language, produced many deaf publications, and held meetings.

Certain social perceptions have been advanced regarding people who were deaf. One social perception has been that people who were deaf were lower in intelligence or "feeble-minded." This perception was based on the assumption that hearing and speech were critical elements to higher understanding and comprehension. Those lacking speech were historically assumed to be "dumb." For those who hear, the silence of those who were deaf has always carried meanings, such as that they were less intelligent and were less capable of understanding. Although over the centuries people accepted the notion that people who were deaf could be educated, it was not commonly thought that they were able to comprehend ideas and concepts as well as those who could hear. Speech was viewed as critical to knowledge and the lack of it has implied to many that the person simply did not have the ability to think and reason (Jackson, 1990). Because people have assumed they were incapable of sophisticated thought and reason, people who were deaf were perceived as being locked in a state of childhood, similar to those people who had developmental disabilities. Even experts who worked extensively with students who were deaf, such as Abbé Sicard, Itard, De Gérando, and Gallaudet saw and treated students who were deaf as being childlike.

The hearing world has historically viewed deafness as silent and thus empty. They see people who are deaf as lacking something in their lives. They view silence as leading to isolation. Many famous educators, such as Sicard and Itard, thought that people who were deaf lived in isolation. The author of a definitive nineteenth century text on deaf education, Baron de Gérando, characterized their lives as unattached, isolated, detached, fickle, and superficial (Lane, 1992). Another association the hearing make is that silence is a dark existence. The hearing associate silence with darkness. To be without sound, they assumed was to live in isolation and to be shut off from the world.

People who are deaf have been perceived as needing to be restricted. They have been historically, similar to people with leprosy or mental illness, been subjected to legal restrictions regarding their rights to be full members in their respective societies. History is full of examples of efforts to restrict them. For example, according to Gardner (1993), the Romans placed more restrictions on people who were deaf than those who were blind. Much of the focus on these early restrictions was on legal and religious rights of people (Moores, 1987). Efforts to restrict people surfaced in many legal documents over the centuries. For example, the *Code of Justinian*, written in the sixth century and influential during the Middle Ages, distinguished between people born deaf and those people who lost hearing after they had learned speech. Later in the same tradition, medieval law failed to grant the traditional rights of primogeniture (property inheritance) to oldest sons, if they were deaf (Silverman, 1978). However, the medieval church permitted them to marry.

Of course there were communities that fully integrated people who were deaf and granted them all rights and responsibilities of others. Saint-Loup (1993) observed that during the Middle Ages customs varied. For example, in Wales, Saint-Loup reported they lacked inheritance rights but in northern France they could make their own wills. Another variation was that for 250 years deaf and hearing residents of Martha's Vineyard lived in harmony with little difficulty and no special restrictions of people who were deaf (Groce, 1985). On Martha's Vineyard, legal rights applied to all people, regardless of auditory capability. There is little evidence that this was the rule and most societies restricted people who were deaf in one way or another.

The Audist (Oral) Versus Signing Debate

Many of the documents and records available today to focus on the enduring issue of how to best educate people who are deaf. This issue serves as a central theme that has shaped the written history of people who are deaf. It continues to be debated and has ramifications today. The audist versus signing debate on the education of deaf people has been intense for over 200 hundred years and has generated much controversy (Winefield, 1987). According to Turkington and Sussman (1992: 144), the crux of the debate has been, "...on the place in society in which a deaf person should fit."

The audist approach has traditionally opposed the segregation of people who were deaf from the hearing world. Audist methods emphasize the student's auditory skills in the areas of speech, speechreading, and residual hearing. The audist approach believes that almost all people process language auditorially. Audists believe that people who were deaf should live their lives similar to people who hear and contend that communication should occur through speech and speechreading. Audists believe that sign language limits deaf peoples' ability to integrate and communicate with the larger hearing world. Audists believe that reliance on sign language isolates and segregates deaf people from a speaking and hearing world. Audists focus on lipreading and teaching people to speak. The desire of audists is to help students obtain a level of communication skills that allow them to fully integrate with the hearing society.

The audist approach gained significant political ground at the close of the nineteenth century. The approach found a ready ally in the theory of evolution. The connection between Darwin's theory of evolution and the audist movement was well established by the end of the nineteenth century (Baynton, 1993; Widell, 1993). The Social Darwinists considered sign language to be at a lower stage of human evolution that was eventually abandoned for a higher stage of spoken language. Sign language became associated with animalistic forms of communication and hence more "primitive." Some educators proposed that only through the use of oral language could people move up the evolutionary scale.

The opponents to the audist approach argued that maintaining a deaf culture and means of communication were important. Those arguing in favor of signing believe that it is the only method by which deaf people could truly communicate. Signing has been around and used for communication since the beginning of history. For example, the ancient Greeks noted that some people used signing to communicate. Later, Saint Jerome in the fifth century, argued that people could gain faith through the use of signs. Historical evidence indicates that forms of sign language was used in the late Middle Ages (Neisser, 1990). Groce (1985) noted that examples and references of sign language used among deaf people can be found in medieval works. Before the 1500s, there are reports of deaf children of wealthy Spanish being taught to communicate (Stroman, 1982). Fischer and Lane (1993) found an early thirteenth century gesture of a man executing a hand sign possibly meaning to keep away evil in a tympanum of the Portal of the Princes in Bamburg, Germany. Over 300 hundred years later, King James I of England tried to establish signing as a professorship in the 1630s. Samuel Pepys described sign language in 1666. Sir Edward Gostwicke (1620-1671) was a fluent user of sign language (Jackson, 1990). Proponents of signing have argued that audist education interferes with learning by deaf children, as it is stressful and requires too much effort compared with signing. Sign language proponents believe that many people could not learn to speak or speechread well enough to rely on either for communication.. Proponents argue that signing is a more natural language for people who are deaf.

Efforts to restrict the educational rights of people who were deaf are scattered throughout history. Two of the most dramatic were the shift from signing to audist instruction fueled by the Paris Exposition of 1878 and Milan Conference in 1880. These events had a dramatic effect on schools, teaching, and ultimately students who were deaf. They were a concerted effort to restrict how people were instructed and how they should communicate. The Milan Conference outlawed sign language, the preferred method of communication for many people who were deaf, in preference to orally based communication and educational techniques. In the decades that followed signing was repressed or at least discouraged. The magnitude of this change was massive. Lane (1992:113) commented, "In America, there were 26 institutions for the education of deaf children in 1867, and ASL was the language of instruction in all; by 1907, there were 139 schools for deaf children, and ASL was allowed in none."

EXPLANATIONS FOR DEAFNESS

Public and medical explanations for why some people are deaf have spanned a wide spectrum. Ancient societies frequently mention divine will as a cause of deafness. Others have taken a secular slant and have suggested maternal fright caused deafness. This view attributed deafness to the experiences and fears of pregnant women. The belief was that any pregnant woman who would come into contact with a deaf person and might become fearful that her unborn child would be born deaf. Her material fright at this prospect would result in her giving birth to the very thing she feared, a deaf child. In the sixteenth century, scholars began to formally recognize the connection between heredity and deafness. Werner (1932) identified the sixteenth century German physician Johannes Schenk as being the first researcher to make reference to familial deafness. Authorities on deafness also credit Felix Platter (1530-1614) as making the first reference to hereditary as a factor in deafness (Moores, 1987). With little doubt, people were well aware of the relationship between certain families and deafness long before the topic received scientific attention. Although they were unaware of the role of heredity as we know it today, they realized that some families were more likely than others to give birth to children who were deaf.

Today, we know that most people who are able to hear at birth gradually lose some of their hearing as they age, particularly when they become very old. Deafness can be caused by a number of factors, such as disease, sickness, aging, genetics, and the quality of health care. In 1980, researchers had identified over 150 genetic causes for deafness (Moores, 1987). Common causes include cytomegalovirus (CMV) infection, meningitis, mother-child blood incompatibility, and premature birth. Deafness and hearing impairments also can be caused by goiter, severe cases of mumps, encephalitis, pneumonia, influenza, pertussis, whooping cough, scarlet fever, staph infections, and maternal rubella (German Measles). Congenital causes can also cause deafness, such as Rh Factor, endocrine disorders, retinitis pigmentosa, and albinism. Injury and trauma, such as anoxia, also may lead to deafness.

It is quite possible that acquired deafness was more common in the past than it is today. A variety of diseases and illnesses contributed to the numbers of hearing impaired. In the past mumps, measles, meningitis, scarlet fever, smallpox, and other ailments led to hearing impairments. The situation found in nineteenth century France might serve as a useful backdrop on the extent of deafness in prior times. Mirzoeff (1992) noted, so numerous were the hearing impaired artists in the eighteenth century, they established a deaf quarter in Paris. By the mid-1880s, the population of France was estimated to be about 37 million of whom 25,000 were identified as being deaf

(Lane, 1984a; Quartararo, 1993). The introduction of antibiotics has greatly reduced the frequency of deafness resulting from illness, such as meningitis and scarlet fever. It is also true that increased mobility of populations may have decreased the frequency of deafness due to inbreeding.

PEOPLE WHO WERE DEAF IN ANTIQUITY

Evidence shows that ancient societies made special provisions for people who were deaf. As noted previously, the ancient *Babylonian Codes of Hammurabi* contain some of the earliest known references to deafness. The *Code* placed social restrictions of children born deaf (Groce, 1985). The ancient Hebrews, Egyptians, and Persians allowed deaf children to live but did very little for them other than restrict their rights. The Egyptians tolerated and were concerned with people with disabilities, including those who were deaf. They were the first to document their interest in people with disabilities. They, unlike many of their contemporaries, forbade infanticide of children with disabilities by decree. The Egyptians were greatly interested in causes and cures, such as ointments, lotions and the well-being of individuals (Moores, 1987).

The ancient Jewish *Talmud* did not allow people who were deaf to own property, since legally they were considered to have the same status as children. The Jewish *Talmud's* story of Herodotus' tale of the deaf son of Croesus, the King of Lydia, represents an early writing about people who were deaf. In Jewish rabbinical law, people who were deaf were classified with people of lower intelligence and minors (Deshen, 1992). People saw them as unresponsive to treatment and instruction. Other ancient Hebrew texts, such as the *Mosaic Code of Holiness*, referred to their limited rights. The Hebrews also enacted laws to excuse deaf-mute people from responsibility for their actions. These laws distinguished between different levels of hearing impairments. Property rights varied and people not hearing and speaking totally lacked all property rights (Hand, 1980).

Hebrew laws classified people who were deaf and/or speechless with people with mental disabilities and children under the assumption they could not assume "normal" adult responsibility for their actions. The laws instructed that they were not complete witnesses in legal matters. Under the laws, marriage of people who were deaf and speechless was not considered valid, but in practice rabbis sanctioned these marriages (Bender, 1970). Overall, the Jewish tradition treated people who were deaf with ambivalence (Di Carlo, 1964; Mann, 1983) in that they were seen as helpless but worthy of help and charity. However, full agreement on their legal and social status in ancient Jewish societies does not exist. Specifically, Zwiebel (1993) provides evidence that some who were deaf were able to attain high positions within Jewish society. In addition, some of the social positions Zwiebel was able to identify required systematic deaf education, inferring that people who were deaf were seen as being capable of learning and having meaningful participation in society.

The Greeks also thought and wrote about people who were deaf. The writings of some of the great Greek philosophers shed light on how people who were deaf were perceived. Aristotle (384 - 324 BC) and later Pliny the Elder (23/4-79 AD) connected congenital disorders with deafness and the lack of speech. Aristotle placed emphasis on sound (speech) as the primary vehicle for transferring thought. He linked the concept of deafness with dumbness, the latter meaning to him a person without speech. He believed dumbness was the result of deafness. Unfortunately, dumbness would come to mean the lack of intelligence and would be used negatively to stigmatize people who were deaf for the centuries that followed.

Aristotle also forwarded the misconception that symbols had to be auditory for understanding. Aristotle viewed speech as the key to human education and knowledge. If hearing was absent, he argued learning was impossible. This basic assumption would have lasting impact on people who were deaf than any other idea in the following centuries. It served as a rationale for repressing attempts to teach them because they were viewed as not being capable of understanding. This misconception would survive until it was seriously questioned in the seventeenth century and reluctantly surrendered during the nineteenth century. Today scholars agree that Aristotle was taken out of context. In a similar vein, Lucretius (c. 99-55 BC) stated, "To instruct the deaf no art could ever reach. No care improve them and no wisdom teach." Deland (1968:7) concluded that Lucretius was referring to people who chose not to hear rather than people who were deaf. About the same time this and other proclamations and observations about the abilities of people were being made. Socrates (469-399 BC) observed that they were able to communicate through gestures and signs. The Greeks even developed a system of manual numeration and later the Romans used finger spelling to communicate. Plato (429-347) wrote about his observations of people using sign language. Ironically, some Greek scholars seem to have stressed the inabilities of those who were deaf to communicate and learn while at the same time they observed people using sign languages and gestures to communicate.

Ancient Roman literature sheds little light on how people who were deaf lived (Radutsky, 1993). It is known that the Romans inherited from Greek philosophy the notion that thought occurred only through the articulated word and that the ability to speak was instinctive rather than acquired. The

Romans did not consider deafness separate from mutism, thus all people who were deaf were incapable of being educated or capable of speech. Radutsky (1993) found that ancient Roman law classified people who were deaf as *mentecatti furiosi* or raving maniacs who were uneducable.

Whereas the ancient Greeks focused on change and new ideas, the Romans were law makers and much of what we know about their perception of people who were deaf is represented in their laws and regulations. Some authorities have suggested that they had few rights under Roman law (Bender, 1970), but this is not the case. The Romans lumped them with people with mental illness and treated them as having the same rights as the insane (Silverman, 1978). They could not own property, make contracts or wills, and had a few legal rights and obligations. Romans who were deaf and speechless could not make but could be benefactors of legal wills. However, if they had acquired speech before becoming deaf, they maintained some of their rights (Stroman, 1982).

Historians have uncovered evidence that the Greeks and Romans exposed weak and deformed infants to die. It has been said that the ancient Romans put infants with disabilities, such as deafness, to death upon committee review. Bender (1970) has questioned whether the Romans actually killed children who were deaf. The diagnosis of deafness at birth would have been difficult if not impossible, so it is likely that they waited until the child was at least three years old before acting. The Greeks may not have destroyed children, as some authorities have proposed (Moores, 1987). Nevertheless, some may have been killed which necessitated the creation of laws to protect them. For example, the legendary founder of Rome, Romulus forbade the destruction of children with deafness under age three, which was the cultural practice according to the writings of Dionysius (Bender, 1970).

The Romans essentially viewed people who were deaf and especially those who became deaf after they had learned to speak, as being limited. For example, the famous physician Galen assumed that they had very little native ability (Bernard, 1993). This belief, coupled with others, fueled the creation of the set of laws that distinguished them from other Roman citizens. Roman law, similar to other ancient laws, attempted to restrict the rights of people who were deaf. The Roman scholar Ulpian provided a legal rationale for restricting rights when he wrote:

> A dumb man, a deaf, someone mad, someone whose goods are retrained by court order (se. a prodigious, spendthrift), cannot make a will. The dumb man cannot, because he cannot utter the words of the nuncupation; the deaf man, because he cannot hear the words of the familiae emptor (nominal buyer of the estate). [Cited by Gardner, 1993: 160]

Deafness disqualified people from becoming judges in ancient Roman law. Legal references to the appointment of curators for deaf and dumb persons suggest their deafness was regarded as a more serious disability for handling their affairs than blindness (Gardner, 1993: 161). Under Roman law they were given a curator to look after their affairs. Under Roman law people born deaf remained covered by legal guardianship for their entire lives (Bernard, 1993).

The Christian tradition has played a major role in shaping the history of people who were deaf. Biblical references to people who were deaf are present in Old and New Testaments. For example the Old Testament Books of Exodus, Leviticus, Psalms, Isaiah, and Micah refer to deafness. Exodus 4:2 states, "Who hath man man's mouth? or who maketh man dumb, or deaf, or seeing, or blind? Is it not I the Lord?" This passage is one of the first known formal references to people who were deaf in western society. The New Testament books of Matthew, Mark, and Luke also refer to deafness.

A central theme in the Christian tradition has been the role of speech in the creation of humans. Saint-Loup (1993) found that within this tradition, when God created Adam, he blew his spirit into him through divine breath or symbolically the gift of speech. Only humans were provided the gift of speech which separates them from other animals. Numerous medieval Christian illustrations and works of art depict this belief, such as illustrations based on the themes that God's word is to be devoured and God's word is made flesh. Saint-Loup noted that there were other links between speech and hearing in the Christian tradition. For example, it was believed that the immaculate conception occurred via God's word to Mary's ear.

During the early Christian periods leading to the Middle Ages, there is little mention of an educated person who was born deaf. Many believed the Christian church held out no hope for people who were deaf. The Apostle Paul wrote, "Faith cometh by hearing." Many Christians believed that people who were deaf could not be taught the Christian faith (Plann, 1993). Later, during the medieval period, people who were deaf, with a few exceptions, were not allowed by the church to confess their sins (Moores, 1987). Relying on Aristotelian philosophy, Saint Augustine (354-430 AD) believed the church could only comfort people who were deaf, as they had no means to learn about God and acquire faith. Saint Augustine thought that deaf people were not endowed with knowledge and believed that no attempts should be made to educate them, as they could not learn. They were lost souls. Saint Augustine wrote that faith was not possible for people who were deaf because they could not learn faith without spoken language. He has been given credit for the cannon law that excluded them from the privilege of Mass. However, contemporary scholars have questioned whether Saint Augustine was misinterpreted. They believe he did not imply that people who were deaf were denied immortality (Moores, 1987). According to Deland (1968:6), "This law prevailed during the Middle Ages, because it was considered necessary that the words of the Consecration of the Eucharist be pronounced in order that the transubstantiation be affected, but St. Augustine had nothing to do with it." Other early Christian leaders argued that people who were deaf could understand. Some early Christian scholars, such as the fifth century influential Saint Jerome, argued people who were deaf could understand Christianity through the use of signs (Saint-Loup, 1993).

The Emperor Justinian (527-565 AD) protected people with deafness but also placed restrictions on them. The *Code* classified people who were deaf in great detail and grouped them with "idiots." The traditional practice of distinguishing among different degrees of deafness continued in *Justinian's Code*. According to the *Code*, the more severe the degree of deafness and capacity for speech, the more restricted were the rights of the individual. Those people who had become deaf after acquiring speech had more rights than those born deaf. *Justinian's Code* recognized different forms of deafness by making a general distinction between mutism and deafness. People who could write had legal rights and those who could not did not. Under the *Code*, society did not permit them to make wills or become legal guardians (Deland, 1968). Under the code, Byzantine authorities appointed guardians who had complete control over their affairs. Werner (1932) found that individuals with deafness were numerous in the Byzantine army. Werner reported that the *Justinian Code* contained special conditions for the testaments of soldiers who were deaf. However, the traditional assumption that they could not learn continued. For example, it was never assumed that a person born deaf would ever become literate. Byzantine records contain no references to efforts to educate them. Although some had their rights restricted, they lead fairly normal lives in Byzantine society.

PEOPLE WHO WERE DEAF DURING THE MIDDLE AGES

If antiquity was characterized by benign neglect or restriction of people who were deaf, during the Middle Ages conditions worsened. They were probably numerous, given many of the medical problems present during the era but scant attention was paid to them. Saint-Loup (1993) concluded that deafness was seldom dealt with in medieval references. When people who were deaf were addressed, Saint-Loup noted they were portrayed in two ways, as living on the fringes of society. They were viewed as social outcasts and linked with others such as beggars, thieves, unemployed mercenaries, and invalids. In the second group they were seen as needy children.

Little medieval attention was paid to people who were deaf other than to restrict their rights. Medieval societies made little to no effort to help improve their lives or educate them. Keeping with tradition, most medieval citizens believed that people who were deaf could not be educated. The old assumption that hearing was crucial to knowledge and learning persisted in the Middle Ages. People also assumed that people who were deaf were mentally deficient and treated them as if they were so. During this era they were generally classified with people having developmental disabilities and those judged to be insane. The history of people who were deaf is the story of escape from this classification.

Much of what we can gather about their lives in the Middle Ages is reduced to the laws established to restrict or protect them. The ability to speak continued to have significance to people. Legally, speech was the line of demarcation between people having rights and those lacking rights (Lane, 1984). For example, authorities did not permit people who were deaf to marry until the 12th century. Radutsky (1993:239) succinctly summarized the medieval social context:

> When the German barbarians overthrew Rome severe civil and religious restrictions were imposed on deaf people. Feudalism cast them aside because their deafness prevented them from military service, the prime concern of the feudal lords. They were deprived of their rights of inheritance, rights to celebrate mass, and even the right of many without special papal dispensation. Despite these restrictions, however, they were not ignored. There was frequently lively discussion over whether deaf people could discern right from wrong and thus be tried for crimes, whether they should be allowed to be godfathers, become monks, and even if they could be subject to torture.

The English monk and historian, the Venerable Bede (672-735), wrote about an early medieval attempt to help a person who was deaf in his *Ecclesiastical History of England*. In this book, Bede told of St. John of Beverley, the Archbishop of York (d. 721), who allegedly was successful in teaching a youth who was deaf to speak (Siraisi, 1990). Bede's account does not refer to deafness but historians have generally assumed that the individual was deaf. Bede's account mentions only the recovery of speech, suggesting a case of aphasia rather than deafness (Pritchard, 1963). Regardless of the accuracy of Bede's description, people took the notion of educating people who were deaf at face value over the next centuries. The story of St. John of Beverley's supported the idea that people who were deaf could be educated.

Medieval treatments and cures for deafness ran the gamut of medieval folk and medical practices. Cures for deafness included the widespread belief that saints could heal deafness or mutism by touch or sight. Numerous accounts of saints touching people's tongues to cure deafness were common. Church officials also used holy relics to cure deafness and raise funds (Saint-Loup, 1993). The efforts of the church parallel the competing but compatible belief that members of royal families, specifically kings, could cure by royal touch. Another medieval theory proposed that the mouth was linked to the Eustachian tube, which in fact it is, and that by shouting into the mouths of people, their deafness could be cured (Radutsky, 1993).

Medical illustrations of deafness and its treatment before the fourteenth century are rare (Saint-Loup, 1993), but some texts contain references to deafness and the ear. For example, the Arabic physician Avicenna's (987-1037) *Canon,* which was translated in the thirteenth century, has an illustration of a doctor explaining the functioning of the ears. Saint-Loup's (1993) review of medieval art found themes that shed light on how people who were deaf were viewed. One fourteenth century medical text shows a man shouting at another who is deaf. The assumption the artist is making fun at is that shouting somehow helps the man hear. The drawing shows the lack of sensitivity to the person's deafness.

Middle eastern and European doctors attributed deafness to a number of causes that fell under the category of obstruction. Medieval physicians believed obstructions were caused by traumas, parasites, food, unstable fluids, age, and a number of other causes. For example, some suggested that worms resided in the person's ear and could be enticed to crawl out by fruit. Many medieval authorities also believed speechlessness was due to some obstruction that kept the person from communicating. Doctors believed if this obstruction could be removed, speech could be restored. Treatments were varied and were virtually the same as those used to cure illness and disease. Doctors and surgeons used surgery, drainage, purgatives, bloodletting, plasters, potions, and musical therapy to treat people. Religious interventions also were available to believers. St. Claire (1194-1253) and Saint Elizabeth worked with people who were deaf. The latter saint reportedly healed several people. Probably one of the most renowned practitioners was Saint Hildegard of Bingen. Lynn Thorndike (1923, Vol II: 145-146), provided insight into how this noted medieval scholar treated deafness. According to Saint Hildegard, "...deafness may be remedied by cutting off a lion's right ear and holding it over the patient's ear just long enough to say, "Hear, adimacus, by the living God and the keen virtue of a lion's hearing." She also suggested the heart of a weasel, dried and placed with wax in the ear, benefited headache or deafness.

212   *Social Perceptions of People with Disabilities*

The following illustration from the *Prayer Book of Hildegard of Bingen* from the late twelfth century shows a popular belief that Christ miraculously could heal people who were deaf, typically through sight or touch (Mark 7:31). The event was more than the miraculous curing of deafness, it was also the story of the symbolic conversion to Christianity. In many, including the fol-

Figure 33. Unknown Artist, Illustration from the *Prayer Book of Hildegard of Bingen*, late twelfth century, Bayerische Staatsbibliothek, Munich.

lowing depictions, the subject being healed is shown at the moment of conversion. For some Christians, implied was the notion that people who were deaf to the word of Christ (including those of the Jewish faith) could be converted into Christians. Saint-Loup (1993:394) made several insightful observations about this illustration, such as Christ and the subject are alone and their relationship is intimate. Another observation was that the man was not belittled, as was often the case of nonbelievers. Third, the healing process was accomplished more through sight than touch. In addition, Christ touches the man's mouth while the subject points to his ear. The caption for this illustration reads, "Spirit, from this possessed deaf and dumb man, be gone." Other illustrations of the miraculous healing include illustrations from the ninth century Münster church and a fourteenth century English Bible found at the Bodleian Library and described by Saint-Loup (1993) as well as the artist Thomas Davidson's (1842-1910) nineteenth century *Ephphatha*.

As medieval Christianity developed, opportunities for increased participation by people who were deaf increased. Gradually, the church opened new avenues for their involvement. Saint-Loup (1993) summarized they were able to be baptized in the fifth century, married in the eleventh, give penance in the thirteen, and take monastic vows in the sixteenth centuries. In should be noted that in the Jewish tradition, they had these same opportunities much earlier in history, such as the right to marriage (Zwiebel, 1993).

The Renaissance brought about a new dignity to humanity. The increased availability of printed materials sparked an interest in educating people. Eventually, educating people who were deaf became of great interest. The Renaissance introduced many fresh ideas about the education of people who were deaf. Bernard (1993) concluded that during the Renaissance new philosophical and cultural streams favorable to people who were deaf developed. Rudolph Agricola (1443-1485) and Jerome Cardan or Girolamo Cardano (1501-1576) challenged traditional assumptions about people's abilities to learn. Rudolf Agricola, in his *De Inventione Dialectia* (1521), provided a foundation for deaf education that many educators used over the centuries. Cardan concluded that people without hearing and speech could learn to write and read. He believed they could be taught to write once they learned to attach significance to words. Cardan thought it was important for them to learn to read and write. Although he wrote extensively on the subject, he never attempted to instruct students who were deaf.

The Renaissance artist, Leonardo da Vinci (1452-1519) observed that some deaf and speechless people could understand conversations of others by watching their lips. He wrote, "I once saw in Florence a man who had become deaf, who could not understand you if you spoke to him loudly, while if you spoke softly without letting the voice utter any sound he understood you merely from the movement of the lips" (Di Carlo, 1964 14). The subtleties of manual communication present in Renaissance Italy among people who were deaf were not lost on Leonardo da Vinci. He recommended to artists:

> By copying the motions of the deaf and dumb, who speak with movements of their hands and eyes and eyebrows and their whole person, in their desire to express that which is in their minds. Do not laugh at me because I proposed a teacher without speech to you, for he will teach you better through facts than will all other masters through words. [Cited by Mirzoeff, 1992]

The great Renaissance artist Raphaël painted a portrait of a woman who was deaf and speechless. The popular assumption of the time was that speech was strongly associated with intelligence. Raphaël's painting, executed in 1506, shows a well-dressed and dignified woman. Without knowing the title of the work, the viewer would not be aware that she was deaf. Her emotional stance is somber and her individuality is obvious. She was not an icon or symbol but a person with a characteristic.

PEOPLE WHO WERE DEAF DURING MODERN TIMES

At the close of the Middle Ages, the possibility of people who were deaf being able to learn and understand became difficult for traditionalists to deny. The door had been set ajar and time was ripe for change. The sixteenth century witnessed increasing number of authorities believing that people who were deaf could be educated. The sixteenth century ushered in many formal attempts to educate people who were deaf. It was during the sixteenth century that scholars first realized that speech was not instinctual but learned. Scholars concluded that people who were deaf did not acquire speech because they could not hear the spoken language around them (Savage, Evans, & Savage, 1981).

In addition to changes in attitude toward educating people, sixteenth century advancements in science led to better understanding of the ear and sense of hearing. Bartolomeo Eustachi (1512-1574) was the first to describe the Eustachian tubes. Felix Platter (1536-1614), a Swiss physician interested in deafness, illustrated the human body. He provided a description of the functions of the bones of the ear and how they conducted sound. He concluded that deafness caused by the brain was incurable. Mirzoeff (1992: 210) noted:

Figure 34. Raphaël, *The Dumb Woman,* 1506, National Gallery of Urbino.

Indeed, as modern medicine developed, deafness came to be seen less as a fascinating problem—how could one know the world with only four senses and what kind of world was thereby known?—than as a medical condition requiring treatment. Previously, such conditions as blindness, deafness and madness were taken to be afflictions sent by God for which there could be no cure, except by miraculous intervention. But as doctors increasingly came to think of the body as a machine, these problems came to be seen as defects to be rectified.

Spain was first to develop formally organized systems for educating people who were deaf. A Benedictine monk named Pedro Ponce de León (1520-1584) was the first well-documented educator of deaf students (Di Carlo; 1964; Winefield, 1987). Benedictine monasteries were noted for their silence during services, while reading holy texts, meals, and at bedtime. To communicate, monks relied on a system of discreet gestures and signs (Presneau, 1993). Pedro Ponce de León believed that people who were deaf could be instructed at a time when few held any hope that they could learn. Often, scholars trace the audist approach to educating people to de León but others have argued that he may have used signs (Plann, 1993).

De León started instructing deaf people when the church prohibited a deaf person from becoming a monk. Upset with this restriction, he proceeded to teach the individual to speak so that he could eventually join the monastery. De León went on to teach wealthy members of the Spanish court. For example, Francisco and Pedro de Valaseo, were deaf brothers who hired de vto teach them to read, write, and speak. Deafness was common among the nobility and aristocracy and wealthy of Spain. Wealthy families had the resources to hire tutors to educate their deaf offspring. It was important for noble Spanish families to teach their children to speak and read, so that they would gain their rights under the law. Spanish society did not recognize people unable to speak and they had no rights to property, titles, or wealth (Sacks, 1989). Restrictions on people also extended to the church. The one exception being when in 1604 St. Francis de Sales was the first to admit a person who was deaf and without speech to communion (Deland, 1968).

De León's work helped convince doubting minds that deaf people could learn, an idea that was not fully accepted. In his time many people clung to Aristotle's belief that they could not learn and with few exceptions, society thought people who were deaf were hopeless. Later de León's works would influence Juan Pablo Bonet who successfully taught the deaf brother of his patron, the Constable of Castile. Juan Bonet wrote the first book on the instruction of people who were deaf in 1620. His *The Reduction of Letters and the Art of Teaching the Mute to Speak* contains ideas that were progressive, even by today's standards, as he argued for early intervention and the importance of building communications and language skills. Scholars consider this work to be the first published description of a systematic method for educating people who were deaf. Juan Pablo Bonet described a one-handed finger spelling method and refined methods of instructing the deaf developed by de León.

In the sixteenth and seventeenth centuries few benefited from early deaf education because of the high cost of instruction and the lack of instructors. It would be much later before authorities would make deaf education available to the general public on a limited basis. From the 1600s to 1755, educators used combinations of signing and oral communication to instruct people who were deaf (Winefield, 1987). Francis Bacon (1561-1626) and John Locke (1632-1704) provided the philosophical foundation for education (Di Carlo, 1964). John Locke's and Francis Bacon's ideas led to viewing students who were deaf as capable of learning and being taught. By the mid-seventeenth century scientists and medical experts increasingly believed that they were capable of learning but no consensus was reached. Education of people who were deaf in the seventeenth century was more of an intellectual and philosophical curiosity than social expectation or obligation. During the seventeenth century, other educators advanced ideas on how to educate people who were deaf. Giovanni Bonifacio (1616) *L' Arte de Cenni* (Art of Signs), John Wallis' (1669) *Elements of Speech*, and Johann Conrad Amman's (1692) *Surdus Loquens* outlined different methods of deaf instruction.

During this period, John Bulwer wrote an early book on using sign language titled *Chirologia: The Art of Manual Rhetoric, The Natural Language of the Hand* (1644-1648). In 1648, he also published *Philosophus: or the Deafe and Dumbe Man's Friend*. In this work, he proposed that a special school to teach people who were deaf be established. By substituting one sense for another, Bulwer believed it was possible for them to learn lipreading and speech. He preferred using signs and manual alphabets as ways to communicate. He thought it was possible to teach people who were deaf and speechless to learn speechreading and speech. He also thought that sign language might be more practical (Turkington & Sussman, 1992). He noted that people who were deaf were looked down by others and were perceived as being little better than "dumbe animals" (Bulwer, 1648: 102).

Sign language methods of communication were clearly used by people, whether formally educated or not during the sixteenth and seventeenth centuries. The need of people to communicate, no matter the method, has always been strong and present. Authors made references to the use of sign language and methods of communicating in communities. For example, in a survey of Cornwall, England written in 1602, reference is made to sign language use:

> He was deaf from his cradle, and consequently dumb, (Nature cannot give out what it hath not received) yet could learn and express to his master any news that was stirring in the country. ...There was one Kemp, not living far off, defected accordingly; on whose meetings there were such embracements, such strange, often earnest tokenings and such hearty laughters and

other passionate gestures, that their want of a tongue seemed rather a hindrance to others conceiving them, than to their conceiving one another. [Cited by Groce, 1985:72]

Following Bulwer, the educator Johann Konrad Amman in 1669, proposed audist techniques as methods of instruction. Other educators during the same period argued for alternative approaches, such as Dalgarno (1680) who outlined training strategies for mothers to teach young children in the home in his *Didascalocophus* or *Deaf-Mute's Preceptor*. He assumed that people who were deaf could more easily learn to read than those who were blind. He suggested a very contemporary-sounding idea that mothers use finger spelling on young children in the cradle. The following late sixteenth century painting by the Flemish painter Jacob de Gheyn (1556-1629) is a presentation of a youth who was deaf and his teacher. The painting shows the use of the two-handed alphabet by the instructor. The painting draws the observer into the work by emphasizing the effort to communicate by the two fingers.

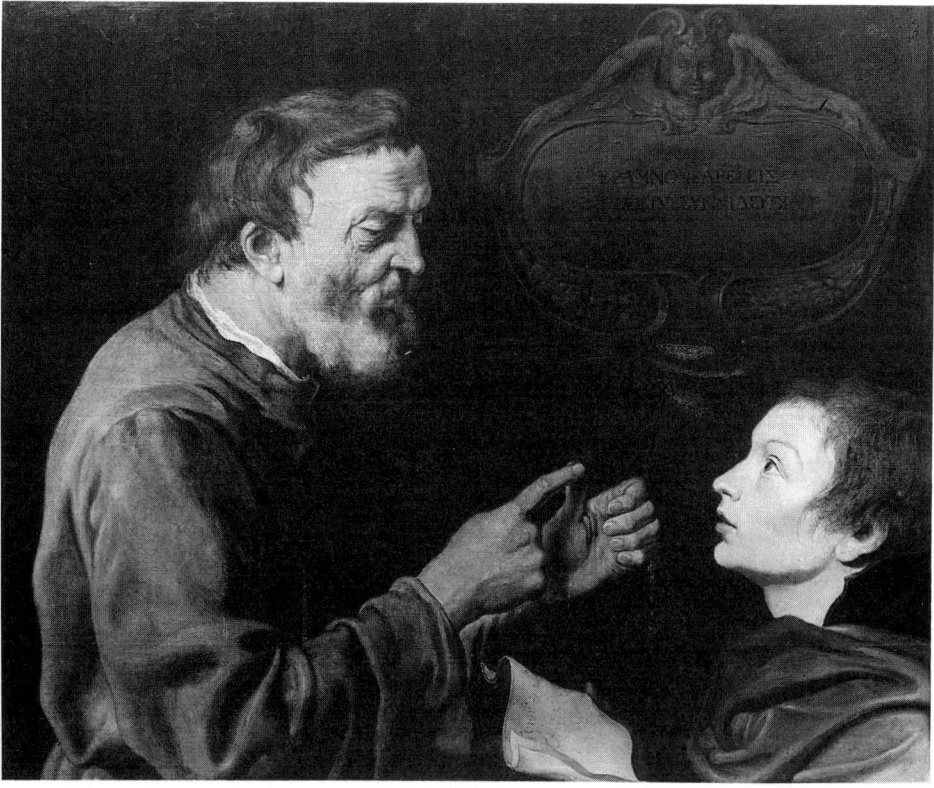

Figure 35. Jacob de Gheyn, *Master and Pupil,* 1599, Manchester City Art Galleries, Manchester, England.

The eighteenth century Enlightenment sparked even more curiosity about the individual and the workings of the human mind. This was a time of enormous intellectual inquiry, global exploration, and general excitement. Pinel had just written his book on psychiatric diagnosis and Jenner found that people could be protected from disease. It was the exciting period just before the French Revolution and the social climate was ripe for the development of sign languages in Europe and particularly France. People were generally open to new ideas and it was within this context, deaf education became more readily available to the general public. However, in spite of advances in understanding and increased social tolerance, people who were deaf continued to be looked upon with suspicion and their sign languages puzzled scholars. Presneau (1993) concluded the upper classes did not appreciate sign languages and considered those who used them as savages and sign language as uncivilized. Presneau (1993:414) summarized:

> For cultured people, a Deaf person was a peculiar, incomprehensible human being. He lives like an animal or a machine, wrote Fontenelle (1703), a member of the Royal Academy of Sciences; he is like a child, replied the empiricist philosopher Condillac (1746). The deaf persons' minds were considered primitive, particularly dependent on the senses of sight or touch. They did not seem to have abstract ideas. A Deaf person was often considered a falsifier.

Yet, people who were deaf made great progress during the eighteenth century, as the social context shifted to one of more tolerance and understanding. Although European scholars, such as the influential French philosopher Condillac, had not fully accepted the notion that people who were deaf could learn, schools for children with deafness began to emerge in Paris, Leipez, and Edinburgh in the 1760s and 1770s. One milestone of the progress made was at the close of the eighteenth century, when the Frenchman Pierre Desloges, himself deaf wrote the first book by a author who was deaf entitled *Elementary Course of Education for Deaf Mutes* in 1779.

According to Sacks (1989), before 1750, for almost all people born deaf, there was no hope for literacy or getting a formal education. All of this would eventually change during the mid-eighteenth century with the notion that people who were deaf were capable of learning and communicating (Sacks, 1989). Children who were deaf were increasingly educated in monasteries and convents, which kept them out of sight during much of the eighteenth century (Presneau, 1993). By the late eighteenth century, officials began to implement national systems for educating people. In making the shift, deaf education became more visible and public than it had been in the past when it was conducted often in the confines of monasteries or convents.

Most famous of all deaf educators during this period of growth were the French Abbe Charles Michel l' Epée (1712-1789) and Abbe Roch-Ambroise Sicard (1742-1822).

Before l' Epée, people who were deaf were denied their rights as citizens, such as the opportunity to attend public schools (Lane, 1977). Parents typically hid, abandoned, or institutionalized their children who were deaf. Some of the more fortunate children were sent to trade schools but faced lives of ridicule and fear. All of this would change, thanks to the efforts of Abbe de L' Epée. While moving about the streets of eighteenth century Paris, the Abbe de L' Epée observed people using a form of sign language they had developed (Di Carlo, 1964). He used these observations of street life into practice. L' Epée also established the first public school for deaf children in Paris in 1755. The school was the first to receive public financial support. Years later, in 1776, he published a book on his instructional techniques titled, *Instruction of Deaf Mutes by Means of Methodological Signs*, which was the first distinct book on sign language. L' Epée also developed a manual alphabet as a teaching tool and published his text *La Veritable Maniere* in 1784. Abbe de l' Epée proposed that rules of grammar be added to signing to form a language. L' Epée believed that the language of signs was the natural language for people who were deaf. He adopted the sign language and took it a step further by adding his own cumbersome system that hampered as much as helped students who were deaf (Lane, 1977). L' Epée wanted to teach the deaf to communicate so that they could take their religious vows. He taught speech and lipreading but did not emphasize either and focused on signing.

L' Epée's work and teaching innovations occurred in a social context of ignorance, disbelief, and wonderment (Lane, 1984b). This was a time when there was a strong belief that the environment caused mental retardation. If mental retardation was caused by the environment, then a cure was possible. In a similar vein, if deafness was environmental, it also could be cured (Vernon & Wallrabenstein, 1988). Abbe de l' Epée would capitalize on this context by staging public presentations of successful students. He used public displays to enlighten society on the possibilities of deaf education. He staged these displays to build public support, financial and otherwise, for his school. Both Epée and later Sicard had prize students demonstrate their learning accomplishments across Europe. They held the shows to demonstrate what could be accomplished with the students. Many notables of the time attended these presentations , such as Catherine the Great of Russia, Marie-Antoinette of France, and Joseph the II of Austria who were impressed (Mirzoeff, 1992). What was not evident to the audiences was often Epée's students were simply copying his signs without any comprehension or understanding. Epée simply gave students signs without meanings and thought he had completed his work (Lane, 1977). Vernon and Wallrabenstein (1988:21) commenting on the Abbe wrote:

> The Abbe de l' Epée would then give performances for the public in which he would dictate in his "methodical" sign language and have his students copy in written French what he had signed. The public was duly impressed and Abbe de l' Epée became famous. No one realized that the deaf children on display had no concept of the meaning of the French that they had written than does the parrot which repeats the obscenities of the sailor who owns him. Although the Abbe de l' Epée knew that what he was doing was a tour de force, he kept this to himself and enjoyed his new found fame and income.

The De l' Epée legacy, according to Lane (1977), was the formation of the deaf community and the calling of attention to that community. Prior to his efforts, people who were deaf were on their own and had little support from the public. His establishment of the school brought together sufficient numbers of students to form a visible and critical mass. Through his campaigning on their behalf and perhaps to some degree his own benefit, people who were deaf became more visible to a larger segment of society. Following his

Figure 36. Unknown Artist, Abbe Epée, Date Unknown, Institut National de Jeunes Sourds de Paris, Paris, France.

efforts, schools for children who were deaf were opened throughout Europe. These schools would eventually play a critical role in the formation of a Deaf Culture. The following print from the Institut National de Jeunes Sourds in Paris shows the Abbe instructing a small group of male students. The instructor points to a chart of signs and corresponding letters in the background. A member of France's aristocracy sits and watches. Demonstrations were important in gaining financial and social support for early schools.

Following the lead of Epée, the challenge for educators was to move students away from simply being copyists (Lane, 1977). Jean Massieu (1772-1846) was instrumental in moving education in this direction. Jean Massieu, himself deaf, was both a student and instructor at Epée's school. He was influential in shaping the course of deaf education and taught the later influential instructors Abbe Sicard, Laurent Clerc, and Thomas Hopkins Gallaudet. Massieu helped develop many of his instructional methods in conjunction with the Abbe Sicard, who he taught sign language (Lane, 1977). At the close of the eighteenth century, Massieu wrote an autobiographical account of what it was like to grow up deaf before the establishment of special schools for children who were deaf. His account was one in which children who were deaf were pretty much on their own. To him, society did not perceive them as being capable of learning. Massieu was fortunate in having five brothers and sisters that were also deaf with whom he could communicate. The family developed their own sign language. In contrast, most children who were deaf were isolated. It was only through the establishment of the schools that some deaf children were able to have prolonged contact with others (Lane, 1984a; Padden & Humphries, 1988).

Massieu wrote down many of his thoughts and experiences that provide a useful description of what life might have been like for some people who were deaf in the late eighteenth and early nineteenth centuries in France. He wrote:

> I was born at Semens in the department of La Gironde. My father died in 1791. My mother is still alive. There were six deaf-mutes in my family: three boys and three girls. Until the age of 13 years 9 months, I stayed in my region without receiving any sort of instruction. I was in the dark. I expressed my ideas through manual signs and my gestures, which I employed to communicate with my parents and brothers and sisters. These signs were quite different from those of educated deaf people. Strangers did not understand me when I expressed myself in this way, but neighbors understood me well enough. [Cited by Lane, 1977: 6]

Abbe Roch Ambroise Sicard (1742-1822) was another of the early pioneers in the instruction of people who were deaf. Abbe Sicard developed a sign language and method that combined writing and a system of "methodical signs," which was first developed by Epée. Sicard also emphasized teaching grammatical rules to his students. At the height of the French Revolution, several activists in France pushed hard for the education of the deaf. Before this, only the very well-to-do had any opportunity for an education. During the height of the French Revolution, the Revolutionary Commune arrested and imprisoned Abbe Sicard because of his official ties to the French court. Fellow instructor Jean Massieu spoke to a judicial tribunal in defense of the beloved Sicard. Massieu convincingly pointed out that Sicard had helped numerous children. Even though he made his point and the group agreed to free Sicard, they did not release him but led him to his execution. At the last moment Sicard pled his own case before the angry mob and they set him free. In 1791, the French National Assembly established state-funded education for hearing impaired and visually impaired people.

Alternative approaches and schools were developing throughout Europe. Where Sicard and Epée focused on hand signs for communication, some of their contemporaries placed emphasis on teaching people to speak. Jacob Rodriques Pereire (1715-1780) also known as Pereira or by one of the other seven spellings of his name, developed and used an alternative method. His method fell into the category known as the audist tradition, where the instructor placed emphasis on lipreading and the spoken word. Pereire would criticize Epée's work and helped establish the persistent debate on which of the two approaches was the best method (Mirzoeff, 1992). Pereire demonstrated that people who were deaf could speak and be taught to communicate. Typical of many presentations of people who were deaf was the depiction of the student and instructor. The following painting from the Institut National de Jeunes Sourds de Paris shows a young child and the instructor Pereire conforms with many presentations. What is striking about the painting is the young child's focus on the eyes of the instructor. The viewer is drawn to the child face and high degree of attention. The instructor is almost equally focused on the eyes of the child. He gently holds the hands of the child as an act of compassion and communication. One senses a social and emotional bond between student and instructor.

Thomas Braidwood (1715-1806), in the audist tradition, taught the hearing impaired in Edinburgh, Scotland in 1760. His school would become the central school for teaching in the audist tradition in the eighteenth century. Although he was famous for his techniques, he was equally renown for keeping his techniques secret from outsiders. He only shared them with members of his family. The Braidwood Academy held a monopoly on teaching in England and Scotland in the eighteenth and much of the nineteenth centuries. This secrecy dramatically shaped the approach to deaf education

Figure 37. Unknown Artist, *J.R. Pereire and His Pupil Marie Marois*, Unknown, Institut National de Jeunes Sourds.

used in the United States. When the influential educator Thomas Hopkins Gallaudet traveled to Europe to study Braidwood's audist methods, Braidwood refused to help him. Consequently, Gallaudet turned to the French schools who more openly shared their methods, which at the time were based on sign language. Upon his return to the United States, Gallaudet would use the French methods as the foundation for his instruction, in favor of Braidwood's audist approach.

The German, Johann Conrad Amman (1669-1724) also taught deaf students in the audist tradition. He believed that speech was of divine origin and that all people, including those who were deaf, could learn to speak. The educator, Samuel Heinicke (1727-1790) also believed speech was necessary in order to develop abstract thought. He taught speech and lipreading and believed that only through oral language could thought be possible (Savage, Evans, & Savage, 1981). He spent much of his energy debating l' Epée, the founder of the manual approach, on the merits of his audist approach over signing.

The famous French educator, Jean Marc Itard (1774-1838) worked with a young boy found in the French woods who had lived on his own for year known as the Wild Boy of Aveyron. Itard was obsessed with the notion that deafness could be cured and made many radical attempts to correct deafness to no avail. He tried purgatives, eardrops, applied electricity to the ears, bleeding, leeching, placing hot buttons behind ears, fractured skulls behind the ears, used setons, and eventually gave up. Lane (1992: 213) provided a description of some of the radical techniques Itard used to treat deafness:

> With the other students he tried a regime of daily purgatives, still others had their ears covered with bandage soaked in a blistering agent. Within a few days, the ear lost all of its skin, oozed pus, and was excruciatingly painful. When it scabbed, Itard reapplied the bandage and the wound reopened. Then the cycle was repeated, with caustic soda spread on the skin behind the ear. All of this was to no avail.

The nineteenth century witnessed the expansion of mass schooling. Education for students who were deaf became increasingly available to a larger segment of the population. Mass schooling of children, although a boon for some children, including those who were deaf, nevertheless tended to accentuate the dependent status of people who were deaf (Winzer, 1986). Nineteenth century educators were very interested in the nature of and thought processes of children with deafness. Many children did not begin their formal education until they had reached age 10 (Moores, 1987). Consequently, what they knew about the world was a function of what they had observed or experienced. This prior learning posed a pedagogical question for educators as to how and what these children knew and learned.

Efforts of teaching were occurring outside France. For example, Francis Green (1742-1809) advocated for the deaf education in Boston. Laurent Clerc (1785-1869) and Thomas Hopkins Gallaudet established the American Asylum for the Deaf and Dumb (Hartford School for the Deaf) in Connecticut in 1817. Thomas Hopkins Gallaudet (1787-1851) was a Connecticut theologian who pioneered deaf education in the United States. Gallaudet had spent time in Europe learning techniques, such as those promoted by the Abbe Sicard, Jean Massieu, and Larent Clerc. Originally, he was an audist but because of contacts with Laurent Clerc and others with the Paris school who focused more on signing and the reluctance of the Braidwood schools to share their techniques, he became a major proponent of sign language (Lane, 1977).

The main task for Gallaudet was to start deaf education in the United States (Lane, 1977). Part of this task was to convince Americans that deafness was not an individual problem but a social problem and that people who were deaf needed to be brought together for instruction (Lane, 1993). He eventually established a school that was the first permanent school in the United States. While in France, Gallaudet encountered Larent Clerc who was a student and instructor at the National Institution for the Deaf-Mutes in Paris. Gallaudet recruited Clerc to Hartford where Clerc introduced sign language as the medium of deaf instruction of America. Under Clerc and Gallaudet's guidance, the American Asylum at Hartford trained many instructors for deaf schools in the United States. After 1817, deaf schools flourished across the country (Padden & Humphries, 1988). A critical feature of the Hartford and later schools was that they were residential. The schools' dormitories introduced deaf students to other deaf students and became the hubs of the deaf communities.

Thomas Hopkins Gallaudet and other principals of schools and asylums viewed people who were deaf as children and reacted to them paternalistically (Valentine, 1993). Gallaudet came from a successful Protestant background that influenced his perception of people he viewed less fortunate. Valentine (1993:54) commented, "Thomas Hopkins Gallaudet always believed that the deaf people who were his students at the American Asylum for the Deaf and Dumb should be treated like his own children: with a father's kindly watchfulness and firm authority." Valentine also noted that there is little evidence that suggests that his students reacted negatively to this perception, possibly out of fear that they would be denied an education at his school. Probably the most famous American student who was deaf during the nineteenth century was Laura Bridgeman (1829-1889) who was deaf and blind. The educator and activist, Samuel Gridley Howe, met her in 1837. Howe became her instructor and was successful in communicating with her and teaching her how to communicate with others. She would travel about the country with Howe to demonstrate what she had learned and garner support.

During the Civil War in 1864, Congress authorized the establishment of a college for students who were deaf in Washington DC. For the next 100 years, the Columbia Institution for the Deaf and the Blind (Gallaudet College) in Washington would be a leader in deaf education. Gallaudet College was at the time the world's only college designed exclusively for students who were deaf. Prior to Gallaudet College, educators designed schools to teach students the necessary skills that would allow them to succeed in the working world (Moores, 1987). Students typically devoted their final year of education to vocational training rather than college preparation. The college's first principal was Edward Miner Gallaudet (1837-1917), who was the son of Thomas Hopkins Gallaudet. Edward Gallaudet saw value to audist schools but concluded that signing produced the best results. Edward Gallaudet fought for a combined system of educating people that included audist as well as manual approaches. Other educators of the time, such as Samuel Gridley Howe and Horace Mann, argued for eliminating sign language because they believed that it isolated and limited people.

Gallaudet's main adversary was Alexander Graham Bell (1847-1922), the well-known inventor of the telephone. Bell was to play a key role in nineteenth century views of the deaf and deaf culture. Bell, whose father Alexander Melville Bell had created a method of education in the audist tradition, would lead an international campaign to eliminate sign language. Bell was deeply interested in deaf education because both his spouse and mother were deaf. The invention of the telephone in the nineteenth century was the result of Bell's attempts to develop a hearing aid for his spouse (Farrell, 1956). Bell firmly believed that audist education was the best and only way to educate the people.

Bell wanted to know whether deafness was biologically inherited. He headed a research team for five years that attempted to prove that deafness was genetically inherited. Much of this effort was directed to reviewing local records for cases of deafness. Martha's Vineyard received much of Bell's attention because of the high prevalence of deafness among the people who lived there. Bell's research resulted in the publication of the highly controversial *Memoir Upon the Formation of a Deaf Variety of the Human Race*. Bell thought that grouping deaf people together was a bad idea because inbreeding would result in more deafness among children (Groce, 1985). He also suggested that deaf people should never be permitted to intermarry for this same reason. He concluded that people who were deaf and used sign language tended to marry each other and have higher birth rates than those taught using audist techniques. He assumed students in deaf schools resorted to instinct and animal passions to guide their behavior. Consequently, he decided that signing could create a sizable population in the future. This was an outcome that he found to be undesirable within the context of nineteenth century Social Darwinism and public concern over the immigration of people to the United States (Mirzoeff, 1992).

In Bell's time, many people believed that human traits, such as deafness or blindness, were biologically inherited. They believed parents passed on traits to their offspring. However, with deafness seemingly appearing and then disappearing within a family line, people wondered how could inheritance explain changes in deafness? While people recognized that deafness did occur more frequently among biologically-related individuals, it was also true that hearing parents would have deaf children and deaf parents could have hearing children. Recessive genetic patterns were not fully understood until the work of Gregor Mendel was accepted by the scientific community around 1900.

The Victorians placed pressure on minorities to conform. It was a era of oppressiveness, intolerance, and society looked down on people with disabilities. Winzer (1986: 30) noted in the nineteenth century, "Stereotypes painted deaf individuals as inferior creatures and acted to complicate their already grave problems further." Society also pressured people with disabilities to fit into the "normal" Victorian society. For the those who were deaf, the emphasis was to force them into becoming oral. The Victorians were obsessed with sexual morality, at least in word if not deed. Not only were people who were deaf subjected to the same attitudes and values common to the typical Victorian citizen, they received special attention. A commonly-held belief was that they were more passionate than hearing people. Consequently, they were more likely to engage in immoral sexual activity and give birth to even more children who were deaf. Thus, efforts to sexually segregate and prohibit intermarriages among people who were deaf were proposed. Mirzoeff (1992: 24) noted:

> In concert with the rise of eugenic science—over thirty states passed legislation allowing medical authorities to sterilize the "unfit." It was permissible to sterilize people under eleven categories, including the deaf, the blind, the diseased, the insane and feebleminded and even orphans.

He later observes the United States Supreme Court in 1927 would later rule this legislation constitutional and that by 1941 over 36,000 people had been sterilized. The United States did not have a monopoly over the notion of sterilization of those who were disabled. Hitler passed the Eugenic Sterilization Act in 1933 that provided for mandatory sterilization of hereditary disabilities, including deafness. According to Mirzoeff (1992), Hitler carried out about 320,000 sterilizations, of which 17,000 were applied to people who were deaf.

The medical profession also sought conformity. Physicians advanced new surgical techniques for some forms of hearing impairments in the eighteenth and nineteenth centuries. Consequently, Mirzoeff (1992) noted physicians subjected them to numerous seemingly violent treatments. Doctors gave them treatments, such as electrical shocks, injections, and surgery to clear out blockages thought to cause deafness. The following nineteenth century illustration of the use of electricity to cure deafness underscores the extent to

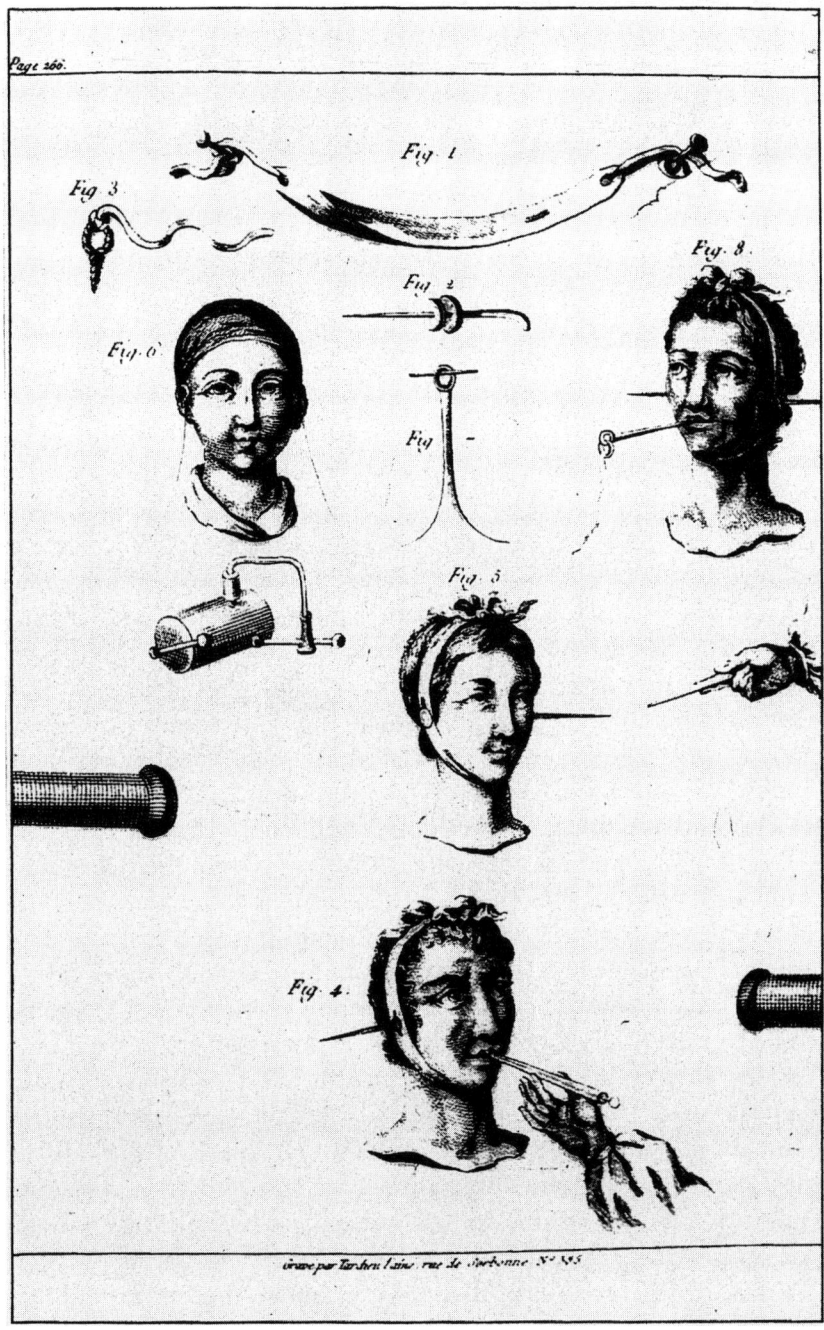

Figure 38. Unknown Artist, *Treatment by Electricity*, Eighteenth century France, Institut National de Jeunes Sourds.

which the medical community attempted to cure deafness. The line between physical torture and humane treatment was often crossed in the interest of curing deafness. The idea that medical people would expose people to such extreme treatments illustrates their lack of acceptance of people who were deaf and their deafness.

The openness toward sign language present at the close of the eighteenth century would eventually erode with the rise of industrial society. About 1880, rigid reforms in schools and instructional methods would be imposed on people who were deaf (Widell, 1993). The benchmark of this shift was the 1880 Congress of Educators of the Deaf held in Milan where conferees voted to support the audist method of teaching. The consequence was that signing was de-emphasized and many teachers who were themselves deaf were replaced with hearing teachers. Ironically, that same year the National Association of the Deaf, which has worked for the rights of people who are deaf, was also founded.

Several state residential schools for the deaf were established during the nineteenth century. Children basically received their entire education at the schools. Emphasis was placed on teaching students to learn basic skills needed for survival. The schools typically had mini-industries, that produced marketable household items, such as brooms, that were then sold to help support the schools and theoretically teach the students work skills. For many students, the schools represented the first significant opportunity to socialize and live with other children who were deaf. When audist instruction was not dominant, the schools exposed students to adult instructors who were deaf. The residential schools were social enclaves in their communities and provided opportunities for students to become in touch with deaf culture and form lasting relationships with other students.

Eventually Day schools would expand in the United States by 1900. These schools relied heavily on audist methods of instruction. Residential schools relied on sign language. With the emphasis on mainstreaming students that developed in the twentieth century, the schools increasingly became questioned. The debate continues today between proponents of the schools and those dead set against them. The net result of the debate has been a decline in enrollments in residential schools and an increase in students being schooled in nonresidential settings. The following nineteenth century print shows a group of small children at a residential school learning to sign the Lord's Prayer. All of the children are clothed in the uniform of the school.

Figure 39. Unknown Artist, *Illustrating the Lord's Prayer with Signs*, nineteenth century, Gallaudet University Archives, Washington, DC.

PEOPLE WHO WERE DEAF OVER THE CENTURIES

The importance of communication to the human species cannot be overstated. Without the ability and opportunity to communicate with other human beings, we as a species decline. The history of people who were deaf has been one of struggle to communicate. Throughout antiquity and the Middle Ages, the general assumption was that people who were deaf were incapable of understanding or even learning. Consequently, with the exception of a few special legal provisions, they were largely ignored and assumed to be "dumb." We do know that from a few rare observations by classic scholars that they indeed developed means of communicating, such as gesturing and signing.

Early Christian scholars concluded or at least were misinterpreted to have concluded that people who were deaf could not understand God and gain faith. The later conclusion was most likely based on the misinterpretation of the writings of the influential Saint Augustine and ancient Greek and Hebrew texts. Regardless, people over the centuries treated people who were deaf as if they could not know God. They were not permitted to play active roles in the church. Their perceived inability to understand God or to take positions of authority in society negated early efforts to educate them.

The recognition that people who were deaf could be educated and taught to communicate came fairly late in western history. The sixteenth century witnessed a few attempts to educate them with mixed degrees of success. In general, many people still thought it was, albeit an interesting endeavor, a waste of effort. This public pessimism regarding the prospects of educating people did not dismay early educators from their belief that people who were deaf could be educated. At first educators tried whatever worked and operated on assumptions they formulated in a hearing world. Over the years this would change and educators turned more to people who were deaf and their communities for answers. Often these answers were rooted in the use of signs and gestures.

Moores (1987) concluded educational advancements for deaf education were spearheaded by the Spanish in the sixteenth century, in British in the seventeenth, and French during the eighteenth, with the Germans prevailing in the nineteenth centuries. Much of the competition for scarce resources by different educational approaches was dependent on public demonstrations of the school's effectiveness. The exhibition of high achieving students who were deaf, while successful in generating public support, reinforced existing stereotypes against them. On one hand their accomplishments were viewed as positive, but on the other hand they continued to be viewed as downtrodden, helpless, poor, and needing assistance. Early educators consciously and openly exaggerated their sad plight to secure support for their educational efforts. These demonstrations only exacerbated the distances between the hearing and the deaf world.

Regardless of the approach used, separate schools for people who were deaf developed first in Europe and then in the United States. The historical significance of this is the notion that for most people who were deaf, the experience of attending a separate school for similar students was the first opportunity for them to discover their identity as being deaf. The evolution of separate schools would have a dramatic impact on the development of the deaf culture and individual as well as group identities.

The concepts of deaf culture and deaf community have been critical to the history of people who were deaf. Regarding Deaf Culture, Foster (1989: 234) concluded:

> Historically, the dominant hearing culture has most often assigned deaf people to deviant or outsider social roles, and in response, deaf people developed a shared understanding of these roles. Sometimes this understanding

led them to challenge these interpretations. It also led them to create alternatives for themselves and other deaf people. The deaf community is one such alternative.

Social isolation has been a common theme that has faced people who are deaf throughout history. Even today, they either by choice or by prejudice some remain relatively isolated from the larger hearing society. The history of people who were deaf is one of repression, restriction, and paternalism. Societies have worked hard to get them to conform to a hearing world. In the final analysis the interpretation of silence by the hearing has framed many of the social perceptions of people who do not hear. The hearing have attached a number of negative connotations to the silence such as aggression, unresponsiveness, arrogance, rejection, refusal, indicative of low intelligence, and other negative connotations. Perhaps it was these assumptions and perceptions that fueled the many extreme efforts to treat deafness and force audist educational techniques on them as a group.

Chapter 7

PEOPLE WITH DEVELOPMENTAL DISABILITIES

Developmental disabilities encompass a wide variety of individual characteristics, including a wide range of diagnostic conditions and behaviors. Definitions of developmental disabilities typically identify functional limitations, such as the individual's limited ability for self-care, self-help, self-direction, self-direction, economic independence, and unassisted living. The inability to fully develop the complete capacity for speech is also characteristic of some severe forms of developmental disabilities. Typically, developmental disabilities are assumed to be lifelong and are present at birth or develop early during the lifespan. They typically refer to long-term or lifelong mental and or physical conditions that develop before age 18 to 22 years of age and require specific forms of assistance that may occur over an extended duration. Major forms of developmental disabilities are classified as mental retardation, cerebral palsy, epilepsy, autism, and seizure disorders. People who have mental retardation represent the largest and most significant subgroup of people with developmental disabilities. They represent a subgroup that, as Bogdan and Taylor (1976:47) wrote, "We assume that the mentally retarded possess common characteristics that allow them to be unambiguously distinguished from all others." They typically are thought of stereotypically as opposed to being unique in their own ways.

People knew very little about the treatment of people with developmental disabilities or mental retardation before the nineteenth century (Scheerenberger, 1982). The absence of information is partially due to historically unclear boundaries of what constitutes a developmental disability (Kauffman & Payne, 1975). People who have developmental disabilities were frequently grouped with people having other disabilities, such as mental illness, deafness, and physical disabilities. For example, in seventeenth century Tudor England, MacDonald (1981:5) noted, "Children, idiots, and lunatics were siblings in the eyes of the law, because they lacked the capacity to reason and so could not be economically and legally responsible." This blurring of boundaries resulted in a lack of focused attention and clarity of definition. Finally, and perhaps the most important, is that they did not historically receive much attention from physicians, educators, and scholars because it was assumed for centuries that little could be done to better their lives.

A critical issue regarding the language and terminology about people with developmental disabilities is the distinction between them and people who were identified as fools. Historically, people used the term "fool" to refer to three basic types of people, biblical fools, entertainment fools, and people with developmental disabilities. Fool in the Bible means a person who was unwise or neglected religious duties (Cranefield, 1966). Biblical and Christian references to this type of fool are numerous. The second type of fool was the individual who makes a fool of themselves to entertain others. This form of fool is best characterized as the court jester or fool. This type of fool was sometimes known as artificial fool. Some of the court fools also had developmental disabilities, making distinctions between court fools who were not disabled and those who were difficult. The third type of fool is those people who had developmental disabilities. People in this category of fool were sometimes known as natural fools because they were not viewed as purposely being fools by choice, as in the case of artificial or religious fools. Since the twelfth century, there was a distinction between natural and artificial fools, the latter being similar to contemporary clowns (Robins, 1986). The natural fools encompassed people with mental illness as well as developmental disabilities. In the same vein, medieval scholars also distinguished between born idiots (natural folly) and unnatural folly (Neaman, 1978). This scheme was tied to the way some people thought about Christianity because neither form of folly could find religious salvation. Occasionally, communities characterized natural fools as being "children of God" as they were seen as being innocent, childlike, and creatures of God. During the Middle Ages in England, people used the euphemistic "innocent" to refer to people who were incurably and naturally damaged and judged as being incapable of performing everyday tasks (Rushton, 1988).

Another critical notion that has been unclear is the distinctions between people who have developmental disabilities and those who were mentally ill. This distinction has not always been evident to the western mind. However, Neaman (1978) noted the seventh century, Isidore of Seville (Isidorus), who wrote *Etymologies,* distinguished between insania (insanity) and dementia (mental deficiency). Throughout history, this distinction between people with developmental disabilities and those with mental illness was legally important. For example, under the reign of the English King Edward I (1272-1306-7) society made legal distinctions among idiots, natural fools, and lunatics (Robins, 1986). Legal distinctions were also made between people with developmental disabilities, natural fools, and people with mental illness or lunatics (Clarke & Clarke, 1965:14). Rushton (1988) found that thirteenth century northern English laws distinguished between those people judged to be unfit to inherent wealth because of mental incapacity and those determined to be out of their minds (mentally ill). The philosopher John Locke (1632-1704) also distinguished between idiocy and insanity.

For most of history, people made few distinctions between people with developmental disabilities and others judged as being disadvantaged. Before the nineteenth century, little attention was directed to people with developmental disabilities and there was seldom, if ever, distinctions made between people with mental illness and developmental disabilities (Tyor & Bell, 1984). It was not until the eighteenth century that the medical profession began to pay serious attention to developmental disabilities and specifically mental retardation (Kanner, 1967). By the eighteenth century however, Kanner contends two major changes altered the attention paid to developmental disabilities: the growth in humanitarian reforms and the growing governmental preoccupation with the biological spread of endemic cretinism.

It is also true that for much of history, relatively general categories were used to define developmental disabilities. For example, people once used the terms idiot and cretin to describe all forms of developmental disabilities, with the possible exception of people who had epilepsy. People with developmental disabilities were viewed as having the same underlying condition but to differing degrees of severity, outward appearance, and observed behavior. For example, children with Down Syndrome were grouped with those with endemic thyroid deficiencies (cretinism). The nineteenth century gave rise to increasing refinement and classification or people having developmental disabilities. This might be expected as the period that was one in which scientists and practitioners in numerous fields engaged in refining and specifying their respective endeavors.

EXPLANATIONS FOR DEVELOPMENTAL DISABILITIES

Before the nineteenth century all of the typical explanations available to account for blindness, deafness, disease, heredity and others were also applied to people with developmental disabilities. For example, one of the most enduring explanations for developmental disabilities has been to attribute them to demons, evil spirits, or sin. A case on point is the Hebrew *Torah* which linked certain "afflictions" (disabilities) to sinfulness. People who had developmental disabilities were included in these "smitten" groups. In addition to God, some people believed evil spirits caused developmental disabilities persisted well into the eighteenth century (Scheerenberger, 1982). During the Middle Ages and later centuries, it was commonly believed that having sex with demons or animals would result in malformed or developmentally disabled children. For instance, Eberly (1988:60) noted a case in Denmark where a young mother was burned at the stake for giving birth to a child who was labeled "monkey-headed." The infant was probably anencephalic, which is an infant born with an incomplete brain, defective spinal cord, and or malformed skull.

Children born with deformities or developmental disabilities have historically evoked religious and mythical responses and interpretations. One enduring explanation for developmental disabilities from the Middle Ages through the Enlightenment was the belief that infants born with developmental disabilities or deformities were changelings. People viewed changelings as abnormal children that were not born by their natural parents but rather were the offspring of evil spirits, such as fairies, demons, and elves. Northern European folklore suggested that at night these evil spirits exchanged the changeling for the parent's infant. The evil spirits made exchanges so that their offspring could be raised by humans. The spirits made these exchanges during the night when the family was sleeping. Consequently, a common practice was for families to sleep with their infants. People believed the human parents' real children were either raised or killed by the evil spirits. Haffter (1968:56) summarizes the perceived traits of changelings as:

> ...the changeling was usually peculiar in appearance; its proportions were wrong, its head was too big for its body, its face was ugly or wrinkled, it looked old, according to legend, it was not a child at all but an age-old creature. Sometimes it had a thick throat and was for this reason known in many districts as killcrop. It could not stand or walk but crept around like an animal. It did not laugh or talk but screamed and shouted interminably.

The belief in changelings as an explanation for abnormal children or children who were developmentally disabled was widespread throughout the Middle Ages and the immediate centuries. Haffter (1968:56) concluded, "Mentally retarded children were thus clearly taken for changelings, particularly cases with hydrocephalic or cretinism." This perception was also based on the fact that these children did not laugh or talk and often gave unintelligible sounds.

Reactions to changelings varied from culture to culture. On the positive side, some communities viewed them as bearers of good luck, such as in

Ireland where they were treated well in some communities. However, other communities mistreated these children to reverse the exchange. People believed that if the changeling was treated badly enough the evil spirits would trade the parent's real child back for the changeling. Thus, some parents unwittingly exposed, tortured, neglected, beat, and burned their own children (changelings) in a vain effort to convince evil spirits to trade changelings. Evidence also exists that children who were identified as changelings were killed (DeMause, 1974). Not all responses were abusive or violent and some churches taught that the best defense was early baptism of the newborn (Haffter, 1968).

The church played an important role in defining changelings. At the crux of the church's interpretation was the role demons played in creating abnormal children. The church viewed them as subhuman forms embodying evil and sinister forces. The blame, as was the case for all witchcraft and other disabilities and diseases, was placed on the interplay between demons and the individual. The disability was defined as a struggle between good and evil forces played out through the changeling. Ironically even some saints were thought to be changelings. Saints Stephan, Lawrence, and Bartholomew were thought to have been switched at the cradle for changelings.

The witch-hunting manual, the *Malleus Maleficarium* (1487), devoted sections to the identification and response to changelings. The *Malleus* attributed changelings to the parents of the child because they were the ones that had sinned and consequently created the changeling. God permitted such things to occur because of the moral weaknesses of the parents. Blame for changelings rested with the sins of the parents. The *Malleus* argued that parents should be punished because their sins led to the creation of changeling children. The *Malleus* concluded that changelings were often the product of intercourse with the devil. Mothers of deformed children could be burned at the stake for this assumed association with the devil (Haffter, 1968). During the Reformation, people with developmental disabilities (changelings) became victims of prevailing concerns over demonism. The Catholic Church did not monopolize thoughts on changelings. For example, Martin Luther believed they existed and thought changelings were merely a mass of flesh *(a massa carnis)* with no soul. Luther referred to them in his *Convivio,* characterized them as annoying, and recommended they be thrown into water.

Societies developed other explanations and it was not until the nineteenth century that people made serious inroads into the true causes of developmental disabilities. The nineteenth century would be a period of medical advances and the insights of Sigmund Freud (1856-1939). In spite of advancements, such as those made by Seguin in the late nineteenth century, authorities continued to attribute developmental disabilities and mental retardation to a wide variety of causes. One nineteenth century authority identified the following causes for mental retardation:

> ...drinking water, bad air, exposure of the neck to draft, vicissitudes of temperature, dietary faults, certain salts used in cooking, saltless food, cold water drunk while sweating, exclusive consumption of vegetables and milk, greasy food, parental drunkenness during procreation, lack of sunlight, exertion accompanied by tight clothes around the neck, waywardness, masturbation, inbreeding... [and] racial causes. [Kanner, 1964: 92]

Today, we know that there are numerous diseases, genetic, and environmental causes for developmental disabilities. People acquire some disabilities because of physiological causes. For example, Romberg's disease is a pituitary disorder that develops in adulthood and leads to atrophy of the bone, skin, and face, which gives the individual's face a pushed-in appearance. Metabolic defects, such as PKU (Phenylketonuria) can result in mental retardation and developmental disabilities. Chromosomal abnormalities, such as Down's Syndrome, hypothyroidism (lack of thyroxine), blood incompatibilities (Rh Blood), Turner's Syndrome, Hurler's Syndrome, Hunter's Syndrome, Edward's Syndrome, Klinefelter's Syndrome, Congenital Hypothyroidism, Tay-Sachs, and malformations of the skull may result in developmental disabilities. Infections cause other developmental disabilities, such as rubella during the first four weeks of pregnancy, viral infections, toxoplasmosis, meningitis, syphilis, and cytomegalic inclusion disease can result in deafness, blindness, and developmental disabilities. Environmental causes such as radiation, physical traumas, prenatal anoxia, compression of the umbilical cord, lead poisoning, and alcohol may lead to developmental disabilities. Children and individuals who are understimulated can also develop developmental disabilities.

MAJOR TYPES OF DEVELOPMENTAL DISABILITIES

The types and variety of developmental disabilities are numerous. Some examples of well-known categories of developmental disabilities however warrant attention because they have received more societal attention over the centuries. The most common form of developmental disability is Down Syndrome. The cause of Down Syndrome was unknown until 1959 when researchers discovered that each of the body's cells of people with Down's Syndrome has one too many chromosomes. About one in every 650 babies born has Down Syndrome. Most people with Down Syndrome have eyes that slope up at the outer corners and folds of skin on either side of the nose that cover the inner corners of the eyes. The face and features are small, the tongue is large and tends to protrude, the head has a flattened back and hands are usually short and broad. Children with the syndrome have IQs that range from 30 to 80. All individuals with the syndrome are capable of learning. Down Syndrome has been present for centuries and some archaeological evidence indicates that suspected cases of Down Syndrome have been found in Anglo-Saxon skeletal remains (Rubin, 1974).

Largely influenced by the evolutionary dogma of the period in which he was writing, John Langdon Haydon Down (1828-1896) was the first to scientifically describe the disability named after him, Down Syndrome. Down's "Observations on an Ethnic Classification of Idiots" published in the *Journal of Mental Science* in 1866 presented many of his ideas on the syndrome. In his *Ethnic Classification of Idiots* written in 1886, he laid out his theories of the causes of the syndrome. His description of and theory behind what caused it proved to be inaccurate (Krishef, 1983). Down proposed that perceived "ethnic" features associated with what would later be labeled Down Syndrome were the result of degeneration. Down thought the syndrome was a retrogression into an earlier type of human being. Down proposed that children with Down Syndrome were biological throwbacks to the invasions of the Huns into Europe during the fifth century. Down viewed the syndrome as an atavistic regression to a lower race (Kanner, 1967). Keeping with the popular arguments of Social Darwinism and ethnocentricity of the period, Down viewed people with the syndrome as having much in common with the perceived "inferior people" of Asia, hence the term Mongolism was used. Down Syndrome children represented a Mongolian form of idiocy traced to biological mixing of native populations with the "inferior" invading Huns. This rationale, already very much a part of European folklore, was based on the idea that physical appearances reflected the psychological makeup of individuals. The children, Down thought, looked like people of Asian ancestry because of their shorter stature and facial appearance, which included almond shaped eyes. He attributed other forms of mental disability and further evidence of biological mixing with these inferior (non-European) groups.

Another developmental disability is epilepsy. Epilepsy is characterized by repeated occurrence of seizures that result from recurrent, abnormal, excessive, and synchronous discharges of populations of cerebral neurons. It is rarely fatal and most people with it are able to carry out normal and productive lives. Epilepsy is not a mental illness per se but an episodic disorder that can, in extreme forms during seizures, disable an individual. Individuals who have epilepsy may function very well mentally and be intelligent. Some people who have epilepsy experience relatively minor (petit mal) seizures and others have severe seizures (grand mal) that almost totally disable them. Today, epilepsy continues to stigmatize people who have it. Common causes for epilepsy include trauma, tumors, infections, such as meningitis, and brain defects. Epilepsy, rightly or wrongly, is considered to be a developmental disability.

Throughout the bulk of history, people have explained epilepsy in terms of rational, mystical, supernatural, and empirical forces operating in different mixtures until the nineteenth century. People have assumed that some supernatural force must play a role in its occurrence. The words epilepsy and epileptic are Greek in origin and linked to the concept of to seize or to attack. Epilepsy has been referred to as the sacred disease, caducus, falling sickness, cranke, demoniacs, and falling evil ranke. Typically these expressions for epilepsy touched on the spiritual nature and falling associated with seizures. At the end of the fifteenth century physicians began to more freely discuss magic, possession, and witchcraft, more so than their medieval counterparts (Temkin, 1971). Increasingly, physicians in the sixteenth and seventeenth centuries viewed their task to differentiate between demonic possession and true epilepsy. It was during the nineteenth century that the science of neurology began to understand the true nature of epilepsy. According to McGrew (1985:111), "Epilepsy is now understood to be a condition resulting from the dysfunction of cerebral nerve cells manifested in sudden and repeated mental disturbances, alterations in the state of consciousness, disordered sensory activity, or convulsions, loss of consciousness, falling down, shaking limbs, and spontaneous evacuation of bowels and bladder are characteristic of grand mal epilepsy." A second type, petit mal, involves momentary lapses in awareness, while focal seizures produce localized movements or sensations in particular parts of the body.

More than another other disease, Temkin (1971) concluded that epilepsy was subject to interpretation both as a physiological process and as an effect of spiritual influences. People have linked it with evil, saintliness, genius, and normality but evil is the most ubiquitous image (Ozer, 1992). People with epilepsy have been perceived in a positive sense as being prophetic but epilepsy has been and continues to be stigmatizing for many people. Some modern scholars have even linked the folk belief in lycanthropy, which is the perceived transformation of individuals into werewolves, as being epilepsy (Drake, 1992) but others disagree (Ozer, 1992). The possible link between transformations into werewolves is an old and ancient notion; and scholars such as the seventh century physician Paulus Aegineta and others, believed it occurred (Drake, 1992).

Initially the Greeks viewed epilepsy as a sacred disease (Rosen, 1968). They identified seizures and convulsions as caused by religious and divine forces. They started the tradition of viewing epilepsy as a sacred illness, a theme that endured until the seventeenth century (McGrew, 1985). However, this view was not universally held. The Hippocratic writings (400 BC) rejected the notion that epilepsy was caused by divine intervention but proposed that it was a product of too much phlegm. The Romans believed in demonic possession and saw epileptic attacks as bad omens (Temkin, 1971). Roman public assemblies disbanded when members had epileptic seizures because attendees assumed that demons were present (Haggard, 1932). Having epilepsy did not always hinder people from being successful in Roman society. Julius Caesar and Caligula had epileptic seizures. Following the treatments outlined by Hipprocrates and Galen, over the next 1500 years physicians would treat epilepsy by bleeding to balance the bodily humors.

Biblical accounts of cases of epilepsy can be found in the *New Testament* books of Mark, Matthew, and Luke. Christians, similar to the Greeks and Romans, generally viewed epilepsy as an outward sign of possession. By possession, the individual becomes the instrument of evil. Temkin (1971) noted that people with epilepsy were seen as being contaminated by the devil or demons and consequently were frequently associated with uncleanliness. People have often attributed uncleanliness to people with disabilities. Anyone touching a person with epilepsy could fall prey to demons and become possessed. People with epilepsy were thus seen as being highly contagious and measures were taken to prevent its spread, such as avoidance, segregation, not sharing dishes, and spitting at them. Numerous descriptions of spitting at people who had epilepsy exist in the literature until the sixteenth century (Temkin, 1971). McGrew (1985) noted that they were also feared and shunned.

Medieval scholars attributed epilepsy to demonic possession. For example, the late fifteenth century witch-hunting manual entitled the *Malleus Maleficarum* linked it to witchcraft. Given this perspective, the clergy and general public frequently called on patron saints John and Valentine to help cure epilepsy. Other responses were available during the Middle Ages such as cauterization, folk cures, reading the gospel, using the hair from white dogs, bleeding, and an assortment of other treatments. Some medieval surgeons trepanned skulls to release demons from peoples' heads, a practice that continued until the seventeenth century.

Following the Middle Ages, great scholars on mental illness, such as Tissot (1728-1797), Pinel (1745-1826), and Chiarugi (1759-1820), paid attention to epilepsy. The physician Tissot published his *Treatise on Epilepsy* in 1770. A variety of treatments continued until the mid-nineteenth century, which brought about the first real changes in how epilepsy was perceived. However, misunderstandings continued in the nineteenth century. For example, in 1815, the French psychiatrist, Esquirol, founded a special hospital (wing) for people with epilepsy. He did so out of concern they would infect other patients at the hospital. He believed that the simple sight of an epileptic seizure could spawn other people who were mentally ill to model their behavior. Segregation became the rule from that point onward. In 1857 the use of bromides by Sir Charles Locock reduced the frequency of epileptic attacks.

Endemic thyroid deficiency or cretinism (endemic goiter) is a developmental disability that develops over time due to thyroid deficiencies. It is a hyperthyroid condition that is characterized by large protruding tongue, puffy eyelids, baggy cheeks, depressed noses, large abdomen, small stature, intellectual delays, stunted growth and mental impairments. Historical descriptions and accounts of people with cretinism, although not numerous, are nevertheless scattered throughout western history. For example, Pliny the Elder (23/4-79 AD) provided one of the first descriptions of endemic thyroid deficiency. Medical interest has been sporadic and rare regarding people with the disability (Kanner, 1964). The medieval scholar Jacques de Vitry's *Historia Orientalis et Occidentalis* (1220) identified people with cretinism. During the Renaissance Leonardo da Vinci drew an example of a person with endemic thyroid deficiency. The sixteenth century mystic and medical practitioner Paracelsus provided a fairly clear description of cretinism in 1530 (Cranefield, 1966). He found that cretinism was frequently linked to endemic goiter. Swiss physician Felix Platter (1536-1614) provided another early description of cretinism in 1602. He was the first to label endemic cretinism as a congenital developmental disability in 1614.

The term cretin is based on the Latin *creta* which means chalk that was thought to be the color of the skin of people with the characteristic (Benda, 1949). In romantic languages, the word cret means dwarf or little. Cretin may have also come from the term chretien which is tied to the belief that people with cretinism were children of God (Eberly, 1988). Francois Emmanuel Fodere (1764-1835) speculated that the word cretin was a corruption of the chretien or Christian because of the simplicity of their minds made them incapable of sinning. In southern France the term cagot was used to refer to people thought to have cretinism. Known as cagots in the Pyrenees Mountains since the eleventh century, people have speculated that they were the descendants of the intruding Saracens (Haffter, 1968). Isolated communities of people with thyroid deficiency existed and thrived in certain regions of southern France and parts of northern Spain. The French used terms such as *caffo, gahets,* and *caffets* to refer to people thought to have cretinism. However, scholars have raised questions about whether these communities were populated by people with endemic thyroid deficiency or were simply differed in other respects (Kanner, 1964). During the Middle Ages and following centuries some thought they were subhuman and descendants of "primitive" peoples.

In the eighteenth century Francois Emmanuel Fodder believed the saturation of stagnant air with moisture caused thyroid deficiency in people. He also hypothesized that inadequate air, vapors, sulfurous vapors, marshy or specific miasma, saltless food, greasy food, lack of sunlight, lack of electricity, race, absence of civilization, and other assorted factors contributed to thyroid deficiency. His solution was a change in lifestyle including a combination of improved diet and living in pure mountain air. He based the later solution on the observation that proportionately few people with thyroid deficiency lived in higher elevations. His treatise on the subject published in 1781 on cretins in western Europe increased public apprehension of people with the characteristic. Consequently, Napoleon Bonaparte ordered a census be taken of people with endemic thyroid deficiency or as they were known to Napoleon as cretins in 1811. Concern over cretinism moved Napoleon to order French families with children with cretinism to move from the valleys to the mountains. His push for a census and moving people failed because of local resistance and his loss of power due to war.

For the most part at least up to the eighteenth century, medical professionals neglected people with endemic thyroid deficiencies. By the eighteenth century, literature began to appear that focused on physiological characteristics of people. The literature of the eighteenth century continued the traditional view of people with thyroid deficiencies by not recognizing them as human beings. The nineteenth century witnessed increased interest in people with the deficiency. It was a period of active interest in the causes of endemic thyroid deficiency. Scholars suggested it was caused by poor diet, genetics, and the environment.

Over the centuries up to the end of the nineteenth century, cretinism and idiocy were judged to be interchangeable. The early leader in the education of people with developmental disabilities Johann Jakob Guggenbuhl referred people, regardless of forms of developmental disabilities, as cretins. He believed all forms of developmental disabilities were at their base cretinism. Troxler defined endemic goiter, albinism, deaf mutism and idiocy as simply different forms of people with cretinism. In the nineteenth century, experts regarded cretinism and mental deficiency as synonymous. The following print from Lavater's *Fragmente* (1774-1778) shows a young girl who had a endemic thyroid deficiency. The accompanying text provides a description of her intellectual and developmental abilities. Lavater heavily ascribed to the pseudo-science of physiognomy which held that outward appearances represented one's state of being and mind. The text provides a description of her characteristics. (Note: The letter "s" in the type set of the period looks similar to the cursive *f* in contemporary type set.)

Figure 40. Daniel Chodowiecki, untitled group of people from Johann Gaspar Lavater's *Fragmente*, 1774-1778, Special Collections, University of Colorado Library, Boulder.

Hydrocephalus is caused by excessive fluid in the skull which results in an enlargement of the head and intellectual impairment. It is a structural malformation that causes fluid to be trapped in the cavities of the brain. The increasing pressure from the buildup of fluid causes the skull to enlarge and result in mental retardation and differing degrees of paralysis. The pressure on the brain can result in severe and chronic pain for people. In the past, experts understood very little on how to treat the condition. Some practitioners used trepanning to relieve pressure but this would have been a temporary solution and not permanent cure. With modern medicine came surgical techniques that can be effective when performed early enough to minimize brain damage. The technique is to shunt the excess cerebrospinal fluid into the blood stream, thus reducing pressure on the brain and swelling.

For centuries in folklore, hydrocephalic children were treated as changelings and thus were seen as subhuman creations of evil spirits (Haffter, 1968). Evidence of their existence is sparse in history. The physician Celsus probably described hydrocephaly in the fourth book of his *De Medicina* written during the first century. It is probably the disorder described in European folklore regarding changelings with oversized heads (Eberly, 1988). One of the earliest systematic descriptions of hydrocephaly was included in Jean Astruc's 1746 book entitled *Diseases of Children*. Hospital records from London show that several cases of hydrocephalic children were present from the sixteenth century to the early nineteenth century. Referred to as watery head, horseshoe head, head-mould shot, water on the brain, and dropsy on the brain, it may have represented one out of eight deaths of children under age five in the early nineteenth century (Forbes, 1979). In the nineteenth century, public schools in the United States refused to admit hydrocephalic children (Scheerenberger, 1982). The result was their segregation from mainstream society. With no place for them to go, many residential schools simply kept them until they died.

We know even less about people who were microcephalic. People called them pinheads because the tops of their skulls were narrow (pointed) relative to people who do not have the characteristic. Historical references in literature and art to individuals who were microcephalic exist but are rare. We also know that people with the disability have historically been used for entertainment. This was particularly true during the nineteenth century when many of them found their way into sideshows and exhibitions. As a group, their low intelligence and outward physical appearances made them ideal candidates for exhibition.

PEOPLE WITH DEVELOPMENTAL DISABILITIES IN ANTIQUITY

There is evidence that people with developmental disabilities lived in many antiquarian societies. For example, Egyptian mummies occasionally have skeletal anomalies associated with developmental disabilities (Harris & Weeks, 1973). Reactions to people with developmental disabilities in antiquity ran the gamut from providing care to infanticide. Overall, we continue to know very little about how ancient societies cared for and reacted to people with developmental disabilities. Typically, contemporary social scientists have concluded that people with developmental disabilities were treated with indifference or cruelty in antiquity (Evans, 1983). The most striking act of cruelty attributed to ancient societies was to abandon or kill children or people with obvious developmental disabilities. Although some ancient communities used infanticide to deal with children with obvious disabilities, there is no indication that it was widely practiced, at least by the Egyptians (Scheerenberger, 1982). Besides the efforts of the family, there may have been early efforts to protect children with developmental disabilities from harm. Some historians have found evidence that the Egyptians made provisions for caring for people through healing temples, where they could go and find comfort (Bullough & Bullough, 1969). In addition to temples, the practice of trepanning to release demons and pressure from the brain was used in prehistoric Egyptian, Greek, and Roman societies.

This same sense of Egyptian compassion toward people with developmental disabilities is not evident in ancient Greece. The Greeks placed great value on the physical perfection and the beauty of the human body. It's reasonable that when the physical characteristics of some forms of developmental disabilities were recognized, communities would have rejected people. For example, children with Down's Syndrome would have not conformed to the Greek ideal body type. How this translated into social reaction is unknown, however, documents indicate that the Spartans aggressively practiced infanticide against those judged deformed or different in a move to purifying their societies. The term idiot is derived from Greek and means a peculiar or private person, one who is cut off from relationships with others and is alone. Greece was essentially a country of politicians and present was the idea that every citizen was to serve in official capacity and to hold office. The Greeks assumed that public officials were more distinguished and of higher intelligence than private citizens who were ignorant (Skinner, 1961). A few people, however, cared little to participate in the political process and preferred to live as private citizens. To distinguish them from the public officials, they were labeled *idiotai*. It implied an unsophisticated person with no or little professional knowledge was an ill-informed person. Typically, idiots did not vote nor participate in democratic government. Over time the term became referred to people of degraded intellect or mental defect. The *idiotai* of Greek life were merely those who chose to avoid the official public servant life in favor for a private life (Haggard, 1932). The term found some use as a general application to all people with developmental disabilities. In English, *idiotai* became idiot in a developmental disability sense, and still finds use in slang.

Historians disagree on how people with developmental disabilities were treated during the thirteen centuries of Roman rule. Greek and Roman medical authorities rarely mentioned developmental disabilities even though they did describe a wide variety of disorders (Cranefield, 1966; Kanner, 1960-61). Scheerenberger (1982) concluded treatment varied by ruler and social class, with the wealthy treating their own considerably better than those less fortunate. Other historians have concluded that the Romans typically eliminated people with developmental disabilities or at least used them for entertainment or as servants (Kanner, 1964; Krishef, 1983). It's known that wealthy Romans commonly kept a "fool" or "jester" in the home for amusement, some of these entertainers had developmental disabilities (Baumeister & Butterfield, 1970). For example, the Roman Seneca as early as the fourth century BC kept people with disabilities in his home to amuse and entertain his guests (Evans, 1983). Some of these "fools" became quite famous, as was the case for the "fool" of the emperor Augustus, who was named Gabba.

The Romans showed a degree of legal sensitivity toward people with developmental disabilities. The Romans were lawmakers and people with developmental disabilities received attention from Roman lawmakers. The current system of guardianship laws can trace its origin to the Romans. The laws were based on the concern that some people were unable to handle their own affairs and needed guardians to protect their interests (Krishef, 1983). The Romans legally grouped people with developmental disabilities with other people whom they judged as being unable to take care of themselves. These laws were not designed to punish people for their disabilities but for their protection from exploitation by others. The Romans also made special provisions for people with developmental disabilities and established charitable institutions to provide care. Children were admitted to these facilities to avoid their dying of exposure. Soranus of Ephesus of the second century AD established a hospital for people who were mentally ill or had developmental disabilities. The Romans also took steps to try to cure people. Roman treatments included bloodletting, whipping, herbs, purges, castration, and other punitive and ineffective treatments. The typical person with developmental disabilities would have been better off being medically neglected than have received such harsh and ineffective treatments.

PEOPLE WHO HAD DEVELOPMENTAL DISABILITIES DURING THE MIDDLE AGES

The treatment of people with developmental disabilities during the Middle Ages ranged from benign tolerance to outright persecution (Scheerenberger, 1982). During the Middle Ages, the belief that people with developmental disabilities were possessed by evil spirits was commonly held (Cleland & Swartz, 1993). Consequently, religious factions punished and killed them. People also saw foolishness as naivetÈ of evil and fools were unsophisticated. The notion of the "fool" as God's simpleton had existed since the thirteenth century (Neaman, 1978). This belief contributed to the many exorcisms and beatings of people who had developmental disabilities, such as epilepsy. Within the same medieval context and in sharp contrast, people with developmental disabilities were also referred to as *enfants dieu* (Children of God). They were seen as innocent creations of God who wandered through the streets of Europe (Robins, 1986). For instance, the English author Langland wrote of simpletons that wandered the countryside as "God's boyes." When perceived this way, they were treated with kindness or at least benign neglect. According to Bernard Farber (1968), idiots appear in English literature around 1300 as grossly deficient people. Chaucer used the term in this fashion in his *Canterbury Tales* (1387) and Sir Anthony Fitz-Herbert in 1534.

Under the encouragement and auspices of the church, people more frequently acted charitable and showed compassion toward people. For example, evidence indicates that church-based hospitals and asylums were built for the sick and destitute, including people with developmental disabilities. For instance in the fourth century, Saint Nicholas of Thaumaturgos the Bishop of Myra provided care to people with developmental disabilities (Evans, 1983; Krishef, 1983). Historians have described the bishop as a protector of the "feeble-minded." His name would eventually be modernized into the familiar Santa Claus or Saint Nick. Doll (1967) found that during the Emperor Justinian's rule, some facilities had resident doctors, priests, and caretakers. In addition, having a disability was not necessarily a barrier to earning a living because some handicraft occupations were open to all.

In twelfth century France, communities held feasts of fools that permitted free reign to those who wished to act out their most base desires to drink and behave in inappropriate ways (Krishef, 1983). Anyone could be an artificial fool during these celebrations, including people with developmental disabilities. Fool societies arose, in which people wore the bell-capped garments of the court fool so that they could not be held responsible for any of their words or deeds (Krishef, 1983). In addition, holidays arose throughout

Europe that focused on the fool. For example, during the late Middle Ages Circumcision Day was celebrated on January first of each year and was also known as the *Festum Stulorum* or feast of fools. People with developmental disabilities, being considered natural fools, were undoubtedly active participants in these festivals. Sander Gilman (1988) notes, that the restorative and curing aspects of dance was a theme present in many works depicting fools and dance was thought to cure foolishness.

During the Middle Ages, great demand for fools was present in royal courts of Europe. Fools or buffoons were common in the royal courtyards of medieval France, as they were also in Germany, where they were labeled *hofnarren*. For instance, King Charles V of France (1337-1380) was fond of fools and awarded the Province of Champagne the exclusive right to supply fools to the royal court (Kanner, 1964). Similar to the Romans, some of these fools became famous, as was the case with Triboulet and Brusquet of the court of King Frances I of France (1494-1547). Besides being viewed as entertaining, some medieval societies viewed them as being incompetent and therefore dependent upon others. Under medieval English law, the monarch was recognized as having control over the possessions, property, and affairs of "idiots" and other people judged to be incompetent to manage their lives. As Krishef (1983: 166) noted, "...under his guardianship people with developmental disabilities essentially held the status of chattel." They were little more than objects that required minimal oversight. In addition, medical writers and scholars neglected them, as they had in the past centuries. Consequently, there were no systematic descriptions of people with developmental disabilities in medieval literature (Kanner, 1964).

The primary responsibility for caring for people with developmental disabilities mostly rested with family and friends (Clay, 1909; Evans, 1983; Kanner, 1964; Rosen, 1968) and somewhat with the community (Alexander & Selesnick, 1966). During the Middle Ages, those not cared for were free to roam about unmolested in the countryside. However, those judged to be dangerous or threatening were incarcerated or punished. For example, Scheerenberger (1982) reported that they were frequently jailed in Prussia. Medieval organizations, such as monasteries, only cared for a fraction of the people with developmental disabilities. In general, medieval authorities took only limited responsibility for them. These modest efforts would decline when Protestants closed several monastic hospitals. Medical care, when provided, consisted of a wide variety of techniques based on folklore, Christian scripture, superstition, and cultural practices. People were known to have used dunking, amulets, beatings, purges, exorcisms, incantations, and other treatments without much success.

In Gheel, Belgium legend had it that several "idiots" had been miraculously cured while watching a princess be executed. The story spread across

Europe and resulted in numerous people flocking to Gheel with the hope of being cured. Gheel became flooded with people who had developmental disabilities. In response, wealthy townspeople started taking them into their homes, as they were thought to be children of God. They were also viewed as a source of cheap household labor. Whatever the motive, the situation in Gheel was more humane than what occurred elsewhere in Europe. Gheel established an institution that cared for children. Many children were boarded out to and adopted by sympathetic families in the community.

Medieval literature contains terms and expressions such as Simple Simon, village idiot, fool, and bumpkin to refer to people with developmental disabilities. Inferred in all of these expressions was the notion of a person who functioned at a lower level of intelligence. Also common in literature was the divine fool, whom achieves the greatest statute during the Renaissance (Neaman, 1978). With the divine fool, the emphasis was not on the figure's abilities or disabilities but on the relationship between the individual and God. The figure of Folly was another major personification during the Renaissance. The connection between divine fools and folly with people with developmental disabilities was not typically made. Artistic presentations of people with developmental disabilities are uncommon during the Middle Ages and most depictions were of artificial fools. During the Renaissance, Leonardo da Vinci sketched many cartoons and characters that may have been based on his observations of real people with developmental disabilities. Some of these drawings suggest developmental disabilities but one cannot be sure. Da Vinci clearly drew some of them in a playful manner pushing the limits of his imagination. Clear and unrefutable presentations of people with developmental disabilities would begin to appear in the modern era during the sixteenth century in northern Europe.

PEOPLE WITH DEVELOPMENTAL DISABILITIES DURING THE MODERN PERIOD

Changes in social perceptions and attitudes toward people with developmental disabilities shifted little immediately following the Middle Ages. There were some exceptions, such as Paracelsus (1493-1541) who wrote the first medical written document on developmental disabilities entitled *De Generatione Stultorum (On the Begetting of Fools)* in 1530. The work focuses on the religious question of how could God create people ("fools") who did not have the capability for understanding God's existence? In addition, how is it humans gave birth to "fools" when other creatures did not? Paracelsus attributed the answer to these questions to the original sin and the fall of

Adam. After the fall, people with problems, such as developmental disabilities, were born. He also concluded that humans only provided the raw materials for children and that "vulcani" carved people from these raw materials into normal beings and beings with disabilities. Paracelsus thought that natural "fools" had unspoiled souls and were therefore innocent.

More dramatic changes occurred in the seventeenth century as increasing attention was paid to people with developmental disabilities and particularly those with mental retardation. A text entitled Archipathologica published in 1614 by a Portuguese physician named Filipe Montalto, described the diagnosis, prognosis, and cure of mental retardation. Woolfson (1984) concluded that Montalto's work represented an early and systematic attempt to understand people with developmental disabilities (mental retardation). In the book, Montalto addressed the issues of the causes of mental retardation and mental illness and possible cures. He believed that mental retardation could arise from birth defects or postnatal causes, including coldness of the brain. In the second section of the book, he discussed some of the cures and medical practices of his time. These medical practices relied on a mix of folklore, alchemy, superstition, and science. He thought the environment must be conducive to cure, purging, and internal and external medicines (Woolfson, 1984). Later in the seventeenth century, Thomas Willis (1621-1675) developed his thoughts on developmental disabilities in 1672. Willis believed the physical welfare of the individual should be considered in conjunction with educational therapy. Willis (1621-1675) described mental deficiency:

> Some being wholly fools in the learning of letters, or the liberal sciences, are yet able enough for mechanical arts. Others, of either of these incapable, yet easily comprehend agriculture, or husbandry and country business. Others, unfit almost for all affairs, are only able to learn what belongs to eating or the common means of living: others merely dolts or driveling fools, scarce understand anything at all, or do anything knowingly. [Cited by Cranefield, 1961: 301]

Johann Gaspar Lavater published a three-volume set in 1774-1778 to support his theoretical ideas about physiognomy. The volumes contain numerous illustrations by Daniel Chodowiecki of people real and imagined that allegedly support his theory that psychological characteristics are revealed through a person's outward appearance. Many of these illustrations were drawn with no information about the appearances of people but with a bias toward proving Lavater's point of view. In the following drawing an assortment of people in all shapes and sizes is presented by Lavater. The work encompasses a wide variety of people with differences to help underscore

Lavater's observation on the variety of human forms. All of the representations reflect stereotypical and traditional ideas about people with developmental disabilities, physical deformities, dwarfism, or mental illness. For example, the fool is depicted with feathers and another with the staff of the fool. Melancholics are stereotypically shown. Sander Gilman (1982) noted that Lavater's debt to older images of mental illness is clear from the work.

194   FRAGMENT THIRD.

ADDITION B.

I fubjoin the profile of a girl of fixteen, whofe ftature fcarcely exceeded two feet. Her phyfionomy fuggefts abfolutely no other idea but that of a *confolidated infancy*. The forehead bent forward, indicates the phyfical imperfections of the firft ftage of human life, and the hollow inflexion of the root of the nofe is the infallible fign of mental weaknefs, or want of vigour. This head, notwithftanding, prefents a certain air of maturity, which feems to have *precipitated* itfelf, if I may ufe the expreffion, into the under part of the face, and which predominates from the under lip to the neck. The experienced Phyfionomift will eafily diftinguifh, in the whole, what is childifh from what is mature.

This dwarf, however, did not want fenfe, or rather, fhe could prattle, and had a retentive memory: the eye and the mouth are fufficient evidence of this; but her form and features are equally incompatible with the graces and the delicacy of fentiment.

Figure 41. Daniel Chodowiecki, untitled plate of girl from Johann Gaspar Lavater's *Fragmente,* 1774-1778, Special Collections, University of Colorado Library, Boulder.

European attitudes toward people with developmental disabilities were transported to the colonies with little or no change. Belief in divine retribution as a cause for disabilities, including developmental, persisted in the modern period. For example, the Puritans in New England believed in divine retribution. Governor Winthrop reported a "monsterous birth," a child with two mouths, which may have been an anencephalic child (Groce, 1985:122). Such occurrences were attributed to God's wrath on the sinful. The Puritan Increase Mather (1684) cited several causes of disabilities including divine retribution.

After the Middle Ages, artists occasionally chose people with developmental disabilities to be the subjects of their works. For example, the sixteenth century artist Hans Baldung, called Grien, drew a black chalk drawing of a head of a fool. Baldung did not draw the subject in a fool's costume that clearly indicates that this was a drawing of a person with mental retardation. The subject wears a hood and has a protruding lower lip, which Baldung used to suggest to the viewer low intelligence. The drawing is realistic and represents a sketch from an individual that Baldung may have encountered. Frans Hals (1580-1666) drawing entitled *Idiot* is another example of an artist's rendition of a person with developmental disabilities.

The great Spanish artist Diego Velasquez (1599-1662) painted several individuals from the Court of Philip IV of Spain. King Philip reported treating these members of his court with compassion, even though they were his servants (Evans, 1983). Velasquez's works during his tenure as court painter include, *El Nino de Valleca, El Primo, Antonio el Ingles* and the developmental disabled *El Bobo di Coria and Don Sebastian de Morra.* The following painting by Velasquez entitled Juan de Calabazas was of the court fool Calabazas. The Court of Philip IV had many people who were dwarfs and or had developmental disabilities. The royal family kept them for amusement and companionship. Typical of Velasquez, the style is faithful to Spanish realism and provides the viewer with an accurate depiction of a relatively well-off person with a developmental disability who was included in the seventeenth century Spanish Court. Most people with developmental disabilities would not have lived in such luxury. Calabazas holds the traditional pinwheel of madness in his left hand as he poses for the painter. The distinction between insanity and developmental disability are somewhat blurred.

Literature of the modern era also depicted people with developmental disabilities. For instance, nineteenth century literature makes numerous references to people with developmental disabilities. For example, Victor Hugo's Quasimodo from the *Hunchback of Notre Dame* (1834) competes at a fair to become the pope of fools by grimacing at a festival. Edgar Allan Poe's (1847) *Hop-Frog* was set during the Renaissance. Its main character is a court fool of small stature with a unique gait. Charles Dickens included many refer-

Figure 42. Diego Rodrquez de Silva y Velasquez, *The Jester Calabazas,* c. 1633, The Cleveland Museum of Art, Leonard C. Hanna, Jr. Fund, 1965.15, Cleveland, Ohio.

ences to children and adults with mental or physical disabilities. Dickens used the character Miss Moucher in *David Copperfield* to depict a person of small stature. Mr. Dick, in the same work, portrays mental disability. Dickens' was besieged by the poverty, misfortunes, ailments, and disabilities of Victorian England. He incorporated disabilities in his characters as a way to attack the social injustices of his times.

The responsibility to care and provide for people with developmental disabilities have historically rested on family and community, with the exceptions being for those people judged to be a danger to the community. Consequently, people with developmental disabilities, similar to those with other disabilities were free to roam about so long as they were not viewed as threatening to others. Dangerous people were either warehoused with others in jails (gaols) or driven from their communities. Thus, nondangerous people with developmental disabilities would have been familiar in many communities. As Trent (1994) noted, they were quite familiar to the general populace for many centuries. This was certainly true in post-revolutionary America where they were expected to participate in the community. Those having limitations that prohibited them from earning a living were either supported by the family or community at large. Similar provision of care by families and communities existed in Europe.

Care and treatment of people with developmental disabilities during the sixteenth and seventeenth centuries essentially remained medieval in character. They were basically cared for and treated in the same ways as those with other disabilities. They continued to be grouped and housed with people who were mentally ill. A case on point was how the Bicître in Paris was used. It was built in 1411 by Louis III as a hospice for invalid soldiers. Later, its function shifted and it began to serve a wide variety of people including those with developmental disabilities in 1654. Basically, all people were colocated at the Bicître until 1828 when a separate ward was established. Over time the Bicître, along with other asylums, evolved from temporary sanctuaries to houses for confinement for people with disabilities.

In Europe, religious organizations provided much of the care available in the seventeenth and eighteenth centuries. Whatever institutional care was provided was poor and resembled punishment rather than humane treatment. One notable exception was Saint Vincent de Paul (1581-1660) who gathered people together and attempted to teach them (Schreenberger, 1982). He was the exception and not the rule and many people with developmental disabilities did not fare particularly well. Similar to Europe, the colonials treated them as criminals, either locking them up or running them out of town. Others were placed out to households who would be paid fees to provide care. While some probably were cared for relatively well, others were exploited as low cost labor for household, farm, and cottage industries.

Corporal punishment was also inflicted on them. Communities were known to have encouraged and sometimes forced them to move to other communities to prevent them from becoming local nuisances. Those not leaving town were subjected to corporal punishment. For instance, Krishef (1983) found that one New York law of 1721 allowed for 36 lashes on the bare back of a man and 25 on a woman, if they did not heed the request for them to leave town. Other punishments included incarceration and abandonment (Deutsch, 1949). This would change in the latter half of the eighteenth century as reform efforts were made on their behalf.

Interest in developmental disabilities flared up during the first half of the nineteenth century. A number of factors fueled this interest, such as an increased public concern over oppressed people including slaves, prisoners, poor, and people with disabilities (Kanner, 1964). Around 1800, the almshouse method of treatment and care began to emerge in the United States (Krishef, 1983). Almshouse treatment, well-intentioned as it might have been, was inadequate. There was no separation of the sexes, food was poor, little to no bathing occurred, and people were punished as a means of control. The effect of the almshouses, whether stated or not, was to remove people, and more specifically those at risk of becoming paupers, from society. Other options were becoming available for people with developmental disabilities. In 1818, the American Asylum for the Deaf and Dumb of Hartford started accepting limited numbers of people. In 1821, the Commercial Hospital and Lunatic Asylum in Cincinnati also began admitting them on a limited basis. In Paris, Salpêtriére opened a section for women with developmental disabilities in 1831. This early effort was not to benefit the women so much as to separate them from the other patients. Parallel developments in almshouses and the expansion of existing institutes occurred in Europe.

The emphasis of these early facilities was not on training people but simply housing them, as the assumption was that they, similar to people who were deaf, could not benefit from instruction. Not everyone bought into the notion that they could not benefit from efforts to educate them. The Frenchman Gaspard Itard (1774-1838) undertook one of the earliest and most famous attempts to systematically educate a child with developmental disabilities. Itard tried to help a young boy known as the Victor of Aveyron or the Wolf Boy of Aveyron. In 1798, hunters captured a boy who was found wandering in the woods naked and alone. The boy was about age 11, dirty, had involuntary muscle contractions, had a short attention span, made guttural sounds, lacked language skills, and was unable to control his emotions. He walked on fours, scratched people, and otherwise acted as a wild animal. His appearance and behavior fit folklore that told of wild or feral children living in the woods and it was speculated he was raised by wild animals.

The boy was sent to Paris in 1798 and was eventually placed under the care of Dr. Jean Itard who taught students who were deaf. Itard, building on the ideas of Locke and Condillac, thought that by changing the environment, one could shape a student's life. Itard firmly believed that because the boy's behaviors were caused by the environment, it was possible to correct his behaviors. The hope was to teach him to be able to function in French society. After five years of effort, Itard failed in reaching his goals for the boy. Victor was able to use limited speech and control his behavior somewhat but a discouraged Itard finally concluded that little more could be accomplished. Victor would always require care and died in 1828.

The importance of Itard's' work with Victor was that he demonstrated that even the most difficult of individuals could be improved through education. This represented a quantum leap in the understanding of and perception of people with developmental disabilities. Itard (1774-1838) influenced teaching and general public attitudes toward people with developmental disabilities. His was the first documented attempt to systematically educate a person with developmental disability (Doll, 1967). Itard's greatest accomplishment was to help do away with the public sense of hopelessness regarding the potential of people with developmental disabilities (Kanner, 1967). Itard's work would be continued by scores of optimistic educators, including Edouard Seguin later in the nineteenth century.

Although they never worked directly with people with developmental disabilities, other eighteenth and nineteenth century educators of people who were deaf, such as Jacob Rodriques Pereire (1715-1780) and Abbe de L' Epée (1712-1789) were influential in creating a climate of optimism for people interested in teaching people with developmental disabilities. Although they did not specifically educate developmentally disabled people, their successes with students who were deaf were inspirational to educators, such as Itard and Seguin. Given the early successes of the schools for children with deafness, people increasingly saw the possibility of educating people with developmental disabilities. Many of the techniques used to teach people with deafness were modified to teach people with developmental disabilities.

Itard was not the only pioneer in educating people with developmental disabilities. In Europe, the Swiss physician Johann Jacob Guggenbühl (1816-1863) became interested in what he termed cretinism. Cretinism, "idiocy" and "imbecility" were all considered to be the same phenomenon with the only differences being the degree and presence of physical deformities (Kanner, 1964). Consequently, if cretinism could be successfully cured or people educated, then the techniques could be used on other forms of developmental disabilities. Before Guggenbühl, people with developmental disabilities were handled through schools for people who were deaf, blind, or mentally ill. They frequently assumed secondary roles, almost as after-

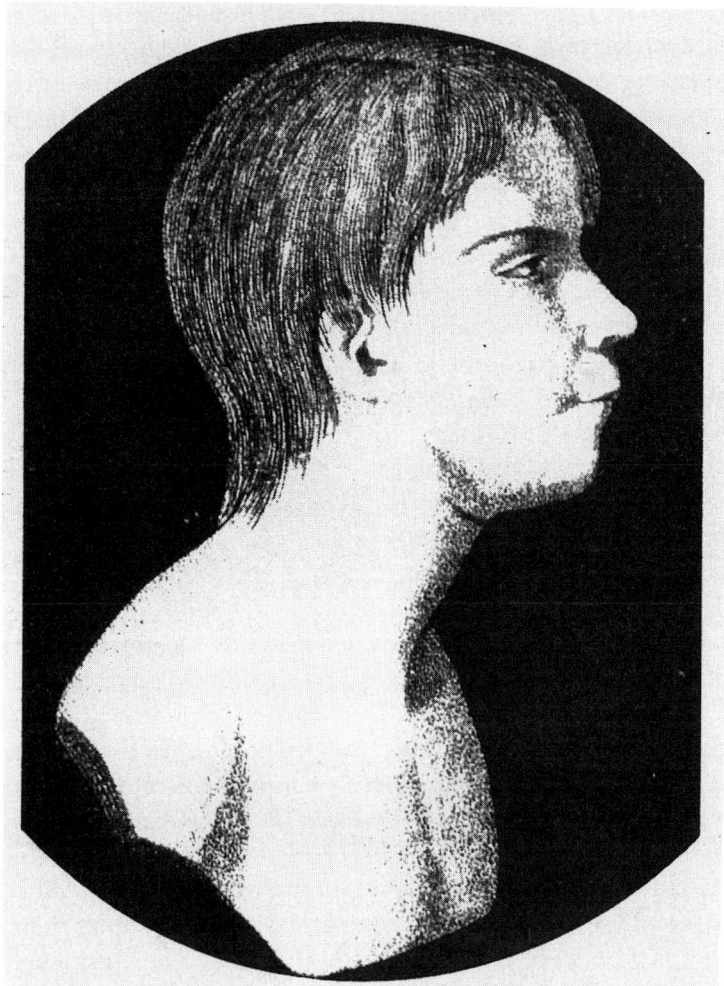

Figure 43. Unknown Artist, *Wild Boy of Averon*, unknown, Institut National de Jeunes Sourds de Paris, Paris, France.

thoughts of the people operating the schools and little energy was directed to educating them. Educators and medical personnel simply wrote them off as being able to change. Physicians and educators paid more attention to people with mental illness because they assumed that more could be accomplished.

Guggenbühl and Saegert in Germany developed systems for educating people with developmental disabilities. Guggenbühl found little information was available about the care and treatment of cretinism. He believed that residential care was essential for the treatment of cretinism. Guggenbühl believed that mountain air, good diet, and medications could, in combination, cure cretinism. Guggenbühl founded what many believe to be the first homelike residential facility for cretinism in Abendberg, Switzerland in 1839. At this facility he tried a number of educational techniques, such as carving letters from wood and connecting them with sounds to build up words (Doll, 1967). He dedicated his life to the "cure and prophylaxis" of cretinism (Kanner, 1967: 166). He was optimistic that successful cures and education were possible. His enthusiasm carried over and influenced many educators of the period.

Initially, the world credited Guggenbühl and the hospital with remarkable success and his fame spread throughout Europe. An influx of people from all over the world traveled to the institute. Guggenbühl needed to be away from the hospital over extended periods of time for fund raising and promoting the hospital. Eventually, people realized that Guggenbühl could not cure developmental disabilities and his claims were unsupported. Eventually, students and his school became the object of ridicule by the mid-nineteenth century. Mismanagement, neglect, fraudulent activities, such as claims of cures coupled with unfavorable inspections by authorities resulted in its decline in public support. Guggenbühl would be discredited as a fraud and quack. However, he is generally credited for instituting the first centrally located gathering place for people with developmental disabilities.

Following the claims and examples advanced by Guggenbühl, educators and administrators believed that people with developmental disabilities could be cured and that "normalcy" could be attained. By the first half of the nineteenth century, interest increased in educating people with developmental disabilities. This was sparked by increased public compassion toward neglected groups of people (Kanner, 1960-1961). Educators were highly optimistic during the last half of the nineteenth century. The nineteenth century gave rise to several independent efforts in Germany, Scotland, Ireland, the Netherlands, Switzerland, Denmark, Norway and eastern Europe to provide care and education for people with developmental disabilities. According to Scheerenberger (1982), the first special education class established as part of a public school system began in 1859 in Halle Germany. In spite of opposition in Germany, the concept spread to other German communities. During the last quarter of the nineteenth and first of the twentieth centuries, Norway (1874), Switzerland (1888), Prussia (1892), Austria (1895), England, 1898), Denmark (1900), Holland (1900), Belgium (1900), Sweden (1904), Italy (1900), and finally France 1909 established special education programs (Scheerenberger, 1982).

In the United States, the status and support of people with developmental disabilities was minimal. Some communities simply transported people to other communities or scared them out of town. Eventually chasing people to other communities lost favor to simply confining them in institutions to live under deplorable conditions. By 1818, there was an attempt at the Hartford Asylum for the Deaf and Dumb to teach developmental disabled people, but this was a modest effort. However, there were encouraging developments, such as the efforts of the nineteenth century reformers like Samuel Gridley Howe who was famous for his work with people with disabilities. Howe (1801-1876) was a physician who directed the Perkins Institution for the Blind in Boston until his death in 1876. Howe placed children with developmental disabilities in his Perkins Institute, a school primarily focused on educating children with blindness. In 1848, Howe persuaded the Massachusetts legislature to fund an experimental school for "idiots" in a wing of the Perkins Institute for the Blind. In 1851, a school was opened in Albany and was titled the State Asylum for Idiots, which would later become the Syracuse State Institution for the Feeble-Minded. In 1855, the Massachusetts School for the Idiotic and Feeble-Minded Youth was founded in Boston following a trial three-year period. Schools were later opened in Pennsylvania in 1853 and in 1857 in Columbus, Ohio. These early nineteenth century American schools drew on humanitarian and reformist values but little on scientific understanding of how to educate and work with people with developmental disabilities. They were highly optimistic that they could dramatically help their students (Tyor & Bell, 1984). These early facilities and others like them were established on an experimental basis rather than as custodial institutions. Superintendents used highly restrictive admission policies to assure that only those individuals most likely to benefit were admitted. The idea was to provide students with special education and return them to their families and communities (Morris & Morris, 1993). Statistics show that very few actually returned.

In 1848, Howe defined feebleminded persons as, persons (not) absolutely devoid of mind, but merely persons of feeblemind. He labeled those people capable of simple reasoning as simpletons. People have used the term simpleton, at least since the seventeenth century, to mean someone who was deficient in sense of intelligence or a simple, foolish person. Those people less capable were called fools, and the least capable were thought of as mere organisms and called idiots. One of Howe's most famous students was Laura Bridgeman, who arrived at Howe's school in 1837. Much has been written about his star student who was both deaf and blind, Laura Bridgeman. Under his instruction, Ms. Bridgeman was to become internationally famous for what she was capable of doing. Ms. Bridgeman's accomplishments added credibility to Howe's work and helped garner support for his efforts to help others. Bridgeman, Howe's most successful and famous student died at the school in 1889 (Trent, 1994). Howe was instrumental not only in championing the rights of an education for the seeing and hearing impaired, but also the developmentally disabled. During the nineteenth century, schools created for blind and/or deaf children also served as anchors for educators working with people with developmental disabilities.

Another nineteenth century reformer was Dorthea Dix, who was well-known as a champion of social causes. In 1841, the reformer, Dorthea Dix started a campaign to change attitudes and treatment of people with mental illness or developmental disabilities. She visited jails and almshouses and attempted to remove people and place them in mental hospitals. Dix (1843) observed:

> More than 9,000 idiots, epileptics, and insane in the US destitute of the appropriate care and protection, bound with galling chains, bowed beneath fetters and heavy iron balls attached to drag chains, lacerated with ropes, scourged with rods and terrified beneath storms of excrement and cruel blows; now subject to jibes and scorn and torturing tricks; now abandoned to the most outrageous violations. [Cited by Farber, 1968:43]

The American schools established in the 1850s represented an optimistic effort to rehabilitate and educate people with developmental disabilities. The key words to describe the attitudes of the times were innovation and reform. It was believed people could be taught to become self-sufficient and productive citizens. They could learn to live and function in society. Supervisors of these small schools were like father figures for people with developmental disabilities. Similar to efforts to rehabilitate juvenile delinquents in the nineteenth century, the emphasis was on creating family-like settings where students could learn the skills necessary to live independently. School staffs were dedicated and optimistic that they could significantly help students learn survival skills. Administrators turned away only the most severe cases.

The nineteenth century represents a period of major growth of facilities and schools specifically designed to train and care for people with developmental disabilities. The United States, for the most part, had lagged behind European countries in establishing schools and facilities for this population. A number of factors contributed to the explosive front-end growth of schools and facilities. For example, by the mid-1840s, local "idiots" became a major concern for officials and reformers. People were alarmed by census data (from 1840 census) that reported large numbers of "idiots" were being housed in jails and almshouses (Trent, 1994). When coupled with reports from Europe that people with developmental disabilities could successfully be educated to return to the community, American reformers increasingly pushed for the establishment of special schools and facilities. In addition, once established, superintendents and reformers pushed the boundaries of the facilities and schools to include a broader range of people. The facilities and schools admitted adults and other groups that communities and families were at a loss to understand and provide care. Overall, these institutions did not reflect thoughtful planning but shifts in the political and social structure of society at large (Farber, 1968).

When reformers and officials established the schools and facilities, they generally believed they would be able to return students back to their communities. Thus, they emphasized training for reentry into the community. However, for those students that could return to the community, they were not always welcomed back. The back-end of the system became closed to people. Poor labor conditions, economic downturns, professionalization, and fear of moral degeneracy suppressed the return of people with developmental disabilities and other "dependent" populations from returning to their communities. With more people being admitted and more not being permitted to leave, the net result was a dramatic increase in the populations in the facilities. This was exacerbated by changes in superintendent attitudes that focused on expansion rather than on returning people to communities. Increasingly, when people entered facilities their fates were set.

According to Kanner (1964), debates regarding people with developmental disabilities of the period included theological issues such as should people with developmental disabilities be confirmed. In addition, people were also concerned with how to strengthen the Christian character of people. They debated whether an "idiot" could swear in as a court witness. (It was decided they could be a witness but could not be sworn in.) By the last quarter of the nineteenth century, after a series of failures, authorities realized that people with developmental disabilities could not be "cured" in the dramatic fashion that Guggenbühl and others had proposed. Institutions for their education increasingly became viewed as permanent homes rather than transitional centers. Educators and their schools shifted from the individual needs of students to the perceived needs of society, which focused on protection and productivity with an emphasis on the former. Schools became more custodial in design and function. By the 1870s, Kanner (1964:85) concludes, "The mental detectives were viewed as a menace to civilization, incorrigible at home, burdens to the school, sexually promiscuous, breeders of feeble-minded offspring, victims and spreaders of poverty, degeneracy, crime and disease." Consequently, people increasingly called for their separation from the rest of society in an effort to "purify" society. Thus, people with developmental disabilities were cast in the same lot as people who were poor, of color, of newly immigrant cultures, with other disabilities, and other groups defined by the majority or those in power as social outcasts.

Following in the footsteps of Itard was Dr. Edouard Onesimus Seguin (1812-1880) who studied under Esquirol. Seguin is often credited for founding special education in the United States. Seguin treated children at the hospice des Incurables and at the Bicître in Paris. Dr. Seguin was idealistic and had a great love for humanity. He was optimistic that he could successfully treat and cure people with developmental disabilities. Seguin took an optimistic view of people with developmental disabilities and assumed that institutional care could help people become "normal" or function at a higher level.

Seguin was medically trained and used the basic medical design of diagnosis, prescription, and summary of the outcome for his model of educating developmentally disabled people (Talbot, 1967). Seguin (1812-1880) regarded them as one of the most neglected populations in society (Farber, 1968). A student of Itard methods, he openly credited him with many of his ideas on education. He developed a sequential system of education students' muscular and nervous systems. He believed that sensory motor training could be used to develop the central nervous system. He started with the proposition, " ...the education of the senses must precede the education of the mind" (Raymond, 1948:82). He believed emphasizing the development of the sense organs would help people with developmental disabilities, consequently physiological stimuli were incorporated into his approach. He believed that much could be accomplished through physical therapy, diet, and training of students to make increasing sensory discriminations. He labeled his techniques "Physiological Education." In 1837, he attempted to educate a developmentally disabled boy in a context where leading authorities such as Jean Etienne Esquirol who believed that working with "idiotic" people was useless (Kanner, 1960-1961). Seguin's student showed improvement and Esquirol would eventually admit to the success of Seguin but also questioned whether the individual was really a true "idiot." In 1846, Seguin published his influential *The Moral Treatment, Hygiene, and Education of Idiots and Other Backward Children* which was the definitive work on developmental disabilities for decades. During his lifetime he moved from France to the United States, and in 1852 he joined the Experimental School in Boston. This move ensured that his ideas were transferred to the United States. Seguin argued for regimentation, personalized treatment, no uniforms, self-sufficiency, and harmonious living. These basic ideas were influential in how schools were operated in Europe and the United States (Doll, 1967; Farber, 1968).

About the same time Seguin moved to the United States, others were working to develop facilities for people who had developmental disabilities. For example, Dr. Hervey B. Wilbur (1820-1883) Hervey Wilbur founded a school in Syracuse New York in 1854 (Raymond, 1948). Other state schools followed in New York (1851), Pennsylvania (1853), Connecticut (1858), and Ohio (1859). The growth of populations in these small facilities and schools quickly outgrew the funding available to support them towards the end of the nineteenth century in the United States. Increasingly, administrators warehoused people without public scrutiny or concern about what happened in facilities. The facilities afforded people little to no privacy, few if any programs, and no treatments. The general public opinion was that people with developmental disabilities were helpless, hopeless, burdensome, and dangerous to society at large. White and Wolfensberger (1969) characterize the operations of institutes and schools as passing through three phases. From 1850 to 1880, there was an honest attempt to make the "deviant nondeviant." From 1870 to 1890, it was to shelter the deviant from society and from 1880 to 1900, to protect society.

By the mid 1880s professionals were attempting to prevent the causes of developmental disabilities. The posture of professionals was proactivist because they believed they could change the course of events. Professionals classified the types of developmental disabilities as either "profoundly retarded" who were denied admission to public schools, "feeble-minded women" of child-bearing age, and "moral imbeciles." The selection of classifications sheds light on how people were perceived. People considered profoundly retarded to be developmentally disabled. The second category reflected a concern that young women who might have had developmental or learning disabilities were vulnerable and not capable of making good decisions. The latter category of moral imbeciles was a broad classification reflecting social concerns regarding people who were simply deviant. This latter group was seen as a threat to the existing socioeconomic order and an undue burden on society. It was a catchall category for people who were poor, abused substances, were criminal, or otherwise deviant. It would be safe to say that the three groups had little in common other than being viewed as needing institutionalization.

The connection between being an imbecile and having impaired moral judgment would be refined during the late nineteenth century. During the Victorian period, authorities made distinctions between degrees of imbecility. At one end were the feebleminded, then weak-minded, and at the extreme the imbecile (mental defect). Idiocy was a term reserved for conditions affecting all faculties (Gilman, 1988: 274). The concept of the moral imbecile would gain favor during the 1880s through the 1890s. Imbecility became more than impaired mental functioning or reasoning, as it became increasingly linked to one's morality. Consequently, it was applied to a wider range of human behaviors and deviants in general, as opposed to the more restricted meanings it had in the past. Issac N. Kerlin (1890) defined the moral imbecile as "...the fundamental disorder is manifested in the derangement of the moral perceptions or emotional nature rather than in the intellectual life, which not frequently is precocious," (Tyor & Bell, 1984: 80). Kerlin classified moral imbeciles into four categories: alcoholics, tramps, prostitutes, and habitual criminals. All had the common characteristic of being perceived as dangerous.

Highly influential during the latter quarter of the nineteenth and early twentieth centuries was the work of Charles Darwin. Charles Darwin's *Expressions of the Emotions in Man and Animals* (1873) argued there was an evolutionary hierarchy of emotions. Darwin drew upon the works of Bell and Dr. Browne with the insane. Darwin (1873: 245) wrote:

> Dr. Maudsley, after detailing various strange animal-like traits in idiots, asks whether these are not due to the reappearance of primitive instincts - " a faint echo from a far distant past, testifying to a kinship which man has almost outgrown."

Darwin was not alone in his thoughts on insanity and developmental disabilities. Among these scholars was the French psychiatrist Benedict Morel (1809-1873) who concluded that heredity accounted for a number of disorders that became more serious with each generation. He labeled these disorders "degeneration." Although he did not eliminate environmental factors leading to degeneration, his focus was on heredity. In 1857, Morel proposed the varieties of insanity and mental deficiencies were related. He hypothesized that both were hereditary and that over the successive generations, groups of people would degenerate and eventually become sterile. Morel associated mental disorders with sterility and viewed the process the "loss of vital energy." This vital energy dissipated with each generation until a state of idiocy was reached. Morel believed that environmental and social factors, such as poor housing, inadequate diet, poor working conditions caused genetic deterioration. Morel also believed that the environment could cause or help prevent genetic deterioration. He believed improvements in living conditions could slow if not halt the degeneration in populations. Morel believed that much could be accomplished by changing their living environments.

Others took his theory and combined it with the works of Charles Darwin. Social Darwinists led to two conceptions of people with developmental disabilities: races of humanity had evolved at different rates and degenerated races had been subjected to environmental influences that diminished their ability to survive. They concluded that people living under poor conditions were already degenerate. Evidence of their degeneracy was the fact that they were already living in poor conditions (Farber, 1968). Those with the strongest survival skills would be able to cope with the world. Those with the weakest or degenerate skills were destined to live in poverty.

Nineteenth century researchers sought to find evidence of degeneracy and looked to racial, foreign-born, and northern versus southern populations to support their theories. They wanted to justify what we would not view as essentially a racist and ethnocentric perception of people from different cultures. It should come as no surprise that people of color, living in southern states, or recent immigrants to northern cities would be found by nineteenth century researchers to be degenerate. In 1865, Sir Francis Galton expressed concern about the degeneration of the human race and later (1883) coined the term "Eugenics." The eugenics movement, as it would become known, argued for the sterilization of people judged to be genetically inferior during the twentieth century. In 1877, Richard Dugsdale (1841-1883) published his influential study, *The Jukes: A Study of Crime, Pauperism, Disease, and Heredity*. This study tied various forms of behavior of one family, the "Jukes" to numerous forms of deviance. The Juke family had a high proportion of social problems, such as developmental disabilities, low moral standards, crime, etc. Oscar Culloch and Henry Goddard echoed Dugsdale's conclusions. Goddard's (1914) study of the "Kallikak" family mirrored Dugsdale. Goddard claimed to have proof that descendants of Martin Kallikak had transmitted feeblemindedness.

The eugenics movement budded during the 1880s fueled by the federal census, prevention of the spread of (growth) in the "defective" population (Tyor & Bell, 1984). Consequently, the 1880s and 1890s witnessed increased pressures to institutionalize and retain people with developmental disabilities. Experts placed emphasis was on the custodial and maintenance functions of institutions that resulted in an inward focus on institutional life. The institution became the end in and of itself. Superintendents of institutions did not view their facilities as preparing people for the outside world but simply as maintaining people. In the 1930s, the eugenics surfaced and became powerful as a major social concern. In the thirties, the overemphasis on biological and genetic inheritance set back some of the optimism people held for education of people with developmental disabilities. This was view reinforced when the first generation of professionals, such as Howe and Seguin died, they left a leadership void that was filled by a new set of school superintendents. The new superintendents reformed the system of institutions into one that focused on custodial rather than in developing self-sufficiency and independent living concerns. In addition, facilities became more depersonalized in their treatment and care of people. Their goal became to make people as happy as they could be within institutionalized settings rather than train them to function in the outside world.

By the turn of the century a significant change occurred and there was a rise in the large custodial facilities. These facilities had little commitment to teaching independent living and more or less focused inward on the task of simply caring for people with developmental disabilities. Administrators emphasized teaching people limited tasks to make their lifelong stay at the facility somewhat useful. People were taught maintenance and chores to help contribute for their care. The basic mission of these facilities, as stated by Tyor and Bell (1984: xi), "...was the segregation of the deficient from the wider society." The facilities were really minisocieties with chapels, dormitories, gyms, auditoriums, power stations, kitchens, gardens, farms, playgrounds, and fences. They could operate almost independently of the larger society in their rural and isolated settings.

At the close of the nineteenth century, the foundations for the eugenics movement had been firmly laid. Led by Charles B. Davenport, Francis Galton, and Karl Pearson, the eugenics movement was an effort to improve inborn characteristics of man by the study of human heredity and application of those studies of human propagation. At the turn of the century, a period known as the "eugenics scare," resulted in the creation of numerous laws in the United States to restrict and control people with developmental disabilities. During the twentieth century the eugenics movement would gain strength, due in part to the advent of intellectual testing. Segregation and marriage restrictions were implemented. Some proposed that they be sterilized to check populations and also prevent masturbation. Proponents of the sterilization argued the last decade of the nineteenth and first four decades of the twentieth centuries that the procedure helped maintain order in facilities, eugenic control, and helped limit the growth of institutional populations (Trent, 1993). It would peak from 1900 to 1910 in the United States and added fuel to the Nazi movement that followed in Germany. For example, in 1905, Pennsylvania enacted a sterilization law. Almost 30,000 people would be sterilized over the next 50 years in the United States (Krishef, 1983). Eugenics was readily accepted by society at large because of the view that people with developmental disabilities were a social menace and left unchecked would breed and cause society to decline. Harry C. Sharp, an American physician who was the first to castrate an inmate to eliminate the individual's masturbation and control population growth wrote in 1907:

> Idiots, imbeciles and degenerate criminals are prolific, and their defects are transmissible. Each person is a unit of the nation, and the nation is strong and pure and sane, or weak and corrupt and insane in proportion that the mentally and physically healthy exceed the diseased, nor can any nation live if there is a reverse ratio. So we owe if not only to ourselves, but the future of our race and nation, to see that the defective and diseased do not multiply. (Cited by Tyor & Bell, 1984:102)

PEOPLE WHO HAD DEVELOPMENTAL DISABILITIES OVER THE CENTURIES

Comparatively little is known about how people with developmental disabilities lived in the past. What is known suggests that there have been many misconceptions about people with developmental disabilities. These misconceptions, while sometimes positive in tone, were nevertheless overwhelmingly negative and had major consequences for people. For centuries mental illness and mental retardation were viewed as one and the same. Even after differences were noted, people with developmental disabilities were grouped with criminals, the poor, people who were ill or had mental illness.

People with developmental disabilities have faced numerous social stereotypes. Contemporary scholars have identified several enduring social perceptions and stereotypes about people who had developmental disabilities (Evans, 1983; Krishef, 1983; Tyor & Bell, 1984). For example, Kanner (1960-61) identified social reactions to people who have developmental disabilities including neglect, toleration, and kindness. In contrast, Trent (1994) identified perceptions and reactions such as teasing, being subjects of humor or the butt of jokes, disgust, pity, benevolence, and being children of nature. Most of these social perceptions and stereotypes attached to people with developmental disabilities, regardless of how they are classified, carried negative connotations.

People with developmental disabilities increasingly became viewed as medical phenomena as the medical profession grew and expanded. Increasingly, experts viewed them as being sick or diseased and treated them as patients. People were to be viewed as within a medical lexicon of being cases, residing in wards or hospitals, subject to cures, called patients, and having treatments along with other medical expressions similar to people who were ill. Today, most of these historical terms are not used and would be considered offensive and negative.

People with developmental disabilities have been confronted with a variety of moves to control and restrict their actions. For example, guardianship, involuntary sterilization, prohibition of marriage, and incarceration have all been applied to people with developmental disabilities. Sometimes these moves have been well-intentioned but mostly they were made out of fear, misunderstanding, or apathy. The irony is that while many people with developmental disabilities sought to integrate into their respective societies, these same societies placed restrictions on their ability to integrate. At times they were denied rights afforded others, such as marriage, to have offspring, hold property, and acquire wealth through inheritance.

There has been no sustained reforming drive or passion to aid people with developmental disabilities. The overpowering stigma attached to developmental disabilities has discouraged reform and interest. There has been a widespread perception that developmental disabilities can be altered but never cured. Consequently, for some people there has been a general sense of hopelessness. They were written off as being hopeless and helpless for centuries. People did not believe that they could be taught or could function well in society. Consequently, they were essentially on their own and were the responsibility of their families or friends. They were seen as a domestic matter and correspondingly, no "mad doctors" and asylum superintendents offered them care, as was the case for people who were mentally ill. Thus, few asylums over history at least up to the last third of the eighteenth century admitted those people determined to be "idiots" (Rushton, 1988). The family and community continued to be the first resort for their care and support. For those not able to secure family or community support, one can only speculate that life was probably tough for many. There is little evidence that they lived particularly well. Rushton (1988:39) observed that in northeastern England, "...most of the problems of idiocy stemmed from family poverty and the failure to arrange an effective system of domestic care." Idiocy, he adds, was an accepted cause of poverty.

It was comparatively late in history before the notion that they might benefit from humane treatment and education arose. This pattern was similar to that for people who were deaf, although deaf education started almost two centuries before efforts to educate people with mental retardation. In the early part of the nineteenth century there was a rise of residential institutions and special schools for people with developmental disabilities that would dramatically change public perceptions. An outcome of the asylum movement was that sufficient numbers of people were brought together in single locations. Their concentration allowed for observation and the beginning of treatment and systematic understanding. These facilities also fueled beliefs that they not only were different from the rest of society but more importantly that they should be separate from the general populace. From then after, separation was the operating assumption when thinking of people with developmental disabilities. In the twentieth century, the move became to reduce these institutional populations by reintroducing people back into their communities or preventing their removal in the first place. The issue became the lack of equal access to educational and other programs in mainstream society.

The late nineteenth and early twentieth centuries' emphasis on genetic inheritance through the lens of Social Darwinism, dengenerationist, or eugenics theories probably impacted people with developmental disabilities and specifically mental retardation dramatically. Underlying this emphasis was the selfish motive of the middle class to maintain the status quo and eliminate anything that threatened the socialeconomic order. People with developmental disabilities, with deafness, from different cultures, working classes, the poor, and people of color were all perceived as representing a threat to the order of things. People with developmental disabilities, perhaps more or at least as much as any group, were not only restricted but socially and medically punished for having disabilities.

EPILOGUE

It should be apparent from these chapters that common threads run through the social history of disabilities. One such thread has been that some of the social perceptions and stereotypes about people with disabilities have been shared. Social perceptions of people with disabilities as being less than human, gifted, deviant, scapegoats, entertaining, evil, gifted, fascinating, beggars, dependent, depressed, naive, and destined to a life of poverty were present in the past and continue to surface in contemporary society. These social perceptions are grounded in long-term notions and misunderstandings about disabilities that have persisted over the centuries. Today, few would argue that the social environment is more favorable than it was in the past for people with disabilities. But much more needs to be done to break down some of the enduring negative social perceptions and responses that continue to affect people.

Numerous factors influenced the creation and maintenance of these social perceptions. The evolution of the moral order, most noticeably through the rise of Christianity, certainly helped frame the social context in which these perceptions arose. Before Christianity evidence suggests that while some societies, such as the ancient Egyptians, responded to disabilities in some surprisingly positive ways, the overall picture for people with disabilities was not particularly favorable. Although no one knows how many people were mistreated or killed, it is clear that ancient laws and customs in many societies permitted families and communities to harm children and adults judged to be different because of their disabilities. With a few brief exceptions, there is little evidence of mass destruction of people with disabilities in history. Rather, people with disabilities were very much a part on the social landscape and if anything were generally treated with ambivalence. We know that people survived and in cases coped with otherwise hostile social conditions and customs. Undoubtedly, as is the case today, many people became disabled over the course of their lives and probably represented a sizable group in earlier societies. The many images of people with physical disabilities scattered through the art of the centuries and medical as well as archeological evidence provides testament of the extent to which people with disabilities were active members of their respective societies.

Evidence suggests that the rise of Christianity resulted in more compassionate, empathetic, and humane responses to people with disabilities. Christianity provided a moral framework in which disabilities were measured and judged. Initially, disabilities were viewed as the product of God's will and evidence of sin. Disabilities and the people with them were seen as sinners and were being punished. This was particularly true for people who had severe developmental disabilities, had leprosy, or were mentally ill. The underlying assumption was that they made moral choices that resulted in their disabilities. When this interpretation was dominant, people with disabilities did not fare well under the cloak of Christianity. Early Christians equated disability with sin and labeled them as sinners (similar to some people's contemporary views on AIDS). Implied is the notion that one should not accept themselves if they have a disability, as they are sinners. Rather than self-acceptance, they should seek forgiveness and miracles to cure themselves.

As Christianity developed and spread, it increasingly called for more compassion for people with disabilities. People were not to be seen as sinners but as God's creations, for better or worse. All Christians were viewed as God's creation and thus shared a common bond. It was within this context that the church took an active role in building early systems of care and treatment. In western social history, the development of church-supported care stands as a landmark and generally positive shift in the interpretation and reaction to people with disabilities. A shift that would be altered with the Protestant Reformation, which pulled back established mechanisms for care, and helped move society to systems of more secular-based care.

Although Christianity eventually taught tolerance and acceptance, the formal church traditionally restricted people who had disabilities from participating as full-blown members in the activities of the church and those social activities it sanctioned, such as marriage. In addition, during times of uncertainty, calamity, reform, economic decline, fear, pestilence, plague, and fervent soul-searching, the church could and did turn against the interests and well-being of people with disabilities. Evidence suggests that at times the church, be it Catholic or Protestant, limited, scapegoated, blamed, restricted, and most importantly punished people because of their disabilities. The punishment or sending of people with physical deformities, developmental disabilities, and those who were mentally ill to their deaths in the name of God occurred, perhaps more so for those with mental illness. When the need arose, people with disabilities could be ideal tools for the church as benevolent benefactor or as enforcer of morality. In the final analysis, there have been mixed messages from Christianity regarding people with disabilities.

In reviewing what has been written and what we know about the lives of people with disabilities in the past, a possible conclusion one can reach was that people with disabilities may have been more familiar to the general public in the past than they are today. It is also true that for many centuries the absence of institutional options allowed people to live, sometimes well and other times not so well, in the mainstream of their respective societies. Only those judged to be dangerous or posing threats were confined or punished. This implies that many people with disabilities before the rise of institutions and asylums were both familiar and integrated into the social fabric of their times. The rise of institutional care and treatment has been identified by numerous historians and scholars as being a critical development in the history of many types of populations, including those with disabilities. The motives for institutionalizing people have varied. Notions of fear, misunderstanding, control, compassion, personal gain, humanity, segregation, fear of contagion, sense of obligation, punishment, among others seem to flavor much of what occurred in the past. Regardless of motive, the bottom line is that by confining or isolating people, they become less familiar and even more vulnerable to social stereotypes, which are likely to be negative and harmful.

Historically, societies have put far more energy into restricting people with disabilities than providing them with opportunities. The notion that people with disabilities had rights was comparatively slow to develop. Rather laws, policies, and social practices focused on restricting people. For example, the many restrictions on people with the disabling disease of leprosy, the limited roles people who were deaf were allowed to play in religious affairs, the sterilization of people with developmental disabilities, the prohibition of marriage, the limitations placed on inheritance, the political barriers to people who had leprosy, restrictions on housing and burials, and countless other examples bear testament to the restrictions that have been placed on people. Today, some restrictions continue to be in place but much has been gained by people with disabilities. A strong argument can be made that in history the French Revolution represented a major shift in western thinking about the rights of people, including those with disabilities.

In addition, key shifts in western history such as the Renaissance which emphasized the importance of the individual and focused on the human form and function, played an influential role in shaping social perceptions of people with disabilities. The Enlightenment introduced logic and reason to the equation although it was often misdirected until the rise of modern science and medicine. It was during the Enlightenment that people began to question age-old assumptions about the learning potential of people with disabilities. For example, scholars and educators increasingly came to question the assumption that most people who were deaf, blind, or developmentally disabled could not learn. The idea that people with these characteristics could, should, and eventually had a right to learn was born during this time. This shift in social perception represents a quantum leap in how people with these or other disabilities were viewed and treated in the centuries that followed.

Later, the notion that groups of people with disabilities could be taught was eventually linked to industrialization. Increasingly, societies judged one's worth and status on their ability to work. Begging became an unacceptable way for people to support themselves. Those who couldn't or didn't work were judged to be vagrants and social outcasts. Thus, considerable effort became directed toward the training of people to function and work in society. Societies became less tolerant of the traditional role many people with severe disabilities had, that of beggar. Although some were able to gain employment, jobs and other meaningful social roles were limited by the state of the economy and the wishes of social groups, such as public officials, labor unions, and social reformers.

The rise of genetics and Darwin's Theory of Evolution resulted in a major shift in the social history of disabilities. Apart from the scientific and theoretical merits of both, societies applied genetic and evolutionary understandings initially not to help people but to restrict, control, and otherwise eliminate people with disabilities. Social Darwinism and the theory of degeneration legitimized racism, ethnocentrism, classism, and prejudice and discrimination against people with some types of disabilities. People born with characteristics that resulted in disabilities were judged to be degenerate and inferior and were treated as if they were. This occurred to the extent that some families broke off or hid their links to family members with disabilities. Today genetics, medicine, and science are making great strides in helping prevent or manage biologically-caused sources of disabilities. The negative connotations of congenital and other inherited disabilities does not carry the same meanings as they did in the past.

Once the idea that people with disabilities could be cured or treated became ingrained in western thought, it became an obsession. One only needs to review the chapters on mental illness or deafness in this volume to get a taste of the extremes to which well-intentioned people have tried to cure and treat disabilities. The line between corporal punishment and treatment for much of history was often blurred. With a few exceptions, most people would prefer to not have disabilities, so in general such efforts were motivated by a just purpose. However, the treatments were often more the obsession of the practitioner than the person with the disability. The many radical and misdirected efforts, such as bleeding, purging, use of water, electricity, chains, whips, crude ear surgeries, and confinement underscore the extent to which people were willing to subject those with disabilities to treatment. Rather than helping people adjust to and accept their disabilities, the historical emphasis has been to minimize and/or remove disabilities as characteristics. Implied with this obsession is the notion that there is something unacceptable about having a disability. People who seek cures or miracles are wanting to change something about themselves that they do not like. Many learned that they should not accept their disabilities and themselves for what they were but strive toward being something or be someone they couldn't.

Many voids in information exist regarding the history of disabilities. For one, the role of the family and the community in caring for people with severe disabilities is virtually uncharted territory. Historians have written volumes about institutional settings but little about people with disabilities within their families or host communities. This is ironic as most people with disabilities, even those that were quite severe, were not institutionalized or hospitalized but were cared for by their friends and families. A second void is while volumes have been written about mental illness, deafness, or blindness, comparatively little is available on other people with other disabilities such as those that are developmental or physical.

We are entering a period when societies are re-familiarizing themselves with people who have disabilities. This is occurring on several fronts. One is an increasing awareness that many people become disabled over the course of their life spans. Disability is not something that happens to someone else but happens to us. Second, with the steady integration of people with disabilities into their communities, they are more likely to be among the general population and hence more familiar. Improvements in technology, medical advances, and a number of other changes have increased the opportunities for people to move about and participate in their respective societies. This trend will likely continue and one result of it is that disabilities and people with them will be more commonplace and more familiar, as they were centuries before. In addition, laws have been established that guarantee the rights of people with disabilities to participate as full members in their respective societies. Finally, contemporary popular culture seems to have embraced and romanticized people with disabilities. For example, in recent years many leading figures in the movies have had disabilities. Examples from the films include, *The Rain Man, Nell, Shine, My Left Foot, Silence of the Lambs, The English Patient, The Piano,* and *Scent of a Woman.* All of these films main characters had disabilities. All of the actors in these parts either won or were nominated for academy awards. The ongoing western fascination with people with disabilities continues today.

Today, the language of disability remains an important force in how people with disabilities relate to their world and the world relates to them. Much of the terminology associated with disability initially was cast with moral and religious overtones. Over time this shifted to be simply negative. With the rise of professional treatment, education, care, and knowledge the negativism declined but remains with us today. Many of the terms finding use in the past remain with us today and are part of the historical heritage of disabilities. People are still referred to as gimps, geeks, vegetables, wheelchair-bound, morons, midgets, idiots, fools, nuts, basket cases, and so forth. Until the last couple of decades, people with disabilities have had little input into the terms and language used to describe them and their lives. However, a significant shift has started to occur as people have become more sensitive to the power language and terms have over the lives of people. Those most affected by the language of disability, that is those with the disabilities, need to and will take an active role in shaping the nature of this language.

Although the historical trail is weak and often difficult to follow, the more familiar one becomes with the history of disabilities, the more one gains a sense that there is an untold story waiting to be told about the many unseen number of people with disabilities who got by, survived, and in some cases thrived throughout western history. These are the ordinary everyday people who never became Beethovens, or Tamberlaines, but nevertheless found ways to adapt to their disabilities in times less tolerant than today. The human spirit must have flowed through their veins.

REFERENCES

Abramov, I. 1993. History of the Deaf in Russia, myths and realities. In Fischer, R. & Lane, H. (Eds.) 1993. *Looking Back: A Reader on the History of Deaf Communities and their Sign Languages.* Hamburg, Germany: Signum, p. 199-205.

Abt, I. 1965. History of Pediatrics. Philadelphia, Pennsylvania: W.B. Saunders.

Alderidge, P. 1985b. Bedlam: Fact or fantasy? In W.F., Porter, R. & Shepherd, M. (Eds.) *The Anatomy of Madness: Essays in the History of Psychiatry, Vol. II, Institutions and Society.* London: Tavistock Publications. Pp. 17-33.

Alexander, F. G. & Selesnick, S. T. 1966. *The History of Psychiatry: An Evaluation of Psychiatric Thought and Practice from Prehistoric Times to the Present.* New York: Harper & Row.

Andreski, S. 1989. *Syphilis, Puritanism and Witchhunt: Historical Explanations in the Light of Medicine and Psychoanalysis with a Forecast About AIDS.* New York: St. Martin's Press.

Angier, N. 1993. Creativity's darker side: Link to mental disorders confirmed, *The Denver Post,* October 12, 1993: 2a-6a.

Anonymous, 1977. Exorcising the leper. *The Medical Journal of Australia,* 2: (11) 345-347.

Anonymous, 1978. News and notes. *International Journal of Leprosy,* 46: (1) 72-73.

Appelboom, T., de Boelpaepe, C., Ehrlich, G. E. & Famaey, J. 1981. Rubens and the question of antiquity of rheumatoid arthritis. *Journal of the American Medical Association,* 245: (Feb.) 483-486.

Aries, P. 1974. *Western Attitudes Toward Death: From the Middle Ages to the Present.* Baltimore, MD: Johns Hopkins University Press.

Aries. P. 1985. Images of Man and Death. Cambridge, MA: Harvard University Press.

Arrizabalaga, J. 1993. Syphilis, In Kiple, K. F. (Ed.) *The Cambridge World History of Human Disease.* Cambridge: Cambridge University Press, p. 1025-1033.

Barker, R. G. 1948. The social psychology of physical disability. *The Journal of Social Issues,* 4: (No. 4) 28-38.

Barker, R. G. 1971. The social psychology physical disability. In Sagarin, E. (Ed.), *The Other Minorities.* Waltham, MA: Xerox College Publishing, p. 210-224.

Baskett, J. & Snelgrove, D. 1978. *The Drawings of Thomas Rowlandson in the Paul Mellon Collection.* New York: Brandywine Press.

Baynton, D. C. 1993. Savages and deaf-mutes: Evolutionary theory and the campaign against sign language in the nineteenth century. In Van Cleve, J. V. (Ed.)

Deaf History Unveiled: Interpretations from the New Scholarship, Washington, DC: Gallaudet University Press, p. 92-112.

Bayless, J.H. 1977. Leprosy in medieval England, *Leprosy Review,* 48: 291-292.

Benda, C. E. 1949. *Mongolism and Cretinism.* New York: Grune & Straton.

Bender, R. E. 1970. *The Conquest of Deafness: A History of the Long Struggle to Make Possible Normal Living to Those Handicapped by Lack of Normal Hearing.* Cleveland, OH: The Press of Case Western University.

Bernard, Y. 1993. Silent artists. In Fischer, R. & Lane, H. (Eds.) 1993. *Looking Back: A Reader on the History of Deaf Communities and their Sign Languages.* Hamburg, Germany: Signum, p. 75-87.

Bernheimer, R. 1952. *Wildmen in the Middle Ages: A Study in Art Sentiment and Demonology.* Cambridge: Harvard University Press.

Best, H. 1934. *Blindness and the Blind in the United States.* New York: Macmillan Co.

Bixenstine, L. 1989. Tender moments: The mother/child paintings of Mary Cassatt. *Kaleidoscope,* 18: 10-13.

Bogdan, R. & Taylor, S. 1976. The judged, not the judges: An insider's view of mental retardation, *American Psychologist,* 31: 47-52.

Bogdan, R. and Biklen, D. 1977. Handicappism. *Social Policy* 7: (No. 4) 14-19.

Bogdan, R., Biklen, D., Shapiro, A., & Spelkoman, D. 1982. The disabled: media's monster. *Social Policy* 13: (No. 2) 32-35.

Bogdan, R. 1986. Exhibiting mentally retarded people for amusement and profit, 1850-1940. *American Journal of Mental Deficiency* 91: (No.2) 120-126.

Bogdan, R. & Taylor, S. 1989. Relationship with severely disabled people: The social construction of humanness. *Social Problems* 36: (No. 2) 135-148.

Brody, S. N. 1974. *The disease of the Soul: Leprosy in Medieval Literature.* Ithaca, NY: Cornell University Press.

Brooke, C. 1985. The structure of mediaeval society. In Evans, J. (Ed.), *The Flowering of the Middle Ages.* New York: Bonanza Books, p. 12-34.

Browne, J. 1985. Darwin and the face of madness. In Bynum, W.F., Porter, R., & Shepherd, M. (Eds.) *The Anatomy of Madness: Essays in the History of Psychiatry, Vol. II, Institutions and society.* London: Tavistock Publications, p. 151-165.

Browne, S.G. 1990. How old is leprosy? *International Journal of Dermatology* 19: (9) 530 - 532.

Bullough, V. & Bullough, B. 1969. *The Emergence of Modern Nursing* (2nd Ed). New York: Macmillan.

Bulwer, J. 1644. *Chirologia: or, The Natural Language of the Hand.* London: R. Whitaker.

Bulwer, J. 1648. *Philocophus: Or the Deaf and Dumbe Mans Friend.* London: Humphrey Moseley. (Media 604).

Burrow, J.A. 1986. *The Ages of Man: A Study in Medieval Writing and Thought.* Oxford, England: Clarendon Press.

Burstein, S. R. 1956. Demonology and medicine in the sixteenth and seventeenth centuries. *Folklore* 67: (No. 1) 16-33.

Burt, J. R. 1982. *Selected Themes and Icons from Medieval Spanish Literature: Of Beards, Shoes, Cucumbers and Leprosy.* Madrid, Spain: Jose Porrua Turanzas.

Bynum, W.F., Porter, R., & Shepherd, M. (Eds.), 1988. *The Anatomy of Madness: Essays in the History of Psychiatry, Vol. III, The Asylum and its Psychiatry.* London: Routledge.

Calvert, K. 1992. *Children in the House: The Material Culture of Early Childhood, 1600-1900.* Boston: Northeastern University Press.

Camporesi, P. 1989. Bread of dreams, *History Today* 39: (April) 14-21.

Carmichael, A. G. 1993. Leprosy. In Kiple, K. F. (Ed.) *The Cambridge World History of Human Disease.* Cambridge: Cambridge University Press, p. 834-839.

Cavina, A. O. 1989. Annibal Carracci's Paintings of the Blind: An Addition. *The Burlington Magazine* 131: 27-28.

Cheyene, G. 1733/1976. *The English Malady.* New York: Scholar's Facsimiles and Reprints, Inc.

Chough, S. 1983. The deaf community: Our sociological perspective. *The Deaf American* 35: 2-6.

Clair, C. 1968. *Human Curiosities.* New York: Abellard-Schuman.

Clarke, A.M. & Clarke, A.D.B. 1965 (Eds.) *Mental Deficiency: The Changing Outlook.* New York: The Free Press.

Clay, R. M. 1909. *The Mediaeval Hospitals of England.* London: Methuen.

Cleland, C. C. & Swartz, J. D. 1993. *Exceptionalities Through the Lifespan: An Introduction.* New York: Macmillan.

Cohn, J. P. 1989. Leprosy out of the dark ages, *FDA Consumer* 23: (No. 7) 24-27.

Copplestone, T. 1983. *Art in Society.* Englewood, NJ: Prentice-Hall.

Covey, H. C. 1991. *Images of Older People in Western Art and Society.* New York: Praeger.

Cranefield, P. F. 1961. A seventeenth century view of mental deficiency and schizophrenia: Thomas Willis on Stupidity or Foolishness. *Bulletin of the History of Medicine* 35: 291-316.

Cranefield, P. F. 1966. Historical perspectives. In Philips, I. (Ed.) *Prevention and Treatment of Mental Retardation.* New York: Basic Books, Inc., p. 3-14.

Crittenden, J. B. 1993. The culture and identity of deafness. In Paul, P. V. & Jackson, D. W. (Eds.) *Toward a Psychology of Deafness: Theoretical and Empirical Perspectives.* Boston, MA: Allyn & Bacon, p. 215-235.

Crouch, B. A. 1986. Alienation and the mid-nineteenth century deaf community: A response. *American Annals of the Deaf* 131: 322-324.

Darwin, C. 1873. *The Expression of Emotions in Man and Animals.* New York: D. Appleton.

Davis, F. 1961. Deviance disavowal: The management of strained interaction by the visibly handicapped, *Social Problems* 9: (No. 2) 120-132.

DeBeauvior, S. S. 1972. *The Coming of Age.* New York: G.P. Putnam's Sons.

Deland, F. 1968. *The Story of Lip-Reading: Its Genesis and Development.* Washington, DC: The Alexander Graham Bell Association for the Deaf, Inc.

de Mause, L. (Ed.) 1974. *The History of Childhood: The Untold History of Child Abuse.* London: Bellew.

de Mause, L. 1974a. The evolution of childhood. In de Mause, L. (Ed.) *The History of Childhood: The Untold History of Child Abuse.* London: Bellew Publishing, p. 1-73.

Demos, J. 1986. *Past, Present, and Personal.* New York: Oxford University Press.

Deshen, S. A. 1992. *Blind People: The Private and Public Life of Sightless Israelis.* Albany, New York: State University of New York Press.

Despert, J. L. 1965. *The Emotionally Disturbed Child -Then and Now.* New York: Robert Brunner, Inc.

Deutsch, A. 1949. *The Mentally Ill in America: A History of Their Care and Treatment from Colonial Times.* New York: Columbia University Press.

Di Carlo, L. M. 1964. *The Deaf.* Englewood Cliffs, NJ: Prentice-Hall, Inc.

Dickens, C. 1874. *The Old Curiosity Shop.* New York: G.W. Carlton and Company.

Dickens, C. 1981. *Cricket on the Hearth.* Dunwood, Georgia: Genesis.

Doll, E. E. 1967. Trends and problems in the education of the mentally retarded: 1800-1940. *American Journal of Mental Deficiency* 72: (No. 2) 175-183.

Dols, M. W. 1979. Leprosy in medieval Arabic medicine. *Journal of the History of Medicine and Allied Sciences* 34: (3) 314-333.

Dols, M. W. 1983. The leper in medieval Islamic society. *Speculum* 58 (4) 891-916..

Dove, M. 1986. *The Perfect Age of Man's Life.* Cambridge: Cambridge University Press.

Drake, M. E., Jr. 1992. Medical and neuropsychiatric aspects of lycanthropy. *Journal of Medical Humanities* 13: (No.1) 5-15.

Duncan, H. & Leisen, J. C.C. 1993. Arthritis (Rheumatoid). In Kiple, K. F. (Ed.) *The Cambridge World History of Human Disease.* Cambridge: Cambridge University Press, p. 599-603.

Dunning, A.J. 1992. *Extremes.* New York: Harcourt Brace Jovanovich Publishers.

Eberly, S. S. 1988. Fairies and the folklore of disability: Changelings, hybrids and the solitary fairy. *Folklore* 99: (i) 58-77.

Ehrlich, G. E. 1986. The arthritis of Peter Paul Rubens as a perspective of his time. *Medical Heritage* 2: (5) 334-339.

Evans, D. P. 1983. *The Lives of Mentally Retarded People.* Boulder, CO: Westview Press.

Farber, B. 1968. *Mental Retardation: Its Social Context and Social Consequences.* Boston: Houghton Mifflin.

Faber, B. 1986. Historical contexts of research on families with mentally retarded members. In Gallagher, J.J. & Vietze, P. M. (Eds.) *Families of Handicapped Persons.* Baltimore, MD: Paul H. Brooks, p.-23.

Farrell, G. 1956. *The Story of Blindness.* Cambridge: Harvard University Press.

Feder, L. 1980. *Madness in Literature.* Princeton, NJ: Princeton University Press.

Fiedler, L. 1978. *Freaks: Myths and Images of the Secret Self.* New York: Simon and Schuster.

Fischer, D.H. 1978. *Growing Old in America.* Oxford, England: Oxford University Press.

Fischer, R. & Lane, H. (Eds.) 1993. *Looking Back: A Reader on the History of Deaf Communities and their Sign Languages.* Hamburg, Germany: Signum.

Foucault, M. 1965. *Madness and Civilization: A History of Insanity in the Age of Reason.* New York: Random House.

Forbes, T. R. 1979. By what disease or casualty: The changing face of death in London. In Webster, C. (Ed.) *Health, Medicine and Morality in the Sixteenth Century.* Cambridge: Cambridge University Press, p. 117-139.

Foster, S. 1989. Social alienation and peer identification: A study of the social construction of deafness. *Human Organization* 48: (No. 3) 226-235.

Frazer, J. G. 1935. *The Golden Bough: A Study in Magic and Religion* (3rd Ed). New York: Macmillan.

Freeman, J.T. 1965. Medieval perspectives in aging (12th-19th centuries). *Gerontologist* 5: 1-24.

French, R. S. 1932. *From Homer to Helen Keller: A Social and Educational Study of the Blind.* New York: American Foundation for the Blind.

French, R. K. 1993a. Scrofula. In Kiple, K. F. (Ed.) *The Cambridge World History of Human Disease.* Cambridge: Cambridge University Press, p. 998-1000.

Funk, R. 1987. Disability rights: From caste to class in the context of civil rights. In Gartner, A. & Joe, T. (Eds.) *Images of the Disabled, Disabling Images.* New York: Praeger, p. 7-30.

Gardner, J. F. 1993. *Being a Roman Citizen.* London: Routledge.

Gareau, M. 1992. *Charles Le Brun: First Painter to King Louis XIV.* New York: Harry N. Abrams.

Garrison, F. H. 1960. *An Introduction to the History of Medicine* (4th Ed). Philadelphia: W.B. Saunder.

Gartner, A. & Joe, T. (Eds.) 1987. *Images of the Disabled, Disabling Images.* New York: Praeger.

Gauthier, M. 1964. *The Louvre Paintings.* New York: Meredith Press.

Gilman, S. L. 1982. *Seeing the Insane: A Cultural History of Madness.* New York: J. Wiley.

Gilman, S. L. 1988. *Disease and Representation: Images of Illness from Madness to AIDS.* Ithaca: Cornell University Press.

Gliedman, J. & Roth, W. 1980. *The Unexpected Minority.* New York: Harcourt, Brace, Jovanovich.

Goffman, E. 1963. *Stigma: Notes on the Management of Spoiled Identity.* Englewood Cliffs, NJ: Prentice-Hall.

Gordon, E. 1991. Accidents among medieval children as seen from miracles of six English saints and martyrs. *Medical History* 35: 145-163.

Gowman, A. G. 1957. *The War Blind in American Social Structure.* New York: American Foundation for the Blind.

Grob, G. N. 1994. *The Mad Among Us: A History of the Care of America's Mentally Ill.* New York: The Free Press.

Groce, N. E. 1985. *Everyone Here Spoke Sign Language: Hereditary Deafness on Martha's Vineyard.* Cambridge, Massachusetts: Harvard University Press.

Gron, K. 1973. Leprosy in literature and art. *International Journal of Leprosy* 46: (1) 249 - 283.

Gussow, Z. 1989. *Leprosy, Racism, and Public Health.* Boulder, Colorado: Westview Press.

Gussow, Z. & Tracy, G. S. 1970. Stigma and the Leprosy Phenomenon: The social history of a disease in the nineteenth and twentieth centuries. *Bulletin of Historical Medicine* 46: 425-449.

Gussow, Z. & Tracy, G. S. 1971a. Status, ideology, and adaptation to stigmatized illness: A study of leprosy. In Sagarin, E. (Ed.) *The Other Minorities.* Waltham, Mass: Xerox College, p. 242-262.

Gussow, Z. and Tracy, G. S. 1971b. The use of archival materials in the analysis and interpretation of field data: A case study in the institutionalization of the myth of leprosy as "leper." *American Anthropologist* 73: (3) 695-709.

Haffter, C. 1968. The changeling: History and psychodynamics of attitudes to handicapped children in European folklore. *Journal of the History of the Behavioral Sciences* 4: (No. 1) 55-61.

Haggard, H. W. 1932. *The Lame, the Halt, and the Blind: The Vital Role of Medicine in the History of Civilization.* New York: Harper Brothers.

Hall, E. T. 1966. *The Hidden Dimension.* Garden City, NY: Doubleday Anchor.

Haller, J. S. Jr. 1993. Ergotism. In Kiple, K. F. (Ed.) *The Cambridge World History of Human Disease.* Cambridge: Cambridge University Press, p. 718-719.

Hand, W. D. 1980. *Magical Medicine: The Folkloric Component of Medicine in the Folk Belief, Custom, and Ritual of the Peoples or Europe and America.* Berkeley: University of California Press.

Hanks, J. R. & Hanks, L..M. Jr. 1948. The physically handicapped in certain non-occidental societies. *Journal of Social Issues* 4: (No. 4) 11-20.

Harris, J.E. & Weeks, K.R. 1973. *X-Raying the Pharaohs.* New York: Charles Scribner's Sons.

Held, J. S. & Posner, D. 1971. *17th and 18th Century Art.* New York: Harry N. Abrams, Inc.

Herzlich, C. & Pierret, J. 1985. The social construction of the patient: patients and illnesses in other ages. *Social Science and Medicine* 20: (2) 145-151.

Higgins, P. C. 1980. *Outsiders in a Hearing World: A Sociology of Deafness.* Beverly Hills, CA: Sage Publications.

Hughes, R. & Bianconi, P. 1967. *The Complete Paintings of Bruegel.* New York: Harry N. Abrams.

Huizinga, J. 1952. *The Waning of the Middle Ages.* London: Edward Arnold.

Jablonski, E. 1966. Man's conquest of blindness. *Blind Digest* Feb.: 2-6, 8.

Jackson, P. W. 1990. *Britain's Deaf Heritage.* Edinburgh, Scotland: The Pentland Press Limited.

Jacquart, D. & Thomasset, C. 1988. *Sexuality and Medicine in the Middle Ages.* Princeton, NJ: Princeton University Press.

Jamison, K. R. 1993. *Touched by Fire: Manic Depressive Illness and the Artistic Temperament.* New York: Free Press.

Johnson, D. 1993. *Jacques-Louis David: Art in Metamorphosis.* Princeton, NJ: Princeton University Press.

Jones, C. 1980. The new treatment of the insane in Paris: The formation of the lunatic asylum under the French revolution. *History Today* 30: (Oct.) 5-10.

Jones, E. W. 1980. Richard III's disfigurement: A medical postscript. *Folklore* 91: (ii) 211-227.

Kalisch, P. A. 1972. The strange case of John Early: A study of the stigma of leprosy. *International Journal of Leprosy* 40: (3) 291-305.

Kalisch, P. A. 1975. An overview of research on the history of leprosy - Part 1 from Celsus to Simpson, Circa 1 AD - Part 2 From Virchow to Moller-Christensen, 1845- 1973. *International Journal of Leprosy* 43: (2) 129-144.

Kamenetz, H. L. 1969. A brief history of the wheelchair. *Journal of the History of Medicine and Allied Sciences* 24: (2) 205-210.

Kanner, L. 1960-61. Itard, Seguin, Howe–Three pioneers in the education of retarded children. *American Journal of Mental Deficiency* 65: 2-10.

Kanner, L. 1964. *History of the Care and Study of the Mentally Retarded*. Springfield, IL: Charles C Thomas.

Kanner, L. 1967. Medicine in the history of mental retardation: 1800-1965. *American Journal of Mental Deficiency* 72: (No. 2) 165-170.

Karacostas, A. 1993. Fragments of "glottophagia:" Ferdinand Berthier and the birth of the Deaf movement in France. In Fischer, R. & Lane, H. (Eds.) *Looking Back: A Reader on the History of Deaf Communities and their Sign Languages*. Hamburg, Germany: Signum, p. 133-142.

Karasch, M. C. 1993. Ophthalmia (Conjunctivitis and Trachoma). In Kiple, K. F. (Ed.) *The Cambridge World History of Human Disease*. Cambridge: Cambridge University Press, p. 871-875.

Karp, D. R. 1985. *Ars Medica: Art, Medicine and the Human Condition*. Philadelphia: University of Pennsylvania Press.

Kastenbaum, R. & Ross, B. 1975. Historical perspectives on care. In Howells, J.G. (Ed.) *Modern Perspectives in the Psychiatry of Old Age*. New York: Brunner-Mazel.

Kauffman, J. M. & Payne, J. S. 1975. *Mental Retardation: Introduction and Personal Perspectives*. Columbus, OH: Charles Merrill.

Kealey, E. J. 1981. *Medieval Medicus: A Social History of Anglo-Norman Medicine*. Baltimore, MD: The Johns Hopkins University Press.

Kim-Farley, R. J. 1993. Measles. In Kiple, K. F. (Ed.) *The Cambridge World History of Human Disease*. Cambridge: Cambridge University Press, p. 897-906.

Koestler, F. 1976. *The Unseen Minority: A Social History of Blindness in America*. David McKay.

Kriegel, L. 1987. The cripple in literature. In Gartner, A. & Joe, T. (Eds.) *Images of the Disabled, Disabling Images*. New York: Praeger Publishers p. 31-46.

Krishef, C. H. 1983. *An Introduction to Mental Retardation*. Springfield, IL: Charles C Thomas.

Lane, H. 1977. Notes for a psycho-history of American sign language. *The Deaf American* 30: 3-7.

Lane, H. 1984a. *When the Mind Hears*. New York: Random House.

Lane, H. 1984b. *The Deaf Experience: Classics in Language and Education*. Cambridge, MA: Harvard University Press.

Lane, H. 1992. *The Mask of Benevolence: Disabling the Deaf Community*. New York: Alfred A. Knopf.

Lane, H. 1993. Constructions of deafness. *A Deaf American Monograph: Deafness: 1993-2013*. 43:73-81.

Larner, C. 1981. Witch beliefs and witch-hunting in England and Scotland. *History Today* 31: (Feb.) 32-37.

Larsen, O. 1973. Gerhard Henrik Armauer Hansen seen through his own eyes: A review of his memoirs. *International Journal of Leprosy* 41: (2) 208-214.

Lavater, J. C. 1789. *Essays on Physiognomy, Designed to Promote the Knowledge and the Love of Mankind*, Vol. 1-5. London: John Murray.

Le Goff, J. 1990. *Medieval History: 400-1500*. New York: Basil Blackwell.

Levy, W. H. 1872. *Blindness and the Blind: or, a Treatise on the Science of Typology*. London: Chapman & Hall.

Lewis, G. 1987. A lesson from Leviticus: Leprosy. *Man* 22: (No. 4) 593-612.

Lindfors, B. 1983. Circus Africans. *Journal of American Culture* 6: (No. 2) 9-14.

Lindfors, B. 1984. P.T. Barnum and Africa. *Studies in Popular Culture* 7: 18-25.

Longmore, P. K. 1985a. A note on language and the social identity of disabled people. *American Behavioral Scientist* 28: (No. 3) 419-423.

Longmore, P. K. 1985b. Screening stereotypes: Images of disabled people. *Social Policy* 16: 31-37.

Mac Arthur, W. 1953. Medieval leprosy in the British Isles. *Leprosy Review* 24: 8-19.

MacDonald, M. 1981. *Mystical Bedlam: Madness, Anxiety, and Healing in Seventeenth Century England*. Cambridge: Cambridge University Press.

MacFarlane, A. 1970. *Witchcraft in Tudor and Stuart England: A regional and comparative study*. London: Routledge & Kegan Paul.

MacKinney, L. 1965. *Medical Illustrations in Medieval Manuscripts*. Berkeley: University of California Press.

Maher, W.B. & Maher, B. 1983. The ship of fools: Stultifera navis or ignis fatuus? *American Psychologist* 37: 756-761.

Malley, G. 1993. The long road to self-confidence of the Deaf in Germany. In Fischer, R. & Lane, H. (Eds.) *Looking Back: A Reader on the History of Deaf Communities and their Sign Languages*. Hamburg, Germany: Signum. Pp. 177-198.

Manchester, K. 1984. Tuberculosis and leprosy in antiquity: An interpretation. *Medical History* 28: (No. 2) 162-173.

Mann, L. 1983. *History of Childhood Exceptionally and Special Education*. Baltimore, MD: University Park Press.

Marcus, S. 1974. *Engels, Manchester, and the Working Class*. New York: Vintage.

Marijnissen, R.H. 1969. *Bruegel the Elder*. Brussels, Belgium: Arcade.

Marvick, E. W. 1974. Nature versus nurture: Patterns and trends in seventeenth-century French child-rearing. In de Mause, L. (Ed.) *The History of Childhood: The Untold Story of Child Abuse*. London: Bellew, p. 259-301.

McBride, M.F. 1985. *Chaucer's Physician and Fourteenth Century Medicine*. Bristol, IN: Wyndham Hall Press.

McGrew, R. E. 1985. *Encyclopedia of Medical History*. New York: McGraw-Hill.

McNeill, W. H. 1976. *Plagues and Peoples*. New York: Anchor Press.

Meaney, A. L. 1992. The Anglo-Saxon view of the causes of illness. In Campbell, S., Hall, B., & Klausner, D. (Eds.) *Health, Disease, and Healing in Medieval Culture*. New York: St. Martin's Press, p. 12-33.

Menden, J. F.C. 1969. Operation for stones in the head. *Journal of the History of Medicine and Applied Sciences* 24: (2) 210-211.

Meyerson, L. 1948. Physical disability as a social psychological problem. *Journal of Social Issues* 4: (No. 4) 2-10.

Midelfort, E. 1980. Madness and civilization in early modern Europe: A reappraisal of Michel Foucault. In Malament, BC (Ed.) *After the Reformation*. Philadelphia: University of Pennsylvania Press.

Mignon, E. 1947. *Crabbed Age and Youth: The Old Men and Women in Restoration Comedy of Manners*. Durham, NC: Duke University Press.

Minott, C. I. 1971. *Martin Schongauer*. New York: Collectors Editions.

Mirzoeff, N. 1992. The silent mind: Learning from deafness *History Today*, 42: (July) 19-25.

Monbeck, M. E. 1973. *The Meaning of Blindness: Attitudes Toward Blindness and Blind People*. Bloomington, IN: Indiana University Press.

Montagu, A. 1971. *The Elephant Man: A Study in Human Dignity*. New York: Outerbridge & Dienstfrey.

Moores, D. F. 1987. *Educating the Deaf: Psychology, Principles and Practices* (3rd Ed). Boston: Houghton Mifflin.

Morris, R. J. & Morris, Y. 1993. Developmental disabilities: Mental retardation and autism. In Eisenberg, M. G., Glueckauf, R. L., & Zaretsky, H. H. (Eds.) *Medical Aspects of Disability*. New York: Spring, p. 161-176.

Mosokowitz, I. (Ed.) 1962. *Great Drawings of All Time, Volume 2*. New York: Shorewood.

Mottez, B. 1993. The deaf-mute banquets and the birth of the deaf movement. In Van Cleve, J. V. (Ed.) *Deaf History Unveiled: Interpretations from the New Scholarship*. Washington, DC: Gallaudet University Press, p. 27-39.

Nash, J. E. & Nash, A. 1981. *Deafness in Society*. Lexington, MA: Lexington Books.

Neaman, J. S. 1978. *Suggestion of the Devil: Insanity in the Middle Ages and the Twentieth Century*. New York: Octagon Books.

Neisser, A. 1990. *Other Side of Silence: Sign Language and the Deaf Community in America*. Washington, DC: Gallaudet University Press.

Nelson, J. A (Ed.) 1994. The Disabled, the Media, and the Information Age. Westport, CT: Greenwood Press.

Nelson, J. A. 1994a. Broken images: Portrayals of those with disabilities in American media. In Nelson, Jack A. (Ed.) *The Disabled, the Media, and the Information Age*. Westport, Connecticut: Greenwood Press, p. 1-24.

Newman, J. 1991. Handicapped persons and their families: Historical, legislative, and philosophical perspectives. In Seligman, M. (Ed.) *The Family with a Handicapped Child* (2nd Ed). Boston, MA: Allyn & Bacon, p. 1-26.

Newton, R. 1989. Hephaestus: The limping paradox of Mt. Olympus. *Kaleidoscope* 18: 19-23.

Nikiforuk, A. 1993. *The Fourth Horseman: A Short History of Epidemics, Plagues, Famine and Other Scourges*. New York: M. Evans.

Ozer, I. J. 1992. Why not a werewolf? The wandering epileptic: Response to Miles E. Drake, Jr. M.D. Medical and neuropsychiatric aspects of lycanthropy. *Journal of Medical Humanities* 13: (No.1) 17-19.

Padden, C. 1980. The deaf community and the culture of deaf people. In Baker, C. & Battison, R. (Eds.) *Sign Language and the Deaf Community.* Silver Springs, MD: National Association of the Deaf, p. 80-130.

Padden, C. & Humphries, T. 1988. *Deaf in America: Voices from a Culture.* Cambridge, Massachusetts: Harvard University Press.

Panofsky, E. 1967. *Studies in Iconology: Humanistic Themes in the Art of the Renaissance.* Oxford: Oxford University Press.

Park, K. 1991. Healing the poor: Hospitals and medical assistance in Renaissance Florence. In Barry, J. & Jones, C. (Eds.) *Medicine and Charity Before the Welfare State.* London: Routledge, p. 26-45.

Parkinson, C. N. 1977. Charles I's dwarf. *History Today* 27: (No.6) 380-384.

Parr, J. 1945. Cresseid's leprosy again. Modern Language Notes 60: 487-491.

Paulson, W. R. 1987. *Enlightenment, Romanticism, and the Blind in France.* Princeton, NJ: Princeton University Press.

Paxton, F. S. 1992. Anointing the sick and the dying in Christian antiquity and the early medieval west. In Campbell, S., Hall, B., & Klausner, D. (Eds.) *Health, Disease, and Healing in Medieval Culture.* New York: St. Martin's Press, p. 93-102.

Payne, G. H. 1916. *The Child in Human Progress.* New York: G.P. Putnam's Sons.

Phillips, M. J. 1990. Damaged goods: Oral narratives of the experience of disability in American culture. *Social Science and Medicine* 30: (No. 8) 849-857.

Plann, S. 1993. Pedro Ponce de León: Myth and reality. In Van Cleve, J. V. (Ed.) *Deaf History Unveiled: Interpretations from the New Scholarship.* Washington, DC: Gallaudet University Press, p. 1-12.

Porter, R. 1987. *A Social History of Madness: The World Through the Eyes of the Insane.* New York: Weidenfeld and Nicolson.

Pouchelle, M. C. 1990. *The Body and Surgery in the Middle Ages.* New Brunswick, NJ: Rutgers University Press.

Presneau, J. R. 1993. The schools, the Deaf and the language of signs in France in the 18th century. In Fischer, R., & Lane, H. (Eds.) *Looking Back: A Reader on the History of Deaf Communities and their Sign Languages.* Hamburg, Germany: Signum, p. 413-421.

Pressman, J. D. 1993. Concepts of mental illness in the West. In Kiple, K. F. (Ed.) *The Cambridge World History of Human Disease.* Cambridge: Cambridge University Press, p. 59-85.

Pritchard, D.G. 1963. *Education and the Handicapped, 1760-1960.* London: Routledge & Kegan Paul.

Quartararo, A. T. 1993. Republicanism, deaf identity, and the career of Henri Gaillard in late-nineteenth-century France. In Van Cleve, J.V. (Ed.) *Deaf History Unveiled: Interpretations from the New Scholarship.* Washington, DC: Gallaudet University Press. p. 40-52.

Quetel, C. 1990. *History of Syphilis.* Baltimore, MD: The Johns Hopkins University Press.

Radutzky, E. 1993. The education of deaf people in Italy and the use of Italian sign language. In Van Cleve, J. V. (Ed.) *Deaf History Unveiled: Interpretations from the New Scholarship.* Washington, DC: Gallaudet University Press, p. 237-251.

Ranson, N. 1986. Dickens and Disability: David Copperfield. *Kaleidoscope* 13: (Summer/Fall) 11-15.

Ravin, J. G. 1987. Monet's cataracts. *Kaleidoscope* 15: (Winter/Spring) 6-11.

Ravin, J. G. 1990. Monet's cataracts. *Kaleidoscope* 20: (Winter/Spring) 90-97.

Rawcliffe, C. 1984. The hospitals of later medieval London. *Medical History* 28: (No.1) 1-21.

Raymond, C. S. 1948. The development of the program for the mentally defective in Massachusetts for the past one hundred years (1848-1948). *American Journal of Mental Deficiency* 53: 80-91.

Reagan, T. 1990. Cultural considerations in the education of deaf children. In Moores D. & Meadow-Orlans, K. (Eds.) *Educational and Developmental Aspects of Deafness*. Washington, DC: Gallaudet University Press, p. 73-84.

Richards, J. 1983. The riddle of Richard III. *History Today* 33 : 18-25.

Richards, P. 1977. *The Medieval Leper and his Northern Heirs*. Cambridge, England: D.S. Brewer, Ltd.

Richardson, G. 1779. *Iconology, Volume III*. New York: Garland.

Robins, J. 1986. *Fools and Mad: A History of the Insane in Ireland*. Dublin: Institute of Public Administration.

Rogers, L. & Muir, E. 1946. *Leprosy*. Baltimore, MA: Williams & Wilkins.

Rosen, G. 1968. *Madness in Society: Chapters in the Historical Sociology of Mental Illness*. Chicago: The University of Chicago Press.

Rosenblum, N. 1989. *A World History of Photography*. New York: Abbeville Press.

Ross, I. 1951. *Journey into Light: The Story of the Education of the Blind*. New York: Appleton-Century-Crofts, Inc.

Roth, H. & Cromie, R. 1980. *The Little People*. New York: Everest House.

Rothman, D. 1971. The Discovery of the Asylum: Social Order and Disorder in the New Republic. Boston: Little, Brown.

Rousselot, J. (Ed.) 1967. *Medicine in Art: A Cultural History*. New York: McGraw Hill.

Rowling, M. 1968. *Life in Medieval Times*. New York: G.P. Putnam's Sons.

Rubin, S. 1974. *Medieval English Medicine*. London: David & Charles Newton Abbot.

Rushton, P. 1988. Lunatics and Idiots: Mental Disability, the Community, and the Poor Law in North-East England, 1600-1800. *Medical History* 32: 34-50.

Sacks, O. 1989. *Seeing Voices: A Journey into the World of the Deaf.* Berkeley, California: University of California Press.

Sagarin, E. (Ed.) 1971. *The Other Minorities: Nonethnic Collectivities Conceptualized as Minority Groups*. Waltham, MA: Xerox College.

Sanchez, A. E. P., & Sayre, E. A. 1989. *Goya and the Spirit of Enlightenment*. Boston: Bulfinch Press.

Saint-Loup, A. 1993. Images of the Deaf in medieval western Europe. In Fischer, R. & Lane, H. (Eds.) *Looking Back: A Reader on the History of Deaf Communities and their Sign Languages*. Hamburg, Germany: Signum, p. 379-402.

Savage, R. D., Evans, L., & Savage, J. F. 1981. *Psychology and Communication in Deaf Children*. Sydney, Australia: Grune & Stratton.

Schadewaldt, H. 1967a. Art and medicine in ancient Egypt. In Roussolot, J. (Ed.) *Medicine in Art: A Cultural History*. New York: Mc-Graw Hill, p. 32-41.

Schadewaldt, H. 1967b. Art and medicine in ancient Greece and Rome. In Rousselot, J. (Ed.) *Medicine in Art: A Cultural History.* New York: Mc-Graw Hill, p. 42-65.

Schadewaldt, H. 1967c. Art and medicine in the Middle Ages. In Rousselot, J. (Ed.) *Medicine in Art: A Cultural History.* New York: Mc-Graw Hill, p. 80-121.

Scheer, J. & Groce, N. 1988. Impairment as a human constant: Cross-cultural and historical perspectives on variation. *Journal of Social Issues* 44: (No. 1) 23-37.

Scheerenberger, R. C. 1982. Treatment from ancient times to the present. In Cegelka, P.T., Prehm, H. J. (Eds.) *Mental Retardation: From Categories to People.* Columbus, OH: Charles E. Merrill, p. 44-75.

Schickel, R. 1968. *The World of Goya: 1746-1828.* New York: Time-Life Books.

Scott, R. A. 1969. *The Making of Blind Men.* New York: Russell Sage Foundation.

Screech, M.A. 1985. Good madness in Christendom. In Bynum, W.F., Porter, R., & Shepherd, M. (Eds.) *The Anatomy of Madness: Essays in the History of Psychiatry, Vol. I, People and Ideas.* London: Tavistock, p. 25- 39.

Scull, A. T 1979. *Museums of Madness: The Social Organization of Insanity in Nineteenth Century England.* London: Allen Lane.

Scull, A. T. 1989. *Social Order/Mental Disorder: Anglo-American Psychiatry in Historical Perspective.* Berkeley: University of California Press.

Scull, A. T. 1993. *The Most Solitary of Afflictions: Madness and Society in Britain 1700-1900.* New Haven, CT: Yale University Press.

Seguin, E. 1907. *Idiocy: and its Treatment.* New York: Columbia University.

Seidel, M. & Marijnissen, R.H. 1971. *Pieter Bruegel.* New York: G.P. Putnam's Sons.

Shapiro, H.A. 1984. Notes on Greek dwarfs. *American Journal of Archaeology* 88: 391-392.

Shapiro, J. P. 1993. *No Pity: People with Disabilities Forging a New Civil Rights Movement.* New York: Times Books.

Showalter, E. 1985. *The Female Malady, Women, Madness, and English Culture, 1830-1980.* New York: Pantheon Books.

Silverman, S.R. 1978. From Aristotle to Bell - and beyond. In Hollowell, D. & Silverman, S. R. (Eds.) *Hearing and Deafness* (3rd Ed). New York: Holt, Rinehart & Winston, p. 421-432.

Siraisi, N. G. 1990. *Medieval and Early Renaissance Medicine: An Introduction to Knowledge and Practice.* Chicago: The University of Chicago Press.

Skinner, H. A. 1961. *The Origin of Medical Terms* (2nd. Ed). Baltimore, Maryland: Williams & Wilkins.

Skinsnes, O. K. 1964a. Leprosy in society: I. leprosy has appeared on the face. *Leprosy Review* 35: (1) 21-35.

Skinsnes, O. K. 1964b. Leprosy in society: II. The pattern of concept and reaction to leprosy in oriental antiquity. *Leprosy Review* 35: (3) 106-122.

Skinsnes, O. K. 1964c. Leprosy in society: III. The relationship of the social to the medical pathology of leprosy. *Leprosy Review* 35: (4) 175-181.

Solomon, L. M. 1968. Quasimodo's diagnosis. *Journal of American Medical Association* 204: 190-191.

Stage, W. 1987. La vie boheme: Syphilis and artists before penicillin. *Kaleidoscope* 15: 16-20.

Stanndard, J. 1977. *The Puritan Way of Death*. New York: Oxford university Press.

Stannard, J. 1985. The theoretical bases of medieval herbalism. *Medical Heritage 1:* (3) 186-198.

Stearns, M. 1944. Robert Henryson and the leper Cresseid. *Modern Language Notes* 59: 265-269.

Steinbock, R. T. 1993. Rickets and Osteomalacia. In Kiple, K. F. (Ed.) *The Cambridge World History of Human Disease*. Cambridge: Cambridge University Press, p. 978-980.

Stone, D. A. 1984. The Disabled State. Philadelphia: Temple University Press.

Stringer, T.A. 1973. Leprosy and "A disease called leprosy." *Leprosy Review* 44: (2) 70-74.

Stroman, D. F. 1982. *The Awakening Minorities: The Physically Handicapped*. Washington, DC: University Press of America.

Sullivan, J. S. 1986. The medical history of Shakespeare's Sir John Falstaff. *Medical Heritage* 2: (6) 391-401.

Szasz, T. 1961. *The Myth of Mental Illness: Foundations of a Theory of Personal Conduct*. New York: Hoeber - Harper.

Szasz, T. 1970. *The Manufacture of Madness*. London: Routledge & Kegan Paul.

Talbot, C. H. 1967a. *Medicine in Medieval England*. London: Oldbourne.

Talbot, M. 1967. Edouard Seguin. *American Journal of Mental Deficiency* 72: (No. 2) 184-189.

Temkin, O. 1971. *The Falling Sickness: A History of Epilepsy from the Greeks to the Beginnings of Modern Neurology* (2nd Ed). Baltimore, MD: Johns Hopkins University Press.

Thomas, K. 1971. *Religion and the Decline of Magic*. New York: Scribner.

Thorndike, L. 1923. *A History of Magic and Experimental Science - Vol. 1-2*. New York: MacMillan.

Tomory, P. 1972. *The Life and Art of Henry Fuseli*. New York: Praeger.

Trent, J. W. 1993. To cut and control: Institutional preservation and the sterilization of mentally retarded people in the United States, 1892-1947. *Journal of Historical Sociology* 6: (No. 1) 56-73.

Trent, J. W. 1994. *Inventing the Feeble Mind: A History of Mental Retardation in the United States*. Berkeley, CA: University of California Press.

Tristram, P. 1976. *Figures of Life and Death in Medieval English Literature*. New York: New York University Press.

Turkington, C. & Sussman, A. E. 1992. *The Encyclopedia of Deafness and Hearing Disorders*. New York: Facts on File.

Tullis, J. L. 1977. Annual discourse—Don't eat the quails. *The New England Journal of Medicine* 297: (9) 472- 475.

Ty, P. L. & Zainald, J. S. 1979. Lunacy in the industrial revolution: A study of asylum admissions in Lancashire, 1848-1850. *Journal of Social History* 13: (Fall) 1-22.

Tyor, P. L. & Bell, L. V. 1984. *Caring for the Retarded in America: A History*. Westport, CT: Greenwood Press.

Valentine, P. 1993. Thomas Hopkins Gallaudet: Benevolent paternalism and the origins of the American asylum. In Van Cleve, J. V. (Ed.) *Deaf History Unveiled: Interpretations from the New Scholarship.* Washington, DC: Gallaudet University Press, p. 53-73.

Van Cleve, J. & Crouch, B. 1989. *A Place of Their Own.* Washington, DC: Gallaudet University Press.

Van Cleve, J. V. (Ed.) 1993. *Deaf History Unveiled: Interpretations from the New Scholarship.* Washington, DC: Gallaudet University Press.

Vernon, M. & Wallrabenstein, J. M. 1988. Historical, cultural, psychological and educational Aspects of American Sign Language. *The Deaf American* 38: 21-24.

Volinn, I. J. 1989. Issues of definitions and their implications: Aids and leprosy. *Social Science Medicine* 29: (10) 1157-1162.

Von Hentig, H. 1948. Physical disability, mental conflict and social crisis. *The Journal of Social Issues* 4: (No. 4) 21-27.

Vukanovic, T.P. 1985. Neolithic blind and Balkan folklore of the blind. *Folklore* 96: (ii) 184-189.

Wells, C. 1964. *Bones, Bodies and Disease: Evidence of Disease and Abnormality in Early Man.* London: Thames & Hudson.

Werner, H. 1932. *History of the Problem of Deaf Mutism Until the 17th Century.* Jena: Verlag Von Gustav Fisher.

White, W.D. & Wolfensberger, N. 1969. The evolution of dehumanization in our institutions. *Mental Retardation* 7: 5-9.

Widell, J. 1993. The Danish Deaf culture in European and western society. In Fischer, R. & Lane, H. (Eds.) *Looking Back: A Reader on the History of Deaf Communities and their Sign Languages.* Hamburg, Germany: Signum, p. 457-478.

Winefield, R. 1981. *Never the Twain Shall Meet: Bell, Gallaudet, and the Communications Debate.* Washington, DC: Gallaudet University Press.

Winthrop, J. 1959. *Winthrop's Journal.* New York: Barnes & Noble.

Winzer, M. 1986. Deaf-Mutia: Responses to alienation by the Deaf in the mid-nineteenth century. American Annals of the Deaf 131: (5) 29-32.

Woolfson, R. C. 1984. Historical perspective on mental retardation. *American Journal of Mental Deficiency* 89:(No. 3) 231-235.

Wortley, J. 1992. Three not so miraculous miracles. In Campbell, S., Hall, B., & Klausner, D. (Eds.) *Health, Disease, and Healing in Medieval Culture.* New York: St. Martin's Press, p. 159-168.

Zivanovic, S. 1982. *Ancient Diseases: The Elements of Palaeopathology.* New York: Pica Press.

Zwiebel, A. 1993. The status of the Deaf in the light of Jewish sources: A comparison with the state of the art. In Fischer, R. & Lane, H. (Eds.) *Looking Back: A Reader on the History of Deaf Communities and their Sign Languages.* Hamburg, Germany: Signum, p. 403-411.

NAME INDEX

A

Abramov, I., 198
Abt, I., 39
Adam, 84, 253
Aelst, P., 84
Agippa, H. 27
Agricola, R., 213
Ahab, Captain, 10
Ahijah, 9
Ajax, 130
Alderidge, P., 142, 143
Alexander, F., 128, 133, 134, 136, 142, 155, 251
Alexander the Great, 93
Amman, C., 217, 218, 224
Anakin, 84
Andreski, S., 69
Angier, N., 9
Angulus, B. 7, 59, 77, 102, 104, 131
Annonymous, 90, 92, 93, 94
Antigon, D., 84
Antoinette, M., 185, 220
Appelboom, T., 78
Aretaeus of Cappadocia, 55
Aries, P., 29, 30,
Aristophanes, 129, 130
Aristotle, 9, 57, 93, 165, 175, 206, 216
Armstrong, A., 81
Arrizabalaga, J., 68
Arithritis, 77
Astruc, J., 247
Avicenna, 55, 167, 211

B

Bacon, F., 10, 217
Bacon, R. 30, 179-180
Bagshaw, M., 55
Baldung, H., 255
Barbier, C., 186
Barker, R., 10
Barnum, P.T., 15
Baudelaire, C., 71

Baumeister, A., 249
Bayless, J., 101
Baynton, D., 202
Bede, V., 98
Belisarius, 169, 189
Bell, A., 227, 267
Bell, C. 154, 155, 156, 157
Bell, L., 237, 262, 266, 268, 269, 270
Benda, C., 244
Bender, R., 56, 205, 207
Bergmaier, H., 73
Bergson, H., 154
Berkeley, G., 183
Bernard, Y., 203, 208, 213
Bernard of Gordon, 102, 103, 104
Bernhardt, S., 154
Bernheimer, R., 7
Berruguete, P., 182
Berthier, J., 197
Best, H., 23
Bevalet, 108, 120
Bezon, 81
Bianconi, P., 20
Biklen, D., 23
Bishop of Exeter, 102
Bishop of Myra, 250
Bixentine, L., 190
Blye, N., 146
Boccaccio, G., 34
Boeck, 118, 120
Bogdan, R., 7, 10, 15, 16, 23, 25, 235
Boilly, L., 171
Bonaparte, N., 245
Bonifacio, G., 217
Bonet, J., 216
Bosch, H., 46, 55, 132, 136, 137, 138,
Botticelli, S., 111
Brahe, T., 9
Braidwood, T., 223, 224
Braille, L., 185, 186
Brandt, S., 70, 136

Bridgeman, L., 188, 226, 262
Brody, S., 90, 92, 94, 96, 97, 98, 102, 103, 107, 110, 118, 121
Bronte, C., 157
Brooke, C., 46
Bronzino, 82
Brothers Grimm, 190
Browne, Dr., 267
Browne, S. 92, 93, 151, 154, 155, 157
Browning, E., 75
Bruegel, P. the Elder, 8, 12, 13, 20, 21, 47, 97, 140, 167, 181, 182
Buchinger, M., 53
Bullough, B., 248
Bullough, V., 248
Bulwer, J., 217, 218
Buoninsegna, D., 32
Burrow, J., 36
Burstein, S., 27, 182
Burtisch, G., 182
Burt, J., 92, 94, 105
Burton, R. 10, 139
Butterfield, E., 249
Buys, C. 20
Bynam, W., 140, 144
Byron, L., 75

C

Caesar, J., 243
Calabazas, J., 255-256
Caldonicus, M., 8
Caligula, 243
Callot, J. 21-22, 62, 63, 64, 65, 66
Calvert, K. 38, 46, 73, 74,
Calvin, J., 34, 71, 129
Camporesi, P., 60
Canute, 169
Caraccio, G., 82
Cardano, G., 184, 213
Carlander, C., 55
Carmichael, A., 89, 92, 93, 102, 104, 107, 108, 111
Carolan, T., 170
Carpaccio, V., 82
Carracci, A., 66-67, 189
Carreno, J., 82
Casanova, G., 71
Cassatt, M., 190, 247

Cavina, A., 189
Celsus, 56, 67
Ceruti, G., 82
Cervantes, M., 71
Charcot, J., 154
Chaucer, G., 110, 250
Cheyne, G., 142, 151
Chiarugi, 243
Chodowiecki, D., 246, 253, 254
Chopin, F., 75
Chough, S., 196
Chrysostom, St. J., 7
Clarke, A. D., 237
Clarke, A. M., 237
Clair, C., 55, 81, 84
Clay, M., 18, 37, 95, 98, 99, 103, 105, 106, 107, 108, 112, 133, 134, 251
Cleland, C., 250
Clerc, L., 222, 225, 226
Cock, H. 47, 48
Cohn, J., 90, 104
Columbus, C. 68-69
Condillac, E., 183, 219, 259
Congreve, W., 30
Conolly, J., 146, 157
Constantine, 36, 77, 110
Copperfield, D., 156, 157, 257
Cornelius of Lithuania, 81
Corot, J., 127
Covey, H. 29, 36
Cowper, W., 97
Cranefield, P., 236, 244, 249, 253
Crazy Ann, 125
Crazy Jane, 124-125, 127
Crazy Kate, 127
Crittenden, J., 196, 197
Cromie, R., 81
Cromwell, O., 84
Crouch, B., 41, 197, 200
Cullough, O., 38, 268

D

Dalgarno, 218
Daniel, 184
Danielssen, 118, 120
Da Panicale, M., 32
Darwin, C., 155, 267
Daudet, A., 71

Daumier, H., 189
Davenport, C., 269
Daviel, J., 179
David, 84
David, J., 169, 170, 189
Davidson, T., 213
da Vinci, L. 34, 213, 214, 244, 252
Davis, F., 23, 25
de Blois, R., 7
de Beauvior, S., 29
de Bry, T., 138
de Chauliac, G. 28
Degas, E., 127
de Gérando, B., 201
de Gheyn, J., 218
de Gower, H., 180
Delacroix, E., 157
Deland, F., 206, 209, 216
de La Tour, G., 170
de León, P., 216
Delilah, 168, 169
de Maupassant, G., 154
de Mause, L., 59, 239
de Medici, C. 81
Democritus, 175, 176
Demos, J., 30
Demodus, 170
Descartes, R., 183
Deschamps, A., 184
Deshen, S., 163, 164, 167, 205
Desloges, P., 219
Despert, J., 14, 143
Deutsch, A., 248
Deutsch, N., 113, 114, 115
de Valaseo, P., 216
de Valaseo, D., 216
de Vigne, A., 181-182
de Vitry, J., 244
de Vitry, J. 33
Diamond, H., 157, 158
di Carlo, L., 205, 213, 216, 217, 220
Dickens, C., 10, 12, 82, 156, 157, 190, 255, 257
Diderot, D., 171, 183, 184, 185
Didymus, 174
Dionysius, 207
Dix, D., 263
Doll, E., 250, 259, 261, 265
Dols, M., 91, 92, 93, 94, 96, 101, 104, 105
Donzello, P., 111
Dove, M., 36
Down, J., 241
Drake, W. 27, 242
Dryden, J., 30
Dugsdale, R. 38, 268
Duncan, H., 77
Dunning, A., 36, 85, 186
Dürer, A., 8, 34, 70, 97, 125-126, 180
Durkheim, E., 154

E

Eberly, S., 28, 29, 79, 238, 244, 247
Ehrlich, G., 36, 77, 78
Elisha, 169
Elsing, W., 180
Emin, 84
Emperor
    Augustus, 80, 249
    Charles V, 180
    Hadrian, 174
    Justinian, 169, 209, 250
Erasmus, D., 70
Esau, 171
Esquirol, E., 145, 154, 157, 244, 264, 265
Etherege, G., 30
Eustachi, B., 214
Evans, D., 8, 24, 127, 248, 249, 250, 251, 255, 270
Evans, L. 214, 225
Evans, W., 84
Eyre, J., 157

F

Fabiola, 58
Fagnani, P., 184
Farber, B., 42, 250, 263, 264, 265, 267
Farrell, G., 23, 86, 169, 175, 180, 184, 188, 227
Father Damien, 119-120
Feder, L., 139, 147, 160, 161
Ferri, N., 81
Fetti, D., 168
Fiedler, L., 6, 14, 80, 81
Fischer, D., 24, 30
Fischer, J., 187

Fischer, R., 198, 203
Fitz-Herbert, Sir A., 250
Fleury, R., 148
Flournoy, J., 197
Fodder, F., 244
Fodere, F., 244
Forbes, T., 74, 247
Foster, S., 196, 197-198, 232
Foucault, M., 112, 136, 140, 143, 146
Fouquet, J., 97
Fracastoro, G., 68, 102
Franklin, B., 180
Frazer, J., 12
Freeman, J., 30
French, R., 18, 19, 56, 57, 75, 170, 174, 176, 177, 178, 180, 186
Freud, S., 154, 175, 239
Funk, R., 39
Fuseli, H., 127

G

Gabba, 249
Galen, 27, 29, 35, 53, 56, 59, 67, 73, 102, 104, 125, 131, 179, 243
Gall, J., 155
Gallaudet, E., 227
Gallaudet, T., 201, 222, 224, 225, 226, 227
Galton, F., 268-269
Garrison, F., 19, 26, 53, 73, 84, 93, 95, 112, 180
Gardner, J., 58, 130, 176, 201, 207, 208
Gareau, .M, 141
Gartner, A., 42
Gauthier, A., 20, 53, 148
Georget, Dr., 157
Géricault, T., 157, 158
Ghirlandaio, B., 180
Gibson, H., 81
Gilman, S., 125, 127 134, 136, 146, 147, 148, 152, 155, 157, 251, 266
Gliedman, J., 41, 81
Goddard, H., 38, 268
Goffman, E., 25
Gog, 85
Gogh, V., 127
Goliath, 84

Gordon, E. 32
Gostwicke, E., 203
Gower, J., 100
Gowman, A., 19, 23, 174, 176
Goya, F. 16, 17, 46, 47, 82, 85, 148, 157, 166, 170, 171, 189
Green, F., 225
Gregory of Tours, 95
Greuter, M., 141
Grob, G., 138, 140, 150
Groce, N., 4, 5, 25, 42, 198, 202, 203, 205, 227, 255
Gron, F., 96, 97, 107, 111
Grunewald, M., 60, 132
Guggenbuhl, J., 245, 259, 260-261
Guille, S., 171
Gussow, Z., 71, 75, 90, 91, 92, 94, 95, 112, 113, 118, 119, 120, 121
Guy de Chauliac, 103-104

H

Haffter, C., 74, 238, 239, 244, 247
Haggard, H., 28, 101, 140, 243, 249
Hall, E., 164
Haller, J., 60
Hals, F., 138, 255
Hamlet, 141
Hand, W., 26, 29, 74, 104, 165, 167, 169, 190, 205
Hanks, J., 39
Hanks, L., 39
Hansen, G., 118
Harris, J., 248
Hartlieb, J., 128
Harvey, W. 36
Haüy, V., 185
Heberden, W., 77
Heinicke, S., 225
Held, J., 169
Hemessen, J., 138
Henrion, 84
Henryson, R., 110
Hephaestus, 57
Herodotus, 205
Herzlich, C., 33, 41
Heyden, P., 168
Higgins, P., 197
Hippocrates, 27, 35, 53, 56, 67,

74, 93, 123,127, 130-131, 165, 175
Hitler, A., 228
Hogarth, W., 147
Holbein, H. the Elder, 96, 113, 180
Holbein, H. the Younger, 115, 116
Homer, 11, 57, 74, 130, 169, 170, 171, 175, 176
Howe, S., 187, 188, 226, 227, 262, 268
Hudson, J., 81
Hughes, A., 20, 125
Hugo, V., 10, 24, 67, 75, 81, 255
Huizinga, J., 29
Humphries, T., 222, 226
Hunter, J., 85
Hunter, W., 85

I

Ingleby, D., 143
Isidore of Seville, 97, 236
Issac, 171
Itard, J., 201, 225, 258, 259, 265

J

Jablonski, E., 176
Jacquart, D., 92, 95, 98, 102, 165
Jackson, P., 201, 203
Jacob, 171
Jamison, K., 9
Jasper, J., 156
Jenner, E., 166
Jeroboam, 9
Job, 96, 97
Joe, T., 42
John of Gaddesden, 103
Johnson, D., 74,
Johnson, H., 15
Jones, C., 15, 62, 144, 145
Jupiter, 176

K

Kaiser, W., 4
Kalisch, P., 93, 103, 111, 113, 120
Kallikak, M., 268
Kamenetz, H., 47
Kanner, L. 34, 237, 240, 241, 244, 249, 251, 258, 259, 261, 264, 265, 270

Karacostas, A., 198
Karasch, M., 166
Karp, D., 47, 116, 171
Kastenbaum, R. 30
Kauffman, J., 235
Kaulbach, W., 148
Kealey, E., 77, 90, 99, 100, 105, 107, 111, 134, 165, 179
Keats, J., 71, 75
Kellogg, J., 153, 165
Kerlin, I., 266
Kim-Farley, R., 104, 167
King,
    Charles I, 81
    Charles II, 55
    Carles V, 81, 101, 251
    Croesus, 205
    Edward I, 99
    Francis I, 251
    Frederick II of Prussia, 84
    George III, 150
    Henry I, 99, 102
    Henry IV, 71
    Henry VI, 62
    Henry VIII, 19, 81
    James I, 81, 203
    John 102
    Joseph II of Prussia, 220
    Lear, 141
    Louis VIII, 106
    Louis IX, 166, 180
    Louis XII, 81
    Louis XIV, 141
    Louis XVI, 185
    Pepin I, 80, 95
    Philip IV of Spain, 82, 255
    Philip V., 81, 101
    Richard III, 4, 9, 10, 62
    Stanislas, 81
    Uzziah, 115
Kingston, W., 55
Klepinger, L., 78
Klein, J., 186
Knox, J., 34
Koch, R., 75, 76
Koestler, F., 9, 25, 164, 174, 175, 188, 190, 191
Krammer, H., 128
Kriegel, L., 9, 12, 62

Krishef, C., 9, 38, 241, 249, 250, 251, 258, 269, 270

L

Lambert, J., 198
Lane, H., 7, 24, 25, 190, 195, 196, 198, 201, 203, 205, 210, 220, 221, 222, 225, 226
Langland, W., 133
Larner, C., 128
Larrey, Dr., 28
Larsen, O., 118
Lavater, J., 151-152, 245, 246, 253, 254
Lazarus, 96, 117
LeBrun, C., 141
LeGoff, J., 16, 18, 95, 99, 100, 101, 106, 111
Leibnitz, G., 183
Leisen, J., 77
Leon, J., 82
L'Epée, A., 220-222, 225, 259
Levy, W., 23, 188
Lewis, G., 91, 93
Lindfors, B., 15, 16,
Little, W., 52
Locke, J., 183, 217, 237, 259
Locock, C., 244
Long John Silver, 10
Longmore, P. 25
Lucia, 124-125
Lucius, 80
Lucretius, 206
Luther, M., 34, 129, 239

M

Mac Arthur, W., 90, 93, 95, 96, 99, 106, 107, 101, 111
MacDonald, M., 15, 125, 129, 132, 139, 235
MacFarlane, A., 128
MacKinney, L., 36, 107, 134
Magog, 85
Maher, B., 136
Maher, W., 136
Malley, G., 198
Manchester, K., 92, 100, 112
Mann, H., 205, 227
Mantegna, A., 82

Marcus, S., 144
Marijnissen, R., 20, 167
Marvick, E., 59
Massaccio, 32
Massieu, J., 222, 223, 225
Massy, Q., 182
Mather, C., 26, 30, 139
Mather, I. 26, 255
Matsy, C., 108
Maudsley, Dr., 267
McBride, M., 5, 134
McGrew, R., 15, 55, 70, 77, 131, 159, 242, 243
McNeil, N., 112
Meadow, K., 197
Meaney, A., 26, 30
Mendel, G., 228
Menden, J., 138
Meville, H. 10, 81
Meyerson, L., 10, 57
Michaelangelo, 34
Midelfort, E., 136, 140
Mignon, E., 30
Millais, J., 125, 171, 173
Milton, J., 10
Minerva, 175
Minott, C., 7
Mirzoeff, N., 204, 214, 220, 223, 227, 228
Monbeck, M., 9, 11, 23, 25, 167, 169, 174, 177, 178
Mondeville, H. 28, 98, 104, 134
Monet, C., 189-190
Monmouth, G. 8
Montagu, A., 194
Montaldo, F., 253
Moon, W., 187
Moores, D., 174, 201, 205, 207, 208, 209, 225, 227, 232
Mora, 82
More, Sir. T., 135
Moreau, P., 184
Morel, B., 267
Morris, Y., 262
Morris, Z., 262
Morrison, A., 154-155
Moses, 177
Moskowitz, I., 47, 115
Mottez, B., 198

Name Index

Mowcher, Ms., 82
Muir, E., 90, 92, 93, 100, 106, 108, 112
Muziano, G., 111

N

Napier, R., 129, 139
Nash, A., 198
Nash, J., 198
Neaman, J., 96, 133-134, 143, 148, 159, 178, 236, 250, 252
Nebuchadnezzar, 6, 46
Neisser, A., 196, 200, 203
Nelson, J., 10, 23,
Newman, J., 39, 125
Newton, R., 57
Nieulandt, A., 117
Nikiforuk, A., 69, 75, 89, 93, 97, 106, 108

O

Odysseus, 130, 176
Oedipus, 141, 175, 176
Orcagna, N., 111
Orley, B., 113
Ossian, 170
Ostade, A., 170
Ozer, I., 242

P

Padden, C., 197, 222, 226
Paganini, N., 75
Paine, A., 84
Panofsky, E., 11, 168
Paracelsus, 27, 103, 244, 252, 253
Pare, A. 28
Park, K., 34, 37, 70
Parkinson, C., 84
Parr, J., 102
Parsons, W., 84
Paul of Aegina, 67
Paulson, W., 19, 23, 175, 178, 183, 190
Paxton, F., 32
Payne, G., 14, 53
Payne, J., 235
Pearson, K., 269
Pepys, S., 203
Pereire, J., 223, 224, 259

Perkins, Mr., 187
Phillips, M., 23, 40
Phineus, 176
Pierret, J., 33, 41
Pigner, A., 186
Pinel, P., 145, 148, 150, 153, 219, 243
Plaerius, J. 28
Plann, S., 208, 216
Plato, 129-130, 175, 206
Platter, F., 204, 214, 244
Pliny the Elder, 206, 244
Plummer, B., 190
Poe, E., 157, 255
Pompey, 93
Pope,
    Alexander III, 100
    Innocent VIII, 128
    Gregory, 97
    John XXII, 128
    Leo X, 180
Porter, R., 123, 132, 139, 141, 144, 147, 150, 153, 155
Posner, D., 169
Pott, P. 62
Pouchelle, M., 6, 30, 98, 104
Praetorius, 176
Presneau, J., 216, 219
Pressman, J., 132
Preti, M., 189
Pritchard, D., 210
Prospero, 77
Pugin, A., 148

Q

Quartararo, A., 205
Quasimodo, 255
Queen
    Catherine the Great, 220
    Elizabeth I, 10, 14, 19, 80, 180
    Henrietta, M., 81
    Matilda, 101
Quetel, C., 67, 68, 70

R

Rabelias, F., 70
Racism, 76, 119, 272
Radutsky, E., 206, 207, 210, 211
Ranson, N., 82, 157
Raphael, S., 82, 180, 214, 215

Rambert, 71-73
Ravin, J., 189, 190
Rawcliffe, C., 37, 99, 121
Raymond, C., 265
Reagan, T., 196
Van Rijn, R., 21, 32, 108, 115, 169, 189
Remus, 6
Renoir, A., 78
Rephaim, 84
Ribera, D., 77
Ribera, J. 53-54
Richards, P., 90, 94, 95, 96, 97, 99, 100, 102, 104, 105, 106, 107, 110, 118
Rickets, 45, 47, 59, 60, 73-74
Robins, J., 81, 95, 128, 132, 134, 142, 236, 237, 250
Robyn, H., 187
Rochester, Ms., 157
Rogers, L., 90, 92, 93, 100, 106, 108, 112
Romanesque, A., 81
Romulus, 6, 207
Roosevelt, F., 4
Roselli, C., 96
Rosen, G., 125, 128, 129, 133, 135, 138, 141, 143, 150, 242, 251
Rosenblum, N., 158
Ross, I., 23, 80, 170, 174, 175, 179
Ross, B., 30
Rosselli, C., 111
Roth, W. 41, 81
Rothman, D., 19, 143
Rousseau, J., 34, 183
Rousselot, J., 111
Rowling, M., 33
Rowlandson, T., 47, 141, 148
Rubens, P., 78, 97, 141
Rubin, S., 26, 56, 90, 95, 96, 98, 99, 102, 103, 104, 106, 107, 111, 112, 134, 165, 179, 241
Rush, B., 150, 153
Rushton, E., 186, 236, 237, 271

S

Sacks, H., 216, 219
Saint-Loup, A., 6, 24, 201, 202, 208, 209, 211, 213
Saint
  Ambrose, 23, 178
  Anne, 113-114
  Anthony, 60, 132, 174
  Anthony's Fire, 60
  Augustine, 208, 209, 231
  Basil, 106, 178
  Bartholomew, 239
  Benard, 178
  Clair, 211
  Dominicus, 59
  Elizabeth, 105, 113, 211
  Francis de Sales, 216
  George, 96
  Gilles, 105
  Gregory, 97
  Herve, 170, 178
  Hildegard of Bingen, 36, 105, 125, 211, 212
  Isidorus, 174
  James, 113-114
  Jerome, 174, 175, 178, 180, 203, 209
  John, 178, 243
  John of Beverley, 210
  Julian, 108
  Lawrence, 239
  Louis, 28
  Martin, 97
  Mary, 105, 208
  Milburga, 105
  Nicholas of Thaumaturgos, 250
  Paul, 110, 208
  Peter, 110
  Roch, 114
  Stephan, 239
  Thomas, 178, 182
  Thuringa, Elizabeth of Thuringa, 12, 13
  Valentine, 243
  Vincent de Paul, 257
Samson, 168, 169
Sanchez, A., 16
Sanzio, R., 62-63
Saragin, E., 91
Savage, E., 214, 225
Savage, J., 214, 225
Sayre, E., 16
Schadewaldt, H., 80, 108, 130

Scheer, J., 4, 5, 25
Scheerrenberger, R., 8, 235, 238, 247, 248, 249, 250, 251, 257, 261
Schenk, J., 204
Schickel, R., 148
Schloss, A., 84
Schongauer, M. 7
Schott, G., 79
Scott, R. 27, 129
Screech, M., 132
Scrofula, (see Tuberculosis)
Scull A. 15, 18, 31, 32, 138, 140, 142, 143, 144, 145, 147, 148, 151, 153, 154, 159, 161
Seguin, E., 239, 259, 264, 268
Seidel, M., 20
Selesnick, S., 128, 133, 134, 136, 142, 155, 251
Seneb, 80
Seneca, 14, 176
Shakespeare, W., 9, 10, 14, 30, 62, 71, 77, 124, 141
Sharp, H., 269
Sharpiro, J., 4, 10, 53, 80, 196
Shelly, M., 24
Showwalter, F., 124, 127, 158
Sicard, A., 201, 220-222, 223, 225
Silverman, S., 201, 207
Siraisi, N., 32, 210
Skinner, H., 248
Skinsnes, O., 92, 93, 94, 102, 106
Smithson, H., 125
Socrates, 206
Sommer, W., 81
Soranus of Ephesus, 249
Spenser, E., 8
Sprenger, J., 128
Stage, W., 67, 68, 71
Stannard, J., 27, 29, 106, 134
Stearns, M., 99, 101, 107
Steen, J., 138, 170
Steinbock, R., 73
Stevenson, R., 10, 75
Stone, D., 18, 19
Stringer, T., 91, 93, 118
Stroman, D., 15, 80, 203, 207
Sullivan, J., 130
Sussman, A., 202, 217
Swift, J., 146

Sydenham, T., 77, 167
Szasz, T., 123 161

T

Talbot, M., 27, 31, 100, 104, 265
Tasso, 157
Taylor, S., 25, 235
Temkin, O., 145, 242, 243
Teniers, D., 117, 170
Teresa, M., 82
Terzi, L., 184
Thersites, 57
Thomas, K., 128
Thomasset, C., 92, 95, 98, 102, 165
Tomory, P., 291
Thoreau, H., 75
Thorndike, L., 36 106, 179, 211
Thyro, 6
Thumb, T., 184
Tiepolo, G., 32
Tissot, S., 153, 243
Titian, 182
Tobias, 182
Tobit, 177
Tomysen, Mrs., 80
Tracy, G., 71, 75, 90, 91, 112, 118, 119, 120
Traini, F. 20, 108
Trent, J., 257, 262, 263, 269, 270
Tribculo, 14
Triboulet, 81
Tristram, P., 29
Trudeau, E., 76
Trumbull, J., 189
Tullis, J, 90, 94, 111
Tuke, W., 144-145
Turkington, C., 202, 217
Turold, 81
Tyor, P., 237, 262, 266, 268, 269, 270

U

Ulpian, 207
Ulysses, 130, 169
Underwood, M., 55

V

Valckert, W., 117
Valentine, P., 226
Valerius, J., 55

SUBJECT INDEX

A

Adaptive Devices, 46-48
American Sign Language, 196
Ars Magna, 35
Arthritis, 77
Asylums, 15, 42, 133-134, 140-143, 148, 157, 258, 271
Audist, 202

B

Begging, 16-23, 47, 48, 101, 138, 169, 276
Blind
  People who had, 4, 8, 11, 14, 18, 19, 20, 22, 25, 28, 32
Blindness, 3, 26, 55, 59, 89, 93, 163, 164, 165, 167,
  as darkness, 10-11
  in antiquity, 174-178
  during the Middle Ages, 178-182
  during the Modern period, 182-190
  explanations for, 164-167
  social perceptions of, 167-173

C

Cerebral Palsy, 52
Changelings, 7, 128, 238-239, 247
Church vii, 18, 19, 23, 31, 32, 33, 34, 41-42, 60, 97, 100, 102, 132, 134, 160, 180, 208, 211, 239, 250
Code of Hammurabi, 56, 205
Code of Justinian, 201, 209
Compensations, 8-9
Consumption (*see* Tuberculosis)
Copper Monday, 115
Corpus Hippocraticum, 35
Cretinism, 237, 244, 254, 261
Cripple(s), 9, 20, 21, 55
Culture, role of, 3-4, 29
Cyclops, 169

D

Darwinism viii, 276
  social, 16, 37-38, 118-120, 202, 227, 228, 241, 267-271, 276
Deaf
  community, 196-198
  culture, 196-197, 232
  during the Middle Ages, 209-214
  during the Modern Period, 214-231
  explanations for, 204-205
  in antiquity, 205-209
  people who were, 4, 6-7, 20, 24, 28,
Deafness, 26, 36
Degeneration, 155, 267-268
Developmental disabilities
  as entertainers, 15-16
  during the Middle Ages, 250-252
  during the Modern Period, 252-269
  explanations for, 237-240
  in antiquity, 248-249
  people with 3, 9, 11, 24, 42
Diabetes mellitus, 55
Disabilities,
  definitions of, 3
  familiarity with, 5
  extent of 4
  causes of, 26-30
  astrological, 29
  God, 26, 31
  old age, 29
  sin, 26, 31, 32, 33, 41, 68
  supernatural, 26
  war, 28
  witches, 26, 27

H

Historical trends affecting,
  humanism, 34
  modern medicine, 35-36

303

other social trends, 38-39
rise of Christianity, 31-34
rise of institutions, 36-37
social Darwinism, 37-38 (see Darwinism, social)
Social perceptions of people with
as beggars, 16-23
as children, 23
as criminals, 23
as dangerous, 10
as economic burdens, 23
as entertaining, 14-16, 20
as evil, 9-11
as liabilities, 25
as maladjusted, 23
as scapegoats, 12-14
as subhuman 6-8, 46
as worthy of pity or charity, 11-12
Down syndrome, 237, 240-241, 248
Dwarfism, 8. 9. 78-84
as subject of art, 81-82
causes for 79
Egyptians, 80, 92-93, 123, 166, 174, 175, 191, 205, 248, 273
Enlightenment, 34, 141, 149, 150, 219
English Disease (see Rickets)
Epilepsy, 241-244
Ergotism, 60
Eugenics, 155, 267-269

F

Family, 18, 24, 38, 42, 132, 179
Feral children, 6

G

Gallaudet College, 226-227
Gender, 124, 127
Gigantism, 78-79
causes of, 84
Greek (s), 24, 34, 36, 47, 53, 56-57, 74, 80, 84, 93, 94, 125, 127, 129-130, 159, 165, 175, 192, 203, 206, 207, 231, 242, 248, 249

H

Handicap, definition of, 3-4
Hansen's Disease (see Leprosy)
HIV, 91, 121
Huizinga, J., 29

Humanism, 34
Humanitarism, 18
Hunchback, (see Scoliosis)
Huntington's Chorea, 56

I

Industrialization, 18, 39-40, 73, 86
Insanity (see mental illness)
Leprosy, 7, 20, 31, 36, 47, 59, 89, 136, 190, 275
causes of, 89-90
forms of, 89-90
decline of, 111-113
during the Middle Ages, 95-113
during Modern Period, 113-118
extent of, 90, 95
in antiquity, 92-94
medieval care of, 103-107
medieval depictions of, 107-111
social perceptions of, 91

M

Malleus Maleficarum, 27, 128, 239, 243
Melancholy, 9, 134, 125-127, 139, 148
Mental Illness,
definition of, 123
diagnosis of, 123
during Middle Ages, 131-138
during Modern Period, 138-158
explanations for, 128-129
female images of, 124-125
in antiquity, 129-131
people with 8, 9
Middle Ages, vii-ix, 6, 7, 8, 14, 16, 18, 19, 24, 29, 31, 32, 34, 49, 58-60, 73, 74, 75, 81, 85-86, 92, 95, 123, 125, 127, 131-138, 159, 160, 161, 169
Modernization, 86
Monster, 7, 29
Multiple sclerosis, 55

N

National Institute of Medicine, 4

P

Parkinson's disease, 56
Perkins Institute, 262
Physical disability, 26, 45-87

depictions of, 12, 13
during Middle Ages, 58-60
during Modern Period, 60
explanations for, 51-56
in antiquity, 56-58
people with, 9, 15
Physical Mobility, 46-51
Physiognomy, 151-153
Piers Plowman, 133
Poliomyelitis, 55
Poor Laws, 19, 39, 180
Potts Disease, 62
Pox (*see* Syphilis)

R

Racism, 76, 119, 272
Reformation, 19, 129, 180
Renaissance, viii, 9, 34, 81, 111, 123, 125, 127, 132, 133, 134, 213, 214, 244, 252, 255
Revolutionary War, 86
Rickets, 45, 47, 59, 60, 73-74
Romans, 47, 57-58, 80, 94, 95, 125, 130-131, 169, 175, 176, 192, 201, 206, 207, 208, 210, 243, 248, 249

S

Scoliosis, 62-67
Scrofula (*see* Tuberculosis)

Sex, 91-92, 102, 125, 153, 175, 238
people with disabilities being oversexed, 8, 24,
Sign language, 203-204
Sin, 136, 146, 160, 164
Spinal,
bifida, 53
cord injuries, 52
Stones of Folly, 136-138
Swaddling, 59, 73-74
Syphilis, 52, 60, 67-73, 86, 90, 120, 166
treatments for, 69-70
use of mercury for, 70

T

Third Latern Council, 100
Tuberculosis, 45, 60, 62, 74-77, 112

U

Urbanization, 18, 86
Utilitarianism, 39-40

V

Victorians, 15, 84, 124-125, 153, 158, 165, 228, 257

W

Witches/ witchcraft, 26-27, 41, 128-129, 132-133, 139, 239

WITHDRAWN
No longer the property of the
Boston Public Library.
Sale of this material benefits the Library.